Massachusetts
THE OTHER
Beyond Boston and Cape Cod

Christina Tree

Countryman Press
Woodstock, Vermont 05091

For Bill Davis

Maps by Richard Widhu
Cover design by Frank Lieberman
Front cover photo of a bicyclist on Coventry Road, Colrain
  Massachusetts by John Martin
Photo of the author by William Davis

Library of Congress Cataloging-in-Publication Data

Tree, Christina.
  The other Massachusetts.

  Includes index.
  1. Massachusetts—Description and travel—1981– —
Guide-books. I. Title.
F62.3.T74 1987   917.440443   86-29080
ISBN 0-88150-075-5 (pbk.)

First Edition

Copyright © 1987 by Christina Tree

All rights reserved. No part of this book may be reproduced in any form or by any electronic or mechanical means including information storage and retrieval systems without permission in writing from the publisher, except by a reviewer who may quote brief passages in a review.

CONTENTS

Introduction ix
What's Where in Massachusetts 1
Calendar of Events 13

UPCOUNTRY MASSACHUSETTS 15
Central Uplands 17
North of Quabbin 31
The Upper Pioneer Valley 42
The Hilltowns 52
Mohawk Trail Country 67
North Berkshire 78

CENTRAL AND SOUTH BERKSHIRES 97

THE PIONEER VALLEY 141
The Five College Area 145
Springfield 165

CENTRAL MASSACHUSETTS 175
Old Sturbridge Village Country 176
Worcester 191
Blackstone River Valley 199
The Nashoba Valley 206

THE MERRIMACK VALLEY 215
Lowell 217
Middlesex Canal 227
Lawrence 230

NORTH SHORE 239
The Salem and Marblehead Area 241
Cape Ann Region 260
The Newburyport Area 289

PLYMOUTH 299

SIPPICAN 315

BRISTOL COUNTY 321
New Bedford 323
Fall River 338

Index 349
Index to Lodging 355

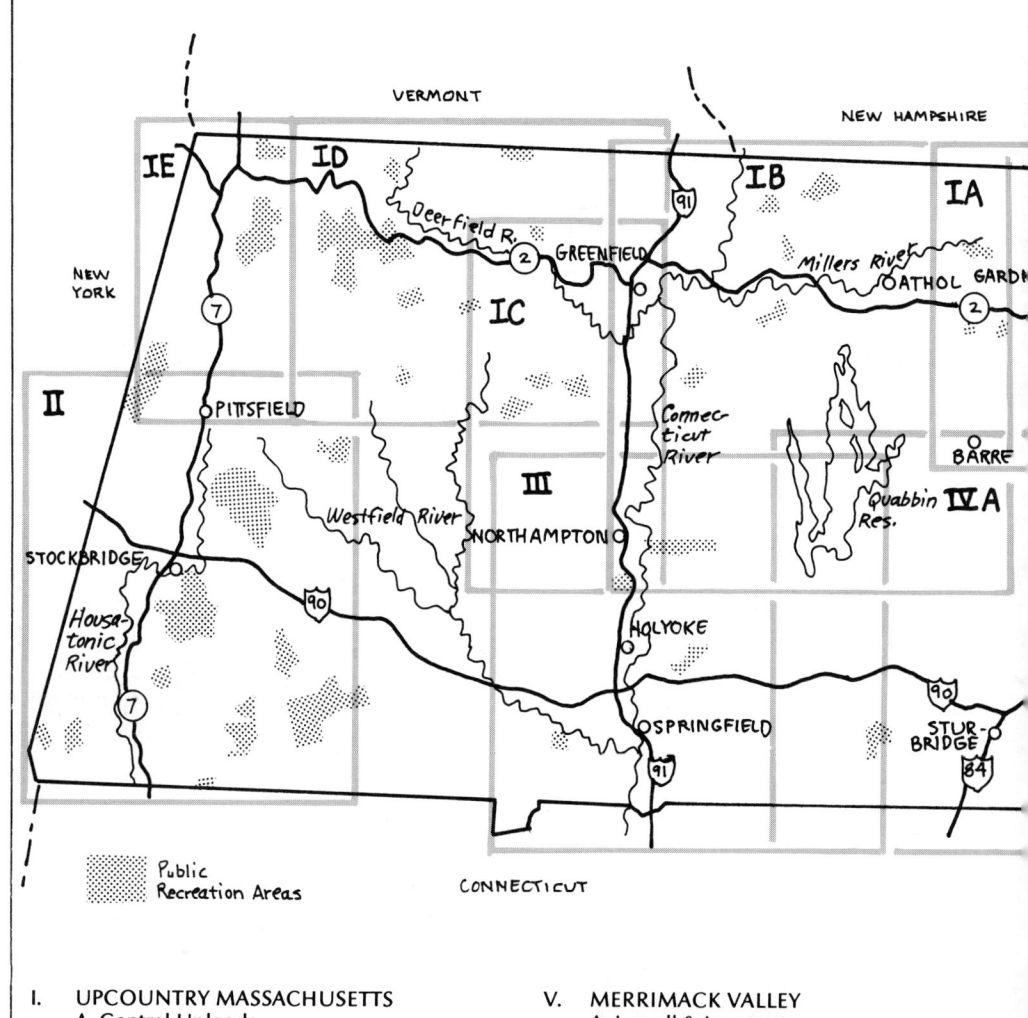

I. UPCOUNTRY MASSACHUSETTS
   A. Central Uplands
   B. Upper Pioneer Valley & North of Quabbin
   C. The Hilltowns
   D. Mohawk Trail Country
   E. North Berkshires
II. CENTRAL AND SOUTH BERKSHIRES
III. THE PIONEER VALLEY
IV. CENTRAL MASSACHUSETTS
   A. Old Sturbridge Village Country
   B. Worcester & The Blackstone River Valley
   C. The Nashoba Valley and North
V. MERRIMACK VALLEY
   A. Lowell & Lawrence
   B. The Middlesex Canal
VI. NORTH SHORE
   A. Salem and Marblehead
   B. Newburyport & The Cape Ann Area
   C. Cape Ann
VII. PLYMOUTH
VIII. SIPPICAN (BUZZARDS BAY)
IX. BRISTOL COUNTY
   A. New Bedford
   B. Fall River

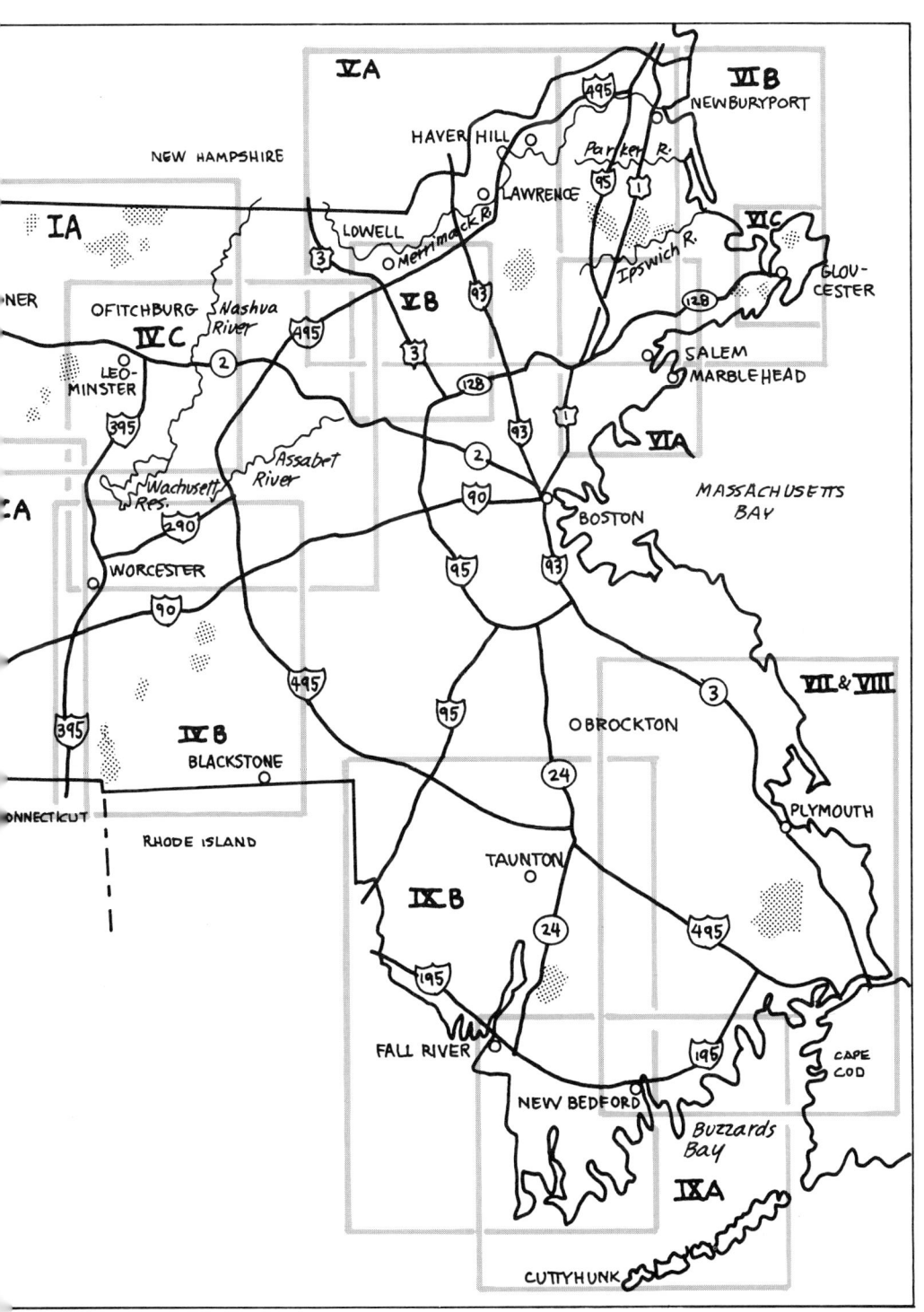

Acknowledgments

I would like to thank the following people, all of whom went far beyond the call of duty in helping me pull together the information for this book: Harry Dodson of Ashfield, Diggory Venn and Mrs. Arthur Shurcliff of Ipswich, Allen Young of Athol, Anna Duphiney and Joan Brownhill of New Bedford, Alan Long and Germaine Vallely of the Department of Environmental Management, Betsy Johnson of *The Advocate* (Williamstown), John Martin of Amherst, Michael Kane and Laura Yudin of the Northern Tier Project, Ann Hamilton of the Franklin County Chamber of Commerce, Sue Coleman of the Greater Gardner Chamber of Commerce, Tom Kussy of the Athol-Orange Chamber, Lillian Davis and Liz Marble of Ashburnham, Mary Taft of Uxbridge, Carolyn and Arnold Westwood of West Cummington, and Lloyd Crawford of West Hawley. There are many more and I am very grateful to you all.

Introduction

"The Other Massachusetts" has finally rolled out its welcome mat. In the past few years hundreds of bed & breakfasts, rural studios and galleries, and shops and restaurants have opened in unexpectedly beautiful places. And a half-dozen Heritage State Parks have begun dramatizing the history of old mill cities through extraordinary exhibits.

Where is The Other Massachusetts? Everyone who lives there, from Rehoboth in the southeast corner of the state to Williamstown in the northwest, from Newburyport in the northeast corner to Mount Washington in the southwest, knows. It applies (geographically) to the two-thirds of the state that lies beyond the Boston/Cape Cod axis.

There are many parts to The Other Massachusetts, very specific regions that do not homogenize into one image. This book attempts to bring them into focus.

Bostonians have traditionally ignored this picture entirely. They assume they live in "The Bay State" because Boston, along with its North and South Shores, overlooks Massachusetts Bay. Half the state's people live within the arc of Route 495, a highway that roughly defines Greater Boston. And these people tend to play on Cape Cod Bay (the state's fastest growing area), if they vacation at all in Massachusetts. Tanglewood aside, they also ignore the Berkshires, a cultural enclave at the western end of the state linked commercially and spiritually to New York state rather than to Boston.

But east of the Berkshires and west of Route 495 lies that vast grey zone variously identified as Central or Western Massachusetts. No wonder Boston, New York, and the rest of the world drives straight on through.

As a travel writer for *The Boston Globe* I limited my Massachusetts explorations to the Bays and the Berkshires for many years. Then a German publisher asked me to write the text for a photo book on Massachusetts. In his Munich-based ignorance, he assumed that visitors might want to know about the entire state.

As I drove around the state I was repeatedly amazed by the unself-conscious beauty of high, rolling countryside and by narrow roads along which little seems to have been built in a century.

Nothing much, I discovered, had been written about the less-touristed two-thirds of Massachusetts since the 1937 WPA Guide. And that included nothing about lodging and dining.

My German photo book was never published, but a few years later The Countryman Press (in their Vermont-based naiveté?) agreed to turn the text into *Massachusetts: An Explorer's Guide*, "a book about things to see and do, places to stay and to eat in ALL of Massachusetts."

Two-thirds of that 1979 book covered the Boston and Cape Cod bases. The second (1981) edition still acknowledged that few tourists ventured farther, "given the scarcity of places to stay and major 'attractions' to see."

Happily, in 1987 we can present a very different picture. Acknowledging that there is no need for another guide to Boston, Cape Cod, or the islands, we can omit them entirely and describe instead the wealth of things to see and do, pleasant places to stay and to dine in the Hampshire Hilltowns and the Five College Area, the Blackstone and Nashoba valleys, and the North Shore. From Plymouth and Bristol County towns, tourists are now opting to explore Boston rather than vice versa.

Because The Other Massachusetts constituted just one-third of the material in the original *Massachusetts: An Explorer's Guide*, I assumed that this project would be a breeze. But I had stumbled on the tip of a quickly emerging phenomenon.

The Other Massachusetts now offers what many vacationers drive far farther north to find: speedy and complete renewal. Whether it happens to be staying in an old townhouse and strolling a cobbled street in a fishing port or sleeping on a farm, swimming in its pond, and biking country roads. It also offers excellent hiking (note the new Mid-State Trail), canoeing, and cross-country skiing. You just have to know where to look—which is where this book will help.

A century ago rural towns like Princeton, Barre, and Ashfield had big summer hotels. And inns were scattered throughout the state along rail lines and old turnpikes. But current highways (notably the Massachusetts Turnpike) now funnel traffic so efficiently that hundreds of towns are bypassed, effectively "backroaded."

The old hotels were, unfortunately, long gone by the time urbanites began combing New England for country inns. And the day of the daytrip is over. Few people seem to enjoy driving for hours to see something and then driving home again. It's no wonder that the superb puppet shows in Lancaster and the sparkling waters in Douglas draw only locals.

Fortunately I can report that within the year required to research this book, dozens of new inns and bed & breakfasts have appeared—many of them on back roads or in classic New England villages that had never lodged a visitor. And Heritage State Parks have opened in Fall River, Holyoke, North Adams, Lowell, and Gardner, drawing visitors to towns that also happen to offer bargain shopping and great ethnic eating.

At the same time The Other Massachusetts remains essentially unchanged. Standout small museums like the Sterling and Clark Institute in Williamstown, Fruitlands in Harvard, and the art collections at Williams, Amherst, Smith, and Mount Holyoke colleges have seemingly always been there, along with the classic town Greens in New Salem and Templeton, Montague and Barre.

Note that we have listed prices—for inns and restaurants as well as admissions. We did this because precise numbers give you a better sense of what to expect than categories, but we realize that they date instantly. Please view them as benchmarks in the rising tide of inflation and phone ahead to confirm both times and rates.

C.T.

The meeting house, Warwick

What's Where in Massachusetts

AGRICULTURAL FAIRS A detailed list of fairs is available from the Massachusetts Department of Food and Agriculture (617-727-3018), 100 Cambridge Street, Boston 02202. The Hardwick, Topsfield, and Tri-County (Northampton) fairs all claim to be the oldest. There are a number of genuine, old-style fairs with ox pulls and livestock judging. Our favorites are those held in Middlefield, Hardwick, and Cummington. The Eastern States Exposition, held every September in West Springfield, is in a class by itself: a six-state event with some 6,000 animals competing for prizes, a midway, concession stands, big name entertainment, and the Avenue of States.

AIR RIDES A map/guide to some 50 public airports is available from the Massachusetts Aeronautics Commission (617-973-7350), 10 Park Plaza, Boston 02116. Most airports offer charters and scenic rides; check out Newburyport, North Adams, and Barre.

ALPINE SLIDES are found at Jiminy Peak in North Berkshire and at Mt. Tom in the Five College Area.

AMUSEMENT AREAS Most were founded in the late nineteenth century by city trolley companies as inducements to ride the cars out to the end of the line. Riverside Park near Springfield is the region's largest, but my favorites are Whalom Park in Lunenburg (Central Uplands) and Mountain Park in Holyoke. Lincoln Park near New Bedford is also good; Salem Willows in Salem is small but pleasant; and there is always the boardwalk in Salisbury Beach (see Newburyport).

ANIMALS New England's largest collection of animals is caged at Southwick's Wild Animal Farm, down a back road in Mendon (see Blackstone Valley). New Bedford has the best of the State's small city zoos. Worcester's animals are divided between the barnyard variety in Green Hill Park and the polar bear, wolves, and wild cats at the Science Center. Springfield and Pittsfield also have small zoos.

ANTIQUES Guides to local antiques groups are available from the Pioneer Valley Association, the Berkshire Visitors Bureau, and the Bristol Country Development Council (see Guidance for those areas). Marblehead and Essex produce their own pamphlet guides. New England's largest antiques shows are in the Sturbridge-area town of Brimfield.

ANTIQUITIES The dispute rages over who discovered Massachusetts. In Berkley you can read the various theories about who carved pictographs on Dighton Rock, a mystery which has been puzzling scholars since Cotton Mather; other sites of dubious origin include the beehive huts in Leverett and Pelham.

APPLES Contact the Massachusetts Department of Food and Agriculture (617-727-3018), 100 Cambridge Street, Boston 02202, for a guide to local orchards which welcome visitors. Note that there are three prime orchard areas in the state: the Nashoba Valley, the Sturbridge area, and the Hampshire Hilltown/Mohawk Trail Country towns.

ART MUSEUMS Williamstown is a pilgrimage point for art lovers from around the world. The Francine Clark Art Institute has an exceptional collection of French Impressionists and late nineteenth-century American Artists, a collection which is complemented by the newly expanded Williams College Art Museum with its American pieces. The Worcester Art Museum also has superb early and nineteenth-century American paintings. In Springfield both the Museum of Fine Arts and the George Walter Vincent Smith Art Museum are well worth visiting. In the Five College Area the Holyoke, Amherst, and Smith college museums all hold surprises. The Berkshire Museum in Pittsfield also has its share of American masterpieces, and the Norman Rockwell Museum in Stockbridge probably draws the biggest crowds of all. In the Nashoba Valley, Fruitlands also has its share of American primitives and landscapes. The Addison Gallery of American Art in Andover is yet another trove of Copleys, Sargents, and Whistlers.

AREA CODE The state is covered by two Area Codes. The code for the western portion of the state is 413 and for the eastern portion is 617. You will find the correct area code for each region of the book listed before Guidance.

BALLOONING The Balloon School of Massachusetts in Brimfield (413-245-7013) offers lessons and rides, and Balloon Adventures of New Bedford (617-636-4846) offers champagne flights. Silver Eagle Balloon (617-549-2660) in North Amherst also takes paying passengers.

BASKETBALL The Basketball Hall of Fame in Springfield has just moved to a brand new building and expanded and the entire city of Springfield celebrates the sport in a variety of ways.

BEACHES In this book we have listed just those strands to which public access is clear. On the saltwater side check out Crane's Beach in Ipswich, Singing Beach in Manchester, Duxbury Beach (described in Plymouth), and Demarest Loyd (described in Fall River). Our pick of the freshwater beaches is Wallum Lake in Douglas.

BED & BREAKFASTS A "B&B" is a private home in which guests pay to stay and to breakfast. Throughout The Other Massachusetts they are providing attractive lodging, much of it in areas which have not welcomed paying guests for upwards of a century. This is especially true in the Hampshire Hilltowns, the Mohawk Trail Country, the Central Uplands, and in the Nashoba and Blackstone Valleys. In the course of researching this book we have visited hundreds of B&Bs and can vouch for the outstanding quality of most. Prices vary but most remain well below those of inns and motels in their areas. A descriptive pamphlet listing B&Bs and *A Look at Bed & Breakfasts in Massachusetts* (geared to both hosts and guests) are available from the Massachusetts Division of Tourism (617-727-3201), 100 Cambridge Street, Boston 02202.

BED & BREAKFAST RESERVATION SERVICES In addition to the individual hosts described in each section, we have noted the services which place guests in private homes, many of which do not advertise themselves as bed & breakfasts. These reservation service organizations are Pineapple Hospitality (based in New Bedford but with host homes throughout the state); Bed and Breakfast in Marblehead and the North Shore and Bed and Breakfasts Associates, Bay Colony, Ltd. (both with North Shore homes); Be Our Guest in the Plymouth Area; Folkstone Bed & Breakfast in Boylston (serving Worcester County); and Berkshire Bed & Breakfast in Williamsburg (with 60 homes in Western Massachusetts).

BICYCLING Lincoln Guide Service (617-259-9204) in Lincoln offers inn-to-inn tours in the Nashoba Valley and east of Quabbin; Berkshire Valley Bicycle Touring (413-298-3160) in Stockbridge; and Calypso Excursions (617-465-7173) in Newburyport also offer guided tours. *Short Bike Rides in Greater Boston and Central Massachusetts* by Howard Stone, The Globe Pequot Press, details a number of rides in Bristol County, the Nashoba Valley, the North Shore, Upcountry Massachusetts and the Pioneer Valley. *Short Rides in the Berkshires* by Lewis Cuyler (Globe Pequot Press) describes 27 routes. We have noted rentals and outstanding bike routes in most sections.

BIRDING The Massachusetts Audubon Society headquartered in Lincoln (617-259-9500) was founded in 1896 in an attempt to discourage using wild bird plumage as hat decorations, and it is the oldest of the country's Audubon groups. Sanctuaries are found in Ipswich, Marshfield, Leominster, Wachusett, Northampton, Hampden, and Lenox; request a pamphlet guide. Other prime birding spots include Plum Island (see Newburyport) and the Holyoke Range State Park (see Five College Area). The prime eagle-watching spot is from Quabbin Park in Belchertown (also Five College Area).

BOAT EXCURSIONS Harbor Tours are available in Newburyport, Salem, and Plymouth; ferries sail from Plymouth (to Provincetown) and New Bedford (both to Martha's Vineyard and to Cuttyhunk). You can tour the canals and Merrimack River in Lowell and cruise a reach of the Connecticut from Northfield Mountain. Also see Whale Watching and Fishing.

BOAT LAUNCHES Sites are detailed in brochures on salt and freshwater fishing available from the Massachusetts Division of Fisheries and Wildlife (617-727-3151), 100 Cambridge Street, Boston 02202.

BOAT RENTALS Sailboat rentals are available in Marblehead (where you can also learn to sail) and Gloucester. Rowboats can be rented at Pontoosac and Onota lakes in Pittsfield, Greenwater Pond in Becket, Hoosuc Lake in Cheshire, Goose Pond and Laurel Lake in Lee, Lake Garfield in Monterey, Prospect Lake in North Egremont, Otis Reservoir in Otis, Lake Quinsigamond in Worcester, and Buttonwood Park, New Bedford. Also see Canoeing.

BOSTON We have not included Massachusetts' capitol and major city because there are already a number of fine guides to Boston. These include: the *I Love Boston Guide* (Collier Books), *Fodor's Boston* (Fodor's Travel Guides), *Frommer's Guide to Boston* (Simon & Schuster) *Blue Guide, Boston and Cambridge* (W. W. Norton & Company), *In and Out of Boston, With (or Without) Children* (Globe Pequot Press), *Historic Walks in Boston* (Globe Pequot Press), and *Historic Walks in Cambridge* (Globe Pequot).

CAMPING The Department of Environmental Management lists State Camping Areas in its *Massachusetts Forests and Parks* brochure available from DEM (617-727-3159), 100 Cambridge Street, Boston 02202. A glossy *Massachusetts Campground Directory* to commercial campgrounds is available from the Massachusetts Division of Tourism (617-727-3200) or write: MACO Spirit, Box 28, Boston 02022.

CANALS The country's first canal is said to have been built in South Hadley in 1794 (scant trace remains). The country's first major canal was the Middlesex, built to connect Boston and Lowell and opened in 1808. The Blackstone Canal which once connected Worcester and Providence, RI is now evolving into a linear park (see Blackstone Valley). The Farmington Canal, which ran from Northampton through Westfield and Southwick on its way to New Haven, is also visible in parts. In Holyoke and Lowell power canals have become important parts of Heritage State Parks, as they will in Turner's Falls.

CANOEING The canoe is making a come back. Early in this century canoeing was a common sight on Massachusetts rivers, and within the last decade canoe lessons and rentals have proliferated. A leaflet guide to the 70-mile trip from the North River at Scituate to Dighton Rock State Park in Berkley is available from the Plymouth County Development Council (see Plymouth area). A newly updated guidebook and a free pamphlet *It's Your River* (showing access points) is available from the Connecticut River Watershed Council (413-584-0057), located at Arcadia Wildlife Sanctuary, Easthampton 01027 (see the Five College Area), which offers guided tours. Both lessons and rentals are offered at nearby Barton Cove.

On the North Shore the Annisquam and

Ipswich rivers are both eminently canoeable. A "Canoeing Map of the Ipswich River" is available from the Ipswich River Watershed Association (see Cape Ann). A similar map/guide to the Merrimac is available from the Merrimac River Watershed Association (see Merrimack Valley). Check the Five College Area, Cape Ann, the Berkshires, Merrimack and Blackstone Valleys for canoe rentals. The *AMC River Guide-Central and Southern New England*, available from the Appalachian Mountain Club, 5 Joy Street, Boston 02108, details river passages and portages throughout the state. Elaborate summer canoe outings are arranged in July and August by Konkapot Kitchens in Mill River (see Berkshires). For canoe races check North of Quabbin and the Blackstone Valley, and for canoe-geared camping check North of Quabbin and Cape Ann.

CAPE COD We have not included Cape Cod because so many other guides do. *Cape Cod, A Guide* (Little, Brown) is the classic. There is *Fodor's Cape Cod* (Fodor's Travel Guides) and from Globe Pequot Press: *Short Walks on Cape Cod and the Vineyard* and *Short Bike Rides of Cape Cod, Nantucket and the Vineyard*.

CHAIR LIFT RIDES All summer and fall you can ride to the top of Mount Tom in Holyoke (see Five College Area) and Mt. Wachusett in Princeton (see Central Uplands).

CHILDREN (especially for) Children's museums are found in Dartmouth (see Fall River) and in Holyoke (Five College Area). The Gloucester Fisherman's Museum (Cape Ann) is also geared to kids. In addition there are doll museums in Sturbridge and Russells Mills (see Fall River) and the Toy Cupboard Theater and Museum in Lancaster is a delight for children of all ages. "Especially for Kids" (a listing of happenings in Bristol County) is available from the Bristol County Development Council (617-997-1250), PO Box BR-197, New Bedford 02741. Also see Animals, Amusement Areas, Swimming, and Water Slides.

CHRISTMAS TREES The Department of Food and Agriculture (617-727-3018), 100 Cambridge Street, Boston 02202, supplies a current list of Christmas Tree Farms at which you can cut-your-own.

COVERED BRIDGES See Charlemont, Colrain, Conway, Greenfield, Pepperell (Groton Street, over the Nashua River), Sheffield (two of them), and Old Sturbridge Village.

CRAFTS The country's largest concentration of craftspeople is said to be found in the Five College Area and surrounding hills. A *Western Massachusetts Craft Directory*, available from the Arts Extension Service, Division of Continuing Education (413-545-2360), University of Massachusetts, Amherst 01003, lists more than 200 galleries and craftspeople who welcome visitors. We have described many of these craftspeople in the Upcountry Massachusetts chapter. The Leverett Craftsmen & Artists and Art Space in Greenfield (see Upper Pioneer Valley), the half-dozen outstanding galleries in Northampton (see Five College Area), Salmon Falls Marketplace in Shelburne Falls (see Mohawk Trail Country), and the Berkshire Artisans Community Center in Pittsfield are all worth checking out. The country's premier craft fair, the A.C.C. Craft Fair, is now held each June at the Eastern States Exposition Grounds in West Springfield, and the quality of crafts displayed at the Deerfield Craft Fairs (June and September) draw discerning crowds.

CRANBERRIES Introduced by the Indians, Pilgrims called them "crane berries," since the pink blossoms reminded them of the heads of cranes. Harvesting in Plymouth County gets underway in late September and is especially colorful if the bog is flooded, making billions of berries bob to the surface. The most famous viewing spot for the harvest is the Edaville RR in South Carver (see Plymouth), scene of an annual Cranberry Festival. The Cranberry World Visitors Center in Plymouth presents the history of the industry.

FACTORY OUTLETS Bristol County

prides itself on being the outlet capital of New England; leaflet guides are available from the Bristol County Development Council (617-997-1250), 70 North Second Street, New Bedford 02714. Worcester County's pamphlet lists more than 100 outlets and is available from the Worcester County Visitors' Bureau, 350 Mechanics Tower, Worcester 01608 (617-753-2920). The Pioneer Valley Convention & Visitors Bureau (413-787-1548), 1500 Main Street, Springfield 01115, also publishes a pamphlet to its area. In this book we have described major outlets under Selective Shopping.

FALL FOLIAGE A *Spirit of Massachusetts Fall Foliage Guide* is available from the Massachusetts Division of Tourism (617-727-3201), 100 Cambridge Street, Boston 02202. Our advice is to follow the roads which branch north and south off Route 2, like the many veins in a leaf.

FARMERS MARKETS A list is available from the Department of Food and Agriculture (617-727-3018), 100 Cambridge Street, Boston 02202.

FISHING The Massachusetts Division of Marine Fisheries (617-727-3193) publishes the *Massachusetts Salt Water Guide*, detailing "How, Where, When and What to Catch," listing launching sites, rental rowboats, bait and tackle shops, licensing requirements, and party boats by town. No license is required and all tackle and bait is supplied if you want to fish in salt water. But for some puzzling reason this state makes it discouragingly difficult to try fishing inland. Just to put a line in the water you have to get a license, nowhere can you rent tackle, and very few places offer lessons on how to put a worm on a hook. Thousands of city folk (unlucky enough to have no grandpa to tell them how) are effectively being discouraged from testing the waters which the state stocks at their expense. In many state parks fishing is the only lure. A *Guide to Fresh Water Fishing* and *Fish and Wildlife Laws* are available from the Division of Fisheries and Wildlife to anyone who sends a self-addressed, stamped, business-size enve-

lope. Quabbin Reservoir (see North of Quabbin and the Five College Area) is the state's premier fishing hole. The Deerfield River (see Mohawk Trail Country) is another favorite.

GOLF We have listed golf courses in each chapter. A list for the entire state is available from the Massachusetts Division of Tourism (617-727-3201), 100 Cambridge Street, Boston 02202.

GUIDANCE The Massachusetts Division of Tourism (617-727-3201), 100 Cambridge Street, Boston 02202, offers a number of useful, free publications: a "Spirit of Massachusetts" Vacation Kit, a seasonal Calendar of Events, a "Ski Massachusetts" brochure, fall foliage information, a Bed & Breakfast Guide, a "Mini-Vacation Packages" brochure, and a Massachusetts road map. Regional Tourist Councils and Chambers of Commerce are listed under Guidance at the head of each chapter.

HANG GLIDING At Aeolus Hang Glider (617-448-5214), Martin's Pond Road, Groton, certified instructors offer lessons year-round. Favored hang gliding spots include Mount Greylock (see North Berkshire), the Hairpin Turn above North Adams (see Mohawk Trail Country), and Skinner State Park in Hadley (see Five College Area).

HAY AND SLEIGH RIDES Both hay and sleigh rides are available in Essex (Cape Ann) and Whately (Upper Pioneer Valley) and at Old Sturbridge Village and the Salem Cross Inn (see Sturbridge Village Country).

HERITAGE STATE PARKS A new way of revitalizing old industrial cities, each "park" revolves around a handsome Visitors Center in which multi-visual exhibits dramatize what makes the community special. In Lowell the state's efforts are upstaged by the National Park, but the state's upgrading of the canal system and excellent exhibits are exceptional. The film in Fall River's riverside, mill-like Visitors Center depicts the way in which ethnic

6 What's Where in Massachusetts

The arts are alive at the Castle Hill Festival, Ipswich

groups have been woven together to form the fabric of the city. In Holyoke a film also dramatizes ethnic and industrial history with an emphasis on the city's extensive canal system. Trains and the Hoosac Tunnel are the focus of the park in North Adams, which is actually built in a defunct railyard. Visitors walk through a simulated tunnel to get the full effect of what it felt like to build it. In Gardner, craftspeople demonstrate the furniture-making skills which put their city on the map, and in Lawrence the stress is, again, on the multi-ethnic mix of people who built the city's massive mills. Each park also draws visitors out into the city. In Fall River there are boat rides and walking tours, in Holyoke a train ride, and in Lawrence a towpath along the canal. In all, the quality of what's been done is impressive and because the parks are so new, their effect is just beginning to be felt. A booklet guide to the burgeoning system (a linear park along the Blackstone Valley is just taking shape, as is the park at Turners Falls) is available from the Department of Environmental Management (617-727-3159), 100 Cambridge Street, Boston 02202.

HIKING The Department of Environmental Management (DEM) has been busy in the forests as well as cities (see Heritage State Parks), blazing long-distance trails across The Other Massachusetts. The Mid-State Trail, incorporating the 1920s Wampack Trail, traverses ridges which run much of the way from Ashby on the New Hampshire line, over Mt. Wachusett, and on down to the Connecticut line. Efforts are underway to provide bed & breakfast lodging for hikers along the way (it's possible already on the northern stretch; see Central Uplands) and a new pedestrian bridge carries the trail across Route 2.

Unfortunately no practical way has yet been found to ford the Connecticut River, but the Metacomet–Monadnock Trail theoretically runs southwest from New Hampshire across the Holyoke Range (incorporating newly upgraded trails and a visitors center) and the Connecticut River to the Mt. Tom Range, on down to Connecticut (see Five College Area). Contact the Trails Program, DEM (617-727-3160),

225 Friend Street, Boston 02114. *Fifty Hikes in Massachusetts* by John Brady & Brian White (Countryman Press) is a well-written guide to trails throughout the state. The Appalachian Mountain Club (617-523-0636), headquartered at 5 Joy Street, Boston, now maintains Bascom Lodge atop Mt. Greylock and offers guided hikes. The AMC *Massachusetts and Rhode Island Trail Guide*, covers the Appalachian Trail through the Berkshires and the Midstate. The *Williams Outing Club Trail Guide* and map, available in Williamstown bookstores, is also a handy guide to Mt. Greylock and surrounding mountains. The Essex County Greenbelt Association's *Passbook* (see Cape Ann) reveals a number of rewarding walks on the North Shore. Also see Yankee Groups for details about Trustees of Reservations, Birding for Massachusetts Audubon, and State Parks.

HISTORIC HOUSES Within the book we have described houses which are open on a regular basis. The Bay State Historical League (617-227-3956), Room 51, State House, Boston 02133, publishes a *Directory of Historical Agencies in Massachusetts*.

HORSEBACK RIDING We are talking here of stables which offer trail riding for a fee. They are described in almost every chapter.

HOSTELING The American hosteling movement began in 1934 in Northfield, where there is still a summer hostel. Although geared to bicyclists hostels are not limited to them. For a mapped guide to New England hostels send a stamped, self-addressed envelope to the Greater Boston Council, AYH, 251 Harvard Street, Brookline 02146 (617-731-5430 or 731-6692 weekdays). For details about the year-round hostel in Littleton see Nashoba Valley.

HUNTING The source for information about licenses, rules, and wildlife management areas is the Massachusetts Division of Fisheries and Wildlife (617-727-3151), 100 Cambridge Street, Boston 02202. Request the current "Abstracts" and a list of the Division's wildlife management areas.

INNS A century ago this state boasted hundreds of inns, scattered along all major stage and rail routes. Dozens can still be found in the Berkshires and some grand old landmarks have recently been restored in unexpected places like Warwick (North of Quabbin), Barre (Old Sturbridge Village Country), Whitinsville (Blackstone Valley), and Princeton (Nashoba Valley). The Old Deerfield Inn (Upper Pioneer Valley) remains inviting. Also see Bed & Breakfasts.

LAKES The state's largest is the man-made Quabbin Reservoir, offering fine fishing; Wachusett Reservoir (the next largest) is also man-made and also good for fishing. The largest lake with public swimming is Lake Chaubunagungamaug in Webster (unfortunately it is not in the book because it falls between the Blackstone Valley and Old Sturbridge Village Area but it is very much there, complete with bathhouse). Other lakes with public access have been described in each chapter.

MAPLE SUGARING Sugaring, a skill learned from the Indians, is thriving today, primarily in the Hampshire Hilltowns, an area with more sugarhouses than the rest of the state put together. During Sugaring Season in March, visitors are welcome to watch producers "boil off" the sap, reducing it to the sweet liquid which is traditionally sampled on ice or snow. A *Maple Sugaring in the Pioneer Valley* guide is available from the Department of Food and Agriculture (617-727-3018), 100 Cambridge Street, Boston 02202.

MARTHA'S VINEYARD We have not included the vineyard in this book, but there are a number of books about the island. *Martha's Vineyard, A Guide* is published by Globe Pequot Press, which also publishes *Short Walks on Cape Cod and the Vineyard* and *Short Bike Rides on Cape Cod, Nantucket and Martha's Vineyard*.

MOUNTAINS Mt. Greylock is the state's highest and you can get to the top (3,491 feet) by car. You can also drive up Mt. Everett (Berkshire), Mt. Wachusett (Central Uplands), Sugarloaf (Upper Pioneer Valley), and Mt. Tom and Mt. Holyoke (Five College Area). All these offer hiking trails, as do Mt. Toby (Upper Pioneer Valley) and Mt. Grace (North of Quabbin). For some dramatic ridge trails see Hiking. Also see Alpine Slides and Chair Lifts.

MUSEUM VILLAGES Old Sturbridge Village, re-creating rural life in the 1830s, is one of New England's biggest tourist attractions and has spawned thousands of adjacent "beds," dozens of shops and restaurants, and some smaller museums in town. Plimoth Plantation is a smaller but equally painstaking reconstruction of the Pilgrim Village of 1627 (note its new visitor center). Hancock Shaker Village is a restored Shaker complex in the Berkshires, and Old Deerfield is an Upper Pioneer Valley restoration of a dozen eighteenth and nineteenth century homes. In East Springfield there is also Storrowtown, one of the country's earliest re-created villages, though it is very small. Fruitlands Museum in the Nashoba Valley is a unique grouping of collections, although not a village as such.

MUSIC Music festivals are a growing phenomena. The oldest (since 1858) is held in Worcester in October. The newest is the summer-long Great Woods Festival in Mansfield, begun in 1986. The best known is the Berkshire Festival at Tanglewood in July and August. Other summer series of note include: South Mountain in Pittsfield, Aston Magna in Great Barrington, the Sevenars in South Worthington, Mohawk Trail Concerts in Charlemont, the Castle Hill Festival in Ipswich, and organ concerts at Hammond Castle.

NANTUCKET We have not included Nantucket in this edition. We recommend *Nantucket, A Guide With Tours*, Globe Pequot Press.

NATURE PRESERVES Public green space ranges from the vast wildlife management areas of the Division of Fisheries and Game to the small but superb spaces maintained by the Trustees of Reservations (see Yankee Groups). Add to this the extensive State Forest and Park System, conserva-

What's Where in Massachusetts 9

Summertime on the Green River, Greenfield

tion areas, town forests, and private preserves like the Norcross Wildlife Sanctuary (see Old Sturbridge Village Area). The Other Massachusetts offers an unsung wealth of inviting walking trails, lake, and riverside areas.

PICK YOUR OWN Listings of places in which you can pick your own apples, blueberries, and strawberries are available from the Department of Food and Agriculture (617-727-3018), 100 Cambridge Street, Boston 02202.

SAILBOARDS Boards can be rented in Magnolia and Manchester (see North Shore).

SAILING Sailing lessons are available and boats can be rented both in Marblehead and Gloucester (see North Shore).

SCUBA DIVING New England Divers (617-922-6951) in Beverly offers diving instruction.

SKIING A *Ski Massachusetts* brochure is available from the Massachusetts Division of Tourism (617-727-3201), 100 Cambridge Street, Boston 02202. Within this book we have described each ski area. In the Berkshires there is Jiminy Peak, Brodie, Bousquet, Catamount, Butternut Basin, and Otis Ridge. In Mohawk Trail Country check out Berkshire East and the newly expanded Berkshire Snow Basin. In the Five College Area there is Mt. Tom, and in the Central Uplands, Mt. Wachusett. There is also Boston Hill in the Merrimack Valley.

SKI TOURING Just 15 years ago the Finns of Fitchburg were about the only Bay Staters skiing through the Massachusetts woods. There are currently more than a dozen commercial touring centers and hundreds of miles of marked cross-country trails in The Other Massachusetts. We have described touring centers in the Merrimack Valley, Central Uplands, Upper Pioneer Valley, Mohawk Trail Country, North Berkshire, Berkshire, and Old Sturbridge Village Country sections. Trails are noted throughout the book under Cross-Country Skiing; also see Green Space, and Forests, Parks, and Reservations. The state's most dependable snow conditions are found in the Western Massachusetts snowbelt which runs North–South through Stump Sprouts (a lodge and touring center) in East Hawley, the Windsor Notch Reservation in Windsor, and Hickory Hill Ski Touring Center in Worthington. A high altitude touring network is presently planned for Greylock Glen in Adams.

STATE FORESTS AND PARKS Massachusetts boasts the nation's SIXTH largest park system, pretty good for the sixth smallest state. The Department of Environmental Management (DEM) is responsible for more than a quarter million acres of public forests and parks. We have described more than 50 forests, parks, and reservations and are continually surprised by their variety. There is ample opportunity for camping (year-round cabins are available in the Savoy Mountain, Willard Brook, and Mohawk Trails State Forests), canoeing, swimming, skiing downhill (at Mt. Wachusett and Butternut) and cross-country, rock climbing, hang gliding, not to mention hiking. DEM continues to ac-

Scrimshaw, New Bedford Whaling Museum

quire new properties (in '86 it was Mosely State Park on the Merrimack River) and to upgrade interpretive programs (witness the new visitors center at the Holyoke Range State Park). The Massachusetts Forest and Park map/guide is a cryptic but indispensable key to this vast system, available from DEM (617-727-3180), 100 Cambridge Street, Boston 02202. For specific information it is best to contact the regional offices: in the Berkshires (413-442-8928); for the Connecticut River Valley (413-549-1461); for Worcester County (617-368-0126); for the Northeast (617-369-3350); and for the Southeast (617-866-2580).

THEATER Summer theaters are located in Beverly (North Shore), Stockbridge (Berkshire), Williamstown (North Berkshire), South Hadley (Five College Area), Gardner and Fitchburg (Central Uplands), and Greenfield. Stage/West in West Springfield is a year-round theater company.

TRAIN EXCURSIONS Mystic Valley Railway Society (617-361-4445, PO Box 486, Hyde Park 02136) runs a Mohawk Trail Express to North Adams on Columbus Day weekend and other excursions throughout the year. Holyoke Heritage State Park (413-534-1723) stages one-hour, round-trip rides on weekends. The Providence and Worcester Railroad (617-799-4475, PO Box 1188, Worcester 01601) runs weekend excursions over the line on which it hauls freight weekdays. Edaville Railroad (617-866-4526), Route 58, South Carver, tours a large cranberry bog (at its brightest in October), and the Berkshire Scenic Railway (413-243-2872) offers spring through fall hour-long trips between Lee and Great Barrington via Stockbridge and Housatanic (weekends and holidays). For details check respective chapters.

TRUSTEES OF RESERVATIONS A nonprofit organization founded in 1891 to preserve the public use and enjoyment of historic places and beautiful tracts of land (much as a person enjoys outstanding paintings in museums), the Trustees of Reservations now owns and manages more than 40 properties described in this book. Several of these are beautifully maintained historic houses (in Stockbridge, New Ashford, and Cummington) but most are exceptional pieces of land, many with waterfalls. A booklet guide to all 69 properties is available from the Trustees of Reservations (617-921-1944), 572 Essex Street, Beverly 01915.

VINEYARDS For details on the three vineyards in The Other Massachusetts check the Nashoba Valley and Plymouth sections.

WATERFALLS Waterfalls can be found in Ashfield, Barre, Becket, Blandford, Cheshire, Chesterfield, Dalton, Middlefield, Mt. Washington, New Marlboro, North Adams, Royalston, Sheffield, Shelburn Falls, Williamsburg, and Worthington.

WHALE WATCHING More than a dozen major whale-watching operators now offer thousands of spring through fall trips to watch the whales who congregate to feed on Stellwagen Bank, a dozen miles off Cape Ann. Check the listings for Newburyport, Cape Ann, and Plymouth. If you are inclined to be seasick opt for a larger, newer boat and be sure to bring a sweater and windbreaker on even a hot day; for many landlubbers these excursions are a first encounter with a small boat on the open sea.

YANKEE GROUPS Many of the state's most historic buildings and most magnificent sites are owned, not by state or federal agencies, but by indomitable old Yankee groups, which in the nineteenth century pioneered the idea of protecting historic and beautiful places. The Trustees of Reservations are doing a splendid job of both preserving and promoting their properties (see above). Massachusetts Audubon seems less enthusiastic about sharing its wealth than in years past, but the Appalachian Mountain Club (see hiking) is reaching out to the public through its publications and through Boston and Bascom Lodge-based programs, as never before.

Lowell's pioneering industrial machinery is being restored and reactivated

A Calendar of Events

Here is a roster of major events that occur each year. A more complete calendar of events, listing precise dates and phone numbers, may be obtained from the Division of Tourism.

JANUARY First Night in Worcester and Springfield; house tours in Lenox; skiing throughout the Berkshires, at Mt. Wachusett, and at Mt. Tom.

FEBRUARY Best month for skiing and ski touring.

MARCH Maple sugaring in the Hampshire Hilltowns and throughout Upcountry Massachusetts.

APRIL River Rat Race in Athol; white water canoe races on the Westfield River; herring run in Pembroke; sheep shearing demonstrations at Plimouth Plantation and Old Sturbridge Village.

MAY Apple Blossom Festival in Harvard; Mother's Day Antique Festival in Brimfield; canoe race in Uxbridge.

JUNE Blessing of the Fleet in Gloucester; ACC Craft Fair in East Springfield; Old Deerfield Summer Craft Fair.

JULY Independence Day observances in Old Sturbridge Village and Historic Deerfield; fireworks and parades in Fitchburg, Grafton, Athol, Pittsfield, and Springfield; opening of the Berkshire Music Festival at Tanglewood; Marblehead Race Week; Susan Anthony Days in Adams.

AUGUST Yankee Homecoming, Newburyport; Pilgrim's Progress in Plymouth; World's People's Dinners, Hancock Shaker Village; Berkshire Crafts Fair, Great Barrington; Center Street Festival, New Bedford; Westfield Fair in Westfield; Indian Pow-Wow in Charlemont; Heritage Week in Salem; Cummington Fair in Cummington.

SEPTEMBER Three County Fair, Northampton; World Kielbasa Festival in Chicopee; Franklin County Fair in Greenfield; The Big "E" in West Springfield; Barrington Fair in Great Barrington.

OCTOBER Horseshed Craft Fair in Lancaster; Mohawk Express to North Adams; Foliage Festivals in Conway and Ashfield; Plimouth Plantation Harvest Celebration; Lenox Apple Squeeze, Lenox; Columbus Day Parade, Worcester; Mount Greylock Ramble, Adams; Apple Festival, Ipswich; Haunted Happenings, Salem.

NOVEMBER Thanksgiving in Old Sturbridge Village; craft fairs in Sturbridge, Leverett, Worcester.

DECEMBER Christmas celebrations in Marblehead, Ipswich, Newburyport, and Lenox.

Upcountry Massachusetts

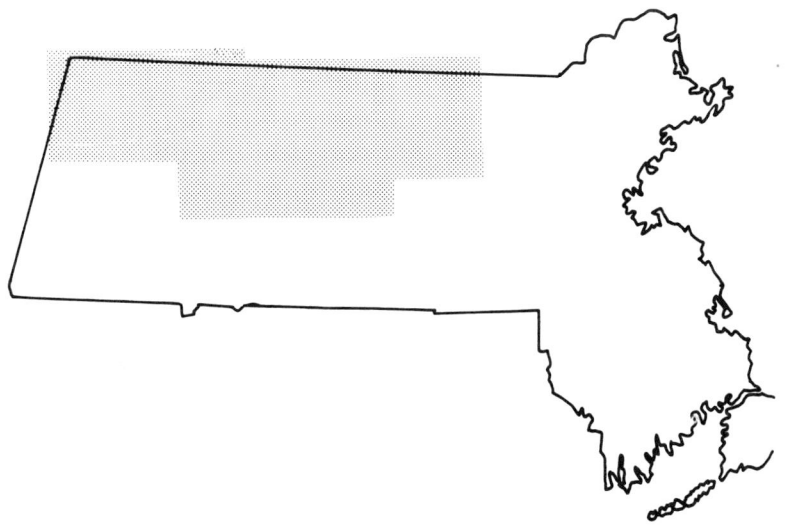

INTRODUCTION

Massachusetts has traditionally been carved into regions which run from north to south; from westernmost Berkshire County (which runs the length of the state) to "Massachusetts Bay" (encompassing Boston and its north and south "shores" on the east).

So the idea of a region stretching from east to west across the state's Northern Tier—from Williamstown in the west to Gardner on the east—is a novel idea. With the exception of the Connecticut River Valley the entire Upcountry Massachusetts region is hilly, lightly populated, economically depressed, and very beautiful. It harbors almost half the Commonwealth's public land but less than three percent of its people. It's not only the state's most rural region, but it is far more rural than most people believe any part of Massachusetts to be.

To promote this area as a destination—rather than just a pass-through zone—the Northern Tier (now incorporated with a director and office in Amherst) has produced a brochure to promote the area. "Come Upcountry. It's nearer than you think" is the message. You don't have to go to Vermont, New Hampshire, or Maine to find miles of wooded backroads, sugarhouses, waterfalls, hiking trails, and antiques. In the past few years a number of farms, renovated inns, and village homes have begun offering bed & breakfast. These hosts are happy to steer guests to local craftspeople, maple producers, and a variety of laid-back, rural pleasures.

The thrust of this chapter is to get you on (and then off of) Route 2, onto the myriad country roads which wander through river towns, by farmstands, up to hilltop orchards, and through covered bridges to one-store villages and fishing holes. I must confess that I have expanded Upcountry Massachusetts by a dozen or so towns (adding the Hampshire Hilltowns and the Montachusett area), fleshing out the natural region which has been only slightly trimmed to fit within political lines.

Central Uplands

The northern tier of Worcester County is a physical extension of New Hampshire's Monadnock Region: it is hilly, largely forested, and has some classic villages and old mills.

The country's furniture industry was centered here in the nineteenth century, thanks to the fortuitous combination of ample water and great stands of hardwood trees. (The 1938 hurricane wiped out most of the hardwoods.) The story of the area's inventors and artisans is well told in the exhibits at the new Gardner Heritage State Park.

The eastern part of this region (the countryside around Fitchburg) is known as Montachusett, a name coined by a Fitchburg newspaperman, for its three visible mountains—Monadnock (just over the New Hampshire line), Watatic on the north, and Wachusett on the south.

Beyond the Boston commuter belt (although accessible by rail), this is genuine country, a fact you realize as much in the small cities of Gardner and Fitchburg as in the byways of Ashburnham and Townsend. The area's many public forests and lakes offer camping and swimming and its back roads are well known to wheelmen. The newly resurrected Mid-State Trail traverses the ridge line which runs down its center.

AREA CODE: 617

GUIDANCE **Greater Gardner Chamber of Commerce** (632-1780), 59 Parker Street, Gardner 01440, open weekdays 9–5, is good for walk-in as well as written information on Ashburnham, Hubbardston, Gardner, Winchendon, Westminster, Winchester, and Templeton.

North Central Massachusetts Chamber of Commerce (343-6487), 344 Main Street, Fitchburg 01420; open weekdays 9–5, is good for walk-in as well as written information on Leominster, Fitchburg, Lunenburg, and Princeton.

Gardner Heritage State Park (630-1497). Walk-in information center open daily 9–4:30; Thursday until 9 PM. Closed Mondays late November through late May.

Department of Environmental Management (DEM), Region 3 (368-0126) can furnish details about area forests and reservations.

Profiles of the Past by Tom Malloy (Millers River Publishing), $8.95, is a lively, nicely illustrated anecdotal history of towns in this region.

GETTING THERE By train: the MBTA Commuter Rail (1-800-392-6099) extends to Gardner with more frequent runs to Fitchburg.

By bus: Vermont Transit runs regularly from Boston's Greyhound Terminal (423-5810), stopping in Gardner and Winchendon. Trailways (343-3064) stops at 221 Main Street in Fitchburg. Wilson Bus Lines serves Fitchburg (345-4829), and Englander Coach Lines (534-0669) stops just off Route 2 in Leominster.

GETTING AROUND Montachusett Area Regional Transit (MART) serves Fitchburg and Leominster (632-7373). Fitchburg & Leominster Street Railway Co. (345-7711) also serves this area.

TO SEE AND DO In **Gardner** Be aware that there is an "Uptown" (junction of Routes 101 and 140), a "Downtown" with worthwhile shops and restaurants, and a South Gardner (route 2A), a separate enclave.

Gardner State Heritage Park Visitors Center (630-1497) in the Lake Street Fire Station (corner of Central Richmond and Lake) is open daily 9–4:30; Thursday until 9 PM; closed Mondays late November through late May. Multimedia exhibits depict the history of furniture production, silversmithing, and the precision timing and fire instruments invented and still manufactured in town. Skilled craftsmen are frequently demonstrating. It also tells of the people—Yankees and immigrants—who have settled in town over the years. A second, modern visitors center at Dunn's Pond is due to open the summer of 1987, complete with changing facilities for the sandy beach. Look for the mammoth wooden chair, a Bicentennial tribute to the city's furniture, which sits in front of the high school on upper Main Street. Also check the furniture outlets under Selective Shopping.

Gardner Museum (632-3277), 28 Pearl Street, housed in the town's former brick, Romanesque-revival library, is open irregularly for special events.

In **Fitchburg:** Like most factory towns, Fitchburg has considerable ethnic diversity, but French-Canadians and Scandinavians are the major groups. The latter includes both Swedes, attracted by the Ivar Johnson Works (a bicycle and later a firearms company), and one of the largest Finnish communities in the country. Thanks to a tradition of philanthropy and a relatively healthy economy, Fitchburg has found it easier to raise money for cultural causes than most towns its size. It has a first-rate local library, an excellent small art museum, a planetarium, and a civic center complex frequently used for both amateur and professional sports and entertainment.

Fitchburg Art Museum (345-4207), 25 Merriam Parkway. Open weekdays 10–4:30; weekends: 1–5; closed Mondays and most of August and September. Free. Interesting collections of early American paintings, nineteenth-century European and twentieth-century American paintings, also special exhibits.

Wallace Civic Center and Planetarium (345-7300 or 343-7900). Open daily, 9–5.

Fitchburg Historical Society (345-1157), 50 Grove Street, open Monday–Thursday, 10–4, Sunday, 2–4. Closed summers. Collection includes a 300-year-old hurdy-gurdy and a 1777 "Vinegar" Bible.

VILLAGES **Ashby** (routes 31 and 119). The **First Parish Meeting House** (now the Unitarian Church) has a Willard clock that has to be wound by hand. Note the **Town Library, Grange Hall** (old town hall), **Ashby Tavern, Congregational Church, General Store**, the town pump and watering trough, and the bandstand where the Ashby Band (organized in 1887) holds forth every Wednesday evening in summer.

Princeton (Routes 31 and 62). This aristocratic old village frames an exceptional common at the southern foot of Mount Wachusett. There is a white steepled **Congregational Church**, built in 1883 but with a Paul Revere bell, a library, and a friendly coffee shop. The ridge road from the village to Mt. Wachusett is lined with 1890s country mansions and former inns (one mansion is now the Inn at Princeton). Also see Redemption Rock, Wachusett Meadows, and Mt. Wachusett State Park under Green Space.

Templeton. Route 2A crests at the Templeton Common, yielding a rare view of rippling hills for many miles to the west. On the common there is a handsome gathering of a Greek revival and a Federal-style church and also a fine old General Store (939–2110), built by Colonel Artemus Lee that is still serving its original purpose (although it now includes an Ice Cream and Christmas Barn). Inquire here about the hours of the handsome, brick historical society across the way. Colonel Lee was also responsible for lining the common with ash trees, which is why it looks leafier than the many town greens that were planted instead with elms.

Townsend, West Townsend, and Townsend Harbor (Route 119). Townsend itself is a classic center with a steepled white church (built in 1731 with a slave balcony), a brick wall, a Victorian town hall, a lineup of shops in nineteenth-century wooden buildings, and a common complete with bandstand. Two-and-a-half miles east of the center look for the **Reed Homestead** complex: a 1780s house with Rufus Porter stenciling (recently restored) and an adjoining gristmill and cooper shop (see Selective Shopping), open weekends in summer.

In West Townsend the **Old Brick Store**, center stage, was con-

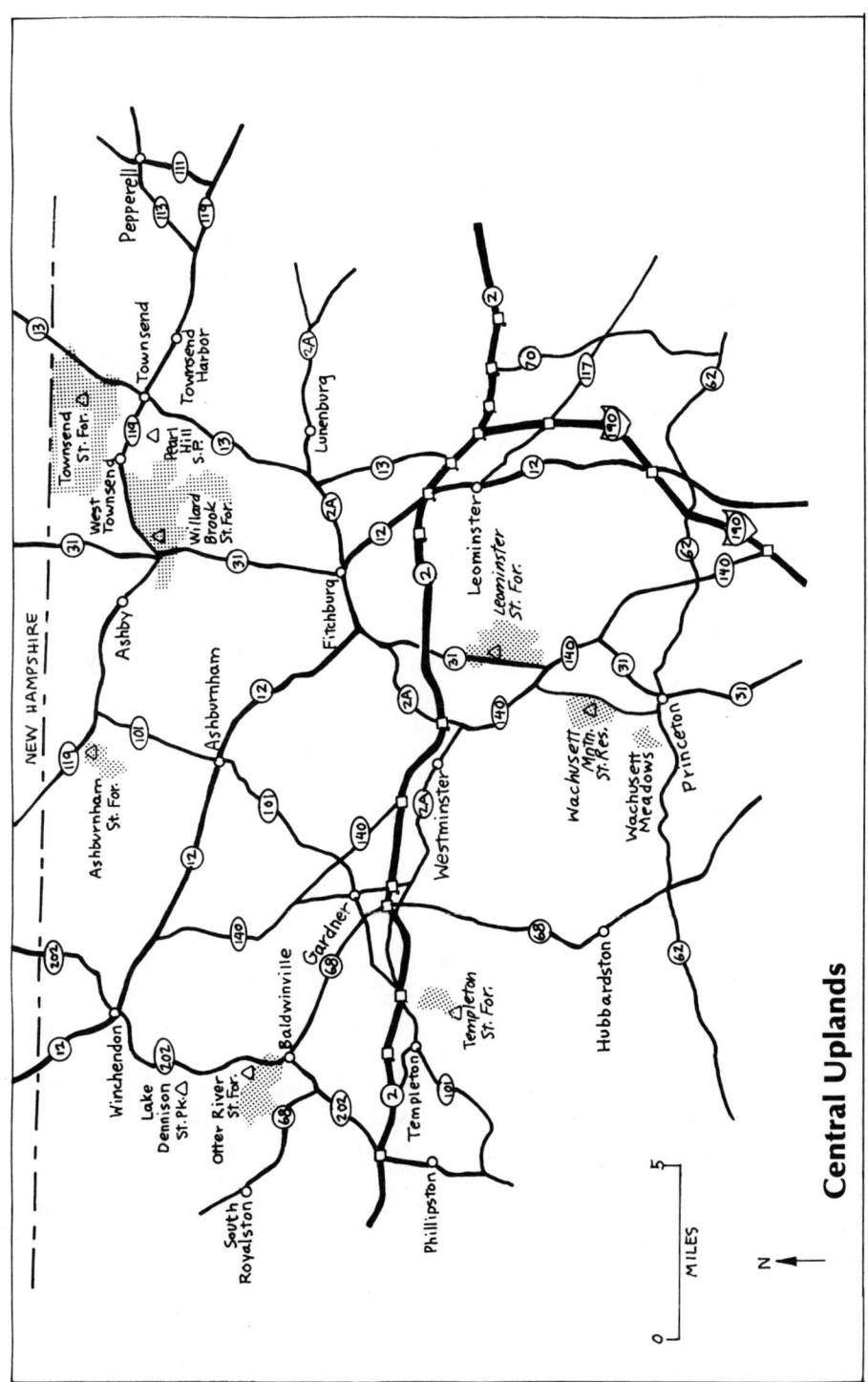

structed as a meetinghouse for the Universalist Restoration Society in 1849. The meeting hall was on the second floor; stores and the post office on the street. The steeple is long gone and the effect is unsettling but nice (the general store hasn't been fancied up).

Townsend Harbor, east of Townsend, contains some unusually handsome houses. It's unclear whether the name stems from the fact that its three fortresses harbored settlers in the early eighteenth century from Indian attacks, or from its status as a stop on the Underground Railroad.

Winchendon is still known as "Toy Town," a name earned when it was a center for the wooden toy industry and shipped its rocking horses all over the world. The toy factories are gone but a giant wooden horse still stands in a local park.

Winchendon Historical Society (297-0412), 50 Pleasant Street, open July and August, Tuesdays, 6:30–8:30 PM and by appointment, exhibits memorabilia.

FARMS TO VISIT In Hubbardston: **Moondance Yogurt & Chris Farm Stand** (928-4732). Commercially marketed yogurt made and sold here at a quality farm stand open April 15–October 15.

Westfield Farm (928-5110). Capri and Herb-Garlic Capri goat cheese made and sold here.

Flagg's Hubbardston Honey (928-3340). Unprocessed honey made and sold.

Sawyer's Berry Farm (928-3379). U-pick strawberries from mid-June until mid-July, raspberries from mid-July into August. Sweet corn from August until October.

Blueberry Hill Farm. U-pick cultivated blueberries from August until September. Picnic tables, drinking water and rest rooms.

Hubbardston Orchards and Flower Shop (928-4488). Flowers May–October, apples and cider in season.

Other: **All Seasons Farm Stand** (386-5539) in Ashby; 42 Fitchburg State Road.

Cambridge Grant Farm (827-4485), 27 Wilker Road, Ashburnham.

Maple Syrup: **Boggastowe Farm** (433-9987) in Pepperell, Routes 119 & 113; barnyard animals in residence.

In Lunenburg: **David's Organic Farm** (582-4824), 386 Mulpus Road and **Ewen's Sleepy Hollow Sugarhouse and Cider Mill** (582-6655), 66 Elmwood Road, a visitor-geared operation.

STATE FORESTS, PARKS, AND RESERVATIONS Ashburnham State Forest (939-8962). 2,000 acres accessible from Route 119 in Ashburnham, good for fishing, hiking, and hunting.

Lake Dennison State Park (297-1609), accessible from New Winchendon Road in Baldwinville, part of the Otter River forest, offers 150 campsites in two distinct areas, a swimming beach with bathhouse, 197 picnic tables and grills, fishing for bass and trout, and cross-country skiing on unplowed roads.

Otter River State Forest (939-8962), accessible from New Winchendon Road, Baldwinville, has 119 campsites and also offers picnicking, swimming, and a summer interpretive program, centered on Beamen Pond.

Pearl Hill State Park (597-8802), accessible via New Fitchburg Road from West Townsend. 1,000 acres with 51 campsites, swimming, fishing, picnicking, and hiking and ski-touring trails.

Willard Brook State Forest (597-8802), Route 119 in Townsend and Ashby, has 21 campsites and four year-round cabins; there's a sandy beach at Damon Pond and miles of hiking and ski trails, including one to Trapp Falls.

Wachusett Mountain State Reservation (464-2987) has a full visitors center. At 2,006 feet Wachusett Mountain is the highest point in Massachusetts east of the Connecticut River. In the late nineteenth century a road was built to the summit, the site of a summer hotel until 1970. From the summit you can see Boston to the east, Mount Tom to the west, and Monadnock to the north. This is a popular hiking goal for local scout groups. There are 20 ways to the top, but most people favor the 1.5-mile Jack Frost Trail. On the other hand you can still drive or, better still, take the chair lift that runs year-round from Wachusett Ski Area (386-6580). The 1,950-acre reservation also includes 17 miles of hiking and cross-country ski trails and picnic facilities. Also see Restaurants and Skiing.

MASSACHUSETTS AUDUBON SOCIETY **Wachusett Meadows Wildlife Sanctuary** (464-2712), Goodnow Road off Route 62, west of the common in Princeton. A 907-acre preserve with a boardwalk "swamp nature trail" and a variety of other walks through uplands, meadows, and woods. $2.00 per adult, $1 per senior citizen and child.

Flat Rock Wildlife Sanctuary (537-9807) in Fitchburg. 315 acres with an excellent trail system. Enter from Flat Rock Road, first right off Scott Road, off Ashby West Road.

Lincoln Woods Wildlife Sanctuary (537-9807), 226 Union Street, Leominster; 65-acre site with several ponds and pronounced glacial topography.

TRUSTEES OF RESERVATIONS **Redemption Rock**, Route 31 in Princeton. Near a parking space in the pines stands a huge, flat table rock where (according to legend) King Philip's Indians agreed to ransom Mary White Rowlandson and her children. That was in 1676 and Mrs. Rowlandson, wife of the first minister of Lancaster, wrote a best-seller about her kidnapping. The Mid-State Trail passes through this spot and continues south to the top of Wachusett Mountain.

Dunn's Pond, a part of the Gardner Heritage State Park, offers picnic tables, a space to stretch, and (as of summer '87) a sandy beach with changing facilities.

AIR RIDES See Nashoba Valley.

AMUSEMENT PARK **Whalom Park** (342-3707). East of Fitchburg on Route 2A in Lunenburg, open Memorial Day to Labor Day except Mondays, 1–10; weekends in spring and September. An old-fashioned family amusement area with picnic tables in a grove, mini train rides, some 50 carnival-style rides, and (across the road) a separate bathhouse and excursion rides on Whalom Lake.

BICYCLING Routes 119, 12, and 31 are all popular and there are endless possibilities along side roads.

GOLF **Gardner Golf Course** (632-9703), Eaton Road, Gardner. 18-hole municipal links.

Grand View Country Club (534-9685), Wachusett Street, Leominster.

Maplewood Golf Course (582-6694) in Lunenburg.

HIKING Note the trails mentioned in Green Space. The **Mid-State Trail** (upgrading the 1920s, 22-mile Wampack Trail) begins at Mt. Watatic, north of Route 119 in Ashby (you can park at the presently closed ski area). It follows the ridge line south to Mount Wachusett, crossing Route 2 on a newly completed overpass. Brochures are available from the **Greater Gardner Chamber of Commerce** (see Guidance) and from the **Trails Program**, DEM, 225 Friend Street, Boston 02114. Detailed maps and USGS sheets are available from **The Mid-State Trail Committee**, PO Box 155, Clinton 01510. It's worth noting that you can bed down along the trail very comfortably. **Timberlost Farm** and **Marble Farm** in Ashburnham, and the **Westminster Village Inn** are right on the trail (see Lodging).

HORSEBACK RIDING **Briarwood Stables** (939-5536) in Templeton.

Smithfield Farm Riding School (582-7748), Lunenburg.

Forty Acre Farm (534-3686), Leominster.

SWIMMING In addition to those noted in State Parks: **Beaman Pond** (386-2427) in Ashby and **Wyman Lake** (874-2769) in Westminster; also note **Dunn's Pond** in Gardner.

ALPINE SKIING **Wachusett Mountain Ski Area** (464-2355), Mountain Road, Princeton. This is a privately operated ski area on DEM land. A striking new base lodge offers gracious as well as cafeteria dining. There is a nursery, rental and ski shop.

Vertical drop: 990 feet

Terrain: two slopes, 13 trails

Lifts: 3 chairs (1 triple), 1 pony lift.

SKIwee program for children aged 5–12 offered weekends and holidays. Tickets: $20, adult; $18, child.

CROSS-COUNTRY SKIING **Wachusett Mountain Ski Area** (464-5101) A

20-kilometer system of groomed trails; rental equipment, instruction and baselodge facilities are offered.

SKYRIDE **Wachusett Mountain Ski Area** (464-2355). Chair lift to the summit operates May–October, Tuesday–Thursday 11 AM–dusk; Saturday and Sunday noon–dusk. $3 round-trip, $2 one-way.

INNS AND BED & BREAKFASTS **Country Inn at Princeton** (464-2030), 30 Mountain Road, Princeton 01541. An 1890, 24-room, Queen Ann-style summer mansion. The inn is decorated in tapestries and floral prints, with oriental carpets and heavy furniture. Beds have antique quilts and the rooms all have their own sitting areas. This is a romantic get-away spot for adults only and the big attraction is the food (see Restaurants). $95–$115 double occupancy B&B.

Timberlost Farm (827-5721), Ashby Road, Ashburnham 01430. Mrs. Lillian Davis welcomes guests to her family homestead, built in 1752. It's a sturdy, homey outpost in the hills, with five snug, sunny guest rooms. They are immaculately clean and furnished with comfortable beds, inherited furniture, and hooked rugs. This is a working farm with beef cattle and horses on the premises. The pond out back is good for a dip and is also stocked with trout. Well-behaved children are welcome. $35 double includes a continental breakfast (frequently homemade doughnuts and preserves). The Mid-State Trail passes through Timberlost's acreage, making it an ideal base from which to strike out either north to Watatic, or to the south.

Wood Farm (597-5019), 40 Worcester Road, Townsend 01469 (a half mile from the common on Route 113). This is the oldest house in town, the old cape section dating from 1716. There are four guest rooms, and guests have the run of the whole 20-room house, usually gathering around the fire in the keeping room, with its eight-foot wide hearth, in winter. A river runs through the 200-acre site, and there is a pond that is good for both skating and swimming. In winter there is cross-country skiing, and in summer your hosts, avid cyclists, are delighted to lead the way through the countryside. $35 double, $25 single, full breakfast included.

Marble Farm (827-5423), 41 Marble Road, Ashburnham 01430. Dick and Liz Marble, who hosted a bed & breakfast for some years in Stonington, Conn., are restoring their old homestead, a mid-eighteenth-century cape with rambling additions. It sits on 200 acres that include Marble Pond, good for fishing and swimming. The farm is within walking distance of Timberlost Farm (see above) and the Mid-State Trail. There is just one guest room at this writing, more to come. $35 double includes a full breakfast.

Inn at Harrington Farm (464-2448), 178 Westminster Street, Princeton 01541. This is a 200-year-old farmhouse on the westerly (backside) slope of Mount Wachusett. There are eight guest rooms (seven doubles and one single) some with stenciled walls, all with antiques. There are two parlors for guests and a pond good for skating; hiking and skiing are just out the door. $50 double, full breakfast included.

MOTELS **Heritage Park Inn** (630-1600), Betty Spring Road, Gardner 01440. A new 109-room resort motel with meeting facilities, a restaurant, health spa, and outdoor pool. From $55 per room.

Westminster Village Inn (874-5911), Route 2, Westminster 01473. Set back just a few hundred feet from the highway, this motel is a surprise. The main house welcomes you with a fireplace in winter, and there is an attractive, pine-paneled, reasonably priced dining room with a small counter that is good for breakfast or soup and a sandwich. There are 31 units (most of them in cottages), six with fireplaces and one efficiency. The Mid-State Trail crosses Route 2 on a new overpass at this point, continues on the inn's property along a ridge and down to Redemption Rock (see Green Space). There is a pool. The inn is under the same ownership as the Old Mill Inn (a five-minute drive) and guests receive discounts on dining there. $40 double, $59.50 for four, with fireplace.

Thunderbird Motor Lodge (342-6001), 299 Lunenburg Street, Fitchburg; 65 units, color TV, phone, air-conditioning, coffee shop, cocktail lounge.

CAMPGROUNDS Note the campsites (almost 250) in the adjoining Lake Denison, Otter River, Pearl Hill, and Willard Brook state parks (see Green Space).

Private campgrounds include **Howe's Camping** in Ashburnham

The Phillipston Fair

(827-4558), **Peaceful Acres** in Hubbardston (928-4288), **Peaceful Pines** in Templeton (939-5004), and **Pine Campgrounds** in Ashby (386-7702).

DINING OUT **Country Inn of Princeton** (464-2030), Mountain Road, Princeton. Chef Frank McClelland has brought his own version of nouvelle cuisine here from L'Espalier in Boston. Meals are long, elaborate, satisfying, and expensive ($50 per person). A six-course tasting menu is usually offered. The wine list is extensive.

Old Mill Restaurant (874-5941), Route 2A, Westminster. A local institution with an attractive old mill setting on a pond (small guests are given bread to feed the ducks). New England specialties include duck and prime rib. Open weekdays, 11–10; weekends and holidays 8–10; Sunday brunch 11–2:30. $8–$12 for dinner.

Four Winds Restaurant (827-6030), 29 High Street, Ashburnham. Housed in an estate where Bette Davis lived, this is the locally preferred dining place. The menu features prime rib and seafood, $7.50–$14. Open for dinner Tuesday–Sunday.

Le Papillon (632-7497), 74–76 Parker Street, Gardner. This find fills two storefronts in downtown Gardner. The decor is brick and stained glass (including a central skylight), with hanging plants. It is very nicely done. The menu is immense. For lunch it can be soup, salad, a seafood omelet, or Chicken Cordon Bleu. Portions are large and the prices reasonable. Live music Friday and Saturday nights. Open daily for lunch and dinner. $6–$12 for dinner.

The Lodge at Mount Wachusett (646-5101). A modern building with soaring ceilings and plenty of glass and wood, this has become one of the region's favorite, year-round dining spots for both lunch and dinner. Lunch can begin with Crab Veronique and progress to Blanquette of Veal, or it can be a salad bar or tuna melt. The menu is reasonably priced and the "sky ride" (chair lift to the top of the mountain) is frequently free with the meal when the ski area isn't open. $8–$14 for dinner.

EATING OUT **Slattery's Back Room** (342-8880), 106 Lunenberg Street, Fitchburg. A full menu from soup and sandwiches to lobsters and prime rib, casual atmosphere, reasonably priced.

Casa LaGrasa Restaurant (632-1986), 26 Central Street, Uptown Gardner. This is the political hub of Gardner. Open for breakfast, lunch, and dinner. The menu features pasta and Italian dishes; large dining room and bar. Reasonably priced.

Casa Giardini (297-0312), 302 Spring Street (Route 12), Winchendon. A local dining landmark, Italian menu.

The Farmer in the Deli (597-8762), 350 Main Street, Townsend. Homemade soups and desserts, wine and beer.

Brookside Restaurant (386-2406), Route 119. Open year-round. A great little roadside dining room, open for lunch and dinner.

Harbour Restaurant (297-2133), 463 Maple Street, Winchendon. Great fried seafood, open for lunch and dinner.

Yankee Restaurant (632-7770), 43 Union Square, Gardner. Steaks, pizza, pub.

Blue Moon Diner (632-4333), 102 Main Street, Gardner. Good for dinner.

Stanley's Lunch (632-9891), 231 Pleasant Street, Gardner. Owned and run by a Lithuanian family for many decades; decor is early 1900s with some '50s renovation. Limited menu, very popular.

Ray's Restaurant (632-9876), 5 Foss Road, Gardner. A solid family restaurant.

Little Town Hall (874-9918), 97 Main Street, Westminster. Best breakfasts in town.

Village Country Store, Princeton Common. A 12-stool lunch counter where a good seafood chowder still costs less than $2. Open 7 AM–3 PM.

Jeanie's Lunch (939-8956), Routes 2A/202 in Templeton. Breakfast from 6 AM on weekdays; from 7 AM on Saturday; and from 8 AM Sunday. Open until 2 PM. Clean, cheerful, and reasonably priced.

ENTERTAINMENT **Theatre at the Mount** (632-3856), La Fonatine Fine Arts Center, Mt. Wachusett Community College, Gardner (Route 140). July and August productions of popular classics by community theater group.

The Guild Players Touring Company (582-9041), The 50 Main Street Playhouse, Lunenburg. Adult and children's productions presented in this 100-seat theater during July and August.

High Tor Summer Theater (342-6888). From Fitchburg take Route 2A/12 north on Main Street, then south on Route 31 for 100 yards, bear right at the Cumberland Farms and follow the sign. A long-established summer theater (July and August) presenting works ranging from Shakespeare, to Moliere, Ibsen, Chekhov, Miller, O'Neill, et al.

SELECTIVE SHOPPING **Warren Barrel Co.**, Townsend Harbor, Route 119. A historic cooperage that now manufactures wooden boxes, planters, toy baskets, animal beds, tables, stools, and more. Open April–Christmas, 10–5 on Friday, Saturday, Sunday.

Priscilla's Candy Shop (632-7148), 9 Pleasant Street, Gardner. Chocolates made on the premises in large copper vats; seasonal specialties.

Goodnow Pearson's (632-6700), 52 Central Street, Gardner. A genuine, old-fashioned department store.

ANTIQUES **A&A Antiques** (939-5445), Athol Road, Templeton.

Chetwood Antique Cooperative (939-8641), Athol Road, Templeton.

Townsend Common Antiques (597-8044), Brookline Street, Townsend. Extensive stock of oak, country, and unusual furnishings. Open Wednesday–Sunday 10–5.

John & Barbara Delaney (597-2231), West Townsend, off Route 119. Specialize in antique clocks but a variety of antiques bought and sold.

West Village Trading Post, 434 Main Street, West Townsend. Open Wednesday–Sunday 10:30–5.

Beehive Restoration (597-6873), 12 New Fitchburg Road, West Townsend.

Toy Town Antiques (297-2411), 178 School Street (Route 12), Winchendon.

Godwin Gallery (433-6205), High Meadow Farm, Pepperell.

Sugar House Antiques (928-4826), Hubbardston. Full line of furnishings. Open most days, 9–5.

The 1818 House (928-4436), Hubbardston. Located in an old inn at the center of the village, open most days.

Auction Houses: **State Line Auction House** (297-2529), Route 12, Winchendon.

Fred's Auction House (534-9004), 92 Pleasant Street, Leominster.

Withington Auction Gallery (354-7126), 2 Ashby Road, Fitchburg.

CRAFTS In Hubbardston: Braided Rugs are made to order by **Nadine Hill** (928-4281); antique porcelain dolls, signed and dated by **Claudette Harty** (928-4446); enameled jewelry is made by **Donald Lytle** (928-4281); wheel-thrown and hand-built stoneware, teapots, table ware, casseroles, and lamps by **Marion Lyon** (928-4414); **Swansea Stoneware Pottery** (632-2036) produces hand-thrown, early American-style crocks, pitchers, lamps, and jugs.

FACTORY OUTLETS Furniture outlets in Gardner: **Chair City Wayside Furniture** (632-1120), Route 2A. This four-story, box-like granite building with a giant ladder-back chair out front is just as unusual as it looks. Here Leonard Curcio makes 10 to 15 hand-turned and fitted chairs a day. It takes him five or six hours to cane a seat, three to four hours to make a rush seat from swamp grass, and about an hour to weave the fiber bottom. Visitors are welcome to watch. "I want people to see that we still make some things well in this country," says Curcio. A ladder-back chair averages $69. Open Monday–Saturday.

The Factory Coop Furniture Center (632-1447), 45 Logan Street, carries a variety of furniture. Open daily.

The Factory Showroom (632-8907), 90 Mechanic Street (behind Burger King). A range of furniture and furnishings, open daily.

The Factory Store (632-2401), 501 West Broadway. Housed in a three-story red brick building, specializing in pine, but stocks a variety of styles.

Juvenile Sales (632-0805), 394 Elm Street. A great place to shop for a crib and other baby furniture. Open daily, housed in a rambling red wood building just off Route 2. Closed Sundays in July and August.

LeChance Furniture & Appliance (632-1930), outlet for Conant Ball Furniture Company of Gardner; showrooms. Closed Sundays.

R. Smith Colonial Furniture (632-3461), 289 South Main Street. Colonial-style furnishings and accessories. Open daily.

Rome Sales Co. (632-0687), contemporary furniture. Closed Sundays.

In Fitchburg: **Anwelt Shoe Factory Outlet** (342-7549), 1 A Oak Hill Road. Shoes for the whole family, 50% off: work boots, Nike sneakers, dress and casual shoes.

Baystate Curtain Manufacturing Outlet Store (342-7314). Custom-made draperies, shower curtains, rods, piece goods, and accessories.

Leather Work Company (343-6629), 655 Water Street. Leather handbags, briefcases, and accessories.

Spindle Stores-Mill Outlet (343-3756), 21 Sheldon Street. Yarns, novelties, craft supplies.

Other: **Templeton Colonial Furniture** (939-5504), Junction Route 2, Baldwinville Road, Templeton. Bedroom, living and dining rooms in maple, oak, cherry, and pine.

Dan's Pine Shop Factory Showroom (939-5687), 20 Elm Street, Baldwinville. A fourteen-room house displaying furniture and accessories. Custom-finishing.

Toy Town Factory Outlet (297-0680), 1 High Street, Winchendon. Household furniture.

Winchendon Furniture Co. (297-0131), Railroad Street, Winchendon; showroom featuring upholstered furniture.

SPECIAL EVENTS June: (first Saturday) **Johnny Appleseed Day**. Leominster's annual salute to native son John Chapman, the Swedenborgian missionary who planted apple trees everywhere.

July: **Independence Day celebrations**, Winchendon. The **Arthur M. Longsjo Jr. Memorial Bike Race**, a 50-mile event that attracts international participants and perpetuates the memory of a local Olympian who was both a cyclist and speed skater. **Yankee Street Fair** (third Wednesday) at the Congregational Church, Westminster. **July 4th** hot air balloon rides, barbecue, music; Wachusett Mountain (464-5101).

August: **Annual Crafts Fair** (third weekend), Templeton. **Annual Ice Cream Festival**, Westminster.

September: **Labor Day** clambake, **Wachusett Mountain** (464-5101). Third weekend, **Annual Flea Market,** Templeton.

Year-round events, ranging from cross-country ski races to summer music, are sponsored by the **Gardner Heritage State Park:** 630-1497.

Late October: **Applefest and Craft Fair,** Wachusett Mountain (464-5101).

MEDICAL EMERGENCY **Burbank Hospital** (343-5000), Nichols Road, Fitchburg.

Henry Heywood Memorial Hospital (632-3420), 242 Green Street, Gardner.

Naukeag Hospital (827-5115), 216 Lake Road, Ashburnham.

North of Quabbin

The northern reaches of Quabbin Reservoir are rimmed by high country. Rural and rolling, some of it is still farmed, but more of it is preserved as public forest.

The hilltop villages—Royalston Center, North Orange, Petersham, New Salem, Phillipston, and Warwick—all possess a haunting beauty. The aristocratic old meetinghouses and town halls stand in lonely splendor, with just a few old houses to testify to the shops, mills, and humbler homes that once supported them.

The Millers River, rising in the wooded hills of Royalston and Winchendon, rushes through the spillways of century-old brick mills in Athol and Orange: two nineteenth-century mill towns which, although a shade shabby, have surprising charm.

The region's "attractions" are its lakes, waterfalls, farms, and wooded trails. Still there is a lot going on here if you like to bike, hike, fish, cross-country ski, canoe, or search out crafts, fresh produce, old books, and antiques.

AREA CODE: 617

GUIDANCE **Greater Athol–Orange Chamber of Commerce** (249-3849/249-7151), 465 Main Street, Athol 01331; open weekdays, 8:30–5. Request a map/guide to the nine-town area, also a list of antique dealers, craftspeople, a "Friends of Quabbin" map ($2.95, $3.95 postpaid), and a copy of the *Metacomet–Monadnock Trail Guide* ($2.75, $3.50 postpaid from Millers River Publishing Co., Box 159, Athol 01331). Millers River Publishing Company is also the source of books on local history and of the temporarily out-of-print *North of Quabbin* by Allen Young, an exceptionally well-written, comprehensive area guide.

GETTING THERE A car is a must in this area, but there is bus service: **Englander Coach Lines** from Boston's Greyhound terminal (423-5810) stops a few times a day at the Sunoco station at the Route 2/202 junction.

VILLAGES **Royalston Common**. Of all the handsome commons in Upcountry Massachusetts, this is the most aristocratic, aptly named for a wealthy Tory, the Hon. Isaac Royal, who fled to England in 1776. Federal and Greek Revival homes, all uniformed in white clapboard, parade down both sides of the wide common and a high-steepled church stands in review. The **Royalston Historic and**

Village Improvement Society (249-2018) maintains a museum in the dome-topped Old Royalston Schoolhouse at the south end of the common. Also see Green Space.

New Salem. This broad, quiet common is framed by some superb buildings: the 1794 Unitarian Church, the 1854 Congregational Church, a former 1839 town hall (now the library), and the buildings of Salem Academy, a widely attended school for 173 years, beginning in 1795. Note the metal plaque recalling the scene here on April 20, 1775, when residents, mustered by alarm bells, gathered and decided to march off to war. A part of town was flooded for Quabbin Reservoir, and three roads from the common dead-end now at Quabbin gates. Gate 35 at the south end of Athol Road is open to hikers, and the path here leads quickly to the water's edge. Near the village, Gate 30 (across from the junction of Route 122 and Orange Road) leads to the Keystone Bridge, beautifully designed and built by Civil War veteran Aldolphus Porter. **The Swift River Valley Historical Association** (see Quabbin) is found on Elm Street, one-half mile west of Route 202.

North Orange. This is a dignified gathering of old country homes near the Community Church of North Orange and Tully, built 1781. Goddard Park, in front of the rectory, is the scene of frequent church suppers, May Day Morris dancing, the August Village Fair, and the December tree lighting.

Petersham. High on a ridge with commanding views, "Peter's ham" (as it's pronounced) was a thriving agricultural community in the 1830s and was rediscovered as a summer resort in the late nineteenth century. The rambling old summer hotel in the middle of town is now Maria Assumpta Academy, but the pillared **Country Store** is a delight to explore, and there are still fine places to dine and lodge in town. **The Petersham Historical Society** (724-3380) has exhibits about the farmers' rebellion led by Daniel Shays. Note the unusual variety of public lands in town and the **Crafts Center**, the showcase for this region's artisans.

Phillipston. This village center is small enough to fit in the snapshot it demands. The Congregational Church, built in 1785, is a beauty, the site of the annual June bazaar and October pumpkin weigh-in.

Warwick. This perfectly preserved old hilltown is just beginning to stir again. A three-sided marker notes that it's 20 miles from here to both Keene, NH and Brattleboro, VT and 8 (precipitously downhill) miles to Northfield on the Connecticut River. You still seem a century from anywhere in this classic cluster, which includes a Unitarian Church, library, historical society building, a fine old fountain, the Warwick Country Store and the fine old double-porched Warwick Inn, newly reopened for bed & breakfast.

MUSEUMS **The Fisher Museum of Forestry** (724-3285), on Route 32 between Petersham and Route 2. Open year-round, 9–5, but sometimes closed for conferences so call ahead. Maintained by Harvard University, along with the 3,000 acres out back, the museum contains a series of dioramas that dramatize the changes in rural Massachusetts' landscape over the past few hundred years. They show the farms of the 1830s (when 75 percent of the land was cleared); the abandonment of the farms in the 1850s; and the succession of land use practices to the present day. Follow the one-and-one-half mile Black Gum Trail to get a sense of how one old farm has changed in a century.

The Athol Historical Society (249-4890), 1307 Main Street, open Wednesdays in summer, 2–4. Housed in the steepled, old town hall this genuinely interesting collection chronicles the town's history from the 1770s through its boom days as "Tooltown USA."

The Orange Historical Society is housed in a high Victorian mansion at 41 North Main Street. The town's first machine-made carpet and other relics of local industrial, as well as exhibits on social life are on display. It is open by appointment and on Sundays, 2–4 in summer, check with the **Wheeler Memorial Library** (544-2295).

Pioneer Valley Museum of Industry (575-0408), next to Town Hall, Orange. Open weekends. Two display halls are filled with inventions, contraptions, and light machinery from the area; exhibits include New Name Sewing Machines made in Orange before the plant moved to Japan.

Also see historical societies noted under Villages.

FARMS TO VISIT **Hamilton Orchards and Apple Barn** (544-6867), marked from Route 202 in New Salem. One of the nicest orchards around: 35 acres of trees yielding a variety of species which you can pick yourself in season. Cider is also pressed in fall. You also can pick raspberries from late August until mid-October, blueberries earlier. Barb Hamilton makes the pies which are for sale and the snack bar serves hot dogs and hamburgers, as well as the famous pies and pancakes with Hamilton-made syrup. The view is off across the Quabbin Reservoir and a nature trail meanders off across the property. Open weekends April through Labor Day; daily Labor Day through mid-October; weekends until mid-December.

Red Apple Farm (249-6763), off Route 2A in Phillipston. There is no pick-your-own here; instead a farm store sells pears and peaches, many varieties of apples (shipped anywhere), and cider pressed in season. Specializing in unusual species. Note cross-country ski trails.

Haley's Orchard (544-2218), North Main Street, Orange. Apple store on Route 2A in season, different species.

SUGARHOUSES **Philip Johnson** (544-3614), off Route 2A on Wheeler Avenue in Orange, is the biggest local producer.

Hamilton Orchards (see Farms to Visit) welcomes visitors during sugaring and serves meals, sugar-on-snow.

Quabbin Maple (544-6939) in New Salem off Route 202 also welcomes visitors.

GREEN SPACE **Quabbin Reservoir.** On the map Quabbin appears as by far the largest blue space in the state, but it's difficult to get a glimpse of its 38.6 miles of watery surface, couched as it is in 119,000 acres of wooded watershed. The Quabbin Visitors Center is at Metropolitan District Commission (MDC) headquarters at the southern end of the reservoir (413-323-7561), but some of the most enjoyable hiking trails are in this northern section. From Gate 35 (off Route 122 in New Salem) you can walk an old railroad bed to the edge of the vast, man-made lake. A self-guided Quabbin nature walk begins at Gate 30, off Route 122 in New Salem. The former town common of Dana is accessible by foot and bike from Gate 40, off Route 32A in Petersham. For one of the best views of the reservoir see **Women's Federated** (recently renamed Federation) **State Forest**.

A total of 2,500 people (living in 650 houses) were evacuated from the towns of Dana, Enfield, Greenwich, and Prescott to create the 18-mile-long reservoir, which was built between 1939 and 1946. The story of the lost towns is told in the photos and memorabilia found in the **Swift River Valley Historical Society** (544-6807), housed in New Salem's Whitaker–Clary House. It's open Wednesday afternoons in summer and by appointment (544-6807); turn at the North New Salem sign on Route 202.

PUBLIC FORESTS **Erving State Forest** (544-3939). The Administration building is on Route 2A. There is swimming, fishing, and boating on Laurel Lake (off Route 2); hiking on Overlook Trail; and camping (tents and small trailers) at 30 sites.

Federation State Forest (939-8962), marked from Route 122 near the Petersham/New Salem line. There are 28 picnic tables and 24 fireplaces from which unmarked trails lead to "wilderness" campsites. There also is trout fishing in Fever Brook.

Harvard Forest. See the Fisher Museum of Forestry (Museums).

Mt. Grace State Forest (544-7474), Winchester Road, Warwick. This 1,617-foot peak has long attracted hikers and for 20 years, beginning in the '40s, the state maintained a four-trail ski area here. At present there is a rickety fire tower on top, yielding a great view. The trail begins at the Route 78 picnic area in a pine grove (50 tables, 25 grills).

Northfield State Forest (544-7474). Accessible on the Wendell Depot Road from Route 2A; 5,000 acres good for hiking and fishing.

Sugarin' time in Sunderland

Petersham State Forest (939-8962), off Route 122. You can fish and canoe here in Riceville Pond.

Royalston State Forest (939-8962). Just 776 acres of forested terrain in the western section of Royalston. Good for hiking, snowmobiling.

Warwick State Forest (544-7474), via Tully Road from Athol or Athol Road from Warwick. Sheomet Lake is a beautiful spot, created by Augustus Bliss in the mid-nineteenth century as a mill pond. There is a boat launch ramp, good for canoes and row boats (no motors permitted). The lake is stocked with trout each spring. Swimming is not allowed.

Wendell State Forest (413-659-3797). Take Wendell Road from Millers Falls. There is swimming and picnicking at Ruggles Pond, fishing and canoeing at Ruggles and Wickett Ponds. The miles of roads through this 7,566-acre forest are the scene of an annual September fat-tire bike race; it's an ideal place for this kind of biking.

Orange State Forest (544-3939). Just 59 acres on the western end of Orange. Good for hiking, cross-country skiing.

James W. Brooks Woodland Preserve on East Street, one mile east of Petersham Common, offers superb ski-touring along the east branch of the Swift River.

Phillipston and Popple Camp Management Areas. Accessible from Route 101 and via Bakers and Narrow lanes: 2,750 acres owned by DEM, Division of Fisheries and Wildlife. Good for hiking and fishing.

Elliott Laurel Reservation, Phillipston (north side, Route 101, just west of Queen Lake). Woodland paths follow stone walls through white pine and hardwood with an extensive understory of mountain laurel.

Swift River Reservation in Petersham. Check with the Trustees of Reservations (537-2377) for details.

Bearsden Woods, entrance from Bearsden Road near Athol Memorial Hospital: 1,000 acres maintained by the Athol Conservation Commission. From the parking lot a dirt road continues to the Millers River and there are a total of 10 miles of hiking trails; a log cabin is used for overnight hikers, and there are nice views from Roundtop Mountain.

Birch Hill Wildlife Area (see Montachusett); 1,000 acres in Royalston, including Beaver Pond and stretches of Stockwell Brook and the Millers River.

WATERFALLS **Bear's Den** in North New Salem. Neilson Road, off Elm Street, three-quarters mile north of Route 202. The Trustees of Reservations guide describes this as a: "Tiny grotto with a sparkling waterfall on the Middle Branch of the Swift River where legend says King Philip gathered with his Indian chieftains in 1675 to plan the march and massacre of settlers in Deerfield."

Doane's Falls in Royalston. Athol Road at Doane Hill Road. Owned by Trustees of Reservations, this is a truly spectacular series of waterfalls. Lawrence Brook flows through a granite gorge crowned with pine and hemlock. A path leads down along the falls, worth following even in winter when the falls are an ice sculpture.

Spirit Falls, owned by Harvard Forest, is one mile west of Royalston Common but a mile hike via a forest road (north from Doane's Hill Road) just east of a bridge across Tully River. The falls is also accessible from a forest road from Route 68; look for a small unmarked turnout where a short footpath leads to a great view of the west branch of the Tully River (this 53 acres is owned by the Trustees of Reservations).

Royalston Falls. Accessible by a 15-minute hike from a parking area, some three miles from the intersection of Falls Road and Route 68. It's a rough drive in, best attempted by high 4-wheel drives. Do not bring small children. Falls Brook flows through a natural gorge and drops nearly 70 spectacular feet.

AIR RIDES **Wings of New England** (544-6715) at Orange Municipal Airport offers charter service and instruction.

CANOEING **The Outdoor Center of New England** (659-3926), 8 Pleasant Street, Millers Falls, offers canoes and instruction. The **Tully Lake Recreation Area** (249-8193) in Royalston has 20 tent sites geared to canoeists who can put into placid Tully Lake and Long Pond. The Millers River between Athol and Orange is comfortable flatwater, putting in at the bridge on Route 2A in downtown Athol and ending just above a power dam in Orange, five miles downstream off East River Street. Canoes also can be launched on Route 2 about a mile east of Erving Center. This is also a famous spring kayaking center (note the River Rat Race under Special Events).

FISHING   The **Quabbin Reservoir**, open for fishing from April to October, yields landlocked salmon, bass, pickerel, perch, and trout. Detailed information on rules and schedules is available from the MDC office: 413-323-7561. The **Millers River** between Athol and Orange is a locally celebrated fishery. **Tully Lake, Lake Mattawa** in Orange, the chain formed by **Lake Rohunta, White Pond, Eagleville Pond**, and **North** and **South Spectacle ponds** (easily accessible from Route 22) are also locally favored. Other spots are noted in Green Space. Boat rentals are available at MDC Gate 31.

Quabbin Reservoir from the Petersham area

GOLF Petersham Country Club (724-3388), 9 holes. **Ellinwood Country Club** (249-9836) in Athol has 18 holes.

HIKING In addition to hiking in the Quabbin watershed, the sometimes poorly marked Metacomet-Monadnock Trail passes through Wendell, Erving, Warwick, and Royalston (a trail guide is available for $2.50, see Guidance). In addition to trails noted above there is also extensive hiking in the Quabbin Watershed; request the "Friends of Quabbin" map (see Guidance). Other hikes are described in Green Space.

CROSS-COUNTRY SKIING Cross-country skiing is noted under Green Space. **Red Apple Farm** (249-6763) in Phillipston also maintains 10 miles of trails and roadways.

SWIMMING Check out **Laurel Lake** in Erving State Forest and **Ruggles Pond** in Wendell State Forest. Town beaches are found at **Lake Ellis** and **Silver Lake** in Athol, **Lake Mattawa** in Orange, **Queen Lake** in Phillipston, and **Moore's Pond** in Warwick.

INNS **Winterwood at Petersham** (724-8885), North Main Street, Petersham 01366. This Greek Revival mansion was built as a summer home in 1842 and now offers five guest rooms, one a two-room suite with twin fireplaces. All are furnished with antiques and have private baths; most have working fireplaces. Innkeepers Robert and Jean Day make guests feel welcome. $60 double, $85 for the two-room suite, continental breakfast included.

Warwick Inn (544-8549), center of Warwick 01364. Built to serve the stage in 1827, this grand old inn was renting rooms for $5 a week until 1985 when Lisa Vanderstelt and Robert Watson spent a year renovating it. They now offer four rooms (two with fireplaces) on a bed & breakfast basis, $39 single, $43 double.

MOTELS **Bald Eagle Motel** (544-2101), junction Routes 202 and 2, Orange 01364. 15 rooms (and adding), cable TV; $25.37 single, $45 for four.

Quabbin Gateway Motel (544-2986), junction Routes 202 and 2, Orange 01364. 15 rooms; $24 single, $35–$38 double with a locally reputable restaurant.

CAMPING Note the public campgrounds at **Barton Cove**, **Tully Lake**, **Erving State Forest**. Private campgrounds include:

Lakeridge Campground (544-7111), 300 Daniel Shays Highway, Orange.

Lamb City Campground (249-9806), Royalston Road, Phillipston.
Pineridge Campground (544-6056), Mountain Road, Erving.
Ranch Campground (544-6270), East River Street, Orange.

DINING OUT **Fox Run** (249-8267), Ward Hill in Phillipston (off Route 2A). Up a side road with a great view. Open April–Thanksgiving for dinner and Sunday brunch; closed Tuesday. The decor is "old farm" and there's a spring-fed well in the Woodshed Lounge. Specialties include Roast Duckling Cerises and Veal Oscar. Minimenus for small eaters (not necessarily children) available. $7–$16.

Batch's Red Rooster Restaurant (544-3300), East Main Street, Orange. Known for its unusual menu, they use local fruit and vegetables in season; open for lunch and dinner. $5–$12.

King Phillip Restaurant (249-6300), Athol Road, Phillipston. Open for dinner, Thursday–Sunday, chef-owned, moderately priced ($10–$12).

The White Pillars (724-3443), on the Common, Petersham. Open for dinner only, Thursday–Sunday, also Tuesday and Wednesday by reservation. This dining landmark is currently specializing in Northern Italian Food. $13.95–$18.95.

Boardroom Restaurant and Executive Lounge (249-2763). Seafood specialties, open Thursday–Sunday for dinner. New and trying hard. $8–$12 for dinner.

EATING OUT   **New Salem Store and Restaurant** (544-7393), Route 202. This is a standout: an attractive dining room with fireplace and deep wooden booths; a range of sandwiches and hot plates made from fresh ingredients, natural foods included. Reasonably priced. Open from 6:30 AM–2:30 PM daily except Tuesdays.

Box Car Restaurant (544-6992), Route 2, Erving. A former railroad car houses this friendly, owner-operated breakfast and lunch stop (dinners during hunting season).

White Cloud (544-6821). Across from the airport. Open 6 AM–3 PM, closed Monday. Interesting plastic decor and creditable food, reasonably priced.

The Gingerbread House (544-8132), 24 South Main Street, Orange. Open for breakfast and lunch, this is the town gossip center. The menu is small but the croissants, soup, and sandwiches are great; serves Bart's ice cream.

Wendell General Store (544-8511), Locks Village Road, has a few tables in back, serves light snacks; inquire about monthly coffeehouses on the nearest Saturday to the full moon.

Cinnamon's (249-8511), 491 Main Street, Athol, serves all three meals, popular locally.

SELECTIVE SHOPPING   **Common Reader Bookshop** (544-7039). Dorothy Johnson has an extensive collection of used books; also specializes in seventeenth–twentieth-century women's history and ephemera.

Armchair Bookshop (575-0424), North Orange. Open daily 10–4 but call ahead; specializes in local town and county history.

Baldwin Hill Bread (249-4691), Route 32A, Phillipston. Distributed throughout New England, these high-fiber breads made from stone-ground wheat are baked here and distributed widely.

ANTIQUES   **Orange Trading Co.** (544-6683), 13 South Main Street, Orange. Gary Moise rebuilds old juke boxes and also has a fascinating assortment of other vintage things.

Upper Pioneer Valley & North of Quabbin

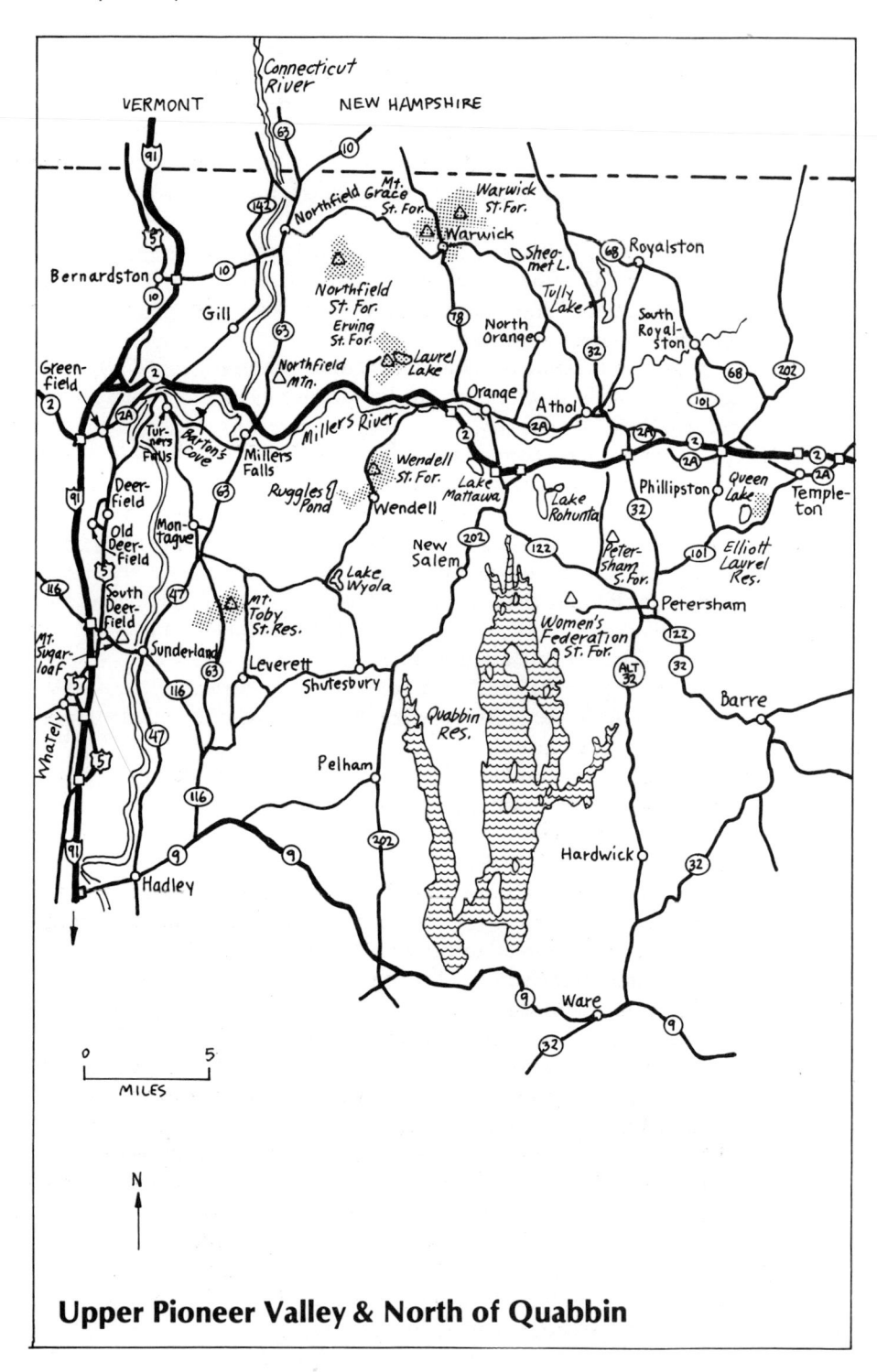

Orange Antiques (544-7009), 139 South Main, Orange.
Ray Sault (544-2826), 325 East Main Street, Orange.
Sawyer's (544-6024), 156 Main Street, Orange.
Edgar Stockwell (249-6541), New Athol Road, Orange, specializing in Oriental porcelains.
In New Salem, **Quiet Lion Antiques** (544-7039) is housed in the old North Salem schoolhouse, and there is also **Federal House Antiques** (544-6158).

CRAFTS **Petersham Crafts Center** (724-3415), off Route 122 in Petersham. Salesroom open Tuesday–Saturday, 1:30–5. This is a long-established, non-profit crafts center which offers classes, stages special exhibits, and displays the best locally made quilts, pottery, greeting cards, candles, jewelry, wreaths, and the like.
Eleanor Voutselas (544-7530) in New Salem makes handwoven scarves, ponchos, baby blankets, and table linens.
Peggy McAndrews (659-3583) in Millers Falls hand knits mittens and scarves.
Jason's Fleece (249-4238) sells wool products: fleece, yarns, hides, hand knit and woven articles.
Michael Humphries (544-2694) in Warwick makes furniture, custom cabinets.
Country Stencil House and Herbe Shoppe (724-6679), North Main Street, Petersham. Open June–August, Wednesday–Sunday 11–5; in September and May, weekends 11–5.
Whittermore's Gift Shop (249-9615), 1042 Templeton Road, Athol. Open daily. Handcrafts, lamps, clocks, and gifts.

SPECIAL EVENTS April: First Saturday: **Athol-to-Orange River Rat Race** (usually attracts more than 300 canoes).
May: **May Day Morris dancing**, North Orange.
June: **Phillipston Craft Fair** (last weekend); **Yankee Engine-unity in Action** steam engine show and experimental fly-in at Orange Municipal Airport.
July: **Independence Day Parade, YMCA Road Race**, Athol.
August: **Royalston Day, North Orange Village Fair**.
September (mid): **New England Fat-tire Road Races** in Wendell State Forest.
October: **Phillipston Pumpkin Commission Weigh-in. Old Home Days** in Warwick, New Salem, Wendell.

MEDICAL EMERGENCY **Athol Memorial Hospital** (249-3511), 2033 Upper Main Street, Athol.

The Upper Pioneer Valley

The Upper Pioneer Valley describes the state's northernmost reach of the Connecticut River Valley. This rich river bottomland, first settled in the seventeenth century, remains rural, spotted with tobacco barns and fine old river towns.

No community illustrates the hazards of pioneering better than Old Deerfield. First settled in 1669 by twenty Dedham families, it stood stark and empty for six years following an Indian attack, but by 1675 the Proprietors of Deerfield were back, harvesting crops and listening to sermons in the square, tower-topped meetinghouse (now reconstructed as a post office). One blustery February night in 1704 Frenchmen and Indians swarmed over the stockade and carried 112 villagers off to Montreal. Many of the survivors actually found their way back, and the homes of a few can still be found in Old Deerfield.

It was thanks to the Connecticut River, of course, that this region was settled more than a century before most of Massachusetts. In 1790 it was still possible to journey by boat from Deerfield to Philadelphia, and well into the nineteenth century the river remained the highway. From Northfield you can still venture out on the river in an excursion boat, and this is the best stretch of the Connecticut in Massachusetts for canoeing.

Greenfield is a solid shire town, a handsome nineteenth-century crossroad with its share of shops, family restaurants, and also some fine buildings. It's big enough to furnish what you want, and small enough to make finding it enjoyable. But Old Deerfield remains the sight to see. Historic Deerfield's dozen museum houses are a treasury of early American art and furnishings and the entire village is suspended in another era.

AREA CODE 413

GUIDANCE **Franklin County Chamber of Commerce** (773-5463), open daily, 24 hours, PO Box 790, Main Street, Greenfield 01302. The Chamber's office at 135 Main Street serves as a walk-in information center weekdays, year-round. June through foliage season an information center at the I-91, Route 2 rotary (in front of Howard Johnson's) also is open.

GETTING THERE By bus: From New York City **Greyhound** (212-635-0800) serves Greenfield, and from Boston **Englander Coach Lines** (617-423-5810) offers frequent service. **Peter Pan** (413-781-3320) also serves Deerfield via Amherst from Boston.

GETTING AROUND   City Cab (773-5600) in Greenfield serves the area. **Franklin Transit Authority** (774-2262) and the **Greenfield-Montague Transportation Authority** (773-9478) connect most valley towns.

TO SEE AND TO DO   In **Historic Deerfield** (marked from Route 5, exit 25 off I-91) more than 50 handsome old buildings still line the mile-long "Street" and stand starkly silhouetted against the surrounding onion and tobacco fields. Preservation efforts began here in 1847 with an unsuccessful attempt to save the Old Indian House. The front door of this building can be seen in **Memorial Hall Museum**, one of the country's oldest historical societies (opened in 1880). The **Frary House** was restored as a historic house museum in the 1890s. Then in 1952 Henry Flynt, a graduate of Deerfield Academy (in town since 1799) bought and reopened the **Deerfield Inn** and began collecting houses. Historic Deerfield, which now owns 22 homes (12 open to the public) is the result.

Historic Deerfield (774-5581), Box 321, Deerfield 01342. The mile-long Street of Old Deerfield Village is marked from Routes 5 and 10. Open all year Monday–Saturday 9:30–4:30; Sunday 11–4:30; July–October until 6 PM. You can buy a three-house ticket for $4.50, and this is about all the touring an average visitor wants in one day because each house is so richly furnished and the tours are detailed. A 20-minute introductory film helps you choose which house to visit. In the **Hall Tavern** (be sure to see the upstairs ballroom) you can also buy a $15 ticket for visiting all 12 buildings (good for a week). Individual houses cost $2 or $3. I suggest that you see:

The Wells-Thorn House (partially built in 1717 and finished in 1751) shows the dramatic changes in the life-styles of the two periods.

The Ashley House (1733) with its elegantly carved cupboards and furnishings depicts the life-style of the village's Tory minister (note his 1730s Yale diploma).

Asa Stebbins House (1799/1810) is the first brick home in town, grandly furnished with French wallpapers, Chinese porcelain, and Federal-era pieces.

The Wright House (1824), another brick mansion, is a mini-museum of early furniture and china.

Sheldon-Hawkes House (1743) is furnished almost exclusively with pieces from the Connecticut River Valley and from Boston, and it is still filled with the spirit of George Sheldon, the town's colorful first historian.

Frary House/Barnard Tavern (1740/1795). This is my favorite because of its classical tavern look, peculiar history, ballroom, and the "touch-it" exhibits which make it the best for children.

Memorial Hall (773-8929). Open May through October 10–4:30 weekdays, 12:30–4:30 weekends. $2 per adult, $1.50 per student, $.75 per child 12 and under. This brick building was designed by Asher Benjamin in 1797 for Deerfield Academy and was purchased by the Pocumtuck Valley Memorial Association in 1878 to house the wealth of things collected by town historian George Sheldon. There are family rooms, a 1797 schoolroom, the Indian House Door (with a tomahawk hole in its center), and a delightful assortment of Indian relics, early paintings, photographs, clothing, and much much more.

Deerfield Academy (772-0421). One of the oldest and most prestigious prep schools in the country offers free tours on request.

The Brick Church, built in 1824, has arched doorways and a closed wooden cupola. It's the scene of frequent concerts and other special events as well as regular (Unitarian) services.

The Old Burying Ground (walk along Albany Road) has many eighteenth-century stones.

In Greenfield: **The Greenfield Public Library** (772-6305), 402 Main Street, designed by Asher Benjamin, is worth noting. If you have youngsters along you may want to visit the outstanding children's room, and the Greenfield Room upstairs contains a historical collection.

Greenfield Historical Society (772-6992), 3 Church Street, by appointment anytime. This 1850s brick mansion has eight rooms filled with furnishings, portraits, early Greenfield artifacts, and photos. Allow one-and-a-half hours for a tour.

Northfield Mountain Recreation and Environmental Center (659-3713/3714), Route 63 in Northfield. April–October bus tours take you to the upper reservoir and underground powerhouse of Northeast Utilities' unusual pumped storage hydroelectric plant. A film about the construction and operation of the plant can be viewed in the visitors center. The project utilizes water from the Connecticut, draws it up into a man-made lake on top of the mountain and uses the stored water to generate power during high-use periods. The powerhouse itself is hidden in a cavern as high as a 10-story building, as wide as a four-lane highway, and longer than a football field. The center also houses special exhibits and a series of lectures and workshops on the area's flora and fauna. June through mid-October the *Quinnetuket II* (a sleek little excursion boat that looks like the *African Queen*) cruises the Connecticut ($5 adults, $2 children under 14, $4 senior citizens).

VILLAGES **Sunderland** is a classic eighteenth-century river town, its homes filing along the Connecticut down one long street. The brick town hall was built to double as the town school in 1867. From Boston I like to approach Deerfield (and shortcut over to Route 116 into the hilltowns) via Routes 63 and 47, past Mt. Toby and tobacco barns rather than around rotaries and down the interstate.

Montague Center, off Route 63 near the junction with Route 47, is a standout common with a Congregational Church designed by Asher Benjamin and a brick town hall which serves as a summer theater (see Theatre 81 under Entertainment). Note the sign on Route 63 for the fish hatchery.

Northfield is another classic river town, one with an unusually wide main street. There are college-size campuses for two prep schools here, founded by the evangelist Rev. Dwight Moody in the late nineteenth century. While there is no trace of Moody's grand old summer hotel, there is a summer Youth Hostel (AYH began here in 1934) and a choice of bed & breakfasts.

SUGARHOUSES   Maple producers who welcome visitors include **River Maple Farm** (648-9676) in Bernardston, **Mt. Toby Sugarhouse** (665-3127) in Sunderland Center, **Brookledge Sugarhouse** (665-3837) and **Fairview Farms** (665-3103) in Whately.

GREEN SPACE   **Poet's Seat**. Off High Street (Route 2A) on Rocky Mountain stands a medieval-looking sandstone tower with an American flag on top. Nineteenth-century local Frederick Goddard Tuckerman liked to sit near this spot, and you understand why when you see the view.

French King Bridge (Route 2 west of Millers Falls) spans a dramatically steep-banked, narrow stretch of the Connecticut, 140 feet above the water. Park at the rest area and walk back onto the bridge (there's a pedestrian walk) for the view. Note the confluence of the Millers River just downstream. The bridge is named for French King Rock below. The king was Louis XV and the rock is said to have been named by one of his subjects. That was in the mid-1700s. It's funny how some names stick.

Mount Sugarloaf State Reservation, off Route 116 in South Deerfield. A road winds up this red sandstone mountain (said to resemble the old loaves into which sugar was shaped) to a modern observation tower on the summit, said to be the site from which King Philip surveyed his prey before the mid-seventeenth-century Bloody Brook Massacre. There are picnic tables and a great view down the valley.

Mount Toby, off Route 47, 0.9 mile south of its junction with Route 63 in Montague. Follow Reservation Road to a small parking area and follow the trail to the fire tower which commands an incredible view of the valley and beyond. It's a three-hour round-trip hike.

BICYCLING   **Northfield Bicycle Barn** (498-2996) rents all speeds.

CANOEING   There is a state boat launching site on the Connecticut at Pauchaug Brook in Northfield.

Inquire at **Northfield Mountain Environmental Center** (659-3713) about the following sites that Northeast Utilities maintains for public access: **Kids' Island** (good for picnicking), **Munn's Ferry Campground** (with Adirondack shelters and tent sites, accessible only by boat), and **River View** (a float dock, picnic tables, and sanitary facilities on the river across from the entrance to Northfield Mountain).

At **Barton Cove** (863-9300) Northeast Utilities maintains tent sites, rents tents and canoes, and offers lessons and interpretive trips.

Below the Turners Falls Dam you can put in at the **Montague City Bridge** (off Poplar Street). There also is an informal access point at the Route 116 bridge on the Sunderland side and at a small park in Whately.

Taylor Rentals (773-8643) in Greenfield rents aluminum canoes.

Outdoor Center of New England (659-3926) in Millers Falls rents canoes and specializes in white water instruction and expeditions.

Guided canoe expeditions are offered by the **Arcadia Wildlife Center** (584-3009) and the **Connecticut River Watershed Council** (584-0057); both organizations are located on Combs Road, Easthampton 01027.

FISHING   At the **Turners Falls Dam** an underground fish viewing facility offers a view of shad and salmon swimming up the fish ladder in spring. Open mid-May to June 30, Wednesday–Sunday, 9–5. The shallow, little-controlled section of the Connecticut River south of the Turners Falls Dam offers good trout fishing. Check with the **Fish and Wildlife Office** in Hadley (586-4416) for detailed fishing advice.

GOLF   **Crumpin-Fox Golf Club** (648-9109), Bernardston, 9 holes.
Thomas Memorial Golf Club (863-8003), Turners Falls, 9 holes.
Mohawk Meadows Golf Club (773-9047) in Deerfield, 9 holes.
Greenfield Country Club (773-7530), 18 holes.
Oak Ridge Golf Club (863-2010) in Gill, 9 holes, par 36.
Northfield Country Club (498-5341), Northfield, 9 holes.

HORSEBACK RIDING   **Mount Toby Stables** (549-1677), Route 63 in Leverett, year-round trail rides.
Top Rail Farms (665-2655), Dickenson Hill in Whately.

SWIMMING   See Erving and Wendell State forests (North of Quabbin). **Lake Wyola** (367-2627) in Shutesbury is a privately maintained sandy, public beach on a wooded lake; there are also picnic tables and campsites.

CROSS-COUNTRY SKIING   **Northfield Mountain Ski Touring Center** (659-3713) offers 25 kilometers of double-tracked trails. Touring equipment and snowshoes rented; $6 adult, $2 ages 7–17 for the 85–86 season.

Northfield Bicycle Barn and Cross-Country Ski Shop (498-2996) also rents skis and maintains a free, five-mile trail out back.

Oak Ridge Ski Touring Center (863-2010) in Gill offers 10 kilometers of varied skiing.

TENNIS The **Amherst Tennis Club** (549-4545) on Route 116 in Sunderland has three indoor and two outdoor clay courts; four racquetball courts.

INNS AND BED & BREAKFASTS **Deerfield Inn** (774-5587), Deerfield 01342; open year-round. A newcomer by Old Deerfield standards (it opened in 1884), this antiques-filled inn is dignified but not stiff. It is THE place to stay when visiting Historic Deerfield, enabling you to steep in the full atmosphere of the village after the visitors have gone. There are 23 rooms (all with private bath), 12 in a new annex added after the 1979 fire (when townspeople and Deerfield Academy students heroically rescued most of the antiques). $72-77 double.

Northfield Country House (498-2692), Northfield 01360. Built in 1901 as a country mansion for a prominent Boston family, the inn is richly paneled, and the downstairs decor is baronial. It is furnished to match with a grand piano, oriental rugs, and luxurious reading nooks. The seven upstairs rooms are furnished exquisitely with high brass bedsteads, and color-coordinated walls, spreads, and sheets. Breakfast is a production, and dinner is served on weekends. The house is above the town on a back road, set in sixteen landscaped acres with hydrangea hedges and a pool. $40–$75 per room, bed & breakfast.

Centennial House (498-5921), Northfield 01360. Built in 1811 and formerly the headmaster's house for Northfield Mount Hermon School, this is a handsome old home with six guest rooms, a gracious living room and dining room, and (the best part) an expansive view of the river valley. The house sits right on Northfield's long, wide main street, which invites strolling. $35–$40 single, including breakfast.

The Bernardston Inn (648-9282), Bernardston 01337. This flat-roofed, three-story old stage coach stop was visibly sagging in 1982 when two Englishmen, Toby Holmes and Steven Pardoe, bought it and began to renovate. The large dining room remains the focal point here, but all rooms have been refurbished, and many have brick fireplaces as well as antique furnishings. Just off exit 28 of I-91, this is a handy spot to land and tune into the beauty of the valley, $30 (single), $40 (double), $58 (triple), B&B.

Sunnyside Farm (665-3113), Whately 01093. Mary Lou and Dick Green welcome visitors to their turn-of-the-century farmhouse, five miles south of Historic Deerfield. There are three guest rooms and a shared bath. A full breakfast is included in $25 single, $35–$40 double.

Also see Mohawk Trail Country and the Hampshire Hilltowns.

MOTELS **Motel 6** (665-2681), South Deerfield. Built as a resort motel but operated by an economy-chain, this is a family find with large, comfortable rooms and an indoor pool. $23 double.

Candlelight Resort Motor Inn (772-0101) at the Route 2/I-91 rotary. Built and maintained as a resort motel with swimming pool, tennis court, and a small golf course. $36–$64 double.

Greenfield Howard Johnson Motel (774-2211), Route 2/I-91 rotary. A standard HoJo's with an outdoor pool. $56–$62 double.

Bernardston Motel (648-9398), South Street. A white Victorian home with six units, $19–$24, suite for $34.

Windmill Motel (648-9152), sixteen units, breakfast served, $25–$35.

Fox Inn (648-9111), Routes 5/10, Bernardston; 30 units, pool, $48 single, $60 double.

Weatherhead's Motel & Cabins (659-3831), Route 2, Millers Falls. 12 units, 8 cabins, restaurant on premises; $30–$45.

French King Motor Lodge (659-3828), Route 2 in Millers Falls. 18 units, swimming pool, restaurant on premises; $39–$44.

OTHER LODGING **American Youth Hostel** (498-5311), at Northfield Mount Hermon School, Northfield, mid-June to mid-August. Munro and Isabel Smith, the founders of AYH, opened America's first youth hostel here in Northfield in an old mansion (since burned). This facility utilizes dorm space, offering 32 beds; $6.50 per person.

CAMPING **Barton Cove Nature and Camping Area** (863-9300) is an unusual facility maintained by Northeast Utilities on a peninsula that juts into the Connecticut River. Wooded tent sites are available and tents can be rented, along with canoes.

White Birch Campgrounds (665-4941), Whately Road. Open year-round, handy to I-91, facilities include hot showers, electric and water hookups, a store, laundry, rec hall, swimming pool, and playground.

Also see **Erving State Forest** (North of Quabbin).

DINING OUT **Deerfield Inn** (774-2359), The Street, Old Deerfield. This is a formal dining room with white tablecloths, Chippendale chairs, and a moderately expensive, ambitious lunch and dinner menu: Deviled Quail or Veal Rigby ($12–$17 for dinner). Lighter meals are available in the pub and there is also a summer coffee shop.

Turnbull's Sunny Farms (773-8203), Route 2/I-91 rotary. Open daily for lunch and dinner. Not a particularly fancy place, this restaurant is our family's favored stop, good for quiche, sandwiches, or for seafood and steaks; great salads, liquor served, moderately priced. $10–$12 dinner range.

Muchmores (648-9107), Huckle Hill Road, Bernardston. This is a locally favored dining place set high on a hill with a panoramic view. The menu includes a range of meat and fish dishes, from Filet Mignon Bearnaise to Shrimp Scampi with Mushrooms, $9–$12 range. There's a good wine list. Open daily for dinner, 11:30–2 on Sundays for brunch. No credit cards.

Bricker's (774-2857), Route 2/I-91 rotary. This is a large restaurant with a number of attractive dining areas and a large moderately priced menu. A favorite place for business lunches, meetings, and wedding receptions. $10–$15 dinner.

Bernardston Inn (648-9282), Route 5, Bernardston. Closed Mondays. The Picadilly Room is open for lunch, dinner, and Sunday brunch. The continental dinner menu may include lamb curry, wienerschnitzel, veal marsala, and baked eggplant ($10–$15 range). Sunday brunch is also attracting an enthusiastic following. Liquor served.

Taylor's Tavern (773-8313), 238 Main Street, Greenfield. Great atmosphere, open for lunch and dinner, modest prices.

Goten Restaurant (665-3628), Route 116, in Sunderland. Open for dinner Tuesday–Saturday, from 2 PM Sunday. A moderately priced Japanese place with a good local reputation. Specialties include hibachi shrimp.

EATING OUT **Famous Bill's Restaurant** (773-9230), 30 Federal Street, Greenfield, open daily 11–11. This is a friendly, family restaurant, moderately priced, liquor served.

The Wok (774-3606), State Road, Deerfield. Open daily for lunch and dinner, Mandarin menu, liquor.

Dimo's Restaurant (665-4444). Italian restaurant featuring veal, lasagna, grinders.

Bart's Cafe (773-3680), 80 School Street, Greenfield. Homemade breakfast, lunch, and superb sundaes; the source of the area's gourmet Bart's Ice Cream.

Rua's Restaurant (498-2292), 79 Main Street, Northfield. A dark, homey family restaurant with home-cooked soups and chowders. Open daily for lunch and dinner.

French King Restaurant (659-3328). A handy Route 2 family restaurant, open daily for lunch and dinner; breakfast in summer.

Weatherhead's Restaurant (659-3831). Daily breakfast, lunch, and dinner; homemade soups and desserts; family restaurant.

Rainbow Bend at the Cove (863-8129) in Gill, Route 2 on Barton's Cove, good for take-out by the water.

Brad's Place (773-8460), 353 Main Street. Open from 6 AM until mid-afternoon; closed Sundays. Fast, friendly local eatery with booths in back.

Steeple Jacks (665-7980), Amherst Road, Sunderland. Open daily for lunch and dinner; full menu, wine & beer.

The Dove's Nest (665-7969), Route 116 in Sunderland. Curvy counter and booths, homemade baked goods; bills itself as the World's Best breakfast; reasonably priced lunch and dinner; beer, wine.

Four Leaf Clover (648-9514), Route 5, Bernardston. Open for lunch and dinner, popular locally. Baked linguini ($4.95), seafood newburg ($6.95), swordfish ($8.56), known for seafood.

ENTERTAINMENT **The Arena Civic Theatre** (773-9891), Box 744, Greenfield 01302, presents musicals and comedies, mid-June through August; tickets: $3.50–$6.

"Music in Deerfield" (773-8929) is a series of concerts performed in the Brick Church Meetinghouse on weekends fall through spring.

Theatre 81 (773-8111), 44 James Street, Greenfield. Summer productions in area sites.

SELECTIVE SHOPPING **The Museum Store**, Historic Deerfield. The J. G. Pratt store is a trove of books, crafts, museum reproductions, gifts, and souvenirs. Open museum hours.

Wilsons, Main Street, Greenfield. The town's long-established, dependable department store.

Yankee Candle, Route 5, South Deerfield. Candles made and sold on the spot; seconds, gifts.

Renovator's Supply (659-3113), Millers Falls, open year-round daily. Best known for its catalog—everything needed to restore a seventeenth- to early twentieth-century house: lights, knobs, hinges, weathervanes, etc. The Old Mill carries unusual and hard to find pieces and the Bargain Basement is a treasure trove.

World Eye Bookshop (772-0844), 60 Federal Street, Greenfield. A well-stocked bookstore serving a wide Upcountry area.

ANTIQUES **Antique Center of Old Deerfield** (773-3620). A collection of 17 shops, closed Mondays.

Lighthouse Antiques (665-2488), Deerfield, specializes in New Englandania.

Ken Miller (498-2749), Northfield, stages auctions on Monday nights (6:30) in summer and fall; on Saturdays (10–5) in the off-season; and also runs a flea market on Sundays, mid-April through October, 7–3.

Goose Lane Antiques (648-9695), Bernardston. Outlet for a group of dealers.

CRAFTS **The Leverett Craftsmen and Artists** (549-6871), Leverett Center, marked from Route 63, showcases some of the best crafts in New England. The majority of its 200 members are in western Massachusetts. The galleries are filled with art-quality weaving, pottery, sculpture, and paintings. Housed in an 1875 box factory in a picturesque village center, it is handy to some interesting hikes (ask at the gallery). Open daily, 12–5; from 10 on Saturdays. Take Bull Hill Road off Route 63, follow signs.

Arts Space (772-6811), 7 Franklin Street, Greenfield. Open Tuesday–Saturday, 10–4; expanded hours before Christmas, less in summer. Changing craft shows representing area artisans.

Individual local craftspeople who welcome visitors are listed in the *Western Massachusetts Craft Directory*, available from Arts Extension Service (545-2360), Division of Continuing Education, University of Massachusetts, Amherst 01003.

SPECIAL EVENTS June: **Deerfield Crafts Fair**

August/September: **Franklin County Fair**, Greenfield. Always the Friday through Monday following Labor Day.

September: **Deerfield Crafts Fair**

MEDICAL EMERGENCY **Franklin Medical Center** (772-0211), 164 High Street, Greenfield; also **Farren Memorial Hospital** (774-3111), Montague City.

The Hilltowns

The Hilltowns are set in gentler country than their neighbors to the north and west. The villages are classic New England centers with white steepled churches, fine commons, and homes. Many hillsides are still farm or pasture land. There are more maple producers here than in the rest of the state put together and there are also orchards, other farms, and craftspeople who welcome visitors. Back roads beckon bicyclists and there are some beautiful hiking trails through state forests and properties maintained by the Trustees of Reservations.

Five years ago this was just a region to pass through. You could count the number of commercial guest rooms on your fingers. Then in 1982 the Hilltown Community Development Corporation placed an ad in local papers, asking people with spare rooms to consider the bed & breakfast business. You can now pick from back-road farms or village mansions: all welcome guests throughout the year. The hilltowns which happen to be in Franklin County (Ashfield, Buckland, and Conway) also now have their share of attractive bed & breakfasts.

The hilltowns have a long tradition of welcoming summer people (witness William Cullen Bryant's summer home and the old hotel, now a rest home, in Ashfield). Now visitors can enjoy the unusual, laid-back beauty of this rural region year-round.

AREA CODE 413

GUIDANCE **Hilltown Community Development Corporation (CDC)** (296-4363), PO Box 17, Chesterfield 01012. Write for information about local craftspeople and artisans. Paintings and crafts are exhibited in the CDC headquarters, behind the general store in Chesterfield (open weekdays, 9–5). For a copy of the brochure "Hampshire Hills Bed & Breakfast" write: Box 307, Williamsburg 01096.

Franklin County Chamber of Commerce (773-5463), PO Box 790, Main Street, Greenfield 01302, publishes pamphlet guides to bed & breakfasts in Ashfield, Buckland, and Conway.

The Pioneer Valley Convention & Visitors Bureau (787-1548), 1500 Main Street, Suite 600, Springfield 01115, publishes a pamphlet guide which covers the remaining towns.

Department of Environmental Management, Region 4 (549-1461)

The Hilltowns

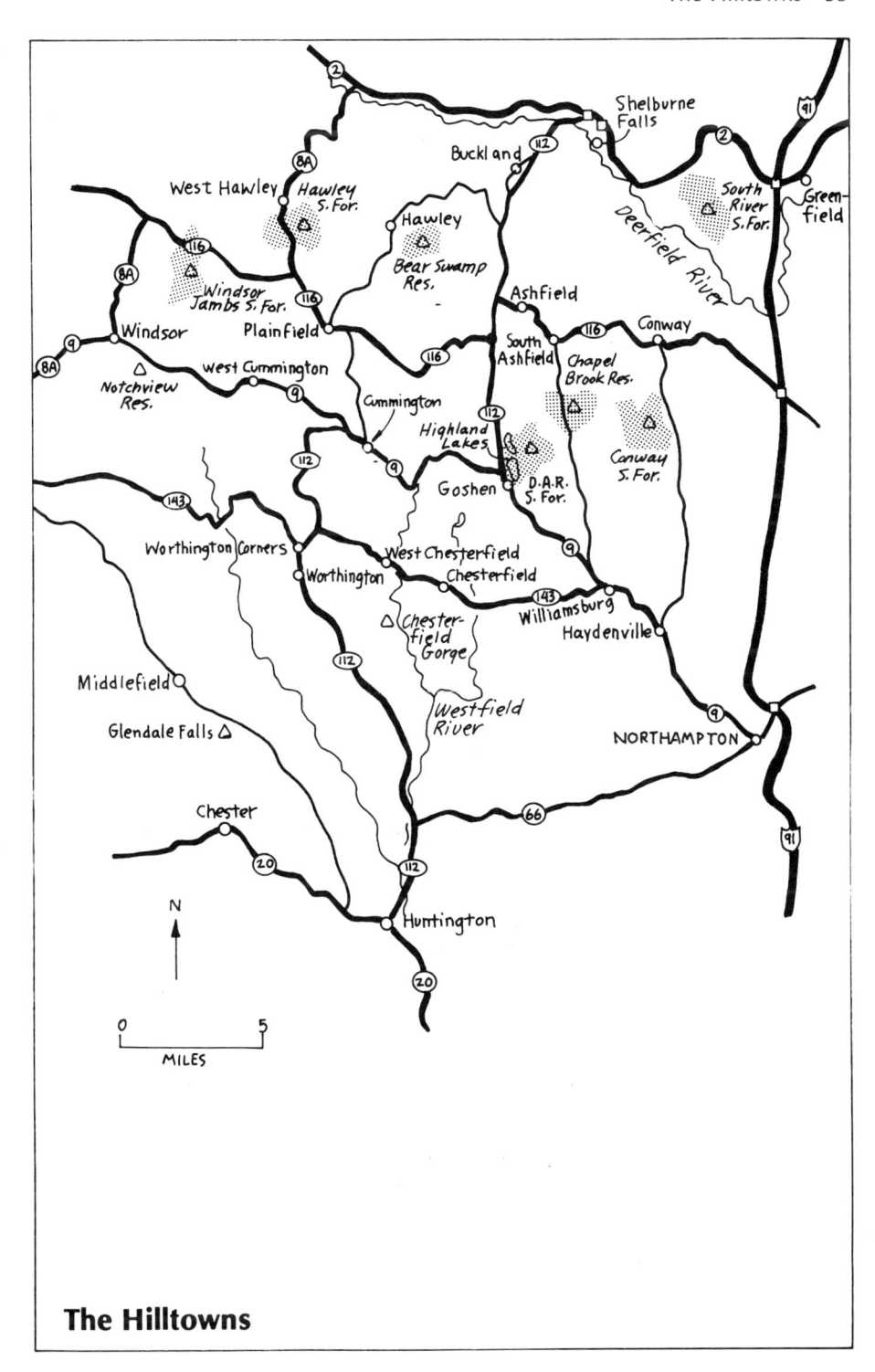

can answer specific questions about the state parks and forests in this area.

TO SEE AND DO **William Cullen Bryant Homestead** (634-2244) in Cummington, south of Route 9 off Route 112. This graceful, 23-room "Dutch Colonial" mansion is set on 189 rolling acres, restored to look precisely as it did during Bryant's last summer here. Built by Bryant's grandfather in 1793, it was home for the writer as a boy (1799–1815) and later became his summer home (1865–1878), when he bought and renovated the old homestead. He raised it an entire floor and filled it with eclectic furnishings and souvenirs toted home from the Middle East, the weights he lifted 100 times a day until he was more than 80, and his books. From the formal parlor to the cottage furniture in the guest rooms, one senses here the exuberant spirit of a colorful nineteenth-century leader (as editor of New York's *Evening Post* for 50 years Bryant wielded immense power) and also the tone of Victorian summer life. The site itself is so beautiful that visitors often linger half a day or come just to sit or stroll in the handsome grounds. Open from the last week in June through Labor Day: Friday, Saturday, Sunday: 1–5; also weekends through Columbus Day. $2.50 per adult, $1 per child.

VILLAGES **Ashfield.** This unusually spirited town of 14,500 publishes *The Ashfield News* (a volunteer effort: 628-4483) and has more than its share of bed & breakfasts. A large, former summer hotel (now the Ashfield Rest Home) still stands in the middle of the village, but most traffic now stops at **Elmer's Store,** which carries the *New York Daily News* and a large selection of wines. The pride of Ashfield remains the Wren-style steeple on its town hall (built as a church in 1814) and the unusual number of both maple producers and craftspeople, most of whom exhibit at the annual Fall Festival. Ashfield is the birthplace of movie director Cecil B. deMille (his parents happened to be staying at the hotel) and has been home for a number of artists and writers, making for an unusually interesting **Historical Society** (623-4541: open Saturday & Sunday in July & August, 2–5). In summer there is swimming at the small town beach right in the village on Ashfield Lake (transients discouraged) and there are two outstanding reservations (see Trustees of Reservations Properties).

Buckland. Buckland's town hall stands just across the **Bridge of Flowers** from Shelburne Falls, and the town's northern line is the Deerfield River. Buckland's Center is, however, a beautiful old gathering of church, historical society, small brick library, and aristocratic eighteenth-century homes (one of them now a bed & breakfast), all set high on a hill a dozen miles south off Route 112. The **Historical Society** (625-6472), open Sunday in summer 2–5, has exhibits about Mary Lyon, the Buckland girl who pioneered education for women in the early nineteenth century and is remembered as the founder of Mount Holyoke College in South Hadley. In the four-square, four-chimney **Major Joseph Griswold House** you can inspect the third-floor ballroom in which Ms. Lyon began her first female academy in 1824. The space has been restored to look as it did then, complete with appropriate books (open Tuesdays in summer but call ahead: 625-2031). The way to the site of Mary Lyon's birthplace is marked from Route 112 but following it is like finding your way to the belly button of the earth.

Chesterfield. This is another classic white clapboard village with an 1835 Congregational Church, an 1848 town hall, and an **Edward Memorial (historical) Museum** (open Saturday, 2–5; June–Labor Day) near the library. But the big attraction in town is Chesterfield Gorge (see Trustees of Reservations Properties).

Conway. Turn off Route 116 and stop long enough at the triangular green to admire the domed **Marshall Field Memorial Library** (369-4646), gift of the native son who founded a Chicago department store. There's a marble rotunda and elaborate detailing within; the historical collection is open Monday, Wednesday, and Friday: 2–5 and 7–9, except holidays. Also note the covered bridge across the South River off Route 116.

Cummington. The classic village center is posted from Route 9, and it is worth stopping to see the **Kingman Tavern** (open Saturday 2–5 in July and August), a lovingly restored combination tavern, fully stocked general store, and post office. There are a dozen period rooms filled with town mementoes like the palm leaf hat and cigar once made here. There is also a barn full of tools and a shed full of horse-drawn vehicles. The big annual event is the **Hillside Agricultural Society Fair**, the last weekend in August.

Plainfield. This beautiful old farming town has a population of 466, which swells to 2,000 in summer. Roads are lined with stone walls and avenues of maples, and the Center has its mid-nineteenth-century white Congregational Church and town hall. The **Shaw-Hudson House** (634-5417) was built in 1833 by Dr. Samuel Shaw, medical partner and brother-in-law of William Cullen Bryant. The personality of the house, especially the medical office with its drug case and books, is worth a stop.

Williamsburg. The southeasternmost of the hilltowns, this is something of a bedroom town for Northampton. The two-street Center straddles the Mill River and invites you to stroll, munching something you've bought at the general store (see Snacks). The **Historical Society** (open Sunday afternoons, June–October and by appointment: 268-7332), housed in the 1841 town hall, exhibits photographs of the 1874 flood that burst a dam three miles above the village, killing 136 residents, collapsing buildings, and wiping

Visions of ice cream and penny candy

out most of the mills. Note the **Brass Works** mill in Haydenville, rebuilt since the flood and recently renovated. An old, three-story gristmill on route 9 is currently under restoration as a **Farm Museum**; the collection of interesting old farm implements is now open by appointment (634-2244).

Worthington Corners. Worthington is altogether an unusual community (note the **Sevenars Concerts**, the vintage 1904 golf course, **Hickory Hill** touring center, the **Sena Auction House** and bed & breakfasts). The Federal-era and Greek-revival homes around a classic general store make this particular four corners stand out.

SUGARHOUSES A brochure with information about the sugaring process and each producer is available from the Massachusetts Maple Producers Association, PO Box 207, Ashfield 01330 (628-3912). The following sugarhouses welcome visitors during the late February/early April boiling-off season, but call before coming. All sell their syrup from their farms year-round.

In Ashfield: **Bear River Sugarhouse** (625-2753); **Gray's Sugarhouse** (625-6559), with dining room service on weekends during sugaring; **Journey's End Farm** (628-3973); **Mollie's Maple** (628-3231); **Olde Tavern Farm** (628-3911); **Orchard Farm** (628-3873); **Sweetwater Farm** (628-3268), with a small maple museum, dining room in season; **Townsley Farm** (625-2668).

In Buckland: **Puringtons' Maple** (625-2780) they still use horses to collect sap; **Shippee Homestead** (625-2952).

In Chester: **Misty Mountain Farm** (354-6337), uses horses to collect sap on weekends.

In Chesterfield: **Bisbee Family Maple** (296–4717); **Daniel Krug** (527-9408), geared to visitors, with roads through the sugarbush, they use wooden buckets to collect sap and a 1910 evaporator.

In Conway: **8-acre Sugarbush** (369-4304); **Boyden Brothers** (369-4637); **Burnett's Sugarhouse** (369-4437); **Poverty Pocket** (369-4629); **South River Sugarhouse** (369-4455); **Walter Truce** (625-6840).

In Cummington: **4-G's Sugarhouse** (634-5358); **Frank Herron** (634-8874); **Howes Brothers** (634-5340); **Maple East Farm** (634-5342); **Maple Heights** (624-5441); **Preston's Sap Shack** (634-5483); and **Tessier's Sugarhouse** (634-5022). **Cumworth Farm** (634-5529) is open in March and early April for pancake breakfasts, weekends: 9–2. Tours of the sugarhouse and sheep barns are also offered.

In Goshen: **Twin Maples Sugarhouse** (268-7124).

In Haydenville: **4-Corner Farm** (268-3266).

In Huntington: **Stonelea Farm** (667-5792); **East Branch Sugarhouse** (559-3766).

In Middlefield: **Whoo-ville Sugarhouse** (623-8347).

In Plainfield: **Bob's Sugarhouse** (534-3548).

In West Chesterfield: **Jack's Sugarhouse** (296-4089).

In West Cummington: **Maple View Farm** (684-3418).

In Worthington: **Cook's Maple Products** (238-5827); **Kinnie Brook Farm** (238-5398); **Red Bucket Sugar Shack** (238-7710), dining room in season; **Windy Hill Farm** (238-5869), dining room in season.

FARMS TO VISIT South Ashfield: **E. & J. Scott Orchards** (628-3327). Late August through May, fresh cider and apples; closed Tuesday.

Worthington: **Tomaselli's Berry Farm** (238-5917).

Chesterfield: **Roberts Blueberries** (296-4762), pick your own.

West Chesterfield: **Adams Apples** (296-4024).

STATE FORESTS **South River State Forest** (268-7098/339-5504), north from Conway Village on the Shelburne Falls and Bardwells Ferry roads. Explore the gorge of the South River to its confluence with the Deerfield River. Near the parking area notice the South River Dam, once used to power the trolley line that carried passengers to and from the New York–New Haven and Hartford Railroad lines, which crossed South River here over the highest trestle in the state (you can see the rail bed and the remains of the trestle).

D.A.R. State Forest (268-7098), Goshen. There are more than 50 campsites, each with a table and a fireplace; 2 sites with picnic tables have been adapted for the handicapped. Upper Highland Lake has a swimming area complete with bathhouse, lifeguards, and a boat ramp (no motors allowed). Trails lead to Moore's Hill, just 1,697 feet high but with an extensive view. A naturalist is employed during the summer to conduct tours and educational programs.

Kenneth Debuque Memorial State Forest. Formerly known as Hawley State Forest (634-8858), just north of Plainfield on Route 8A (turn off the Hallockville Road opposite Hallockville Pond), it offers a fine loop-hike from Basin Brook (on Route 8A; there is a small parking area). Moody Spring, located off Hallockville Road in the forest (Moody Spring Road), is a genuine mineral spring, which you can sample from a metal pipe. A sign proclaims: "This water has proven helpful in cases of sore throat, stomachache, intestinal disorders, rheumatism and all scrofula diseases." Not far from the spring, just off East Hawley Road, stands a well-preserved charcoal kiln. The forest's many miles of dirt roads make for fine winter ski touring; 12 miles are marked with blue triangles and a map is available.

Windsor Jambs State Forest (684-9760). Follow signs from Route 9 in West Cummington, via River Road. There are 24 campsites near Windsor Jambs, a quarter-mile-long gorge (a rock formation known as "jambs"). The state dams the river for swimming and there are bathhouses, 80 picnic tables, and grills. This stretch of the Westfield River is a popular spot for white-water canoeing. There are also many miles of hiking trails.

TRUSTEES OF RESERVATIONS PROPERTIES **Bear Swamp Reservation**, in Ashfield on the Hawley Road (less than two miles west of the junction of Route 116 and 112), is 171 acres with roads and trails and is known for its wildflowers: lady's slippers, painted trillium, cowslips, marsh marigolds, blue gentian, wild azaleas, and flowering dogwood.

Chapelbrook Reservation in South Ashfield, where Route 116 doglegs east, continue south on the Williamsburg Road, two and one-quarter miles. Turn left to find the series of shallow falls that spill into a deep pool, perfect for sliding down and into. Across the road the Chapelbrook Ledges offer superb views of the surrounding countryside.

Glendale Falls, Middlefield, off the Skyline Trail Road onto Clark Wright Road, some three and one-half miles southeast of the village; closed in winter. Glendale Brook drops more than 150 feet over rocky ledges. There are 60 surrounding acres and the Skyline Trail itself is worth the ride. Accessible from Route 143 in Hinsdale and from Route 20 in Chester, the Skyline Trail follows the edge of the Berkshire Plateau.

Chesterfield Gorge. Turn off Route 143 at the West Chesterfield Bridge, one mile south on River Road. Warden: May 25–October 14, weekends, holidays. A deep canyon carved by the Westfield River, the gorge is walled by sheer granite cliffs topped with hemlock, ash, and yellow birch. Swimming is not allowed but the Trustees provide picnic tables. $1 adult, $.50, child.

Notchview Reservation (684-0148). The Budd Visitor Center on Route 9 in Windsor (one mile east of the junction with Route 8A) is open daily, year-round. There are picnic tables and trail maps for the 25 miles of hiking and cross-country trails (5 kilometers are groomed), some of the best trails in the state because of their elevation (1,900 feet to 2,297 feet). Winter trail fee: $3 per adult, $1.25, child.

Petticoat Hill Reservation in Williamsburg, up Petticoat Hill Road from the village. A trail leads to the summit of Scott Hill. Stone walls and cellar holes hint that this was the most populated part of town in the 1700s, but it's now forested; a good spot for wildflowers.

OTHER RESERVATIONS **Devil's Den Brook** in Williamsburg is a rocky gorge off Old Goshen Road. Turn right on Hemenway Road at the western fringe of the Center, branch left onto Old Goshen. If you take the next left, up Brier Hill Road, you come to 70 acres of wooded trails, good for ski touring and hiking. Ask locally about Rheena's Cave.

GOLF There are nine-hole courses in Ashfield (628-4413), in Haydenville (268-7229), and in Worthington (238-9731).

SWIMMING See the Windsor and D.A.R. state forests.

ALPINE SKIING **Berkshire Snow Basin** (634-5318), Route 9, West Cummington, is a newly revitalized family area with a pleasant lodge, ski shop, and ski school. Open weekends and holiday weeks (call ahead).

    Vertical drop: 1,000 feet
    Trails: 15
    Lifts: two T-bars
    Snowmaking added in 1985 to cover 60% of trails
    Rates: $13 adult, $10 junior (under age 12)

    Expansion plans are in the works for a triple chair and two or three more trails, with the longest to be 2½ miles long.

CROSS-COUNTRY SKIING **Hickory Hill Touring Center** (238-5813/5477), Buffington Hill Road, Worthington. This 650-acre spread offers more than 25 kilometers of maintained trails with better than average snow cover thanks to elevations of 1,600 to 1,850 feet. Trails are wide and smooth enough for racers, but there is enough variety to satisfy everyone, ample rental equipment, and a large barn with a fireplace, drinks, and snacks. Lessons and guided ski tours; $5 adults, $2 children under 12.

    Cummington Farm (634-2111), on the Plainfield Road from Cummington Village. The 25 kilometers of groomed trails represent one of the oldest, best-known cross-country systems around. Guided night tours. Check to make sure it is not the scene of group races when you come. Restaurant, dorm and cabin lodging. Rentals. Trail fee: $5.50 adult, $3.50 child under 12.

    Also check **Stump Sprouts** in West Hawley (Mohawk Trail Country); and note the trails in Notchview Reservation and the State Forests.

INNS, BED & BREAKFASTS Note that a pamphlet guide, *"Hampshire Hills Bed & Breakfast,"* is available from Box 307, Williamsburg 01096.

    The Whale Inn (268-7246), Goshen 01032. Built as a parsonage in 1799, the Whale Inn is now primarily a restaurant with a big, attractive dining room serving three meals daily. There are five rooms upstairs in the original house. $21.14 single, $42.28 double, $47.57 for a suite.

    In Cummington 01012: **Windfields Farm** (684-3786), R.R.1, Box 170. This 1860 farmhouse offers life's luxuries: comfortable beds, a book-lined living room with hearth, memorable breakfasts made with just-laid eggs, maple syrup, and fruit all produced on the premises. Out back there are trails for all seasons (great cross-country) and a swimming pond. Add to this two consummate hosts: Arnold Westwood, a retired Unitarian-Universalist minister, and his wife, Carolyn, a prize-winning organic gardener. Rates:

$40 double, $35 single, "winter weekends" with meals available in January and February.

Cumworth Farm (634-5529). All of the McColgan's seven children are grown and have left the fine, 200-year-old farmhouse, which now has five spare rooms. All are furnished with antiques, and two are heated with woodstoves and fireplaces. The core of the house is a big kitchen with hanging baskets, the scene of hearty breakfasts with the McColgan's own syrup, jams, and berries. There is a gracious living room, but guests are drawn outdoors to ski cross-country in winter, to watch the sugaring operation in spring, and to visit with the sheep and wander the meadows in summer. Ed and Mary McColgan are unusually interesting hosts. $35 double, $30 single, $10 per extra cot.

Caldwell's (634-5556). This is a snug old cape right in Cummington Village, a few houses up from the white Congregational Church. With two children grown, the Caldwells have two spare rooms: one comfortable double and one single, overlooking the spacious garden. Both Tom and Ginnie work and so prefer to take guests on weekends. Full breakfasts are included in $35 double, $30 single, $5 for a cot.

The Hill Gallery (238-5914), mailing address: Star Route Box 10AA, Worthington 01098. Located halfway between Hickory Hill and the Berkshire Snow Basin, this modern home (built by owner Walter Korzec) caters to skiers in winter and offers a pool in summer. There are two guest rooms with baths; also extra bunks for children in this multi-level home, which doubles as a gallery for Korzec's prints and paintings. $40 double, $25 single including a full American breakfast.

In Worthington 01098: **Raymond and Helen Magargal** (238-5817). The Magargal home has served variously over the years as a basket factory, a cheese factory, and an inn. Now it can accommodate a total of 11 guests in four delightful upstairs rooms which share a bath. You can walk to the golf course and swimming, and Hickory Hill is handy in winter. The Magargals are the kind of grandparents who instantly adopt guests' children. $40 for the twin bedroom, $30 double, $25 single includes breakfast.

The Franklin Burrs (238-8326). Open May through October. This renovated country home is set on 100 acres. It offers a twin-bedded room with private full bath. No smokers please. $35 double, $25 single, includes continental breakfast. An additional room is sometimes available.

Worthington Inn (238-4441), Old North Road. This 1780 house has been professionally restored. Debbie and Joe Shaw have four guest rooms. On the edge of Worthington Four Corners, it is handy to golf and swimming and also to the Hickory Hill ski trails. $50 with private bath on weekends, $45 midweek; $45 with shared bath on weekends, $40 midweek; $10 less single; includes full breakfast.

In Huntington 01050: Robert and Barbara Paulson (667-3208), off Route 66. Guest facilities are in a solar wing with a view. It contains a library, a screened porch, and a loft room with beds for three and space for sleeping bags. Hiking, skating, cross-country skiing, and a used bookshop are all on the premises. Rates: $50 maximum for up to five; $40 double; and $35 single; full breakfast included.

Colonial Inn (667-8737), Worthington Road. Newly renovated, primarily a restaurant with five guest rooms, $55–$65 depending on shared, private bath.

In Williamsburg 01096: **Carl and Lottie Sylvester** (268-7283). An easy walk to Williamsburg Center but in quiet country. Three bedrooms accommodate five. There is a living room with fireplace and TV for guest use; full breakfast included: $35 double, $30 single.

Twin Maples (268-7925). A restored 200-year-old farmhouse with three guest rooms (one with twin beds, two with doubles, all with antique beds), shared bath, sitting room, and screened porch. A crib and cot are available. $40 double, $30 single including a full breakfast with homemade maple syrup, jams, and jellies.

Helen and Donald Gould (268-7314). A gracious 1812 house within walking distance of the Center, furnished with paintings and artifacts collected during the Goulds' 25-year stay in Latin America. Two bedrooms; gourmet breakfast included: $35 double, $30 single.

"In the Country" Bed & Breakfast Association, PO Box 457, Ashfield 01330 is the source of a pamphlet listing the following bed & breakfasts in the hilltowns that happen to be in Franklin County.

In Ashfield 01330: **Ashfield Inn** (628-4571). This is a Georgian mansion set on four acres, offering five spacious guest rooms. Each is furnished with antiques and garnished with fresh flowers, scented soaps, shampoos, and chocolates (two rooms on a bath). Continental breakfast and candlelight dinner are included in $100 per day double, $60 single, $10 per child.

Hidden Hill Bed & Breakfast (625-2674). Betsy Beebe offers a secluded, old country home on the outskirts of the village. Breakfasts feature home baking, local jams, and homegrown fruit, served on the terrace or in a glass-enclosed room overlooking gardens and hills. Non-smokers please. $30–$34.

Gold Leaf Inn (628-3392). A late Victorian home in the center of the village; walk to swimming, golf, and tennis courts. A full breakfast is served in your room, on the porch, or in the dining room next to the fire. $35–$45.

Bullfrog Bed & Breakfast (628-4493). The Thibaults' home was the first bed & breakfast in Ashfield. It is a snug 200-year-old cape on Route 116 south of South Ashfield, with a lovely back garden and frog pond. Three snug rooms, furnished with antiques, and a lovely common space. $40 per couple.

In Conway 01341: **Hilltop Bed & Breakfast** (369-4928). Bill and Linda Graves welcome guests to their century-old home with spectacular views of farms and forests. Two bedrooms with shared bath enjoy a screened porch; private living and dining rooms with a separate entrance. $30–$35 per room includes a full breakfast.

In Buckland 01338: **The 1797 House** (625-2975 or 625-2697). Janet Turley's classic old home on Buckland's classic green is a standout. There are three double guest rooms, each with private bath. Guests enjoy a large country breakfast by one of the four fireplaces, or on the screened porch. $42 for one, $55 for two, including a full breakfast.

The Scott House (625-6624). Set in a rural area, handy to Shelburne Falls, this home offers a guest room with fireplace and private bath. $35–$50 includes breakfast.

CAMPGROUNDS **Berkshire Green Acres** (634-5385), Ray and Mary Ellen Bolduc, Grant Street, Plainfield 01070. Open all year, 190 sites, lounge, snack bar, recreation hall, swimming; $10.

Berkshire Park Camping Area (238-5918) in Worthington Corners 01098. Open May to mid-October, 85 sites on 216 acres, swimming in a spring-fed pond, free hot showers; $6.50.

SELF-IMPROVING VACATION **Cummington Community of the Arts** (634-2172), Cummington 01026. This non-profit, educational institute provides year-round living and studio space for artists of all disciplines. Facilities include a concert shed, a library, painting and sculpture studios, several small cabins, two main houses, darkroom facilities, an electric kiln, and an organic vegetable garden. In summer some 25 artists and 10 children are accepted on a one- to three-month basis. Children aged 5–14 live together in a renovated barn, with full-time supervision. Fifteen artists are accepted for the seven-month winter term. Reasonably priced.

DINING OUT **New Hope** (625-2338), Apple Valley, Ashfield. Dining is by reservation only. Candlelit country fare with a continental flair in an atmospheric 1794 cape. There is a fixed menu and it's BYOB. Open year-round on Friday, Saturday, and Sunday at 7 PM (November through April; Sunday dinner begins at 2 PM).

Colonial Inn (667-8737), Worthington Road, Huntington. Open for dinner and Sunday brunch, but phone ahead. Newly reopened under the management of a local fish store owner, the specialty is lobster done seven different ways, a variety of seafood, $7–$15.

The Whale Inn (268-7246), Route 9 in Goshen. The large dining room overlooks gardens and adjoins the Marine Cocktail Lounge.

Specialties include homemade soups, steak, chicken, and prime rib. Dinner dancing to live music on Friday and Saturday. Open for breakfast, lunch, and dinner, which is priced from $7.50 to $14.95.

Christmas Inn (268-7511), Williamsburg. Closed January, otherwise open Tuesday through Saturday 5–10; Sunday 12–9. Decorated year-round for Christmas. Turkey dinner with all the trimmings, steak, and scampi are the specialties. $8–$15, children's plates available.

EATING OUT   **Buffalo Village Restaurant** (634-2228), North Street in Plainfield Village. A big bar and booths, reasonably priced pizza, sandwiches, and something different: buffalo burgers, steak, and stew (the buffalo is raised in town).

Country Corners Restaurant (268-7313), Route 9 in Goshen. All three meals, reasonably priced, homemade pies.

Ashfield Lake House (628-3224), open May–Columbus Day for lunch and dinner; full bar by the lake; a local hangout.

SNACKS   **Williamsburg General Store** (268-3687), 12 Main Street, Williamsburg. Baked goods, natural foods, and ice cream parlor.

ENTERTAINMENT   **Sevenars Music Festival** (238-5854), July and early August weekends. The Schrade family and guest musicians perform in the acoustically superb former gym of the old double-porched Worthington Academy, junction of Ireland Street and Route 112. The group, "Sevenars," is named for the seven Schrades, who include Robert (composer of more than 1,000 songs), his wife Rolande, and their children Robelyn, Rhonda-Lee, Rolisa, Randolph, and Rorianne. Twins Rhonda-Lee and Rolisa help out but don't perform. The Schrades are widely acclaimed musicians in their own right and their guests, including occasionally a symphony orchestra, are tops too. No tickets. Donations.

SELECTIVE SHOPPING   **Happy Valley Farm Gift Shop**, Route 9 in Cummington, sells gifts, greeting cards, candles, jellies, cheese, and toys. It's a fine old house by the river with a fireplace and picnic table.

Antiques: Check out the **Brassworks Antiques Cooperative** (268-7985) and **Gaskell's Antiques** (268-3522) in Haydenville; **Country Cricket Village Shop** (238-5366) and **Partridge Hill Antiques** (238-5992) in Worthington; the **Old Brick Store** (634-2215) in Plainfield; **Riverbreeze Shop** (667-3438) and **Second Time Around Shoppe** (667-3131) in Huntington; **Jack Cobb Antiques** (354-6502) in Chester; and **Conway House** (369-4660), with furniture, samplers, and glass, on route 116 in Conway. There is also **Robert L. Merriam's** rare bookstore (369-4052) in Conway, and **Yesterday's Books,** run by Clayton and Ruth Craft, in Ashfield.

Auctions: These occur regularly; contact **Sena's Auction Service**

(238-5377) in Worthington and **George Thomas Lewis and Co.** (268-7513) in Williamsburg.

CRAFTS   Some 40 craftsmen belong to the **Hilltown Artisans Guild** (see Guidance), worth contacting for information about specific crafts or juried shows. The **Williamsburg Country Store** (see Snacks) sells work by many local craftspeople. Our source for the following listing is the *Western Massachusetts Craft Directory*, available from the Arts Extension Service (545-2360), Division of Continuing Education, University of Massachusetts, Amherst 01003.

In Ashfield: **Marcine Appel** (628-3325) makes handwoven cotton women's clothing; **Norvelene Contakos and Elizabeth Heck** (628-4519) make appliqued bed coverings and clothing; **Marianne Hurley** (628-3319) makes collectable toys and dolls; **Dick Muller** (628-3895) designs leather handbags, wallets, and accessories; **Jo An Mulhall** (625-9563) makes jewelry from silver, gold, and porcupine quills; **Stephen Smithers** (628-4591) makes handwrought lighting fixtures; **Popular Toys, Ltd.** (628-3377) is a source of handcrafted wooden toys; and the **Baptist Corner Studio** (625-9748) sells crafts, paintings, and woodcuts.

In Buckland: **Bryan Gregir** (625-2190) makes one-of-a-kind furniture.

In Conway: **Leprechaun Sheepskin** sells sheepskin clothing and accessories; **Jonathan Slytz** (369-4992) designs jewelry; and **Katheryn Wilkes** paints and stencils on wood.

In Goshen: **Marcia Phillips** (268-7155) weaves art-to-wear, hand dyed, tapestry clothing; and **Kit Loney** (268-7892) weaves tapestry hangings and clothing.

In Plainfield: **Tom Patti** (634-5370) makes glass sculpture.

In Haydenville: **Susan Parks** (286-7429) makes handmade ceramic tile; and **Marty Phinney** (268-3228) makes pottery and stoneware ornaments. Artists also exhibit at **The Brassworks** (268-3540).

In Williamsburg: **Tai Ingrid Hazard** (628-3272) makes custom-made furniture; and **Miriam Massano** (268-3240) weaves natural dyed fibers: scarves, pillows, and shawls.

In Huntington: **Linda Siska** (667-8838) makes stoneware in natural tones; **George Peterson** (667-5510) makes hand-thrown tableware; and **Perl Sossaman** (667-3448) makes flower garlands and potpourri.

In Windsor: **High Hollow Pottery** (684-3852) is a source of stoneware and tableware.

In Worthington: **Debora Phillips** (238-5365) makes "welcome slates."

SPECIAL EVENTS   July and early August: **Sevenars Concerts**, Worthington; **Middlefield Fair**; **Goshen Flower Show**.

August: **Hillside Agricultural Society Fair**, organized by a num-

ber of hilltowns, held in Cummington the last weekend in August.
October: **Holiday in the Hills**, Conway (first weekend); **Fall Foliage Festival** (Columbus Day Weekend).

MEDICAL EMERGENCY **Worthington Health Center** (238-5511), Old North Road, Worthington.

Franklin County Public Hospital (772-0211), 164 High Street, Greenfield.

Mohawk Trail Country

East of the Hoosic Valley, mountains rise steeply, gentling into a plateau as you travel east or south. This high, spruce-forested, little-peopled area differs from the neighboring hilltowns. It includes some of the most beautiful and least touristed country in New England.

"Peaks of one or two thousand feet rush up either bank of the river in ranges, thrusting out their shoulders side by side . . . I have never driven through such romantic scenery, where there was such a variety and boldness of mountain shapes as this," observed Nathaniel Hawthorne about the view that you can still enjoy from the wooden observation tower at Whitcomb Summit.

The tower is one of three period pieces still staked along the original Mohawk Trail: 38 miles of Route 2 between Greenfield and North Adams that was formally dedicated in 1914. The Mohawk Trail was the first road in Massachusetts designed specifically for "auto touring." In an era when the quickest way to go was by train, the trail was where Bostonians drove their first cars to explore the most dramatic, least populated part of the state.

While the Mohawk Trail now officially stretches 63 miles (from the New York line to Millers Falls), it is this original 38-mile swatch which, although funky and worn in spots, still smacks of a more romantic era.

Take its very name and theme. Ignoring the century in which this was Massachusetts' second turnpike and its first shunpike, the Mohawk Trail conjures up the narrow path blazed by Indians. And there were plenty of native Americans on hand to greet the 1920s tourists. Shopkeepers imported Indians to sell baskets and beadwork by the road. There are still nine Indian trading posts along the trail, snaring small children with wooden Indians, tepees, plastic buffalos, and real deer.

East of the Hoosac Range the Mohawk Trail follows the Deerfield River through a narrow valley, hemmed by abrupt hills. Charlemont, the old crossroads community here, offers motel rooms and campsites and attracts fishermen in spring, vacationing families in summer, and, thanks to Berkshire East, skiers in winter. Some of the state's best cross-country skiing can be found at Stump Sprouts in West Hawley, south on Route 8A.

Shelburne Falls, eight miles east, is also a stop for all seasons. Long known for its Bridge of Flowers and "glacial" pot holes, it has recently become a showcase for the many craftspeople who have found inspiration and affordable housing in the surrounding hilltowns.

In this section I have included the hilltowns of Rowe, Colrain, and Heath because they are such backcountry villages, divided from the more agricultural communities to the south by Route 2. Although I am presenting the Mohawk Trail as the east-west tourist route that it is, I hope travelers will venture off on the suggested byways and will also venture up and down Route 8A from Charlemont and Route 112 from Shelburne Falls. Search out maple producers, orchards, craftspeople, covered bridges, and old graveyards. The Hilltowns, with their choice of bed & breakfasts, can also serve as a base for exploring this area.

AREA CODE 413

GUIDANCE **The Mohawk Trail Association** (664-6256), PO Box J, Charlemont 01339.

Franklin County Chamber of Commerce (773-5463, daily, 24 hours), PO Box 790, Main Street, Greenfield 01302. Note the information booth at the Route 2/I-91 rotary.

GETTING THERE By bus: **Englander Coach Lines** (662-2016) in North Adams makes frequent daily stops in Charlemont on its Boston–Albany route, connecting with New York City service in Williamstown.

TO SEE AND DO On and off the trail: **The Hairpin Turn** and **Western Summit**. There is no avoiding the well-named Hairpin turn which zigs and zags up the mountain from North Adams. You can pause at the Wigwam Western Summit, a spot from which hang glider pilots launch themselves high above the valley.

At the **Whitcomb Summit** in Florida a wooden observation tower stands in front of the Whitcomb Summit motel and restaurant. The view (described above) is east, back down to the Deerfield Valley. A path leads off to **Moore's Summit** (2,250 feet) highest point on the Mohawk Trail. Florida (pop: 720) is one of the coldest towns in the state, but it was named in 1805 just as the United States was purchasing Florida from Spain. It is now known for its turnips, cause for a Turnip Festival in fall.

Hoosac Tunnel. One-quarter mile east of Whitcomb Summit, past the Elk Memorial (placed here in 1923 by the Elks of Massachusetts), take Whitcomb Hill Road down to the Deerfield River. Turn left on River Road and follow it until it crosses the railroad tracks. Look here for the eastern portal of the Hoosac Tunnel, opened in the 1870s by blasting through granite.

Bear Swamp Project and Visitors Center (625-6321). Keep left on River Road until you come to an extensive picnic area by the

Mohawk Trail Country 69

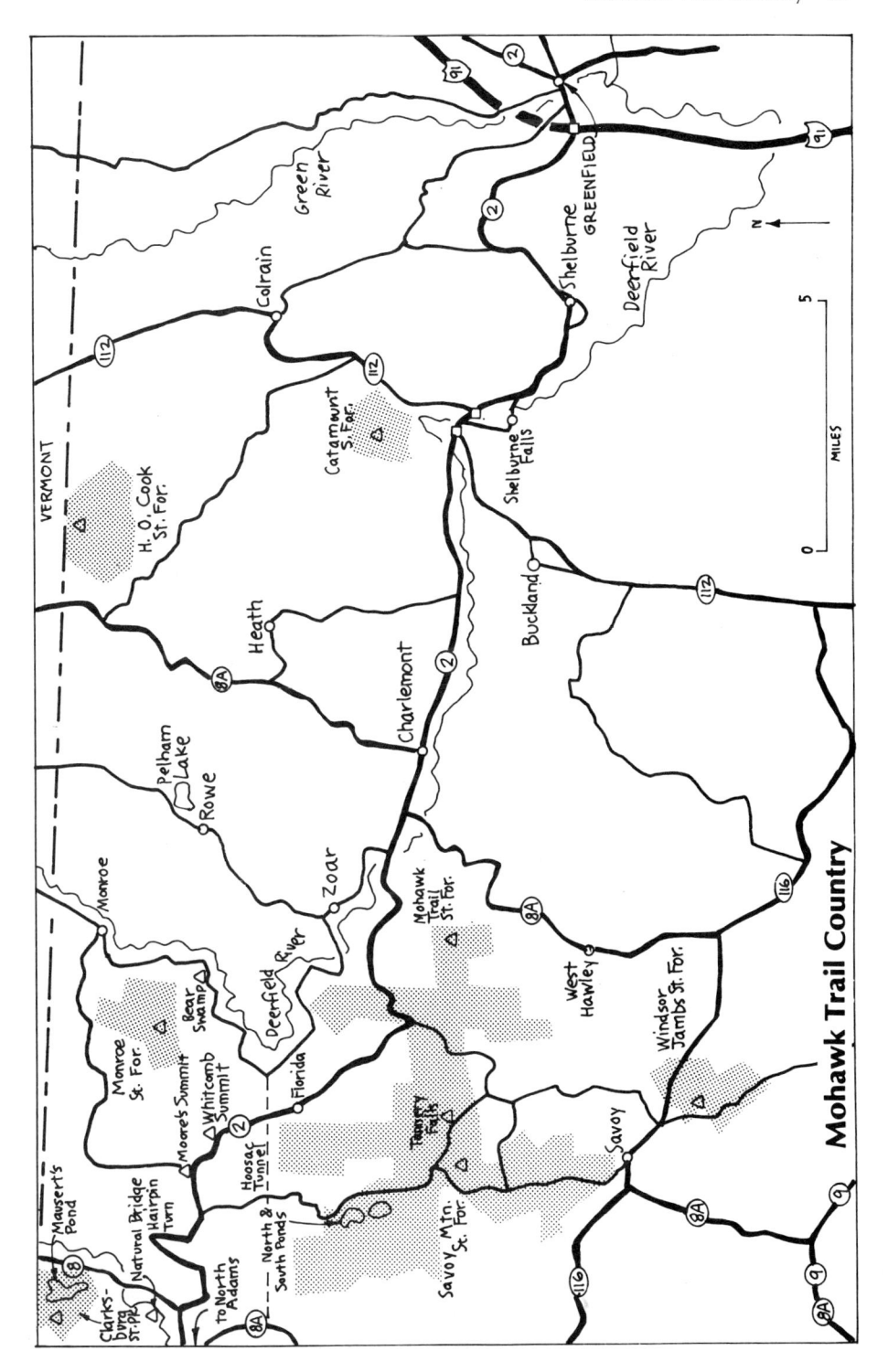

river, maintained by New England Power Company. You are in a sheer gorge, impressive in any season. In an underground visitors center, displays explain the way that two 300-megawatt underground pumps generate power from the Deerfield River as it flows from the upper to the lower reservoir. Ancient Indian artifacts are also displayed. Follow River Road across the iron Bailey Bridge and past another riverside picnic area, to Zoar, a cluster of houses that is actually part of Charlemont. From Zoar you can turn back to Route 2 or detour a bit farther to Rowe.

Rowe (population: 330) is well worth a visit. It has been home for New England's first atomic energy since 1961 and for the Bear Swamp project since 1974—with an obvious effect on the town's budget for civil amenities. Instead of the usual town dump, Rowe has a landscaped "Refuse Garden." Buff plaques label the sites of buildings that stood in town when it bustled: the **Foliated Talc Mill** (1908–22) and **Eddy's Casket Shop** (1846–1948), for example. The Browning Bench Tool Factory has been restored and moved to the shore of Pelham Lake where it serves as an arts and community center. There are picnic tables in 1,000-acre **Pelham Lake Park** and a new gazebo ornaments the common. The **Rowe Historical Society Museum** (open weekends July 4–Columbus Day, 2–5) has an unusually extensive collection, including records and artifacts from eighteenth-century Fort Pelham (the site is marked). To reach Charlemont turn back through Zoar to Route 2. The **Rowe Yankee Atomic Plant** (424-6261) is open to the public, Monday through Friday, 10–4.

Mohawk Memorial Park, Charlemont. A 900-pound bronze Indian stands on a boulder, his arms uplifted to the Great Spirit. The arrowhead shaped tablet at the base reads: "Hail to the Sunrise in Memory of the Mohawk Indian." There is a wishing pool with 100 inscribed stones from the various tribes and councils throughout the country.

Bissel Covered Bridge, Charlemont. Rebuilt in 1951, this 60-foot span is over Mill Brook just off Route 2 on Route 8A.

Charlemont Historical Society Museum, Town Hall (open June–September, Saturday: 1:30–4).

Shelburne Falls. The town's walk-in information center (625-2143) is at the head of the **Bridge of Flowers**, an abandoned trolley bridge (now reserved for foot traffic) that local garden clubs keep flooded with flowers as a war memorial. Technically the two bridges across the Deerfield River link the towns of Shelburne Falls and Buckland, but, despite the fact that Buckland's town hall sits right at the south end of the bridge, both banks are considered part of Shelburne Falls. It's a place to get out and walk around. The wonderfully straightened and shaped "pot holes" at the foot of Salmon

Falls (Deerfield Avenue, off Bridge Street) are no longer considered "glacial" but they are still unusual and worth a look.

The Shelburne Falls Artisan's Guild (774-7204) in the Salmon Falls Marketplace (a converted grain storage building above the falls on Ashfield Street) is also worth a stop to see art-quality crafts.

The Historical Society in the Arms Academy Building (corner of Maple and Church Streets) is open Tuesday afternoons.

Colrain. This town boomed with sheep raising, cotton mills, and an iron foundry in the mid-nineteenth century. The old foundry is still in Foundry Hollow, and there is a covered bridge across the North River (on Lyonsville Road) which is now closed. **Catamount Hill**, site of the first schoolhouse to fly the American flag, has old cellar holes, a monument, and a small lake. The **Colrain Historical Society Museum** is housed in the former First Methodist Church in Colrain Center (open Sundays, 1–4). The 300-acre **Wilderness Wildlife Sanctuary** (624-3218) has hiking paths, and there are guided tours for a small fee. Also see State Forests and Sugarhouses.

Shelburne. The High Ledge Sanctuary, owned by Massachusetts Audubon, offers views down the valley. Ask locally for directions.

Long View Lookout overlooking the Connecticut River Valley is worth a climb. The complex includes a gift store and rest rooms.

SUGARHOUSES   Gould's Sugarhouse (625-6170), Route 2 in Shelburne. Open during foliage, in December, as well as in spring and summer. They offer sit-down meals: waffles, homemade sausage, and sugar-on-snow.

Other Shelburne maple producers who welcome visitors include **Davenport Maple Farm** (625-2866) in Shelburne Center (maple candies and spreads as well as syrup); and **Grave's Sugar House** (625-6178) on the Colrain Road. In West Hawley we can swear by **Harold White's** syrup (339-4426). Stop by his farm on Route 8A two miles south of Route 2. In Colrain there is **Hager Bros.** (624-3214); **W. R. Hillman & Son** (625-2847); **Harold Roberts & Son** (624-8804); and **Harold Truesdell** (624-3980), who offers sit-down meals in season. In Heath there is **Elmer Sherman** (337-4855), off Route 8A on Judd Road. All welcome visitors to their sugar shacks during sugaring season (March), but call before coming to see if the sap is running.

APPLE ORCHARDS   Mohawk Orchards (625-2874), a quarter mile north of Route 2 on the Colrain-Shelburne Road, sells apples year-round; also apple cider, peaches, and pears.

STATE FORESTS AND PARKS   Savoy Mt. State Forest (663-8469), RFD #2, North Adams 01247. From Route 2 in Florida take Shaft Road south to the park supervisor's headquarters; the more direct approach is from Route 116 in Savoy. There is swimming in **North Pond** and camping (45 sites) at **South Pond. Tannery Falls** is past the camping area: at a Y in the road fork right, cross the bridge and turn left at the sign; continue until you reach the picnic area on the left; park and take the short trail to the top of the hill. At the campground there are toilets, showers, picnic sites, and three log cabins ($8–$10 depending on the number of rooms). There are 24 miles of hiking trails, two ski-touring loops and a "crooked forest" of deformed trees. The waters are stocked with fish. In winter cross-country skiers find trail maps at the parking lot near North Pond. The skiing is free and rather challenging; trails have not been maintained since the Williams cross-country ski team stopped training here a half dozen years ago.

Monroe State Forest (339-5504) covers 4,000 acres in the towns of Florida and Monroe. Access is on Monroe Road off Route 2 (just east of Whitcomb Summit). Nine miles of hiking trails and several "pack-in" campsites on the Dumbar Brook Falls Trail. The **Roycroft Lookout** takes in a panorama of the Deerfield River Valley.

Mohawk Trail State Forest (339-5504), Box 7, Charlemont, covers 6,457 acres. It offers more than 50 campsites and five log cabins, swimming in a man-made pool in Cold River, complete with bathhouse, scattered picnic tables, and many miles of hiking trails. Follow trail to Stafford Meadow on the Deerfield River; note the graves of Revolutionary War soldiers.

Catamount (339-5504). Fishing is the big attraction in this 1,125-acre forest in southwestern Colrain and eastern Charlemont with streams and a 34-acre lake. There are also hiking and riding trails.

H.O. Cook State Forest (258-4774). The lure here is fishing for trout in the stream on the western side of the property. There are also hiking and riding trails. Access is off route 8A on State Farm Road in Heath, one-half mile south of the Vermont line.

Also, see the Hilltowns chapter for Dubuque (Hawley) and Windsor State Forests.

BICYCLING The back roads of this region are well suited to biking. Wide-tired rental bikes, ideal for the many miles of dirt roads in neighboring state forests, are available from **Stump Sprouts** (see Skiing).

FISHING The stretch of the Deerfield River in Charlemont lures fishermen throughout the Northeast. There is a catch-and-release section in the village of Hoosac Tunnel (from the Fife Brook Reservoir Dam one and a half miles down river to the railroad trestle). Beware the changing depth of the water throughout this area due to releases from the dam. For details about local fishing check with Herman Prillip at the **Oxbow Inn** (625-6729).

SWIMMING See Mohawk Trail State Forest; also see Windsor State Forest (Hilltowns chapter).

ALPINE SKIING **Berkshire East** (339-6617), Box O, South River Road, Char-

lemont 01339. This is an unusually challenging mountain for its size.
>   Vertical drop: 1,180 feet
>   Terrain: 25 trails, 40% expert, 40% intermediate
>   Lifts: 4 chairs, 2 bars
>   Snowmaking: 90% of terrain
>   Open: daily; night skiing: Wednesday–Saturday.
>   Rates: $20 weekends, $12 junior (under 14), $10 night skiing.
>   Other amenities: nursery, two base lodges, ski school, shop.

CROSS-COUNTRY SKIING **Stump Sprouts** (339-4265), West Hill Road, West Hawley 01339. High on the side of a mountain this 450-acre tract offers some memorable cross-country skiing on wooded trails at 1,500- to 2,000-foot elevations. Snacks and rentals are available in the warming hut, which is part of Lloyd and Suzanne Crawford's home. There are 25 kilometers of trails, lessons, and guided tours. $4 trail fee, $2 under 12. Also see Lodging.

For further cross-country skiing see Savoy Mt. State Forest.

INNS, LODGES, B & Bs **Stump Sprouts** (339-4265), West Hill Road, West Hawley 01339. Lloyd Crawford has built the modern, clapboard lodge almost entirely with his own hands, from timbers he found standing on this 450-acre hilltop spread. He has also built the bunks and much of the furniture inside. A maximum of 20 can be accommodated in a variety of rooms on many levels (there are lofts and wonderful corners with skylights and stained-glass windows). Guest rooms sleep from two to eight, and windows maximize the view of tier upon tier of wooded hills. Frequently full on winter weekends (because this is also a ski-touring center), Stump Sprouts is often empty in other seasons. When enough guests warrant it, Lloyd and Suzanne offer three meals a day ($27–$35 per person with lodging). Even the sauna has a fabulous view. There are lawn games and a variety of hikes that Lloyd has mapped for guests. Bring your own sleeping bags and towels.

Fiske Dairy Farm (625-6375), Zerah Fiske Road, Shelburne Falls 01370. Marion Fiske has been accommodating visitors in her 200-year-old homestead for 20 years. There are six guest rooms (one downstairs with a canopy bed), all sharing one bath. Dinner as well as breakfast is served and it frequently includes homegrown vegetables; breakfast always features homemade preserves. This is a working, 300-acre dairy farm. Children are welcome, and there is plenty of space for hiking and cross-country skiing. $35 per person includes two meals, $25 with breakfast only.

The Charlemont Inn (339-5796), Route 2, Charlemont 01339. A rambling clapboard landmark in the middle of the village dating, in part, from 1787. It has had its ups and downs over the years, has just received a coat of paint and some internal spiffing. There are 14 rooms with shared baths on the second floor, two dining rooms on the first. New owners are downplaying the restaurant, refurbishing rooms. $32–$48 year-round.

Forest Way Farm (337-8321), Route 8A, Charlemont 01339. Jimmie and her husband Paul Snyder have restored this 1820 center-chimney home with a great view and five guest rooms. The Snyders have recently moved up from Texas. There is a pool: $40 double, $35 single.

Country Comfort (625-9877), Shelburne Falls 01370. Eileen and Michael Rauch welcome guests into their Victorian home. They have three guest rooms and include breakfast in the $25–$45 tab.

Parson Hubbard House (625-9730), Shelburne 01370. Jeanne and Dick Bole live in a 1774 parsonage, high on a hill with long views. Three guest rooms share two baths. Full breakfasts that feature their own maple syrup are included in the rate: $40 double, $40 single; non-smokers preferred.

Highland Springs Guest House (625-2648), Route 2, Shelburne 01370. This is a crisp, bright, old-fashioned guest house with four guest rooms with four-posters, one with private bath. Mrs. Sautter charges $12 per room.

Also see Hilltowns for more B&Bs in neighboring towns.

MOTELS **The Oxbow** (625-6729), Charlemont 01339. A 23-room motel with an attractive dining room, pool, and winter ski packages. Owner Herm Prillip is an enthusiastic fisherman who is happy to share his knowledge of local fishing spots and also his knowledge of what's where in this region. Open all year. Year-round weekend package: two nights with breakfast and dinner: $76.50 per person.

Hilltop Motel (625-2587), Shelburne Falls 01370. Motel with seven units, three cottages (six in-room kitchenettes). On Route 2 overlooking the Deerfield River, open year-round, $33 double.

Red Rose Motel (625-2666), Shelburne Falls 01370. A 12-unit motel with pool and playground; open year-round. $32–$36 double.

Whitcomb Summit Motel and Cottages (662-2625), North Adams 01247. 18 motel units, 18 cottages, pool; restaurant on premises. $40–$50 double, $60 for 4.

CAMPGROUNDS **Shady Pines Campground** (743-2694), on Route 116, Savoy. Pool, 10-acre "safari field," store, cross-country ski trails, open year-round, 125 sites, $13 for 2.

Springbrook Family Camp Area (625-6618), Shelburne Center.

The Country Aire Campground (625-2996), East Charlemont. Trailers and tenters.

Mohawk Park (339-4470), on Route 2. 400 acres with 75 sites, playground, river swimming, fishing.

Also see Savoy Mt. and Mohawk Trail State Forests.

SELF-IMPROVEMENT VACATION **Rowe Camp and Conference Center** (339-4216), Kings Highway Road, Rowe 01367. This Unitarian-Universalist center consists of a farmhouse and assorted camp buildings on a quiet back road. On most weekends throughout the year there are speakers (many of them well known) on topics ranging from herb healing to remodeling your home to transactional analysis. An adjoining 1,000-acre town preserve has trails for walking, cross-country skiing, and snowshoeing. Weekends range from $89–$139, depending on your income. Request a current conference calendar. Guests bring their own sleeping bags and the food is "vegetarian gourmet." The summer camp also has special sessions for women, families, and young singles.

DINING OUT **Plantation House** (339-8371), East Hawley Road, Charlemont. An eighteenth-century farmhouse (on the opposite side of the Deerfield River from Route 2) that has long been considered THE place to dine between Williamstown and the Connecticut River. The menu is continental with specialties like Onion Soup au Gratin and Chicken Ruby. Closed Sundays and Mondays; dinner only, $10–$13.

The Sweetheart Restaurant (625-2064), just off Route 2 at 42 South Maple Street in Shelburne Falls; closed Mondays. This dining landmark began in 1916 as a teahouse to serve the Mohawk Trail's first tourists. Today it is a French restaurant with an $8–$15 menu that includes rack of lamb and hazelnut chocolate mousse (open from noon on Sunday but otherwise from 5 PM).

Marty's Riverside Restaurant and Bakery (645-2570), State Street, Shelburne Falls. Open for breakfast, lunch, and dinner. This isn't a formal place but it is so good that Hill Country residents are willing to drive many miles just to eat here. It overlooks the Bridge of Flowers; specializes in homemade baked goods. Reasonably priced. Baked salmon at dinner is $10, but fettuccine Alfredo is just $4.95. Lunch is very reasonable: chile, whole grain breads, soups.

EATING OUT **Gould's Sugarhouse** (625-6170), Route 2, Shelburne. Open daily in spring and fall, 9 AM–7 PM, serving waffles with maple syrup, also sandwiches and hamburgers.

Oxbow Restaurant (625-6729), Route 2, Charlemont. Closed Tuesdays, otherwise breakfast, lunch, and dinner in a cheerful, pine-sided dining room.

Charlemont Inn (339-5796). The original stagecoach stop in Charlemont, still offering meals and lodging.

Railroad Crossing (625-6345), 10 Bridge Street, Shelburne Falls.

Open from 5:30 AM until 9 PM Monday–Friday; Saturday 5:30–10 PM, Sunday 7AM–9 PM. Food is homemade, fresh, moderately priced; child's menu available, bar. Great family find.

Foxtowne Coffee Shoppe (625-6606), 25 Bridge Street, Shelburne Falls, open daily 7 AM–11 PM. Sandwiches, burgers, doughnuts.

SNACKS AND ICE CREAM **McCusker's Market & Deli** (625-9411), Shelburne Falls. This distinctive three-story wooden Odd Fellows Building with the flag on top has become a landmark along the Mohawk Trail. Mike McCusker's store stocks all kinds of gourmet fare and staples (coffees, teas, 110 spices); makes up mouth-watering soups, salads, and deli delights; stocks locally made baked goods and crafts; and sells Bart's Ice Cream. It also serves as a factory outlet for Lamson & Goodnow cutlery, manufactured in town since 1851. In the back are booths and one of the most unusual johns in the East. Open daily, 8 AM–8 PM.

ENTERTAINMENT **Mohawk Trail Concerts** (774-3690) at the Federated Church, Route 2 in Charlemont, Fridays at 7:30, Sundays at 8 PM, during July and August. The church's excellent acoustics and 225-seating capacity creates a fine space for fine music. Fridays are "preview" rehearsals.

SELECTIVE SHOPPING Mohawk Trail Trading Posts: **Mohawk Tepee** in Charlemont (free petting zoo, open year-round); **Indian Plaza** in Charlemont features a narrow gauge railroad from the abandoned Davis Copper Mine in Rowe. There is also **The Outpost** in Shelburne, **The Wigwam** in North Adams, and **Longview**, overlooking the Connecticut River Valley near the western end of the trail.

Bridge Street in Shelburne Falls is lined with shops worth checking: **Larry's Clothing**, **Magical Child** (toys and clothes), **Bridge Street Bookshop**. **Mole Hollow Candles** is a candle factory in a rehabilitated mill overlooking Salmon Falls and the pot holes.

Country Closet in Shelburne on Route 2 sells outlet-priced (last season's) clothes, and the **Antique Center** of Charlemont (closed Mondays) is an outlet for several dealers.

CRAFTS, GALLERIES, AND OPEN STUDIOS **The Shelburne Falls Artisan's Guild** (774-7204) in the Salmon Falls Marketplace (a rehabilitated Agway grain storage building) showcases art-quality local crafts. **Bald Mt'n Pottery** (625-6353) is also located in the Marketplace.

If you call ahead, the following craftspeople will welcome you into their studios.

Shelburne Falls: **North River Glass** (625-6422); **Sandra Lee Ackerman** (625-2312), hand-painted early American folk art.

Shelburne: **Rebecca Ashenden** (625-6844), handwoven wool blankets and shawls, cotton placemats, and tablecloths.

Heath: **Robert Dane** (337-5736), glass sculpture, marbles; **Alan Nichols** (337-6665), chairs, tables.

Colrain: **Cathe Cellana** (624-5596), functional and one-of-a-kind pottery; **Susan Katz** (624-3222), porcelain pottery.

Charlemont: **Ann Brauer** (625-2208), contemporary quilts.

SPECIAL EVENTS March–April: Maple syrup producers welcome visitors in to their sugarhouses to watch the process of "boiling off." (See Sugarhouses.)

May: **Daffodils Day** in Shelburne Falls.

July: **Independence Day** celebrations in Heath and Rowe (great fireworks).

August: **Rodeo** at Charlemont Fairgrounds, **Annual Heath Fair, Annual Indian Pow Wow** at Indian Plaza, Charlemont.

North Berkshire

In North Berkshire steep, isolated valleys are cut by rushing rivers, divided by the massive presence of the state's highest mountain range. Geologically Mr. Greylock is part of New York's Taconic Range, this region's western wall. On the east the highest peaks of the Hoosac Range hedge it from the rest of Massachusetts.

The draw here is Williamstown, a classic New England college town with an internationally acclaimed art museum. Popular as a spa a century ago, it's now known in summer chiefly as home of the Williamstown Theatre Festival. Its year-round resort amenities, which include two golf courses, the original mineral pool, and the state's two biggest ski areas, are virtually unrecognized.

North Adams, a classic New England mill city, is now home of the Western Gateway Heritage State Park. This is a complex of shops, restaurants, and exhibits that dramatize the nineteenth-century saga of building the Hoosac Tunnel—the 4.74-mile passage through the Berkshire Barrier that put North Adams on the map.

Scheduled trains no longer serve North Berkshire, but travelers still pass through as though their wheels were grooved to Routes 2 and 7. Unless it happens to be peak foliage time, few even turn off to drive the spectacular road that snakes up Mt. Greylock from Route 2 in North Adams and from Route 7 in Lanesboro. The Mt. Greylock Reservation is more than 10,000 acres and includes 35 miles of hiking trails.

AREA CODE 413
GUIDANCE **The Berkshire Visitors Bureau** (443-9186), Berkshire Common, Pittsfield 01201 (open weekdays, 9–5), publishes an excellent, free winter and summer "Vacation Guide" for the whole county.

The Northern Berkshire Chamber of Commerce (663-3735), PO Box 267, 69 Main Street, North Adams 01247 (open 9–5 weekdays), is good for specific information.

The Western Gateway Heritage State Park (663-6312), behind City Hall on Route 8 South between State Street and Furnace Street, operates an information desk for the area. Open daily, 10–6, Monday through Wednesday.

Department of Environmental Management (442-8928) in Pittsfield has the answers on all local forests and parks.

North Berkshire

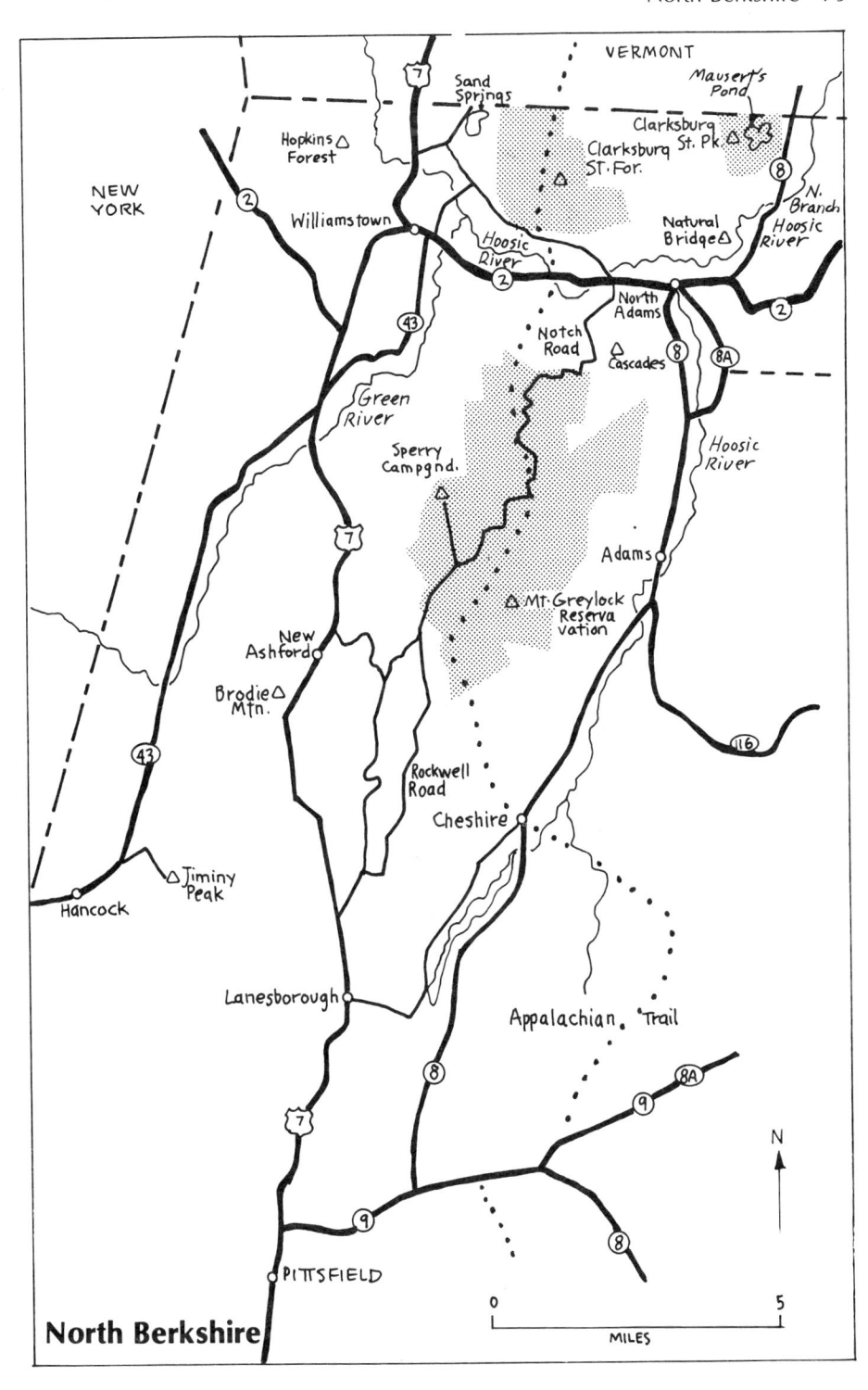

For seasonal walk-in information centers check Guidance under Williamstown and North Adams.

GETTING THERE By bus: Bonanza (in Williamstown: 458-9371) links Williamstown and North Adams with New York City, Albany, South Berkshire, and Connecticut. Englander Coach Lines (based in North Adams: 662-2016) links Williamstown and North Adams with the Greyhound terminal in Boston.

GETTING AROUND Williamstown, North Adams, Adams, Cheshire, and Lanesboro are all served by Berkshire Regional Transit Authority buses (BRTA) (499-2782 or 1-800-292-6636).

IN AND AROUND WILLIAMSTOWN

In 1755 Colonel Ephraim Williams, Jr. wrote a will. It gave the community of West Hoosuck a "Free School forever," provided that the township fall within Massachusetts (it was contested by New York) and that it be named Williamstown. Williams died fighting Frenchmen and Indians, and the conditions of his will were eventually met. Despite its isolation (in 1815 at a low ebb in its finances, townspeople paid to keep the college here, away from the "allurements of dissipation"), Williams continues to maintain its place among the country's top colleges.

As early as the 1830s, local mineral springs began attracting visitors and, by the Civil War, Williamstown was an established resort with some large hotels and palatial summer homes. The old hotels are long gone but there are some comfortable new ones, plus a number of family-run motels and bed & breakfasts.

Sited at the junction of two major highways (Route 2 East/West and Route 7 North/South) the state's northwesternmost town snares most people who pass through.

The Sterling and Francine Clark Art Institute alone is worth a trip and its fine collection is complemented by that of the newly expanded Williams College Museum of Art. But the town deserves more than a pass-through. Circled by mountains, it has an unusual beauty and offers some exceptional lodging, dining, theater, and shopping as well as golf, hiking, biking, swimming, and cross-country and alpine skiing.

AREA CODE 413

GUIDANCE The information booth (junction of Routes 2 and 4) is stocked with pamphlets and open year-round, but it is only staffed from Memorial Day to Columbus Day. Off-season you can still obtain information by contacting the Williamstown Board of Trade (458-3641).

TO SEE AND DO **Sterling and Francine Clark Art Institute** (458-8109, 458-9545), 225 South Street. This collection rivals that of many city museums. There are medieval works like a fifteenth-century panel painting by Piero della Francesca, and works by such masters as Fragonard, Turner, and Goya. But the museum is best known for its French Impressionist paintings (Monet, Degas, Pissarro, and no less than 30 Renoirs) and also for its American period pieces (Winslow Homer, John Singer Sargent, and Frederic Remington). The white marble building and its modern red granite addition contrast nicely with the cows next door, the apple trees out front, and the clapboard farmhouse across the street. In summer there is a cafe out back and a path (used for cross-country skiing in winter) leads over a brook and up Stone Hill. The museum sponsors a series of films and lectures. Open Tuesday–Sunday 10–5; free.

Williams College (597-3031) now enrolls 1,950 students, drawn from throughout the United States and from more than 40 countries (the ratio of men to women is now 55 to 45). Tours of the 75-building, 450-acre campus are available at the Admissions Office (next to the Adams Memorial Theater).

Few other colleges are as entwined with their communities. Be sure to pick up the "Guide to the Campus" with a map that nicely covers half of the town. Buildings of interest to the general public include:

Williams College Museum of Art (597-2429), housed in recently expanded, octagonal Lawrence Hall (1836). There are Greek and Roman statues and Renaissance works, but the standout pieces are American (nineteenth- and twentieth-century) works by Eakins, Hassam, Feininger, Rivers, and Hopper, among others. There are also constantly changing exhibits in the handsome wing designed by Charles Moore. Free, open Monday–Saturday 10–5, Sunday 1–5.

Chapin Library of Rare Books in Stetson Hall sits back behind Thompson Memorial Chapel, across Main Street from the Museum of Art. It's worth visiting to see the college's priceless collection of documents from the American Revolution. An original copy of the Declaration of Independence, the Articles of Confederation, two early versions of the Bill of Rights, and a draft of the Constitution are exhibited (closed Saturday and Sunday).

The Hopkins Observatory (597-2188), dedicated in 1838, is one of the first observatories in the country. Free shows are offered here in the Milham Planetarium most Fridays; since space is limited, make reservations.

Hopkins Forest Farm Museum (597-2347). Exhibits in a barn display changes in local farming and in the landscape over the years.

The Williamstown Theatre Festival (597-3400). 1987 marks the 33rd season of sophisticated productions held in the Adams Memorial Theatre on Main Street. Some 240 performances are staged in July and August; also 45 events, including experimental theater, in **The Extension** (same building); revues by **The Cabaret** (at area restaurants and at the Sterling and Francine Clark Art Institute); and new play readings. For a schedule write: Williamstown Theatre Festival, Box 517 (01267).

The Elizabeth Sanford Botsford Memorial Library (458-5369), Main Street. Built in 1815 as a residence for the college treasurer, this is one of the homiest libraries in the state. The original carved staircase and graceful mantels survive, and there is an extensive historical collection—spinning wheels, Civil War uniforms, old ice skates, and photos—upstairs. Open 9–5 daily, except Sundays.

RECREATION **Alpine Slide at Jiminy Peak** (458-5771), Route 43, Hancock. Memorial Day to Labor Day daily, weekends in May and September; 10:30 AM to 10 PM.

BICYCLING Biking is understandably popular on the back roads around town, especially on Route 43 along the Green River. Rental 10-speeds are available from **Spokes** (458-3456) on Main Street and from **The Mountain Goat** (458-8445) on Water Street, which also rents fat-tired mountain bikes. **Jiminy Peak** (738-5431) also rents 10-speeds in summer.

CANOEING Canoeing can be enjoyed on the Hoosic River. Check with **Berkshire Outfitters** (743-5900), Route 8, Adams.

FISHING Fishing can be rewarding in the **Green River**, also in town-owned **Bridges Pond** and in **Hemlock**, **Broad**, and **Roaring brooks**.

GOLF Golf can be enjoyed on two 18-hole golf links: the **Taconic Golf Club** (458-3997), Meacham Street, open daily mid-April to mid-November; and the **Waubeeka Springs Gold Links** (458-5869), open daily April to mid-November. Also, **North Adams Country Club** (664-9011) in Clarksburg.

HIKING **The Hopkins Experimental Forest and Farm Museum** (597-2346), Northwest Hill Road, is a college-owned preserve of upwards of 2,000 acres with a short nature loop. There are also trails connecting with the **Taconic Crest Trail**, along which you can easily hike from New York into Vermont. Also see Mt. Greylock Reservation.

HORSEBACK RIDING **Clover Hill Farm** (458-8500), Adams Road, offers English riding lessons by appointment.

PICNICKING **Stone Hill**, a 55-acre town park, accessible from Stone Hill Road off South Street, offers wooded trails and a stone seat with a view. Mt. Hope Park (16 acres on Route 43) has picnic tables by the confluence of the Hopper and Green rivers.

SWIMMING **Sands Spring Pool and Spa** (458-5202), Sands Springs Road (off Route 7, north of town about one-quarter mile east of the Cozy Corner motel), is an attractive, family-run pool that is fed by the town's mineral springs. Billed as the oldest spa in the United States (it was formally established in 1813), this old-fashioned complex includes a snack bar, changing rooms, sauna, whirlpool, and video machines. The pool (50 feet × 70 feet) is sparkling clean, 74 degrees, and genuinely exhilarating. Open May–September, weekdays 11–8; weekends 10–8; nominal fee. The **Margaret Lindley Park** (Routes 2 and 7) is a well-kept town pond with changing rooms and picnic tables; daily charge for non-residents. Open during school summer vacation, daily 11–7.

TENNIS There are town courts at the **Green River Linear Park**, Water Street (honor system for an hour). **Williams College** (597-3131) maintains 12 clay and 12 hard top tennis courts (fee), and the public is permitted to use them. **Brodie Mountain Tennis and Racquetball Club** (499-3038), Route 7 in New Ashford, has indoor courts (fee).

ALPINE SKIING **Brodie Mountain** (443-4752), Route 7, New Ashford (10 minutes south of Williamstown). Named for an eighteenth-century Irishman, Brodie is known as Kelly's Irish Alps (it's owned by the Kelly family), famed for its Leprechaun Lounge and its green snow on St. Patrick's Day. It's also a respectable ski hill with lodging and a year-round campground.

Vertical drop: 1,230 feet
Terrain: 23 miles of slopes and trails
Longest run: 2.5 miles
Lifts: four chairs, two tows
Snowmaking: 95% of area
Night Skiing
Nursery: infants accepted
Rates: $25 per adult, weekends; $22 per child 14 and under; cheaper weekdays. Half-day, evening, and night tickets available.

Jiminy Peak (738-5431), Route 43 in Hancock, sits high in the Jericho Valley, a narrow corridor that runs east–west between Route 43 and Route 7 in Hancock. In recent years it has expanded steadily and now is a self-contained winter resort with rental condos and a 105-suite country inn (see Resort Motor Inns).

Vertical drop: 1,200 feet
Terrain: 25 slopes and trails
Longest run: 2 miles
Lifts: four chairs (one triple), one tow
Snowmaking: 80% of area
Night Skiing.
Nursery: 2 years and up
Rates: $26 per adult, $22 per child (12 and under). Night and half-day tickets.

CROSS-COUNTRY SKIING **Brodie Mountain** (443-4752) maintains roughly 16 miles of trails with a great deal of variety. There are the wide, tracked trails (lit at night) that the Williams College Ski Team uses, and there are less formal trails through pastures and up into the wooded Mount Greylock Reservation.

A favorite local tour is along the four-mile **Stone Hill Loop** from the rear of the parking lot of the Clark Art Institute. A network of trails are also maintained in **Hopkins Forest** (see Hiking). Skiers are also welcome on the **Taconic Golf Course**. Also see Mt. Greylock Reservation.

Cross-country rentals are available at **Brodie Mountain** and in Williamstown at **The Mountain Goat** (458-8445) and at **Goff's** (458-3605).

SKATING   The Williams College **Lansing Chapman Rink** (597-2433) is open to the public for a small fee. Outdoor skating at **Bridges Pond** and **Frog Pond**.

RESORT MOTOR INNS   **The Orchards** (458-9611 in MA, 1-800-231-2344 outside), 222 Adams Road, Williamstown. Billing itself as the Berkshires' most gracious country inn, the Orchards was built from scratch in 1985. Its stone, salmon-colored exterior (smack on Route 2 across from a shopping mall) belies the elegance of the interior. You step past a token reception desk into an oriental-carpeted living room with a cupola ceiling, crystal chandelier, and antique Steinway baby grand. The fireplace is green Vermont marble with a medieval-looking mantel. At the appropriate hour, a silver tea service is wheeled in. The idea is to make you feel as though you are a guest at an English country house: there are English soaps and salts in the bathrooms and goose feather pillows on the beds. There are also niceties like climate-controlled rooms, extra sinks and phones in dressing rooms, mini-fridges in the foyer, and color TVs hidden in armoires. There is also a spa room with Jacuzzi and climate chamber. See Dining Out for the good word on its dining room. Rates are $85–$250 per room.

Williams Inn (458-9371), 1090 Main Street, Williamstown (junction of Routes 2 & 7). This is a functional, 1970s, three-story building with 104 motel-style rooms, a red-and-black dining room, function rooms, an indoor pool, a Jacuzzi, and a 3-star Mobil rating. The buses from Boston and New York stop outside, and the inn, which sits on the green right next to the town hall, has become a community gathering place; $72–$82 per day double; group rates.

The Country Inn at Jiminy Peak (738-5500/445-5500), Hancock 01237. The attractive new complex has a formal hotel lobby, but the 105 suites are all condominium units, each with a token kitchen and sitting room (the couch opens up) plus bedroom. Drummonds Restaurant is a pleasant dining room on the third floor (it is operated by the owner of the prestigious Mill on the Floss) and there is a first floor Country Village Recreation Center with a Jacuzzi and exercise room. Larger **Beaver Pond Meadows** condominium units also share these amenities. $90–$190 (for a three-bedroom condo). In summer Jiminy Peak offers an Alpine Slide, a putting green, and 10-speed bikes.

INNS   **The Hancock Inn** (738-5873), Route 43, Hancock 01237. A turn-of-the-century country inn on the New York border, 15 minutes southwest of Williamstown, just one mile from Jiminy Peak. Innkeeper Chester Gorski is an acclaimed chef (see Dining Out), proud of his weekend champagne brunch as well as his dinners.

Le Jardin Inn (458-8032), south on Route 7, is a former estate best known for its French fare (see Dining Out) but also with nine rooms (five with working fireplaces and one with a whirlpool bath), all with views of pines and trout ponds. $60–$90 per room, continental breakfast included.

BED & BREAKFASTS   There are said to be more than 30 bed & breakfasts in town, but some of these can be found only through Berkshire Bed & Breakfast (268-7244) and others list themselves other ways. Only a few hang out their shingle.

River Bend Farm (458-5504 or 3121), 643 Simonds Road, Williamstown, is a red clapboard farmhouse built in 1770 by Colonel Benjamin Simonds, one of the town founders and the leader of the Massachusetts forces at the Battle of Bennington. The house has been reverently restored by Dave and Judy Loomis. Two of the five bedrooms have fireplaces and all are furnished not just with antiques, but with the appropriate antiques (including two rope beds). The rooms share two bathrooms. Rates are $40 double, $30 single, $10 for a cot, including breakfast with homemade bread and River Bend Farm honey. Open April–Thanksgiving.

Steep Acres Farm (458-3774), 520 White Oaks Road, Williamstown, has three double rooms and a single. There is hiking and cross-country skiing on the property, with great views. $45 per room.

Pine Knoll Farm (442-4101), Box 268, Kessler Road, Lanesboro 01237. This 1869 house was a speakeasy during the depression. It sits on 150 acres of meadows and woodlands and can accommodate ten people. In winter its trails connect with Brodie's cross-country network. $40 per night double (shared bath), $60 with private bath; breakfast included.

Townry Farm (443-9285), Greylock Road, Lanesboro 01237. This is a great place for families with small children: a working livestock farm with 160 sheep in the barn, usually a half dozen Labrador retrievers on hand (they are bred and trained here), and some Morgan pleasure horses. The white clapboard farmhouse dates back to 1780 and is sited on the road to Mt. Greylock's summit. It commands some nice views itself and is handy to Brodie Mountain's cross-country trails in winter. It is great any time of year for walking. This is home for Barb and Cliff Feakes, warm hosts who welcome guests to share their den. There are three guest rooms (shared baths). A breakfast of fresh baked breads (Barb has turned the old woodshed into a bakery) is included in the $35 double price ($5 per extra person).

MOTELS   In Williamstown 01267: **Chimney Mirror** (458-5202), 295 State Road. Werner and Marina Bacher have operated this 18-room facility for many years. Rooms are very clean, all with phones and cable color TV. Dining is across Route 2 at Howard Johnson's. Rates are $37–$52 double, $7 each additional person but children under 14 free; studio rooms: $52–$96. Lower rates in winter, free pick up for bus passengers.

Berkshire Hills (458-3950). South on Route 7, a two-story, 21-room motel with cable TV and a pool; $35–$50 double in summer, lower off season.

Elwal Pines Motor Inn (458-8161), south on Route 7, is just 12 rooms with wooded grounds, grills and picnic tables, a pond, pool, and lawn games. $50 double weekends, $45 midweek. Closed in winter.

Four Acres (458-8158). One mile east of the village on Route 2, this 31-room motel has cable TV, picnic tables and grills, and offers free shuttle service to the bus and airport. $45–$65 double.

Northside Inn (458-8107), near the junction of Routes 7 and 2. This is a 30-room, two-story motel with some suites and a playground. Full breakfast served June–November, $44–$48 double.

Jericho Valley (458-5406), nine miles southwest of Williamstown on Route 7, is sited on 250 acres and has seven efficiency cottages with fireplaces, also one two-bedroom apartment with fireplace, and eight standard rooms, some with refrigerators. There is a pool, playground, and lawn games; also grills and picnic tables. A full breakfast is served. $40–$110; weekly rates, ski packages.

The Willows Motel (458-5768), 480 Main Street. A (10-unit) centrally located, homey motel with a pool. $37–$43.

1896 Motel (458-8125), 910 Cold Spring Road. Better known as a long-established restaurant, this motel is set on Hemlock Brook, and offers doubles for $55 ($47 off season), complimentary breakfast included.

DINING OUT   **In Williamstown: Le Jardin Inn** (458-8032), on Routes 2 and 7. Chef-owner Walter R. Hayn has established an enviable reputation for his French fare. Lunch as well as dinner is served and Sunday brunch (10:30–1:30) is popular locally. There is always a wide choice of "Les Poissons," "Les Volailles," and "Les Entrees"; duckling with apples ($14.00) and rack of lamb ($40.00) are among the specialties. Closed occasionally during off months.

1896 House (458-8123), one mile south on Routes 2 and 7. This old dining landmark has recently come under new ownership and is winning praise for its imaginative seasonal menu. You might have chevre in puff pastry ($3.00) as an appetizer, followed by Bouillabaisse ($13.50), or veal chops stuffed with crab ($15.00). Lunch and dinner served.

Le Country Restaurant (458-4000), 101 North Street (Route 7). Many local people consider this chef-owned restaurant the best around. Lunch served Tuesday–Friday; dinner, Tuesday–Sunday. Dinner entrees: $9.95–$15.95.

Three Chefs Taconic Restaurant (458-3090), two miles south on Routes 2 and 7. A well-respected dining spot with an extensive menu, including Frog Legs Provencale ($11.95) and Veal Oscark ($14.50). There's live music on Saturday nights. Dinner served Monday–Saturday, lunch Sunday–Friday.

The Orchards (458-9611). The handsome dining room overlooks the hotel's inner court and in summer you can lunch outside in the garden. A sample meal included perfectly poached salmon ($11.95) and Cornish game hen with pecan wild rice ($14.75). Dessert, coffee, and liqueurs are served upstairs in the living room rather than the dining room.

The Williams Inn (458-9371), on the Green. Traditional New England cuisine like broiled lamb chops ($17.95) and broiled scallops ($12.95) are featured, but there is a full continental menu; all three meals served.

Capers (458-9180), 412 Main Street. "Inventive Cuisine" and live jazz, folk, and light rock music (Thursday–Saturday) are the attractions of this nicely decorated nineteenth-century carriage house, which used to be the British Maid. Average entree: $8.

Captain's Table (458-5645), south of the village on Routes 2 and 7. Open for dinner and Sunday afternoons. A steaks, chops, and seafood place with a good salad bar; moderately expensive.

In Hancock: Hancock Inn (738-5873), Route 43, three miles north of Route 22. This out-of-the-way Victorian-style inn is on the gourmet map. It's been on "Good Morning America," enjoyed a number of rave reviews, and takes it all in stride. Linen napery and candlelight set the tone for veal and shrimp Dijonaise or duckling braised in port wine with grapes. Entrees (including vegetables and bread) run $12.95–$17.95. Leave room for desserts. Dinner served Wednesday through Sunday from 5 PM. Reservations are a must.

In New Ashford: The Springs (458-3465), Route 7. A Berkshire dining landmark, owned and operated by the Grosso family for more than 50 years, serving lunch and dinner daily. Specialties include fetuccine Alfredo ($10.25) and homemade frozen Kahlúa pie ($3.50).

North Adams is known as the City of Spires

The Mill on the Floss (458-9123). A daily prix-fixe menu ($12.50) is served. A la carte specialties include Coquilles St. Jacques and Sweetbreads au Beurre Noir et Capres.

EATING OUT **The River House** (458-4820), Water Street, Williamstown. Candlelight dining here can be as expensive as at the places listed above, but this is also a great spot to come for lighter meals or late night (10–12) burgers, sandwiches, and salads in an old tavern atmosphere.

Mrs. Murphy's Chowder House (458-9165), Route 7 in New Ashford. Family fare and Irish music are the specialties at this local favorite, serving lunch and dinner; closed Monday and Tuesday.

Howard Johnson's (458-4208), Main Street, east of the village in Williamstown. Widely respected for its home cooking and friendly service. Good for all three daily meals; owner operated.

Erasmus (458-5007), 76 Spring Street, Williamstown. A new cafe in the long-established College Bookstore is the place to devour better-than-average sandwiches and delectable pastries, as well as magazines, best-sellers, and a nice range of titles. There are sidewalk tables in warm weather. Open for breakfast, lunch, and dinner.

Papa Charlie's Deli, Spring Street, Williamstown. Open until 11 PM, mostly takeout, but a few tables and varied fare: Greek spinach pie, lentil soup, seafood salad.

Bette's Life and Times (458-5930), 27 Spring Street, Williamstown. Formerly Betty's Lunch, this is a reliable eatery, open for breakfast, lunch, and dinner.

Goodies Cafe, Spring Street, Williamstown, is a with-it eating place with a wall of jelly beans, and gazpacho for $1.50. Dining at small tables and delicacies to go.

ENTERTAINMENT **Williamstown Theater Festival** (597-3400), Adams Theater, Box 517, Williamstown. This festival offers some of the best summer theater in the Northeast; classics and new plays are presented by top actors.

Late June through late August, Tuesday–Friday, 8:30; also Thursday at 2:30, Saturday at 5 and 9. Smaller productions of new works are presented at **The Extension**, same building. **The Cabaret** also performs at area restaurants and at the Clark Art Institute.

The Williamstown Community Theatre and the College's **Williams Theatre** perform during winter months.

A variety of plays, films, and lectures are presented at the **Clark Art Institute**.

Williams College Weekly Calendar is worth checking for films, concerts, and plays.

Images Cinema (458-5612), Williamstown, features foreign and art films as well as new releases.

SELECTIVE SHOPPING **The Potter's Wheel**, 84 Water Street, Williamstown, is the area's standout crafts shop (it now has a branch on Nantucket). It is a handsome gallery featuring a range of quality hand-crafted items from throughout the country: stoneware, cloisonné jewelry, hand-blown glass, wood, and woven art.

Water Street shops are a varied lot and it's worth checking out the street.

MEDICAL EMERGENCY **Williamstown Medical Associates** (458-8182), 197 Adams Road, Williamstown.

Village Ambulance Service (458-5080), Williamstown.

ON AND AROUND MT. GREYLOCK, INCLUDING NORTH ADAMS AND ADAMS

Mt. Greylock is no isolated peak. It is a range containing the three highest mountains in the state and rises steeply on all four sides above the countryside. While the summit of Mt. Greylock itself is technically in Adams, the main approach and information center are on the opposite side of the mountain in Lanesboro, fifteen miles south of Williamstown on Route 7.

At 3,491 feet Mt. Greylock is the highest peak in Massachusetts and it dominates North Berkshire. The wonder is that its 10,000 wooded acres are so little used. They harbor 35 miles of hiking trails, 50 acres of blueberry fields, waterfalls, fish-stocked streams, and campsites.

In the visitors center a slide show reveals that the mountain is 440 million years old and that its status as public land began in 1885 when the Greylock Park Association purchased 400 summit acres, built a road to the top, and erected an open iron observation tower (this was already the third summit tower; the first appeared in 1833).

There are a number of stories about Greylock's name. I favor the theory that it stems from the clouds which so frequently cling to its pate. But on a clear day the 100-mile view encompasses five states.

With the advent of the Western Gateway Heritage State Park, more people are approaching Mt. Greylock from North Adams, a distinctly late nineteenth-century mill city.

During the Civil War, North Adams supplied textiles to the Union troops, but its boom years came with the 24-year-long drilling of the Hoosac Tunnel. In ensuing decades it was the largest community in Berkshire County; its mills turned out shoes, rugs, machinery, boxes, bricks, and biscuits as well as textiles.

Today Adams is still known for textile mills, which are worth inspecting for their varied architecture and outlets. The center of town is McKinley Square, with its bronze statue of President McKinley. His arms are raised as they were in Congress when he argued for passage of his famous tariff, the one which made it difficult for imports to compete with home-produced goods (like textiles from his friend William Plunkett's Berkshire Cotton Manufacturing Company).

Mt. Greylock towers above Adams, and farms were formerly scattered above the town on a high plateau known as Greylock Glen. The state's Department of Environmental Management (DEM) has committed itself to developing a four-season resort on this site, complete with alpine and high-altitude cross-country skiing, golf, swimming, and conference and lodging facilities. At present, however, summit access from Adams is limited to hiking trails.

South of Adams, Route 8 follows the Hoosic River through the alpine-looking farmland around Cheshire. North of North Adams Route 8 trails the north branch of the Hoosic past the Natural Bridge and on into wooded Clarksburg State Park.

AREA CODE 413

GUIDANCE **Western Gateway Heritage State Park** (663-6312), Route 8 south of City Hall in Adams. Open daily 10–6, until 9 PM on Thursdays. Good for general area information.

Greylock Reservation Visitors Center (499-4262), on the Rockwell Road in Lanesboro. Open year-round: Monday–Friday 8:30–4:45; weekends 9–5:30. There is a slide show, a diorama of the reservation, exhibits, and an interpretive program. A resident naturalist at Bascom Lodge at the summit also answers questions and leads hikes and workshops.

TO SEE AND DO **Mt. Greylock Reservation**. The reservation totals 11,119 acres, most of them steep and wooded. In the late 1700s Ash Fort was built halfway up Mt. Greylock and, later, sections of the mountain were cleared for farms and pasture. By the late nineteenth century logging had stripped the entire east face of the mountain, and erosion became a serious problem. This triggered the formation of the Greylock Park Association, a private venture which seeded the public preserve. It's been a part of the state park system since 1966. The chief points of interest include:

The Summit War Memorial Tower, a 90-foot granite structure dedicated to all Massachusetts men killed in war. Originally erected in 1933, it has been rebuilt but still leaks. You can climb the iron stairs to gain the ultimate view.

Bascom Lodge (743-1591). A handsome, rustic wood and stone building, was constructed on the summit in the 1930s by the Civilian Conservation Corps. Currently managed by the Appalachian Mountain Club, it welcomes motorists and hikers alike, offering snacks in its high-ceilinged hall and private and dorm-style rooms for 30 guests. Maps, guides, and hikers' aids are sold; workshops and guided hikes offered. Open mid-May through October (see Lodging).

There are two main roads to the summit: (1) At the Mt. Greylock Reservation sign in Lanesboro turn right and follow Rockwell Road for nine miles; (2) Either from the Heritage State Park in North Adams (via the Reservoir Road) or from Route 2 west of town (look for the Mt. Greylock Reservation sign) take the Notch Road up, also nine miles. In the winter roads are closed to traffic but are used by snowmobilers and cross-country skiers.

The Appalachian Trail traverses the mountain, passing 8.8 miles from Jones Nose to the summit and down the northern flank to Route 2. See Hiking for further suggestions.

Picnic tables are provided at **Stony Ledge**, the dramatic overlook beyond the **Sperry Campgrounds** (35 primitive sites on a first-come, first-serve basis, $5 fee).

The Cascades are a popular one hour's hike from Route 2. Park on Marion Avenue and pick up the path at the end of the street. Cross the foot bridge and follow the path up. A waterfall is formed by Notch Brook as it tumbles into a pool below.

Western Gateway Heritage State Park (663-6312), behind City Hall on Route 8 south. Open daily 10–6, until 9 on Thursdays. This served as a former freight yard. The Visitors Center is housed in the old Fitchburg Railroad Freight Station, built in 1884. Here you enter a tunnel, filled with the sounds of digging. At a press of a button an explosion echoes around you. You learn that many men died (a total of 196 were killed in the course of tunnel construction) before the trick of freezing nitroglycerin was discovered—the day when Nate Smith's sleigh, laden with explosives, overturned and didn't explode. You proceed down the tunnel (the innards of four linked boxcars), hearing and seeing various sides of the tunnel story, from political debates to workmen's ghost stories. The Visitors Center is also a gallery for changing exhibits on aspects of local history and for frequent free lectures, films, and concerts (for the current schedule call: 663-8059). Other components of the park are described under Dining Out and Selective Shopping.

Natural Bridge State Park (663-6312). Take Route 8 north off Route 2 just west of North Adams and look for the sign on the left. Open April through October, 10 AM–dusk. Billed as "the only natural marble bridge in North America" and "150 million years older than Niagara Falls," this formation has been a tourist attraction for more than 150 years. Recently acquired by DEM, it is now easier to appreciate both its beauty and history. The site itself, which includes a pond and marble dam, is a nice spot to linger.

An interpretive program, rest rooms, and picnic tables are provided. $3 per vehicle.

North Adams Public Library (662-2545), on Monument Square, top of Main Street. Built as the Blackinton Mansion in 1869, the building still has large crystal lights in the reading room; a grand, curving staircase; and Victorian furnishings that conjure up the city's boom era.

AIR RIDES Mohawk Valley Aviation (662-2356), Harriman-West Airport, Route 2, North Adams. Scenic 12- to 14-minute trips are offered in two- or four-seater airplanes. Introductory flight and glider instruction are also offered.

FISHING Points North Hunting and Fishing Outfitters (743-4030) in Adams have a large selection of fly-fishing supplies and offer trips and advice. **Mausert's Pond** in Clarksburg State Park is stocked with trout.

HIKING The Mt. Greylock Reservation offers 32 miles of hiking trails. In addition to those mentioned under To See and Do we should mention the portion of the Appalachian Trail on the Notch Road (at the Mt. Williams Reservoir) to the summit; the Bellows Pipe Trail, also from the Notch Road (at the Notch Reservoir); the steep 1.8-mile Thunderbolt Ski Trail from Gould Road (above Adams); and the Cheshire Harbor Trail from W. Mountain Road from Adams. From **Sperry Campground** it's a short hike on Deer Hill Trail to the base of a 40-foot falls, and there is a short Overlook Trail loop from the summit. Inquire at the Reservation information center or at Bascom Lodge about other loops and guided hikes. Pick up a copy of the Williams Outing Club map of the Williams area at local bookstores or at Bascom Lodge.

In **Clarksburg State Park** there are six miles of hiking trails and also an Indian burial ground to explore on Clark Road.

PICNICKING In **Clarksburg State Park** there are 100 picnic sites.

SWIMMING Windsor Lake (known locally as "the fish pond") in North Adams is at the top of Bradley Street (off Church Street), just past North Adams State College. The small lake is sparkling and there are fireplaces, a playground, snack bar, and changing facilities. Nominal admission for non-residents.

In Clarksburg State Park (664-9030), **Mausert's Pond** has a small sandy beach, bathhouse, and changing facilities; $3.

CROSS-COUNTRY SKIING For suggested trails on Mt. Greylock check with the Visitors Center (see Guidance). Also see Williamstown and Mohawk Trail Country.

LODGING Butternut Inn (743-9394), 6 East Street, North Adams 01247. An 1880s Victorian house with cherry woodwork and stained-glass windows, this is a comfortable bed & breakfast with three second-floor guest rooms (one has a private bath, the other two share one). Rates are $40 to $50 per room, $10 for an extra person, including a continental breakfast of homemade muffins and rolls. No children under age six.

Bascom Lodge (743-1591), PO Box 686, Lanesboro 01237. This sturdy 1930s lodge sits atop Mt. Greylock commanding incredible views. The facility is managed by the Appalachian Mountain Club. There are eight guest rooms: three doubles and five dorms sleeping four to six. Linen is supplied but bring a sleeping bag or extra blankets. Reservations are required (with a deposit of $4); $12 per adult, $6 per child under 10; meals are served family-style.

North Adams Inn (664-4561), 40 Main Street, North Adams 01247. A standard motel; facilities include a restaurant and an indoor pool.

CAMPING **Historic Valley Park Family Campground** (664-9228), PO Box 751, North Adams 01247. Sited on Windsor Lake, 100 campsites; beach, canoe rentals, store. $8 for a family of six.

Clarksburg State Park (664-9030), Route 8, north of North Adams, has 47 sites across from Mausert's Pond.

Also note that Mt. Greylock has 35 campsites and see Savoy State Park (Mohawk Trail Country).

DINING OUT **Boston Seafood Restaurant** (663-3870), Oasis Plaza, North Adams. Seafood is the specialty and there is an oyster bar. Chicken and prime rib are also on the menu. Open for lunch and dinner, moderately priced.

North Adams Inn (661-4561) in North Adams. The Richmond Room serves a $1.39 breakfast special, a lunch buffet, and standard dinner menu.

Bounti-Fare (743-0193), Route 8, Adams. There are mountain views and a farm motif. Specialties include baked stuffed shrimp and prime ribs. Lunch served Tuesday–Friday, dinner daily and from noon on Sundays; entrees from $7.50–$15.

Country Charm Restaurant (743-1445), Route 8, Cheshire. Specialties include roast chicken, prime rib, and grapenut pudding, $3.95–$10.95, closed Monday and Tuesday.

La Cocina Mexican Restaurant (664-4757), Route 2 in North Adams near the Williamstown line. Great Mexican food and weekend entertainment.

Freight Yard Pub (663-6547), Heritage State Park, North Adams. Good for burgers to full meals, great salad bar, pudding bar, cut-your-own-bread.

EATING OUT **Capital Restaurant** (664-9185), 57 Main St. The local favorite for good food at great prices.

SELECTIVE SHOPPNG **England's Department Store**, Main Street, North Adams. A branch of the Pittsfield department store, in business since 1857.

The war memorial on Mount Greylock is the highest point in Massachusetts

The Williamsburg Country Store, Heritage State Park, North Adams. Baked goods, health foods, crafts, and gifts.

Heritage Junction, Heritage State Park, North Adams, specializes in new and antique rail memorabilia; also carries a wide selection of gifts, souvenirs.

Williams Bookstore (458-5717), 9 Spring Street, Williamstown. This is the kind of store you expect to find in a college town. It's crammed with classics as well as general titles and the kind of art books which invite browsing.

OUTLETS In North Adams: **International Outlet** (664-4580), 192 State Street, North Adams, sells a variety of kitchen and gift items.

Novtex (664-4207), 459 State Road (Route 2), North Adams. Open daily, weekdays 9–5; Saturday 10–4; Sunday 12–4. Laces, ribbons, craft supplies, and notions at substantial savings.

In Adams: **Waverly Fabrics Outlet Store** (743-1986), 5 Hoosac Street. Fabrics, upholstery, carpets. Open Tuesday–Saturday.

Old Stone Mill (743-1015), Route 8. Savings of up to 75% on a wide variety of wallpapers, many with matching fabrics. Open Monday–Friday 10–4, Saturday 9–4.

The Coat Place (743-0882), Commercial Street, Monday–Saturday 9–5. Wide choice of coats and rainwear.

Harbor Woolens (743-1222), Grove Street. Woolrich, Lee, Levi, and other name brand clothes; irregulars and closeouts.

SPECIAL EVENTS Memorial Day Weekend: **Polka Holiday** at Polanka Pavilion.

Early June: **Polish Picnic** at Polanka Pavilion.

Late June: **St. Stanislaus Kostka Society Polish Picnic**.

Late July–early August: **Susan B. Anthony Days**, commemorating the suffragette who was born in Adams; Main Street is closed off and filled with booths, games, and food; auction. The 1782 Quaker Meetinghouse is open (Maple and Friend Streets).

Early August: **Adams Agricultural Fair**, three days.

Mid and late August: **Polish picnics** on alternating weekends.

First weekend in October: **Northern Berkshire Fall Foliage Festival** begins the last weekend in September; includes races, games, special sales, suppers, and culminates with giant parade.

Columbus Day Weekend: **Mt. Greylock Ramble**—more than 2,000 Adams residents traditionally climb their mountain; everyone is welcome.

MEDICAL EMERGENCY **North Adams Regional Hospital** (663-3701), Hospital Avenue, North Adams.

Central and South Berkshires

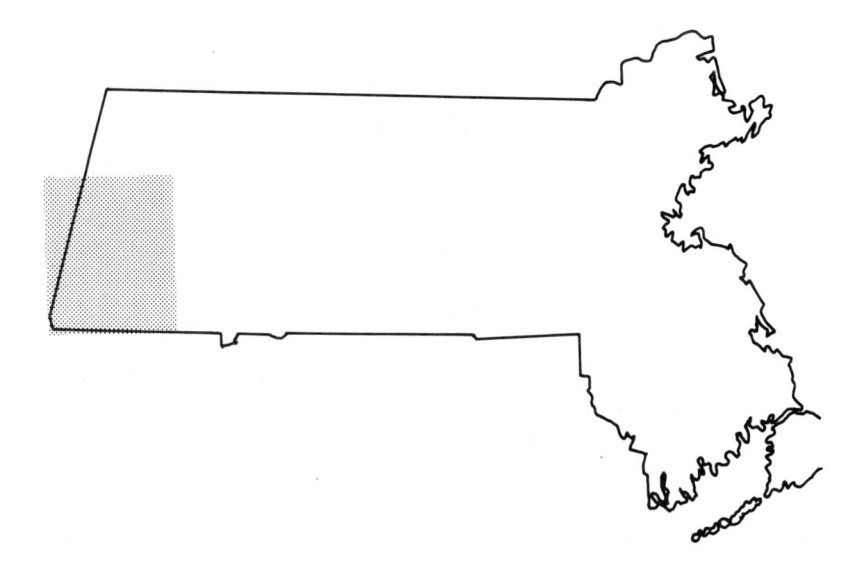

INTRODUCTION

There is a special feel and look to this roll of hill and valley, known collectively as "the Berkshires." Pittsfield, the county seat, is equidistant from both Boston and New York City, but the area has always drawn its visitors and ideas from the south (rather than the east), and it is little influenced by what happens around the state's far away "Bay."

Ask a Lenox man where he lives and the answer is "the Berkshires," not Massachusetts. Lenox is, of course, one among the clutch of towns which people tend to equate with the Berkshires: an elite grouping known the country over for music, dance, theater, and literati past and present.

Writers like Longfellow, Hawthorne, Melville, and Holmes were among the first Berkshire summer residents, and what they wrote helped to attract the very wealthy, who built mansions, terraced cornfields into formal gardens, and—with the advent of World War I and income tax—departed. They were replaced in the 1930s by dancers, musicians, actors, and writers attracted by the Berkshire Playhouse, Jacob's Pillow Dance Festival, and (by far the most famous) the Berkshire Music Festival. These and other summer happenings attract a steady flow of summer traffic.

Happily, this busy cultural scene is staged in tranquil countryside that is far more than a backdrop. Since the 1840s both picnicking and hiking (along bench-spotted paths and up gentle mountains) have been considered the thing to do in the Berkshires. With more than 100,000 acres of state forest and a sizable number of other public preserves, the area remains one of the most inviting to explore on foot.

A number of old mansions are now inns and bed & breakfasts, varying wildly in price. On weekends during "Tanglewood Season" (July and August when the Boston Symphony Orchestra is performing in Lenox) you can pay Manhattan prices for a modest room and queue up for an equally pricey dinner. Yet midweek, even in August, you pay less and don't wait. During the remainder of the year most inns charge much less, the galleries and museums remain, and there are hundreds of miles of cross-country ski trails and four ski areas.

AREA CODE 413

GUIDANCE **The Berkshire Hills Conference-Visitors' Bureau** (443-9186 or outside MA: 1-800-BERKSHR), Berkshire Common West Street Plaza, Pittsfield 01201. Open Monday–Friday 9–5. This is the source of *The Berkshires Vacation Guide*, a thick biannual listing of attractions, lodging, and dining. The bureau also keeps track of vacancies during crunch periods and can refer callers to inns and motels with space. The **Pittsfield Information Booth**, across Main Street at the park, is open June through mid-October, Monday–Saturday 8–8, Sunday 8–5.

Lenox Chamber of Commerce (637-3646), in the old Lenox Academy building, 75 Main Street. Open year-round. In summer: daily from 10–4 Monday–Thursday; 10–6 Friday and Saturday; 10–2 on Sunday. In winter: Thursday–Saturday 9:30–4:30, with a 24-hour answering machine. A very helpful walk-in center, with an extensive pamphlet rack, is also the site of the Berkshire Ticket Booth (see The Arts). Staff make referrals to local lodging places which, during Tanglewood Season, include more than 50 private homes.

Stockbridge Information Booth (298-3344). A kiosk-style booth on Main Street. Open daily in summer months (but only from noon–2 PM on Sundays).

Great Barrington Information Booth (528-1510), at the southern edge of downtown on Main Street (Routes 23 and 7). Open year-round; daily in summer 9–5 (Fridays 9–9), closed Mondays and for lunch in winter. The ladies in charge have a long and grateful following. When commercial rooms fill up they refer to private homes.

Lee Information Booth (243-0852). A seasonal wooden booth at the park in the middle of town on Main Street.

Department of Environmental Management (442-8928) in Pittsfield will answer specific questions on local state forests and parks.

GETTING THERE By air: Pittsfield is 37 miles from Albany Airport. Air Taxi service is available from all major Northeast airports via Berkshire Aviation at Great Barrington Airport (528-1010), Lyon Aviation (443-6700) at Pittsfield Airport, and Sabre-Air (663-7257) at Harriman Airport in North Adams. From Albany Airport you can also take AAA Limousine Service (518-456-5030).

By train: Amtrak's *Lakeshore Limited* from Boston to Chicago stops in Pittsfield. There is no Pittsfield station anymore; the train stops at a shelter on West Street and you buy your ticket aboard.

By bus: From Boston Peter Pan and Greyhound serve Lenox, Lee, and Pittsfield. From New York City, Boston, Albany, and Providence Bonanza serves Great Barrington, Lee, Lenox, and Pittsfield.

GETTING AROUND The **Berkshire Regional Transit Authority** (499-2782) links Great Barrington, Lee, Lenox, and Stockbridge with Pittsfield; hours are geared to commuters rather than visitors. Local taxis include **Abbot's Taxi** (243-1645) in Lee (serves Boston, New York, Albany, and Connecticut airports as well as making local runs); **Michael's Limousine Service** (499-9992) in Lanesboro (the fleet includes an antique white Rolls-Royce with TV, VCR, and wet bar) and **John Tufu** (447-7027); **Blue & White/Red & Gold** (528-0567)

Central and South Berkshires

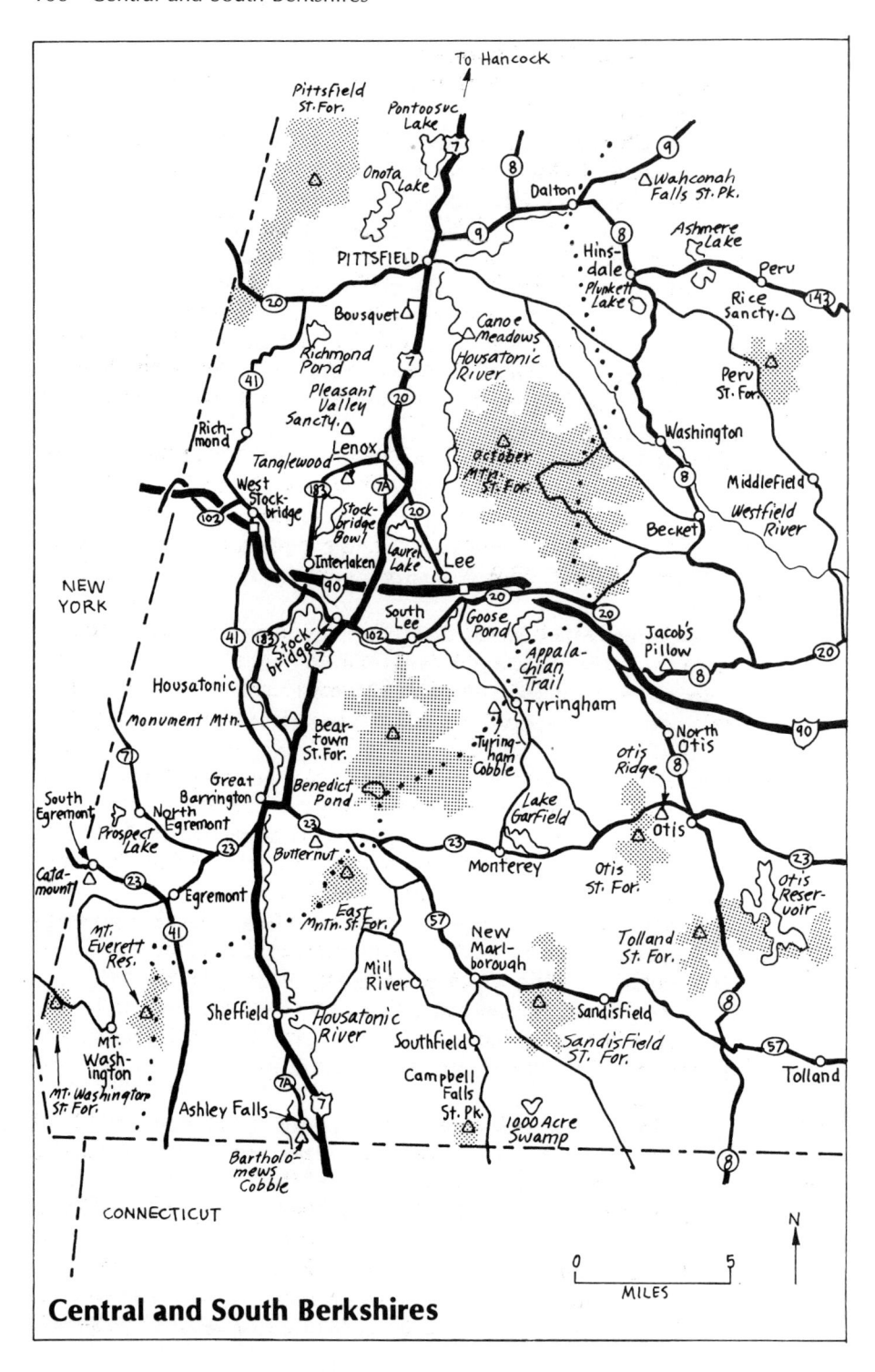

in Great Barrington; **Charlie's Taxi** in Housatonic; and **Rathbun's Taxi** (298-4848) in Stockbridge.

MUSEUMS AND MUSEUM HOUSES **Berkshire Museum** (443-7171), 39 South Street, Pittsfield (Route 7, just south of the Park). An example of what a regional museum should be, this complex was founded in 1903 by Dalton philanthropist Zenas Crane. The 18 galleries display both permanent and changing exhibits and there are frequent films, performances, lectures, and concerts in the 300-seat theater. The permanent collection includes Hudson River School landscapes; early American portraits by Church, Inness, and Copley; and mobiles by Alexander Calder. There are also fifteenth- to eighteenth-century European works; and ancient artifacts, including a 2,000-year-old mummy. Children also love the natural history collection of shells, gemstones, fossils, and the new Aquarium featuring fish from throughout the world. There are also reptiles, spiders, local animals, and birds. A special Berkshire section includes a birchbark canoe. Open Tuesday–Saturday 10–5; Sundays 1–5; open Mondays in July and August. Also note the **Berkshire Atheneum** (442-1558) housed in the new library at 1 Wendell Avenue, around the corner from the museum on Park Square (open Monday–Saturday). The **Herman Melville Memorial Room** contains a fine scrimshaw collection, some of Melville's personal belongings, and a special room is devoted to dozens of Berkshire authors.

Hancock Shaker Village (443-0188), five miles west of Pittsfield on Route 20, junction of Route 41; from Boston take the last exit on the Mass. Pike (Route 41 North). Open daily June through October 9:30–5; admission is $6 per adult, $2 under age 12, free under age 6, $5.50 students & senior citizens. The 22 buildings here seemed doomed to sale to a neighboring racetrack in 1961 when a group of Pittsfield residents rallied to buy them from the last Shaker sisters. Now 20 of the buildings have been restored—including the much-copied round stone barn.

The entire village looks like a primitive painting: set against its own orchard and meadows (the museum owns 1,000 acres) a scattering of tidy buildings gather around the 1830 Brick Dwelling. Founded in 1790, this "City of Peace" prospered in the mid-nineteenth century (some 250 Brethren were divided among six "families" in the 1830s) and survived for 170 years. The guides, craftsmen, and furnishings all tell about the dancing monks and nuns who turned farming, craftsmanship, and invention into visible prayers. Note the frequent special events staged throughout the year. There is a snack bar and picnicking space. Also note the gift shop which sells yarn, herbs, and baked goods made on the premises; no admission ticket required. Inquire about the Shaker Trail that leads into the adjacent Pittsfield State Forest, past the sites of old Shaker dwellings and religious ceremonies, and by the Shaker-built Great Wall of the Berkshires.

Chesterwood (298-3579), two miles west of Stockbridge. Take Route 102, go left on Route 183, and follow signs. Open May through October daily 10–5, admission is $4. This is the 160-acre estate of Daniel Chester French (1850–1931), whose Minute Man statue in Concord established his eminence as a sculptor at age 25. By 1895, when he discovered Stockbridge, he was internationally respected and able to maintain this elaborate summer home and studio, which commands, as he put it, the "best dry view" he'd ever seen. Maintained by the National Trust, the property includes the mansion, a Barn Gallery with special exhibits, and the studio, which is now exhibit space for plaster casts of many of the sculptor's works, including the statue which sits in Lincoln Memorial in Washington, D.C. Visitors are welcome to stroll the grounds, which include a wooded path through the hemlock glade overlooking Monument Mountain. Frequent events are staged throughout the summer and there is also a November sale (at the gift store) and a guided tour.

The Norman Rockwell Museum (298-3822), Main Street, Stockbridge. Open daily (except major holidays and the last two weeks in January) 10–5. America's beloved artist is represented by some 200 works, including many original works done for *Saturday Evening Post* covers. The museum is presently housed in the eighteenth-century Corner House on Main Street, but a new museum will be built on a 40-acre estate north of the village (President Reagan himself is a member of its board). Norman Rockwell lived within walking distance for the past 25 years of his life. The present facility is frequently mobbed in summer, and we frankly resent having to pay $3 per adult, $1 per child for even the briefest visit when groups (who always seem to be clogging the place) pay far less. The museum shop sells Rockwell prints.

Arrowhead (442-1793), 789 Holmes Road, off Routes 7 and 20. Turn at the traffic light just north of the Lenox line. Open Memorial Day through October; Monday–Saturday 10–4:30, Sunday 11–3:30. Melville was 31 in 1850, the year he bought this eighteenth-century house. He had been famous since *Typee* became a best-seller, five years earlier. It was the year that Nathaniel Hawthorne wrote: "on the hither side of Pittsfield sits Herman Melville, shaping out the gigantic conception of his white whale, while the gigantic shape of Greylock looms upon him from his study window." This is a sparsely furnished house but it conveys a sense of Melville in the 13 years he lived here, while writing *Moby Dick* and a number of works which brought him no fame or money in his lifetime. The

Hancock Shaker barn with spinner processing the museum village's own wool

house is headquarters for the Berkshire County Historical Society; a film on Berkshire history is shown and there is a nature trail.

Naumkeag (298-3239), Prospect Hill Road, Stockbridge. Open Memorial Day to mid-October, weekends in the early summer and after Labor Day, Tuesday–Sunday and holidays, 10–5. $3.50 per adult for house and garden, $1 per child. The Trustees of Reservations maintain this gabled and shingled 26-room "cottage." It was designed by McKim, Mead, and White in 1885 for one of the leading lawyers of the day, Joseph Hodges Choate, who endeared himself to his wealthy colleagues by reversing an income tax law that Congress had passed in 1894. The gardens are as exceptional as the house.

Mission House (298-3239), Main Street, Stockbridge. Labor Day through mid-October, Tuesday–Saturday 10–5, Sunday and holidays 11–4; adults $2.50, children $1. John Sergeant, the famous, idealistic young missionary to the Stockbridge Indians, built this house for his bride in 1739. He built it not on Route 102 where it now stands (known as the "Plain" at the time, this was the site of Indian wigwams) but up on the hill where the town's few white families lived, among them the Williamses. Sergeant's wife was Abigail Williams, a lady of pretensions, and the house is elaborately built for its time and place. It was salvaged and moved to this site in 1929 and is now maintained by the Trustees of Reservations.

Colonel John Ashley House (229-8600), in Ashley Falls, well marked from Route 7, south of Sheffield Village. Open Labor Day through mid-October, Wednesday–Sunday and holidays 1–5. $2.50 per adult, $1 per child. The oldest house in Berkshire County (1735), this was the site of the drafting of the Sheffield Resolves, denouncing the British Parliament in 1773. The home is beautifully paneled, restored, and furnished. You learn about Mom Bet, the first Berkshire slave to sue for, and win, her freedom. The house and nearby Batholomew's Cobble (see Other Public Preserves) is maintained by the Trustees of Reservations.

Crane Museum (684-2600), off Route 8, near Pioneer Mill on Housatonic Street, Dalton. Open June–September, Monday–Friday 2–5; free and worth a stop. Housed in the rag room of the Old Stone Mill (1846) by the Housatonic River, its displays tell the story of papermaking and include a fascinating variety of paper money. Crane Paper is the sole supplier of "money paper" to the United States Mint; the company has been in the family for five generations.

Merwin House (298-3039), 39 Main Street, Stockbridge. Open June through mid-October, Tuesday, Thursday, Saturday, and Sunday noon–5; $1.50. A preserved 1825 home with nineteenth-century furnishings. Maintained by the Society for the Protection of New England Antiquities.

Albert Schweitzer Center (528-3124), Hurlburt Road, Great Barrington. Open Tuesday–Sunday 10–4 in summer; weekends in winter. The house was bought with money bequeathed by Schweitzer to Erica Anderson, the internationally known filmmaker who served him in Africa without pay for 15 years. When Schweitzer died (aged 90) in 1965, Miss Anderson moved here and dedicated herself to promoting his philosophy of "Reverence for Life." In addition to a small museum there is the 90-minute film she made of Schweitzer at work in his clinic in Lambarene in French Equatorial Africa. Shorter films are also available and there is a 12-acre wildlife sanctuary out back. Miss Anderson died in 1977.

VILLAGES Lenox has already led three distinct lives. The first was its rise from farm to shire town in 1787, a status which gave it graceful Federal buildings like the **Court House** (the present library with its luxurious reading rooms, gallery, and outdoor reading park), the **Academy** (now housing the Chamber of Commerce), and the **Church on the Hill**. Then, in the 1860s, when the county seat shifted to Pittsfield, Lenox began acquiring a new look: intellectual and literary families from Boston had been spending their summers in town for a decade but now the very rich began buying up huge holdings. By the turn of the century more than 75 elaborate summer "cottages" were scattered along every ridge in town.

But the glory years of this "inland Newport" were brief. The income tax, World War I, and the depression did it in. Lenox the resort might have vanished entirely had it not been for the Berkshire Music Festival, a novel concept in 1934—when music halls were not yet air-conditioned and symphony music ceased with summer. The Boston Symphony selected Lenox as its summer home because Tanglewood (an estate named by Nathaniel Hawthorne during the time he wrote there) was donated to the cause. Most of the other Lenox estates now house inns or non-profit institutions, ranging from the Stevens School of the Bible to The Mount (the former home of Edith Wharton), which now serves as home for Shakespeare & Company and is also open in summer for tours. In recent years a number of shops have opened in the heart of the village.

Stockbridge didn't even begin like other towns: in 1734 it was founded to contain and educate the local Mohicans. Just four white families were permitted to settle, theoretically to "afford civilizing examples to the Indians." But predictably these families multiplied and the Indians dwindled. After distinguishing themselves as the only tribe to serve in the Revolution and the first to be given United

The Mount, former home of novelist Edith Wharton in Lenox, is considered one of the more modest Berkshire "cottages"

States citizenship, the Stockbridge Indians were shipped west, eventually to Wisconsin, where a few hundred descendants still live.

Stockbridge has always been the county aristocrat, spawning the **Laurel Hill Association**—the country's first village improvement society. Today residents tell you that the same number of notables have been summering in Stockbridge for the past hundred years, only the faces change periodically. The rambling wooden **Red Lion Inn** and the **Norman Rockwell Museum** are both at the heart of the village, a short walk from the Mission and Merwin houses. **Naumkeag** is just a short ways up the hill and the **Berkshire Theatre Festival** is on the northern fringe of town.

The village Green is actually west of Route 102's junction with Route 7 and many visitors miss it entirely. Here stand the imposing brick **Congregational Church** (1824), the pillared **Old Town Hall** (1839), and the **Field Chime Tower**, which marks the site of the original Indian mission. The Indian Burial Ground is nearby—the large mound, topped by a stone obelisk that overlooks the golf course. The village cemetery, across from the Green, contains the remains of John Sergeant, Indian Chief John Konkapot, nineteenth-century tycoons like Joseph Choate, and town aristocrats like the Fields and Sedgwicks.

Sheffield. This was the first town to be chartered in the Berkshires; its wide, main street (Route 7) is lined with stately old homes. It's the only town in the state to boast two covered bridges across the Housatanic (one original, one rebuilt), and it has the greatest number of antiques dealers of any town in the Berkshires. The 1770s brick **Dan Raymond House** (open Fridays 1:30–4, also Saturdays same time, in summer), in the center of town, is maintained by the Historical Society to reflect the life-style of this prosperous merchant, his wife, and their nine children. The 1760 **Old Parish Church** is a beauty, the oldest church in Berkshire County, and the site of the annual three-day **Sheffield Antiques Fair**, which is always held the second weekend in August.

Tyringham. Hemmed in on three sides by mountains and not on the way to anywhere else, this was the site of a Shaker community from the 1790s until the 1870s. The picturesque village then began attracting prominent summer residents, including Samuel Clemens. A number of nineteenth-century writers eulogized Tyringham, but the reason most people come today is to see the **Tyringham Galleries**. Built by sculptor Henry Hudson Kitson, it is known as the "Gingerbread House" because it resembles a fairy tale witch's house. Now it is **Tryingham Art Galleries** (243-3260), open daily 10–5; adults $.50, children free.

THE ARTS In no other part of the country are so many quality music, dance, and theater productions found so near to each other. On almost any day of the summer you can choose from a rich menu of live performances, many at prices far below what they would command in New York or Boston. Discount tickets are, moreover, available on the day of performance at the **Berkshire Ticket Booth**, open daily 1–5:30 in the old Academy building, which also houses the Lenox Chamber of Commerce.

Music: **Berkshire Music Festival** (637-1600), Tanglewood, entrance on West Street (Route 183, west of Lenox village). The Boston Symphony Orchestra's series of 28 concerts, beginning the end of June and ending in August, are staged in a fan-shaped, open-sided pavilion called simply "the Shed." This is a bit of Yankee understatement since the 6,000-seat concert hall has marvelous acoustics. More than 14,000 people regularly converge here on weekends, but a concert is never sold out because there is always room beyond the Shed on the manicured grounds (400 acres in all). Many Sunday concert-goers actually prefer the lawn and come several hours before concert-time with elaborate picnic hampers, some with candelabra and flowers to batten their table cloths. In addition to the symphony concerts (Friday and Saturday evenings, Sunday afternoons) there are weekly chamber music concerts and open rehearsals; the annual Festival of Contemporary Music; and concerts by young musicians of the Tanglewood Music Center (almost daily). The Boston Pops performs each summer as well. A detailed schedule and order form is available by contacting the **Tanglewood Ticket Office**. Before May 31: Symphony Hall, Boston 02115 (617-266-1492); after May at: Tanglewood, Lenox 01240 (637-1940). Ticket prices for the shed ranged from $9 to $40, more for special events; $6.50 for the lawn ($7.50 for special events), no discounts for children of any age (I'm sure we're not the only ones to have smuggled in an infant in a picnic basket).

South Mountain (442-2106), one mile south of Pittsfield on Routes 7 and 20. The acoustically excellent, 500-seat concert hall is a colonial-style building built in 1918 and is called the Temple (of music). Here chamber music concerts, performed by internationally known artists, are presented on Saturdays during August and September. A schedule is available from South Mountain Association, PO Box 23, Pittsfield 01202.

Stockbridge Chamber Concerts (443-1138) is a series of July and August chamber music concerts presented at various Berkshire mansions and schools. Each concert has a particular country as its theme and is preceded by a wine and cheese party. Single tickets $15.

The Curtisville Consortium (298-4950 or 298-3316) is a series of

Tanglewood is the cultural heart of the Berkshires

Wednesday evening concerts (8 PM) in the classic old Congregational Church of Interlaken, a village in Stockbridge that was originally known as Curtisville (it's on Route 183 south from Lenox, north from Stockbridge). The musicians are Boston Symphony members and guest artists.

The Berkshire Choral Festival (299-3522), at the Berkshire Choral Institute, Berkshire School in Sheffield. This is a series of five Saturday night choral concerts performed in the concert shed of this private school campus. Each concert is performed by a different group of singers who come from throughout the country and rehearse for a week before the concert.

The Aston Magna Festival (528-3595) is a series of July weekend concerts of seventeenth- and eighteenth-century music performed on original or authentic reproductions of the instruments that were used when the music was composed. Performance sites vary but usually include St. James Church and the Bard College Chapel (both in Great Barrington) and Jacob's Pillow.

Berkshire Opera Company (637-3073). Performances are currently held in the round, stained-glass-walled Pierce Chapel at Cranwell in Lenox in late July and August.

Music at the Pillow (243-0745), Box 287 SB, Lee 01238. Jacob's

Pillow, best known for its dance performances, is also the scene of frequent concerts. In addition to Sunday performances by Aston Magna (see above), there is also a Sunday evening jazz series and an "Inside/Out New Music" series of "downtown" street music. Also see the Hilltowns chapter for the Sevenars Music Festival in Worthington.

Dance: **Jacob's Pillow** (243-0745), Box 287 SB, Lee 01238. The oldest and most famous dance festival in North America, "the Pillow" continues to thrive as a learning and performance center. The core is the 633-seat Ted Shawn Theater, an acoustically fine building, the first built (in 1942) exclusively for dance. It is named for the festival's founder, recognized as the pioneer of male ballet in the United States, who bought this 100-acre farm in 1930. Technically in the town of Becket, its approach from Lee is along a steep, zigzaggy stretch of Route 20 known as "Jacob's Ladder." In the farmhouse garden sits a large, cushion-shaped boulder named "Jacob's Pillow." Shawn himself died in 1972. The festival now includes a wide range of dances by internationally known groups and also avant-garde performances: juggling, clowning, and the music series noted above. The setting is superb, both in the theater and on an outdoor stage. You can come early to dine in the cafe, to picnic, or to stroll through the grounds. Something is happening every night (except Mondays) from late July through August. Tickets are $11 to $18.50.

The Berkshire Ballet (422-1307), 210 Wendell Avenue, Pittsfield. The region's only year-round professional dance company offers a three-week (July and August) series of classical story ballets and also modern and contemporary dance performances.

Theater: **The Berkshire Theatre Festival** (298-5536 before June 1; 298-5576 after), Main Street (Route 102), Stockbridge. The BTF, as it is known, is dedicated to "the presentation and preservation of the American repertory." Founded in 1928 and housed in a white wooden theater that was originally designed by Charles McKim to be a casino, the nine-week (late June through August) festival usually features four plays in which prominent actors perform under well-known directors. It also includes a series of experimental plays in the 100-seat Barn Theater and outdoor Children's Theater (Thursday and Saturday at noon—bring a picnic). Tickets for the Mainstage are $10–$19.

Shakespeare & Company (637-3353), The Mount, Lenox 01240. In an outdoor amphitheater on the grounds of The Mount (the gardens and this 35-room Georgian mansion were built and designed by Edith Wharton in 1902) this resident group performs Shakespeare, usually two plays in the course of its July through August season. Performances are Tuesday–Sunday at 8 PM and the audience begins forming at 6 PM to picnic. The company also produces matinees about the life of Edith Wharton, using material from her writings; these performances extend through October. Shakespeare & Company, a national touring company, salvaged the mansion from the wrecker's ball in 1976 and now rents it from The National Trust. Tours of the house (637-1899) are also offered (June–October) for $3. Adult tickets range from $7.50–$15.

Williamstown Theatre Festival (see North Berkshire, Upcountry Massachusetts chapter).

The Berkshire Public Theatre (445-4634), 30 Union Street, Pittsfield. This is a year-round professional repertory theater that offers a full season of drama, musicals, and comedy. The building is the former Union Square Theatre. Tickets range from $7–$12.

The Lenox Arts Center Music Theatre Group (298-9468) stages productions in the 100-seat Citizens' Hall in Interlaken during July and August. The audience participates in these dramatic happenings. The hall is off Route 183 south from Lenox, north from Stockbridge.

Mixed Company (528-2320) is a year-round company that performs in a 55-seat theater in the restored Granary on Rosseter Street in Great Barrington.

The Robbins-Zust Family Theatre Company (contact Berkshire Ticket Booth) performs Sundays in West Stockbridge, Wednesdays in Pittsfield, and Thursdays in Great Barrington. These are marionette performances by the Zust family: Genie, Richard, and their children Thea, Maia, and Dion. The July and August productions are fairy book classics; $2 for all tickets.

TO SEE AND DO **Berkshire Scenic Railway Museum** (243-2872), PO Box 298, Lee. Fridays through Sundays and holidays, May 25–October 27, with two to four runs a day (more frequent in July and August). The 1920s coaches traverse a 15-mile route from Lee to Great Barrington, stopping in Stockbridge en route. This is a genuinely interesting ride that begins at Sullivan Station (Lee's old station now restored as a restaurant), heads south by the 500-foot-deep white pit owned by Lee Marble Company, and continues on by lily ponds and fields to the elaborate Stockbridge Station (designed by Stanford White). Passengers can debark and stroll around; it's a short walk into the village, the obvious spot to rubberneck since the Great Barrington station is two miles from shops and restaurants. Still we recommend taking the entire ride. $7 adult, $5 seniors, $3 children aged 5 to 12. In Lee there is a museum coach that shows a continuous slide show. Passengers are free to take one run in the morning and return on another in the late afternoon.

Berkshire Cottage Tours (637-1899). Based at Edith Wharton's The Mount, a van makes the rounds of summer mansions in Lenox

The Berkshire Museum combines fine art, historical, and scientific collections with films, lectures, and an aquarium

and Stockbridge, telling the full story behind each. Offered July–August, Thursday–Sunday.

STATE PARKS AND FORESTS **Beartown State Forest** (528-0904) includes a total 10,555 acres. The high tablelands stretching northwesterly from Monterey are known as "Beartown"; the upper end drops down to the Housatonic River in South Lee. Accessible from both Route 102 (in South Lee) and Route 17 (in Monterey), it includes (in Monterey) Benedict Pond, a man-made pond good for swimming (there are sanitary but no changing facilities); picnicking; and boating (no motors). There are also a dozen campsites plus lean-tos along the Appalachian Trail. You can drive or hike to the summit of Mt. Wilcox.

Mount Washington State Forest (582-0330). This 3,289-acre tract fills the southwest corner of Massachusetts. It's best known for Bash Bish Falls, a dramatic 60-foot falls that plunges through a sheer gorge. Access is via Route 23 in South Egremont and then by a wooded, windy road that brings you to a parking lot. Here trails wind down to the falls, where visitors perch on smooth rocks like so many birds. There are 15 miles of hiking trails and 15 primitive, hike-to camping sites ($2 fee) with pit toilets, spring water, and fireplaces. In winter there is cross-country skiing and snowmobiling, and in June the mountain laurel blooms throughout the forest. Also see Mt. Everett State Reservation.

Mount Everett State Reservation (528-0330), also in the town of Mt. Washington, is basically a road to the top of Mt. Everett, the 2,602-foot-high mountain that commands a sweep of the surrounding country. There is dogwood in spring, laurel in June, and blueberrying in August. Guilder Pond, accessible by car, is filled with pink water lilies during late July and much of August. From the auto path near Guilder Pond a path leads to the fire tower. Mt. Washington is, incidentally, the state's smallest town, with a population of less than 50, and its center is marked by the small Union Church (ecumenical, open summers only) and the tiny town hall. The Ann Lee Cottage, a small cape that once housed the Shakers' foundress, stands near the cemetery on West Street.

October Mountain State Forest (243-1178), a total of 15,710 acres accessible from Route 20 in both Lenox and Lee. Camping is the big thing here, but there are just 50 sites ($5). Schermerhorn Gorge is a popular hike and there is boating (no motors); 25 miles of trails are used for winter skiing and snowmobiling. Much of this area was once impounded by Harry Payne Whitney as a game preserve (it included buffalo, moose, and angora sheep as well as smaller animals). Halfway Pond is a good fishing spot.

Otis State Forest (528-0904). Boating (no motors) is permitted in Upper Spectacle Pond, and there are extensive cross-country ski trails, a part of which traverse the original road that Henry Know labored over with cannons in the winter of 1775–76 (off Route 23 on Nash Road onto West Otis).

Tolland State Forest (269-7268), off Route 8 in Otis, offers 90 campsites (85 of them for tents), also picnic space for 100 and swimming, fishing, and boating in Otis Reservoir.

Sandisfield/Cookson State Forests (258-4774). The state forest holdings are scattered around Sandisfield, but the most popular section is just over the New Marlboro line (Route 57) on York Lake: a 40-acre dammed area near the headquarters of Sandy Brook. Here you can swim, boat (no motors), and picnic (there are tables, grills, and fireplaces). There are also ten wilderness campsites.

Campbell Falls State Park (258-4774) is also accessible from Route 57 (in New Marlboro) and then by a forest road to this site: the Whiting River pours over a split ledge and cascades 80 feet down a precipitous declivity. There are picnic tables, toilets, and foot trails.

Pittsfield State Forest (442-8992) totals 9,695 acres. From the corner of Routes 20 and 7 in Pittsfield, drive west on West Street, north on Churchill Street, then west on Cascade to the entrance. $2 day-use fee. A five-mile circular paved road leads along Lulu Brook to Berry Pond, where there is camping (13 sites) and boating (no motors); there are 18 more sites at Parker Brook, with a picnic area across the way, another at the Lulu Brook swimming area. A ski lodge, located near the ski jump, can be rented by groups in summer; it's used as a warming hut in winter. Trails lead to the Taconic Skyline Trail, a spectacular ridge route leading north into Vermont. Tranquility Trail, a paved, ¾-mile loop through spruce woods, has been designed for wheelchair access. There are taped descriptions of flora and fauna. In June the forest harbors 40 acres of azaleas. Balance Rock, a 165-ton boulder poised on another rock, is accessible via Balance Rock Road from Route 7 in Lanesboro. The camping fee is $4 or $5 depending on site.

Wahconah Falls State Park (442-8992), off Route 9 in Dalton, three miles east of town center. A two-minute walk brings you from the parking area down to picnic tables scattered along the smooth rocks above the falls; swimming is permitted in the small pool at their base. Of course the falls are named for an Indian princess and her legend is, for once, a happy one.

Peru State Forest (442-8992), off Route 143 in Peru, south on Curtin Road, one mile from Peru Center. Garnet Hill (2,178 feet) yields a good view of the surrounding country, and there is fishing in Garnet Lake.

OTHER PUBLIC PRESERVES Maintained by the Trustees of Reservations:

Monument Mountain, Route 7 north of Great Barrington. This is one of the most distinctive peaks in the state: a long ridge of pinkish quartzite, scarcely 15 feet wide in some places, 1,700 feet high. The climb is lovely any day, whether by the Hickey or Monument trails. The hillside is covered with red pine and, in June, with flowering mountain laurel. A Bryant poem tells of an Indian maiden, disappointed in love, who hurled herself from "Squaw Peak." Nathaniel Hawthorne, Herman Melville, and O. W. Holmes all picnicked here in 1850.

Bartholomew's Cobble (229-8600), marked from Route 7A in Ashley Falls south of Sheffield. This 200-acre tract takes it name from the high limestone knolls or cobbles of marble and quartzite that border the glass-smooth Housatonic River. We recommend the pine-carpeted Ledges Trail, a (theoretically) 45-minute loop with many seductive side trails down to the river or up into the rocky heights. A booklet guide is available from the naturalist when the property is open (mid-April to mid-October, Wednesday–Sunday and holidays 9–5; $2 adults, $1 children). There are exhibits in the Bailey Trailside Museum.

Tyringham Cobble, one-half mile from Tyringham Center on Jerusalem Road. The Appalachian Trail crosses a portion of this 206-acre property—steep upland pasture and woodland, including a part of Hop Brook with views of the valley and village below. Note that the Trustees also maintain 446-acre **McLennan Reservation** on Fenn Road, two miles south of Tyringham center—steep, wooded slopes with one of the county's most spectacular views.

Massachusetts Audubon Sanctuaries: **Pleasant Valley Wildlife Sanctuary** (637-0320), 472 West Mountain Road, Lenox. This 730-acre property includes part of Lenox Mountain and Yokun Brook. It has beaver ponds and meadows, a hemlock gorge, a hummingbird garden, a summer trailside museum, and seven miles of trails (used in winter for cross-country skiing). $2 admission per adult, $1 per child and senior.

Canoe Meadows Wildlife Sanctuary in Pittsfield (Holmes Road off Route 7) is 242 acres of woods, wetlands, and croplands with five miles of trails. No rest rooms. $1 per adult, $.50 per child and senior.

Other scenic spots: **Race Brook Falls** in Sheffield. A series of five cascades and a picnic area. From Route 41 follow red blazes 1.5 miles.

Umpachene Falls. At the New Marlboro Church in the village center turn south, follow signs to Mill River. Just before the metal bridge there is a dirt road forking right; from here follow signs.

Thousand Acre Swamp. Turn off Norfolk Road south of Southfield, then left on Hotchkiss. A birdwatcher's delight.

Sages Ravine. A strikingly cut chasm with a waterfall 700 feet deep. It is accessible from Salisbury Road, Mt. Washington (taking the hiking trail from Plantain Pond); also from Route 41, via a path beginning just north of the bridge on the New York/Connecticut line. This is also an access trail to the Appalachian Trail, which continues north over Mt. Race.

Laurel Hill, Stockbridge. A path leads from the elementary school on Main Street to a stone seat designed by Daniel Chester French. Marked trails continue across the Housatonic to Ice Glen (a ravine) and to Laura's Tower (a steel tower); another trail leads along the crest of the spur of Beartown Mountain.

Bowker Woods. Route 183 between Stockbridge and Chesterwood; drive in at the sign. There's a pine grove by a small pond, good for picnics.

John D. Kennedy Park, in Lenox on Route 7. The grounds of the former Aspinwall Hotel offer hiking trails; good for cross-country skiing in winter.

Becket Falls. Two-tenths of a mile up Brooker Hill from the Becket Arts Center (Route 8 and Pittsfield Road) there is a shallow turnout in which to park; then it's a steep scramble down to view the 25-foot-high cascade.

Dorothy Frances Rice Wildlife Refuge, in Peru. South Road off Route 143 from the town center. 300 acres, walking trails, self-guided trails; owned by the New England Forestry Foundation.

Berkshire Garden Center (298-3926), Stockbridge, junction Routes 102 and 7. Open year-round. This is a botanical garden on 15 acres that include a pond. There are shrubs, trees, perennial borders, greenhouses, herbs, and periodic lectures and workshops. Admission charged mid-May to mid-October; $2 adults, $1 senior citizens, $.50 children.

ALPINE SLIDE   at Jiminy Peak. (See North Berkshire, Upcountry Massachusetts chapter.)

BICYCLING   There's a fine little book, *Short Bike Rides in the Berkshires* by Lewis C. Cuyler (Globe Pequot Press) that describes twenty-seven routes. Guided tours are available from **Berkshire Valley Bicycle Touring** (298-3160) in Stockbridge. From May through October they also rent bikes; other rentals are available from **Plaine's** (499-0294) in Pittsfield, from **Pedal and Paddle** (229-3033) at the Sheffield Package Store in Sheffield, and from the **Mountain Goat** (458-8445) in Williamstown (see North Berkshire). Also **Ed's Bicycle Shop** (243-1170) in Lee.

BOATING   Rentals are available at Pontoosac Lake in Pittsfield (YMCA/Ponterril Marina: 443-1132), also at **Greenwater Pond** in Becket, **Goose Pond** and **Laurel Lake** in Lee, **Lake Garfield** in Monterey, **Prospect Lake** in North Egremont, **Otis Reservoir** in Otis, and **Richmond Pond** in Richmond. Motorboats can be launced at **Onota Lake** in Pittsfield. The placid Housatonic is ideal for lazy rides down the river. Trips are detailed in the *AMC River Guide—Central/Southern New England* ($7.95). Rentals are available from **U-Drive Boat Rentals** (442-7020), the **YMCA Marina** (443-1132) in Pittsfield, and from **Pedal and Paddle** (229-3033) in Sheffield. Elaborate canoe outings are arranged in July and August by **Konkapot Kitchens** (229-6614) in Mill River. "A Canoe Guide to the Housatonic River: Berkshire County," available for $3 at local booksellers, is a handy guide to the history and nature of the river as well as to put-in points.

FISHING   For a detailed listing of every pond and river stocked with bass, pickerel, perch, hornpout, and trout, check the *Berkshire Visitors Bureau Summer Guide*. **Points North Hunting and Fishing Outfitters** (743-4030) in Adams (see North Berkshire) offer sport-fishing trips.

HIKING   See the trails described above (State Parks and Forests, other Public Preserves); also see North Berkshire.

HORSEBACK RIDING   **Chapman Farm** (442-4491), **Undermountain Farm**

(637-3365) in Lenox, and **Talbot Stables** at Foxhollow (637-2996) offer trail rides, as do **Timberwinds** (684-1592) and **Wohconah Stables** (684-1178) in Dalton. **Whip n' Willow Stables** (528-1363) in Great Barrington offers supervised rides by the hour.

GOLF   The local courses are the 18-hole **Country Club of Pittsfield** (447-8500); 18-hole **Cranwell Golf Course** (637-0441); the 9-hole **Greenock Country Club** (243-3323) in Lee; the 18-hole **Pontoosuc Lake Country Club** (445-4217); the 18-hole **Wahconah Country Club** (684-1333) in Dalton; and the 18-hole **Wyantenuck Country Club** (528-0350) in Great Barrington.

MINIATURE GOLF   For my children a Berkshire trip isn't complete without a visit to the indoor **Rainbow's End Miniature Golf** (18 holes) at the Cove Lanes in Great Barrington (Route 7).

SWIMMING   Under State Parks check **Wahconah Falls, Beartown, Sandisfield, Tolland,** and **Pittsfield.** For a fee you can also swim at: **Prospect Lake Park** (528-4158), a private campground in North Egremont (there are picnic tables in the pines and a float); at the **Egremont Country Club** (528-4222); at **Ashmere Lake** and **Plunkett Lake** in Hinsdale; at **Kinne's Grove on Lake Garfield** in Monterey; at **Onota** and **Pontoosuc Lakes** in Pittsfield; at **Card Lake** in West Stockbridge; and at the **YMCA Ponterril Outdoor Center** (three pools) on Pontoosuc Lake. **The Club at Bousquet** (499-4600) also has a pool and bathhouse. Green River swimming holes can be found one mile west of Great Barrington (off Route 23) and off Hurlburt Road, between Alford Road and Route 71.

TENNIS AND RACQUETBALL   **Tennis Village School,** West Stockbridge, 2 hard-surface courts; **Lakewood Park,** Pittsfield, 2 courts; **Pittsfield High School** (499-1779) 4 courts; **Taconic High School** (499-1248), Pittsfield, 4 courts; **Crosby Middle School** (499-1894), 4 courts; **Herberg Middle School** (499-1864), 4 courts; **Sheffield Racquet Club** (229-7968), 4 clay courts, clubhouse; **Greenock Country Club** (243-3323), Lee, two courts; and **Egremont Country Club** (528-4222), four courts. **The Club at Bousquet** (499-4600) has six indoor courts.

ALPINE SKIING   **Bousquet Ski Area** (442-8316), Pittsfield. Open daily in winter, also nightly except Sunday. Marked from Routes 7 and 20 south of town. The New Haven Railroad's first snow train rolled into Pittsfield in 1935, and 447 New Yorkers braved the quizzical looks on local faces while they herringboned up the open slope at Bousquet's Ski Area. Clarence Bousquet soon installed the country's second ski tow and the area became the first to be lighted for night skiing.

Vertical drop: 750 feet
Terrain: 21 trails
Snowmaking: 85% of area

Lifts: two chairs, five tows, one T-bar

Rates: $21 per adult, $19 junior on weekends; $16 and $14 weekdays.

Other: The Club at Bousquet (see Tennis)

Butternut (528-2000), Great Barrington; west on Route 23. Channing Murdock is one of very few New England ski operators who continues to manage a ski area that he founded. Butternut is now more than 20 years old and has distinguished itself for its grooming and for the beauty of its design—both on and off the slopes. The clubhouse base lodge—with its expansive sun deck and attractive interior—is another exception among ski areas. The view is north to Stockbridge and Lenox.

Vertical drop: 1,000 feet

Terrain: 18 trails

Lifts: one triple, five double chairs

Snowmaking: 98% of area

Rates: $25 adult, $19 Junior, $15 Senior, $8 six and under.

Other: coin-operated giant slalom race course

Catamount (528-1262), South Egremont, Route 23. Catamount straddles the New York/Massachusetts line, overlooking the rolling farm country of the Hudson Valley. It's been in business more than 40 years as a family area. The newly enlarged base lodge is pleasant.

Vertical drop: 1,000 feet

Terrain: 25 slopes and trails

Lifts: four chair lifts, three T-bars

Snowmaking: 85% of area

Rates: $25 per adult, $20 junior, second child $9 on weekends.

Other: night skiing

Otis Ridge (269-4444), Route 23 in Otis. A long-established family ski area which limits lift tickets to 800 and operates a Ski Camp (ages 8–16) near the top of its trails.

Vertical drop: 375 feet

Terrain: 15 slopes and trails

Lifts: one double chair, five tows, two T-bars

Snowmaking: 80% of area

Rates: $13 per adult, $10 per child, $6.50 per senior weekends

Other: Lodging and food at the slope-side Grouse House (269-4446)

CROSS-COUNTRY SKIING **Bucksteep Manor** (443-4752), Washington Mt. Road, Washington. With an 1,800-foot elevation and 25 km. of trails on 400 acres, this is usually snow-covered in winter. Trails are groomed and tracked, and there are rentals, guided tours in October Mountain State Forest, and lodging and dining on the premises.

Butternut (528-0610), Great Barrington. Adjacent to the alpine area are four miles of trails connecting with Beartown State Forest.

Canterbury Farm (634-2111), Fred Snow Road, Becket. Lessons, rentals, and trails on 200 acres.

Foxhollow (637-2000), Route 7, Lenox. Rentals (waxless) and lessons offered on the resort property. There are 14 miles of groomed trails.

Oak N' Spruce (243-3500). Rentals and 6 kilometers of trails (some lighted for night skiing) on the property.

Also note cross-country trails mentioned under State Parks and Forests. Mt. Washington State Forest is off-limits to snowmobiles but offers a marked network of touring trails; start at Forest headquarters on East Street. Trails are also marked in Bartholomew's Cobble and in Beartown, Sandisfield, and Otis State Forests. Kennedy Park, Pleasant Valley, and Canoe Meadows are all popular touring spots for Lenox residents.

LODGING During July and August general Berkshire policy is a minimum two- or three-night stay on weekends. Note that the Lenox Chamber of Commerce refers guests to private homes during this period.

RESORTS **Chanterwood** (243-0585), Box 375, Lee 01238. Open late June to Columbus Day. A low-key hideaway deep in its own woods above Goose Pond. Donald Campion has owned this long-time institution for just a few years but he is preserving the atmosphere of a rustic old family camp. There are concerts in the music room and guests are encouraged to meet around the dinner table (there are also small tables for those who prefer them). In addition to the rustic-style lodge there are 18 cottages of various sizes. Down by the spring-fed lake there are boats and a dock. There are also lawn games and tennis courts, a game room, and a 2,000-book library. $60–$85 per person, $455 per week MAP.

Eastover (637-0625), 430 East Street, Lenox 01240. A resort maintained by the Bisacca family since 1947 with 165 rooms (some in a turn-of-the-century gilded "cottage") most in motel-style annexes. Facilities include a small ski slope with a chair lift, an ice rink, driving range, seven tennis courts, horseback riding, indoor and outdoor pools. Weeks and weekends are tightly programmed, with the unusual twist that some are geared exclusively to singles, others to families, and still others to couples. Weekends are $57–$72 per person per night, including all meals.

Kripalu Center (637-3280), Box 793, Lenox 01240. This is a holistic health and yoga center, offering a structured daily regimen and a variety of weekend, week-long, and longer programs. Kripalu is housed in Shadowbrook, a former Jesuit novitiate on the grounds of Andrew Carnegie's 300-acre estate, which overlooks the Stockbridge Bowl and is within walking distance of Tanglewood. The staff numbers more than 200, and guests average more than 300 on weekends. This is not a place from which to explore the Berkshires; guests come from throughout the country to exercise, meditate, dance, reduce stress, or whatever the program is which has drawn them; they may also come simply for the holistic food, peace, and minimum daily regimen of exercise and yoga. Facilities include whirlpools, saunas, hiking and cross-country trails, beach, boats, and tennis; also a children's program during summer months. Introductory weekends from $65 (lodging and meals included) and week-long programs run from $240–$750 depending on accommodations (which range from dorms to private room and baths).

Foxhollow (637-2000), Route 7, Lenox 01240. A white, wooden mansion once owned by the Westinghouse/Vanderbilt families forms the centerpiece for this resort, which offers swimming (indoor and outdoor), horseback riding, sailing, tennis, and cross-country skiing. Guest rooms are spacious and the dining room is attractive, but on our last visit there was a salesman in every corner selling timesharing. Five weekday packages go for $249–$349 per person and summer weekend rates are $100–$135 per night.

Oak n' Spruce (243-3500; outside MA: 1-800-628-5072), Route 102, South Lee 01260. This moderately priced old place has indoor and outdoor swimming pools, saunas, cross-country skiing in winter. From $18 per person EP, $42 MAP.

Bellefontaine (637-1100), 91 Kemble Street, Lenox 01240. A magnificent gilded cottage forms the centerpiece for a resort that includes 120 suites, 37 condominiums, a restaurant, health spa, indoor pool, and cross-country ski trails on 92 acres. (Opening in 1987.)

Cranwell Resort and Conference Center (637-1364), 55 Lee Road, Lenox 01204. A fine old gilded cottage that was Cranwell School until its recent conversion into a resort and conference center; facilities include an 18-hole golf course. (Opening in 1987.)

INNS

Blantyre (637-3556 after May 1; 637-1728 in winter), East Street, off Route 20 (PO Box 995), Lenox 01240. Built in 1902 to re-create an ancestral home in Scotland, this is a magnificent Stockroker Tudor mansion, lovingly restored to its peak glory by the Fitzpatricks, owners of the Red Lion Inn in Stockbridge. There is a baronial entry hall and a truly graceful music room with crystal chandeliers, sofas covered in petit point, a piano, and a harp. Guests dine in the darkly paneled dining room, either around the long, formal table or "a deus" in the octagonal "More Room" named for the shiny fabric on its walls. Dinner is open to the public by reservation ($50). Guest rooms are impeccably furnished with antiques and most have fireplaces. There are 85 well-kept acres with four tennis courts, a swimming pool (with hot tub and sauna), and competition croquet courts. $150–$350 per room bed & breakfast plus 10 percent service charge.

Wheatleigh (637-0610), West Hawthorne Road, Lenox 01240. This is a yellow brick palazzo built in 1893, set in 22 acres that include a swimming pool and tennis court. We are put off by the "No Trespassing, Violators will be Prosecuted," which is the first thing to greet guests as they turn in the drive. There are 17 rooms, all with private bath. We find the potted palm atmosphere a shade stiff, but that's probably sour grapes because we can't afford it. Breakfast, a light lunch, and dinner are served. $95–$165 per room plus 15 percent service in winter; $145–$275 in summer.

The Red Lion Inn (298-5545), Main Street, Stockbridge 01250. Probably the most famous inn in Massachusetts, a rambling white clapboard beauty built in 1897. Staying here is like stepping into a Norman Rockwell painting, and there isn't a musty or dusty corner in the entire inn. Even the cheapest, shared-bath rooms are carefully furnished with real and reproduction antiques and bright prints, and there are some splendid rooms with canopy beds. The inn's long porch, festooned with flowers and amply furnished with rockers in warm weather, is the true center of Stockbridge in summer as is the hearth in its lobby in winter. There is a large, formal dining room, a cozy pub, and, in summer, a garden cafe by the pool. $65–$195 per room on summer weekends, less midweek and in winter.

The Inn at Stockbridge (298-3337), Route 7, Box 2033, Stockbridge 01262. Open May through October. This is a white pillared mansion built in 1906, set on 12 acres with ample woods and meadow to tramp around in. Flowers, comfortable blue chintz chairs, and books fill the living room, where a fire is lit on rainy days. There's an attractive pool in the garden. Breakfast is served either in the formal dining room or on the back porch. Innkeeper Lee Weitz is an experienced, creative chef and breakfast may be a souffle. There are seven guest rooms, each different, five with private bath. Guests tend to mingle over wine and cheese at 5 PM. $50–$115 per room midweek, $80–$195 on weekends.

Seven Hills (637-0060), 100 Plunkett Street, Lenox 01240. Open April to New Year's Day. This is a 1911 Tudor-style mansion set on 27 acres. In summer the waiters are drawn from top music schools and frequently regroup in the Music Room after dinner to entertain guests. The full staff numbers 50, to serve 110 to 120 guests. Rooms vary from bright, motel-style doubles out in the garden to classic old bedrooms with flowery wallpaper and working fireplaces. Rates include an extravagant noon buffet and full breakfast as well as a multi-course dinner. Facilities include a pool and tennis courts; a path leads down to Laurel Lake. $75–$100 per person with all three meals in summer; $35–$45 per person with breakfast during spring and fall.

Apple Tree Inn (637-1477), 224 West Street, Lenox 01240. This century-old cottage has had its ups and downs and is in fine shape these days. It sits high on a hill overlooking the Stockbridge Bowl, just across from Tanglewood, set among apple trees and rose gardens (owner Greg Smith cultivates no less than 300 varieties). Each of the thirteen rooms in the main house has been imaginatively, lovingly restored and furnished, four with working fireplaces. The 20 rooms in the modern lodge are motel-style but pleasant and handy to the pool, which commands an extraordinary view. The other great view is from the circular, glass-walled dining room, moderately expensive and open to the public. Light meals are also available in the oak-beamed tavern. $80–$240 on summer weekends, $45–$115 on winter weekdays.

The Village Inn (637-0020), 16 Church Street, Lenox 01240. Set back from a quiet back street in Lenox village, the inn offers 27 rooms (24 with private bath), a comfortable screened porch, and a Victorian-style parlor. There is usually someone sitting on the stool in front of the check-in desk, which doubles as a bar. The inn is open to the public for breakfast, tea, and dinner. $65–$110 per room on a summer weekend, $45–$90 in winter, midweek.

The Old Inn on The Green (229-7924), New Marlborough 01230. This is a 1760, double-porched inn in a beautiful village center, off the beaten track. It has been nicely restored, its four bedrooms furnished with antiques and heated with woodstoves (electric heaters are also provided). The prix-fixe dinner menu is available Friday and Saturday; the $60 per room price includes breakfast.

Windflower (528-2720), Box 25, Egremont (Route 23) 02158. This is a turn-of-the-century white clapboard house with shutters and gables. There is a gracious living room with a fireplace and a reading room with books, games, and a piano. A pool, golf links, and tennis courts are just across the road at the country club. Fine dining is the specialty of the house. Barbara Liebert and her daughter Claudia Ryan are the chefs, using berries, herbs, and vegetables from the garden. Everything from soup to dessert is made on the premises. The 13 rooms all have private baths; number 12 has a working fireplace and a four-poster. $50–$70 per person MAP.

The Williamsville Inn (274-6580), Route 41, West Stockbridge 01266. The 1797 house is right by the road but there are 10 acres that include gardens, a pool, and tennis court. Some guest rooms have fireplaces and four-posters and there is both a tavern and reading space by the fire downstairs. The large dining room is open to the public. $85–$95 per room (no meals), $135 for a two-room suite, less in winter.

Gateways Inn and Restaurant (637-2532), 71 Walker Street, Lenox 01240. Built by Harley Procter of Procter and Gamble in 1912 to resemble (the story goes) a cake of ivory soap—which it does—with black shutters. Actually this is an elegant inn, best known as a restaurant, with nine rooms, one suite with two fireplaces. Guests have use of the pool and tennis court at the owners' bed & breakfast five miles away. $80–$200 (for the Fiedler Suite) on summer weekends, $45–$100 on winter weekdays.

The Egremont Inn (528-2111), Box 418, South Egremont 01258. This is a three-story, double-porched landmark in the middle of a classic crossroads village. Dating, in part, from 1780 it now has a comfortable, lived-in atmosphere. There are 23 rooms, all with private baths, flowery paper, white spreads, and passable antiques. Goodale's (the inn restaurant) closes midweek in winter. There is a pool and two tennis courts, and in winter Catamount ski area is just down the road. $60–$75 per person MAP, $100 single on summer weekends, $40 per person (double occupancy), and $40 single midweek.

The Weathervane Inn (528-9580), Route 23, South Egremont 02158. A gracious old home on 10 acres. Rooms all have private bath, antiques. There is a bar in the living room and the dining room is open to the public Thursday–Monday. There's also a TV room and a pool. Monday–Wednesday rates are B&B: $35 per person double

Cross-country skiers in the Berkshire Hills

occupancy; on weekends: $350 for two people, three nights, three breakfasts, two dinners (the minimum stay).

Candlelight Inn (637-1555), Lenox 01240. Better known as a restaurant than an inn, with five guest rooms upstairs, all with private baths. This is a busy place, smack in the heart of Lenox village. $50–$95 per room, no meals in summer. Lunch and dinner are served downstairs, and there is a pub.

Federal House (243-1824), Route 102, South Lee 01260. A columned, 1824 mansion built by the founder of the Hurlbut Paper Company, now widely respected as a restaurant. There are seven nicely furnished guest rooms, all with private baths. A room with double occupancy (breakfast included) ranges from $55–$135, depending on day of the week and season.

The Gables Inn (637-3416), 103 Walker Street, Lenox 01240. This gracious old village home housed Edith Wharton while she was constructing The Mount. While known primarily as a restaurant, it has newly renovated bedrooms with private baths; $75–$100 with breakfast, $100–$130 for three nights.

Westbridge Inn (232-7770), West Stockbridge 01266. This is a rambling, nineteenth-century wooden hotel with 15 rooms, an old-fashioned ice cream parlor, chop house, and pub.

The Morgan House (243-0181), Main Street, Lee 01238. A double-porched old tavern in the middle of town with 13 rooms, 12 with shared baths, thus a relative bargain: $26.42–$58.13 double in summer, more for suites; less off-season; continental breakfast included.

New Boston Inn (258-4477), Sandisfield 01255. A striking old tavern in the middle of the village of New Boston, newly restored, offering eight bedrooms with private baths, a wide board pine taproom and ballroom, which now serve as public dining rooms. $85–$95 double in season, country breakfast included.

BED & BREAKFASTS **Berkshire Bed & Breakfast** (268-7244), Main Street, Williamsburg 01096. This newly reorganized reservation service offers placement in some 60 homes scattered between Sturbridge and the Berkshires—where they include some attractive places not otherwise listed. Rates range from $35 to $65.

In Lenox 01240: **25 Cliffwood Inn** (637-3330) was built in 1904 as the summer home of the American ambassador to France. It's airy and elegant with eight bedrooms, two suites, four with private bath, six with working fireplaces (Room #6 has a fireplace in its bathroom), and the walls are covered with interesting art, on semipermanent loan from a friend's art gallery in Texas. Innkeepers Hector Bellini and Don Thompson ran a restaurant in Texas before coming to Lenox. Breakfast is continental, but dinner, prepared Saturday nights for registered guests who request it, is an event.

$60 per room in summer (breakfast included), special weekend packages in winter.

Garden Gables (637-0193), 141 Main Street (closed March 15–April 20). Marie Veselik has welcomed guests to her charming home since 1951. The triple-gabled white clapboard house set well back from Route 7—but within walking distance of the village shops and restaurants—accommodates 20 people. Rooms are small but bright and comfortable, two are singles, and there are two small efficiency apartments. The ample grounds convey a sense of being out in the country and there is a pool. A single room with shared bath is $40 in July and August, a double with private bath is $70–$85; cheaper other times of the year. The apartments are just $380 a week. Breakfast is not included but is served.

Walker House (637-1271), 74 Walker Street. This is an expanded Federal-era (1804) house with a Victorian feel inside. It is nicely decorated with inviting public rooms and also has a flower-garnished and wicker-furnished veranda overlooking the expansive (more than two acres) back garden. Five of the eight guest rooms, each named for a composer, have fireplaces and all have charm. Breakfast, tea, and bicycles are included in the rates. $80–$110 per room on weekends, $55–$75 midweek in summer; $65–$85 on winter weekends, $45–$65 midweek.

Cornell House (637-0562), Main Street. This is an attractive Victorian house with nine guest rooms, all with private bath, some with fireplaces, but not worth the $110 it commands during Tanglewood season (continental breakfast included); cheaper off-season. There are also four apartments in the old Carriage House.

Brook Farm (637-3013), 15 Hawthorne Street. A friendly, yellow Victorian house on a quiet byway south of the village, Brook Farm is furnished with the abundance of books and art that fits its period (1889), offers eleven guest rooms, six with private baths, four with fireplaces. A full breakfast is served in the elegant, green dining room overlooking gardens. There is a pool to laze around, also comfortable indoor lounging space by fireplaces. $75–$110 depending on day of the week and season (three-night minimum in July and August). Special reasonably priced winter package including dinner.

Whistler's Inn (637-0975), 5 Greenwood Street. The core of this mansion dates to 1820 but it's now a rambling Tudor-style mansion with large, opulent public rooms, which include a ballroom, library, and formal dining room. There are 11 bedrooms, all with private bath; $55–$150 in summer, less in winter (the top price goes for the spacious master bedroom with fireplace). A continental breakfast is served. Innkeeper Richard Mears, author of the novel *Ebb of The River*, divides his time between Lenox and Northern California. The inn is across from the Church on the Hill and an easy walk both from village shops and from the trails in Kennedy Park.

Underledge (637-0236), 76 Cliffwood Street. This is a formal turn-of-the-century home with twelve guest rooms, five with working fireplaces, all with large windows. Located a ways down a mansion-lined street, it borders Kennedy Park with its extensive trails for walking and skiing. The building was the Lanoues' home before they opened it to guests, and there is a friendly feel to the place. Complimentary breakfast is included in the rates. $45–$110 per room in summer, $150–$600 per week. September through November $45–$90. Closed December–Memorial Day.

Amity House (637-0005), 15 Cliffwood Street. An airy, sparely furnished old home with seven guest rooms, gleaming wood floors, and country quilts on the beds. Smoking is not permitted in the bedrooms, but this is one of the few gracious Lenox houses that welcomes children (Hostess Rhoda Crowell has taught school). Twin beds in rooms with a connecting bath are ideal for families. Rates include continental breakfast: $50–$100 (top price is for three) on weekends, less midweek.

East Country Berry Farm (442-2057), 830 East Street. A ways from the village (not within walking distance of Tanglewood) but with a sense of being off in the country, with a pool and horses. Continental breakfast with fresh fruit included in the rates: $65–$105 for the rooms, $125 (four night minimum) for a cottage, $125 for a one-bedroom apartment, $160 for two bedrooms. These are all high season rates. Cheaper in May, June, and rest of the year.

Quincy Lodge (637-9750), 19 Stockbridge Road. Max and Alix Kowler have acquired a loyal following, including many members of the BSO, during the years in which they have opened their gracious home. Breakfast is included.

Strawberry Hill (637-3381), 9 Cliffwood Street. This is an elegant home in which guests breakfast on muffins and breads in the formal, silver-decked dining room. There are floor to ceiling french doors in the bright living room, six rooms upstairs (each with private bath), also a two-bedroom apartment. $110 per room on summer weekends, less midweek, includes a generous continental breakfast. This is no place for children.

In Great Barrington 01230: **Elling's Bed & Breakfast** (528-4103), PO Box 6, Route 23 West. Ray and Jo Elling have been in the bed & breakfast business longer than most people and it has bred an easy, friendly atmosphere. The handsome white clapboard house dates back to 1746 and its guest wing, containing six guest rooms, has its own low-beamed living room with fireplace and TV. The rooms are nicely furnished with antiques; one has a private bath and the others are no more than two on a bath. The house sits high on a knoll above the road, commanding a view of fields backed by hills. There's a deep, sandy swimming hole in the river on the property and plenty of inviting space to roam. Breakfast is buffet-style: fresh baked muffins and homemade jams. Rates: in summer $65 per room with private bath, $50 without; $50 with private bath, $40 without in winter.

Little John Manor (528-2882), PO Box 148, Route 23 at the Newsboy Monument. Built as the gardener's cottage for a former estate, this is a delightful house with four guest rooms, sharing two baths. The hosts, who formerly managed a largish inn in Maine, pride themselves on their full English breakfasts and teas (homemade scones and all). They also bottle and sell their wine vinegar. Rates are $50–$65 double.

The Turning Point (528-4777), RD2 Box 140. Closed in March and April. Built as the Pixley Tavern in 1800, this is a striking old double-doored inn, nicely renovated, offering seven guest rooms and a cheery parlor. There is also a great country kitchen in which guests are permitted to make their coffee and tea. Irv and Shirley Yost have moved to the Berkshires to maintain a healthful life-style for themselves, something they like to share through the ample, whole-grain breakfasts that they serve. No smoking inside the house. In summer there is Lake Buel just down the road and in winter Butternut Basin is a few minutes' drive. $45 single to $85 double on summer weekends; $5 less weekdays.

Seekonk Pines (528-4192), Box 29 AA, RD 1. The dining room has an oil cloth on the table, plastic coffee cups for the guests, and liquor lined along the molding. In the living room there is a "do not touch" sign on a doll house. Guest rooms, however, are pleasant, and there is a swimming pool and a total four acres of lawns and garden. Hostess Linda Best paints the watercolors displayed throughout the house. $42–$60 per room, June through October, $35–$54 in winter, continental breakfast included.

Greenmeadows (528-3897), 117 Division Street. A Victorian farmhouse with large guest rooms, private baths. $60–$80 for two, with country breakfast.

Coffing-Bostwick House (528-4511), junction of Route 41 and Division Street. An 1820s Greek Revival home with space to relax in the library and living room, parlor with cable TV, antiques-furnished guest rooms, full breakfasts included in rates. $60 double on weekends, less weekdays.

Washburn House (528-3344), 75 Taconic Avenue. This is simply an attractive home on a quiet side street with three guest rooms sharing two baths; $40 per couple in summer includes a continental breakfast; it's $5 extra per child.

Berkshire Bed & Breakfast (268-7244). The host welcomes guests in a turn-of-the-century home set in 300 acres. There is a swimming hole in the trout stream and resident animals include horses as well as dogs and a cat. There are double, two twins, and one single rooms, all with shared bath; strictly non-smoking. $60.

In Sheffield 01257: **Staveleigh House** (229-2129), South Main Street. Dorothy Marosy and Marion Whitman, longtime friends, have created a truly homey Berkshire retreat. I don't mean homey as in cluttered and shabby because every wing chair and sofa is brightly, tastefully upholstered, and every room is furnished with flair. There are five guest rooms, one with private bath and two downstairs, off by themselves, overlooking the garden. My favorite is a symphony in blues and whites with a wicker chaise longue and rocker. The house was built as a parsonage in 1818 and it's set back from Route 7 with inviting gardens out back. Breakfast is an event here: puffed pancakes, individually baked and topped with apple slivers, for instance. $60–$65 per room including breakfast.

Ivanhoe Country House (229-2143), on Route 41. This is an exceptional find: gracious, friendly, comfortable. Guests are welcome to play games or the piano, watch TV or dip into the library of the paneled Chestnut Room where a fire burns in winter and french doors create an airy feel in summer. There are nine rooms, three with kitchenettes, all with access to fridges. One two-bedroom unit with a glassed-in porch can sleep a family of five or six. Continental breakfast appears outside each bedroom in the morning. In summer there is a pool, and in winter you can poke around the inn's own 25 acres on skis. $55–$115 (two-bedroom unit with bath) on weekends in summer. Well-behaved dogs are welcome.

Oak Lodge (229-8531), South Main Street. A Victorian-era house on more than three acres of lawn, with four rooms, each with private bath, in the guest wing. A full breakfast is served on the screened porch, if desired. $60 double, $55 single.

Centuryhurst Antiques (229-8131), Main Street, PO Box 486. This old home offers four rooms, $43–$48 including breakfast.

Berkshire Bed & Breakfast (268-7244). The hosts offer two double and three twin rooms, all with private baths, in a log home nestled in pine trees. $75–$80.

In New Marlboro 01230: **Hollister House** (229-8623). A classic 1847 village beauty nicely furnished by Madeline Hunting, who has done much of the upholstery herself. As attractive as many of the better-known and more expensive bed & breakfasts, its three rooms (sharing two baths) are reasonably priced ($40 single, $45 double in summer) and demand no minimum stay. It's on the verge of this lovely town, with a frog pond out back. In winter there are nearby trails through public forests.

Langhaar House (229-2007), Branch Road. Richard Sellew welcomes guests in summer to his grandparents' home. $40–$69 per room, breakfast included.

Millstones Guest House (229-3486), Route 57. There are four guest rooms, each nicely furnished in genuine antiques, one downstairs with a private bath. Continental breakfast is served buffet-style.

In Lee 01238: **Ramsey House** (243-1598), 203 West Park Street. This is a gracious 1895 house on a quiet side street. The five rooms vary but all are furnished with antiques and are color coordinated. The downstairs master bedroom, with a beautifully canopied four-poster, private bath, and sun porch, fetches $90 on weekends in summer; other rooms go for as low as $55; less off-season. Continental breakfast is served on the glass-enclosed porch.

Haus Andreas, R.R. 1, Box 605-B, Stockbridge Road. A majestic mansion with an eighteenth-century core and turn-of-the-century lines (it was landscaped and modernized by George Westinghouse, Jr.). It is now home for Gerhard and Lilliane Schmid, owners of the Gateways Inn in Lenox. All six guest rooms are furnished in antiques and have private baths, three have working fireplaces. There is a pool and tennis court, bikes, and a golf course across the street. $80–$150 Thursday–Sunday in summer, four-day minimum; $55–$90 other days and off-season.

1777 Greylock House (243-1717), 58 Greylock Street. Five rooms in Lee's oldest (somewhat Victorianized) home with a large porch set back above its lawn. There are suites on the first and second floors: $65 to $85 in summer; $35–$45 in winter, continental breakfast included.

Kingsleigh (243-3317), 32 Park Street. A gracious Italianate 1840s house with a comfortable library, parlor, and enclosed porch. There are four guest rooms with private and semi-private baths. $65–$85 on summer weekends, $45–$60 weekdays; $50–$70 winter weekends, $40–$55 winter weekdays.

In Richmond 01254: **Peirson Place** (698-2750), Route 41. This gracious home has been in the same family since 1787. There are 10 rooms and suites, some private baths, two Pullman kitchens. The 200 acres include a swimming pond and sauna, also a great gazebo. Rates include breakfast and a full tea. A-la-carte meals are served by advance reservation on some days. Double rooms range from $60 to $110; singles from $40 to $60 on summer weekends (no meals included); less in winter.

Middlerise Bed & Breakfast (698-2687), Route 41. Carol and Carter White have a fine clapboard home on a hill. There are four guest rooms, choice of shared or private bath. The Whites founded and own Alliance Editions, distinctive clothing carried in top stores. Continental breakfast is served. $50–$60.

Bash Bish Falls mark the south/western corner of Massachusetts

Berkshire Hills Country Inn (698-3379), Dean Hill Road. Sited on 147 hilltop acres with a panoramic view: three double rooms with a shared bath, one with private bath, continental breakfast included in the rates: $45.

Berkshire Bed & Breakfast (268-7244). The hosts offer three double rooms (shared bath) in a converted carriage house, set on 147 acres with views of hills and mountains. A ten-minute drive to Tanglewood. $45.

In Pittsfield 01201: **White Horse Inn** (443-0961), 378 South Street. A fine old house with nine rooms, all with private bath, several with fireplaces. Continental breakfast included in rates: $85–$100 summer and fall weekends; $60–$75 winter, less weekdays.

Munro's American House Guests (442-0503), 306 South Street. A restored 1898 house with matching furnishings. November to June $40; July–October $55. Rates include a continental breakfast served on the sun porch.

Greer Bed & Breakfast (443-3889), 193 Wendell Avenue. An elegantly decorated colonial revival home with three large bedrooms, two with fireplaces, one with private bath. Full breakfast served in a formal dining room. $30–$65 per night in July and August, less off-season.

Other: **Merrell Tavern Inn** (243-1794), Main Street (Route 102), South Lee 01260. This is a standout: a double-porched inn built in 1800, used as a stagecoach stop on the Albany–Boston Pike beginning in 1817. For 34 years prior to 1981 it was a house-museum, but it's far more pleasant as an inn. There are five bedrooms on the first and second floors, four more in the third-floor space that was once a ballroom. Original fabrics and colors have been copied and the antiques are appropriate to the early nineteenth century. Guests breakfast in the tap room, with its original circular bar in the corner. $195–$210 per room for two nights, $250 for three nights on weekends in summer, $55–$60 on weekdays; in winter $160 for two weekend nights with a fireplace, $95–$105 without; $50 on winter weekdays for a room with fireplace.

The Golden Goose (243-3008), Tyringham 01264. This is an inviting old house in the middle of a picturesque hilltop village. The rooms are furnished with antiques and breakfast, which usually includes homemade applesauce and hot biscuits, is served family-style at the oak table. There are private baths and a small efficiency apartment with its own entrance; guests also have access to a fridge and BBQ. The Appalachian Trail is just outside, and there is a nearby swimming pond. The inn is set on its own six acres. $50–$75 (private apartment) in July and August; $5 less the rest of the year.

Canterbury Farm Bed & Breakfast (623-8765), Becket 01223. This early nineteenth-century home stands on its own 200 acres, surrounded by gardens, fields, and woods criss-crossed with ski trails. There are four guest rooms (one with a fireplace) sharing two baths. There are two sitting rooms with a color TV, a piano, and games in the library. $40 per couple includes a full breakfast; $10 for an extra person in the room. 10% less for more than two rooms or for five days.

The Dalton House (684-3854), 955 Main Street, Dalton 01226. The handsome old home was built by a Hessian soldier in 1810. There is a large informal sitting area with old beams, wood lined walls, and a "loafing loft." A breakfast buffet is served in the Garden Room. All rooms have private baths and some have fireplaces. In summer $58–$75, fall: $48–$65, winter: $42–$60, spring: $48–$65.

MOTELS AND OTHER LODGING We do not want to ignore the Berkshires' many fine motels, but these are adequately covered by Mobil and AAA Guides. Listings of sources for cottage and apartment rentals can be found in the Berkshire Visitors Center Guide (see Guidance).

Black Swan Inn (243-2700). A 40-room motor inn with motel-style rooms, a comfortable lobby, and a view of Laurel Lake. There is also a restaurant with a Hungarian menu. $75–$85 on summer weekends, $45–$55 weekdays, MAP rates and packages available.

Hilton Inn Berkshire (499-2000), Berkshire Common at West Street. This is the Berkshires' only high-rise and very much a part of the county seat. There are 175 rooms, an indoor pool, sauna, cafe, and a highly rated restaurant (Encore). $79–$92 double in summer, more for suites, less single; children free in same room; less off-season.

DINING OUT Elegant Dining: **Gateways Inn** (637-2532), 71 Walker Street, Lenox. Chef/owner Gerhard Schmid has won wide acclaim and many awards for his cuisine: classic continental fare with entrees (including salad, vegetables, and rolls) at a fixed price: $21.50. The choice may include Veal Sweetbreads, Filet Mignon, Provincial Rack of Lamb, or game in season. Desserts always include Black Forest Torte. The formal dining rooms fill most of the ground floor of a white mansion built in 1912 by Harley Procter (see Lodging). Open for dinner only.

The Old Mill (528-1421), Route 23, South Egremont. Dining well doesn't cost a fortune at this popular old gristmill by Hubbard Brook. Meals are in the $10–$15 range; specialties include game hen with garlic and herbs, and English mixed grill. No reservations are accepted for less than five people so come early on weekends. Open every night for dinner.

Federal House (243-1824), Route 102, South Lee. Rated highly, the small dining rooms in this 1824 pillared mansion are the place to dine on Escalopine of Veal Gnocchi Italienne ($15.50) or Escalope of Salmon with Caviar ($16.50); Chateaubriand Bouquetiere for two is $38. Open for dinner and Sunday brunch.

Goodale's (528-2111), at the Egremont Inn, offers assorted atmospheres in a number of dining rooms (go for the old tavern) and some exceptionally flavorful dishes. Try the fresh, sauteed trout or veal with a champagne sauce. Entrees run $10.75 (for the trout) to $16 for lamb chops. Open for dinner Wednesday–Sunday, also for Sunday brunch.

Paolo's Auberge (637-2711), 306 Pittsfield-Lenox Road (Routes 7 and 20) at Brushwood Farm. The dining rooms in an early eighteenth-century house are low-beamed and brick-walled, candlelit. Chef/owner Paul Eugster is Swiss born and trained. At dinner a vegetarian entree is $17.50 and veal dishes (a specialty) are $20 plus. A four-course Sunday brunch is $14. Lunch is served weekdays and dinner nightly; closed Sundays in winter and spring.

Church Street Cafe (637-2745), 69 Church Street. The small dining rooms are candlelit, hung with exceptional art and the patio is exceptionally attractive, the right setting for light, zesty chicken and seafood dishes. The desserts are unusually delectable. $10–$12 range. Open for lunch and dinner, closed Sundays in winter.

Wheatleigh (637-0610), West Hawthorne Road. This Florentine Palazzo, within walking distance of Tanglewood, features "creative cuisine": pheasant with cognac sauce, or rack of lamb for instance, $20–$25; also open for lunch and brunch in season; closed Mondays.

Windflower Inn (528-2720). This chef-owned (mother and daughter) and -operated inn features fresh ingredients and everything (from soups and sauces to breads and desserts) made from scratch on the premises. The menu is limited, offering three choices, and you must reserve ahead. No smoking in the dining room; expensive.

Williamsville Inn (274-6580), Route 41, West Stockbridge. Dining by candlelight is from a "Country French" menu; expensive.

Lenox House Restaurant (637-1341), Routes 7 and 20. Candlelight and elegantly set tables; Veal Piccata, Bouillabaise, and roast duckling are the specialties. Open for lunch ($4–$10) and dinner ($14–$20).

Village Inn (637-0020), 16 Church Street, Lenox. The dining room has a pronounced country inn feel; specialties include Whole Smoked Maine Trout and Eggplant Curry ($7.50–$14). Breakfast, tea, and Sunday brunch are also served.

Apple Tree (637-1477), 224 West Street. The round corner dining room, twinkling with small white lights, seems suspended above the Stockbridge Bowl which it overlooks. The specialties are fresh seafood and homemade pasta. Dinner for two runs $30–$35 without wine.

The Red Lion Inn (298-5545), Stockbridge. The formal dining room of this dignified inn is as formal as you would expect, and the menu holds no surprises: Roast Prime Ribs, Veal Oscar, and Fresh Poached Salmon, also New England standbys like Chicken Pot Pie and Yankee Pot Roast. Of course you can have apple pie and Indian pudding for dessert: $8.50–$18 for dinner. It·is also open for breakfast and lunch; less formal dining in Widow Bingham's Tavern and (in summer) in the courtyard.

Elm Court Inn (528-0325), Route 71, North Egremont. Young Swiss chef/owner Joseph Miller has put this old tavern back on the dining map. The large, low-ceilinged dining room gleams with worn, highly polished wood. Veal dishes are the specialty; Wiener schnitzel is usually available. $13–$15. Dinner served except Tuesday and Wednesday.

Westbridge Inn (232-7120), West Stockbridge. The atmosphere is pleasant and the menu is Swiss: fondue and veal dishes. $9–$17.50.

The Old Inn on the Green (229-7924). This classic eighteenth-century stagecoach stop has four small dining rooms, the scene of five course prix-fixe dinners on Friday and Saturday evenings. By reservation only; moderately expensive.

Less Formal Dining Out: **20 Railroad Street** (528-9345), Great Barrington. Railroad Street was still dingy in 1977 when this friendly pub opened. Since then the side street has filled with boutiques and restaurants, but this one still stands out. The menu is big, ranging through soups, chilies, nachos, salads, pocket sandwiches, burgers, rubens, and daily specials like Chicken Marbella or Veal Mariera are featured. The huge wooden bar is said to have been taken from the Commodore Hotel in 1919. Open daily for lunch and dinner, also for Sunday brunch ($6.95).

Konkapot Restaurant (229-6614), Mill River (10 miles from Great Barrington, eight miles from Sheffield). This is a small place featuring homegrown herbs and vegetables, homemade bread, and desserts. Reserve.

Ghinga Sushi Bar (298-4490), Stockbridge Railroad Station. The town's handsome stone railroad station seems the right place to feast on Maki Rolls (six for $1.80), seasoned pieces of octopus ($1.40), and Horse Clam ($1.70) or shrimp Sashimi ($10.90) and "earth-size" Sushi ($13.50).

Embree's (247-3476), Main Street, Housatonic. An attractive, high-ceilinged dining room has been created in the former Housatonic Mills company store. The atmosphere is low-key and trendy. The menu is a mix of nouvelle, Oriental, and healthy: whole-grain breads, sprouts, goat cheese, and spicy curried lamb, not to mention stir fries and tempeh. Open Wednesday–Sunday for dinner, Sunday for brunch. Entrees in the $6–$10 range.

The Morgan House (243-0181), Main Street, Lee. The center of town since stagecoach days, this is a sure bet for either lunch or dinner. Roast duckling is a specialty, and there are children's plates; $3–$8 for lunch, $8–$15 for dinner.

Cork'n Hearth (243-0535), Route 20, Lee–Lenox line. Housed in a converted icehouse overlooking Laurel Lake, this is a long-established dinner spot specializing in Prime Rib, seafood, and poultry with a big salad bar.

Sullivan Station (243-2082). The Lee railroad station (departure point for the Berkshire Scenic Railroad) is an attractive restaurant serving $4.50 burgers for lunch, $10.25 "veal of the day" for dinner, and Sunday brunch. The day we stopped by, a tour group had taken over the place and other customers were rather rudely turned away.

August Moon (528-9363), Route 7, Great Barrington. The parlor of a house has been nicely fitted with simple tables. The menu is natural food/Oriental with specialties like Mushroom-smothered Tofu as well as Beef Lo Mein, Sweet n' Sour Shrimp ($10), and Beef Lo Mein ($5.95). No MSG is used and the emphasis is on fresh ingredients.

Sebastians (528-3469), Route 23, South Egremont. The decor is fresh and striking and the specialty is pasta made on the premises, also light seafood and veal dishes, great desserts, $10.50–$16.

Cafe Lucia (637-2460), 90 Church Street. A gallery setting for light lunches like chilled mussels in white wine ($4.95), a country pate plate ($6.95), Ossobuco ($14.95), or Chicken Saltimbocca ($12.95) at dinner; homemade desserts. Open until 12:30 AM on Friday and Saturday.

Truc Orient Express (232-4204), Main Street, West Stockbridge. A Vietnamese restaurant with a nice, woven-straw decor. The food is as spicy as you specify. Specialties include "singing chicken" and a Mongolian hotpot. Open daily for lunch and dinner ($8.50–$12).

Noodles (528-3003), 12 Railroad Street. This is a pleasant Berkshire-style trattoria featuring homemade pastas and Northern Italian specialties. Open daily for lunch and dinner; moderately expensive.

Shaker Mill Tavern (232-8565), West Stockbridge. This is a large, attractive dining place in which dinner ranges from Eggplant Parmesan ($8.95) to lamb chops ($15.95). Sunday brunch, Friday dancing, and Saturday evening entertainment.

The Restaurant (637-9894), 15 Franklin Street, Lenox. This is an informal, storefront dining room, open for lunch, dinner, and brunch ($5.75 for French toast to $9.95 for crabmeat crepe). Liquor is served.

Dakota (499-7900), Route 7, Lenox/Pittsfield line. There is a large fieldstone fireplace in the dining room, which is supposed to resemble an Adirondack Lodge. Specialties include seafood, hand-cut steaks and mesquite grilled fish. Open for dinner daily.

EATING OUT **Mary's Place** (229-8784), Sheffield. Around in back of the Sheffield package store, Mary's is a find for lunch: a dozen flower-1garnished tables, homemade breads, croque monsieur, chilis, cakes, pies, wine, and beer. Open Tuesday–Friday 11–4.

The Gaslight Store, South Egremont. This old variety store has its original marble counter, at which you can enjoy Gazpacho, tomato curry, or vichyssoise for 70 cents. The tables are covered in red check oil cloth, and there are a variety of sandwiches and Stocsh's ice cream; open 7–4.

Sophia's Restaurant (298-3216), Stockbridge. This friendly, narrow eatery had its day of fame as Alice's Restaurant. Now it's a place for pizza, subs, Greek salad, and Gyro on Pita Bread ($3.35).

Four Brothers (528-9684), Route 7, Great Barrington. This is one in an upstate New York chain, but it doesn't seem that way. The decor is classic Greek, complete with plants and fake grape arbor. Generally regarded as the best pizzas, Greek salads, and lasagna around; there's also fried fish and eggplant casserole ($4.50).

The Deli (528-1482), 282 Main Street, Great Barrington. Breakfast begins at 5:30 AM and there is an amazing choice of omelettes all day, along with zany sandwich combos and homemade soups.

The Highland Restaurant (442-2457), 100 Fenn Street, Pittsfield. Since 1936 this has been a downtown mainstay for office workers. In addition to the spaghetti and scaloppine there are daily specials, and you can always get a hamburger, homemade cream pie, and cocktails. Closed Mondays.

Jimmy's (499-1288), 114 West Housatonic Street. A solid family, Italian restaurant with salads and Italian pu-pu platters for three.

Rachel's (443-9673), 122 North Street. Brick walls, hanging plants, interesting prints, and a large deli-style menu combine to make this an attractive lunch place: fruit and veggie salad is $2.50 and the Quiche du hour, $3.50. It's upstairs in an old office building that has had its innards rejigged into Galleria shops.

Joe's Diner (243-9756), 63 Center Street, Lee. Smack in the middle of Lee is this hole-in-the-wall that's open (usually) 24 hours except Sunday. There are twelve counter stools and several tables but a full menu for all three meals; dinner comes with vegetable, potato, and bread; daily specials. Figure $3 tops for a full breakfast, about the same for lunch, and $4–$6 for a full dinner.

City Front Cafe (528-3860), 10 Castle Street, Great Barrington. Fresh vegetables and respectfully treated fish are the draw at this New Age eatery, a true find. Closed Wednesday and September, otherwise open for lunch, brunch, and dinner.

The Quiet Corner (637-2039), 104 Main Street, Lenox. The fare in this bookstore is surprisingly fine: soups, sandwiches, and desserts all seem prepared with special care.

Duck Soup (443-1106), Route 7, Lanesboro. Not much to recommend it from the outside, this is a find for duck lovers. Try the aromatic, hearty duck soup and the roast duckling.

Laura's Scottish Tea Room (637-1060), Route 7, Lenox, at Lenox House Country Shops. The atmosphere is nil but the food is genuinely Scottish: "bangers" (sausages) and scones are served all day and the meat pies, not to mention mincemeat pies, are memorable.

La Concina (499-4027), 140 Wahconah Street, Pittsfield. Un Hermano of the North Adams eatery by the same name, this is a much loved source of Guacamole, "Quesadilla" (a tortilla filled with chicken, refried beans, and cheese with lettuce and tomato), and Sangria (in this case, wine and fruit juices laced with brandy).

ELEGANT PICNICS The picnic is a Berkshires institution: before Tanglewood concerts or Shakespearean plays, on top of mountains and beside the Housatonic. Picnic provenders take their art seriously.

A Movable Feast (637-1785), 100 Main Street (in the rear courtyard), Lenox. Complete gourmet picnics at a moment's notice, from $8.95.

Molly & Me (637-3161), 83 Church Street, Lenox. Rhubarb flummery, spoonbread, whatever.

The Elegant Picnic (637-1621) at the Curtis, Lenox and (298-4010/4059) in Stockbridge. "Distinctive al fresco" feasts.

Konkapot Restaurant (229-6614), Mill River. Famed for elaborate al fresco expeditions, which include dining on their own smoked duck, salmon and ribs, pates, unusual salads, and homemade desserts.

SELECTIVE SHOPPING **Apple Hill Designs** (528-3458), PO Box 332, Egremont. "Bits & Bites of the Berkshires" is the name of Mimi McDonald's latest business: post and note cards, regional foods, and color slides are all sold through local stores, distributed from her ubiquitous blue van. An authority on its history and craftspeople, Mimi is a source of all things specifically Berkshire. She welcomes inquiries.

Jenifer House (528-1500), Route 7. An "Americana Marketplace": A vast, fascinating melange of country furniture, clothes, gifts, and food.

Country Curtains (298-4938), The Red Lion Inn, Stockbridge. Country Curtains began in the nether parts of the Red Lion (helping to fill the old inn while the Fitzpatricks restored it in the '60s). Both the inn and business have long since outgrown this arrangement, and there are a half dozen Country Curtains stores around New England, selling an incredible array of curtains, spreads, towels, and accessories too. Pick up a catalog at the store at the inn.

Kenver, Ltd. (528-2330), Route 23, South Egremont. Housed in the eighteenth-century Old Egremont Inn, this shop claims to be the largest ski and sportswear shop in the Northeast.

Railroad Street Books (528-1950), 44 Railroad Street. The selection is rich and, since children find plenty to fascinate them, parents are free to browse.

The Bookstore (637-3390), 9 Housatonic Street, Lenox. I always stop by to see if my own books are stocked, never leave without something I hadn't intended to buy. This is a deep, inviting store with a second floor.

Either/Or Bookstore (449-1705), 122 North Street, Pittsfield. A large, satisfying shop with a wide variety of titles.

Shopping Areas (not, shudder, centers): In Stockbridge, don't miss the **Mews** next to The Red Lion Inn.

In Great Barrington, **Railroad Street** harbors a half dozen unusual stores.

In West Stockbridge, a number of shops cluster in old buildings all rehabilitated by one developer.

In Lenox Village, interesting shops line **Main, Church, Walker, Franklin,** and **Housatonic streets,** and more have been formally grouped in the **Village Shopping Centre,** but don't miss the newer clusters north of town on Routes 7 and 20: the **Center at Lenox, Lenox House Country Shops,** and the shops at **Brushwood Farm.**

Food: **Otis Poultry Farm** (269-4438), Route 8, North Otis. Cheeses, homemade chicken and turkey pies, fruit pies, breads, jams, fresh cider, syrup, honey, homemade peanut butter, sheepskin products, "custom laid eggs," turkeys, and chickens.

Monterey Chevre (528-2138), Rawson Brook Farm, two miles off Route 23 on New Marlboro Road in Monterey. Goat cheeses are available from April to December. Visitors are welcome.

Sunset Farm Maple Products (243-3229), Tyringham Road south at the junction of Routes 102 and 20 in Lee. Sugarhouse open daily, year-round.

ANTIQUES More than 50 dealers are listed in the pamphlet guide to dealers published by the Berkshire County Antiques Dealers Association, RD 1, Box 1, Sheffield 01257. Sheffield itself lists 19 dealers and its annual August Antiques Fair is a major event. Ashley Falls (just south) and South Egremont (northwest of Sheffield) each have a dozen dealers too, making this corner of South Berkshire particularly rewarding hunting grounds.

Auctions at **Cropreso Gallery** (243-3424), 136 High Street, Lee, are an event; geared to a wide audience. Paintings, furniture, and furnishings fill the interior of an 1890s church; spectators fill the pews. Quilts and Americana are a specialty. A cafe serves light snacks and items to go for $10–$10,000.

CRAFTS **Great Barrington Pottery** (274-6259), Route 41, Housatonic. The handsome, nicely glazed pieces are fired in a Japanese wood-burning kiln; exquisite silk flowers are also sold, and tea is served ceremoniously (1–4 daily) in a tea house set in a landscaped garden. The Pottery has a smaller shop in **The Mews Gallery** in Stockbridge.

The Dolphin Studio (298-3735), West Main Street, Stockbridge. Look for the big yellow house with mustard (Dijon) shutters and a big dolphin hanging on the porch. The French family makes a kaleidoscopic number of interesting gifts: from ceramic magnets to elaborate ceramic mirrors; a variety of sweaters, hats, and shawls, jewelry, handbags, and stuffed toys to mention but a few (works by a number of their friends are also represented).

Undermountain Weavers (274-6565), Route 41 South, West Stockbridge. In this barn studio you can watch the shuttles fly on century-old Scottish handlooms. The resulting lightweight woolens are designed for suits and skirts, scarves, ties, shawls, and tunics, samples of which can also be purchased.

L&R Wise Goldsmiths (637-1589), 81 Church Street, Lenox. Open daily in season, closed Sundays in winter. Much of the jewelry on exhibit is crafted on the premises; worth a look even if you are not in the market.

Hancock Shaker Village (443-9010), Hancock (see Museums). The Village sells yarn produced from its own herd of twenty Corriedale sheep. It also sells its own herbs and spices and a variety of crafted as well as Shaker-style items.

SPECIAL EVENTS May: **Chesterwood Antiques Auto Show,** Stockbridge; **Memorial Day Parade,** Great Barrington.

July: **Independence Day parade** and celebrations, Pittsfield.

Late July–early August: **World People's Dinners** and **Shaker Kitchen Festival,** Hancock Shaker Village, Hancock.

August: **Berkshire Crafts Fair** (early), Monument Mt. High School, Great Barrington; **Annual Festival of Shaker Crafts and Industries** (mid).

September: **Barrington Fair** at the Great Barrington Fairgrounds; **Great Josh Billings Run-around:** a 29-mile race involving biking, running, and canoeing (late September).

October: **Hancock Shaker Village Antiques Show,** Hancock; **Berkshire Garden Center Harvest Festival,** Stockbridge; **Lenox Apple Squeeze Festival,** Lenox.

November: **Chesterwood Christmas Sale** and tour, Stockbridge; **Annual sale** at Hancock Shaker Village.

December: **Christmas at Hancock Shaker Village,** Hancock; **Christmas in Lenox:** concerts, tree lighting, house tour.

MEDICAL EMERGENCY Berkshire Medical Center (499-4161), 725 North Street, Pittsfield: 24-hour emergency medical and dental care.

Fairview Hospital (528-0790), 29 Lewis Avenue, Great Barrington: 24-hour emergency care.

The Pioneer Valley

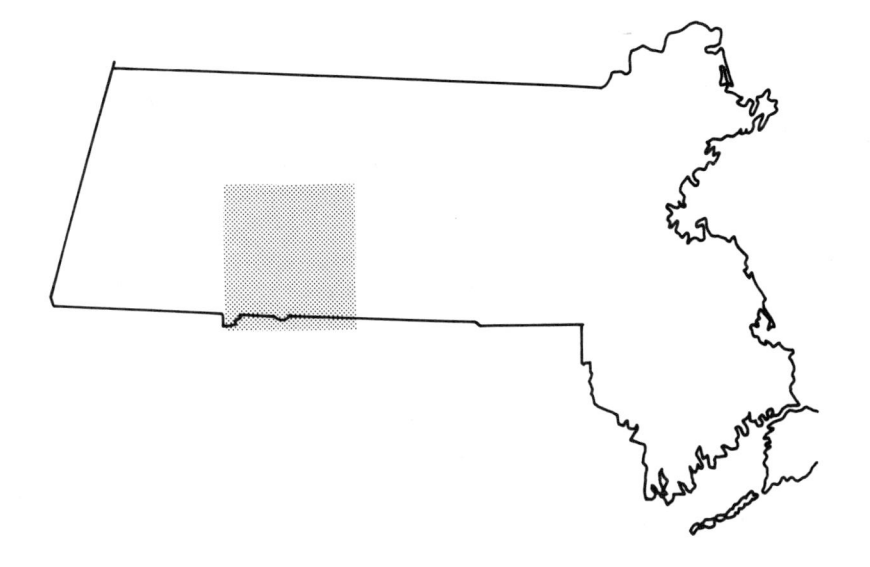

INTRODUCTION

The Pioneer Valley is a 1930s name for the regional tourism association that still serves all of Hampden, Hampshire, and Franklin counties. It's an apt one to the degree that it stresses the Connecticut Valley's role as a center for the 2,500-square-mile region. It reminds us that settlement in the valley predates that of Berkshire to the west and central Massachusetts to the east. But by lumping such a varied area under one name, it downplays the existence of the hill country on either side of the valley and the very real differences within the valley itself.

We have described the Deerfield–Greenfield area as the Upper Pioneer Valley, a section within Upcountry Massachusetts, because of its close link to the surrounding hilltowns and Mohawk Trail.

The Five College area, described within this section, is its own world, one frequently referred to as the center for the New Age culture (or is it post New Age now?) of New England. Each of the colleges—Mount Holyoke, Hampshire, Amherst, Smith, and the University of Massachusetts—is worth visiting simply for the quality of its museums. Together they offer an unbeatable calendar of theater, lectures, and varied entertainment (much of it open to the public). Local restaurants and shops are, of course, student- and faculty-geared (many are run by alumni of the colleges), as are the ample recreational facilities.

Holyoke, a classic nineteenth-century planned mill city, is ignored by most visitors to the college towns, but it shouldn't be. The new Heritage State Park complex is well worth a stop and surrounding mill buildings harbor craft studios and outlets.

Springfield, the largest city in Western Massachusetts, forms the centerpiece for the lower valley. It was founded in 1636 by a group of Puritans from Roxbury but was upstaged by Northampton until 1777, when it was chosen for the site of an armory. Skilled workmen flocked to the spot and speedily began turning out guns, paper cartridges, and cartridge boxes for the Patriot cause. These went down the river.

It is difficult today to grasp the former importance of the Connecticut River. A number of ships were built on West Springfield's Common around 1800, and by the 1830s steamboats were making round-trips between Hartford and the head of navigation at Wells River, Vermont. In 1794 the country's first canal was built around the falls at South Hadley. At the height of the subsequent canal-building craze, Northampton citizens funded construction of a canal system that linked them with New Haven.

The valley today is distinguished by its number of extensive manicured parks, its elaborate stone and brick public buildings,

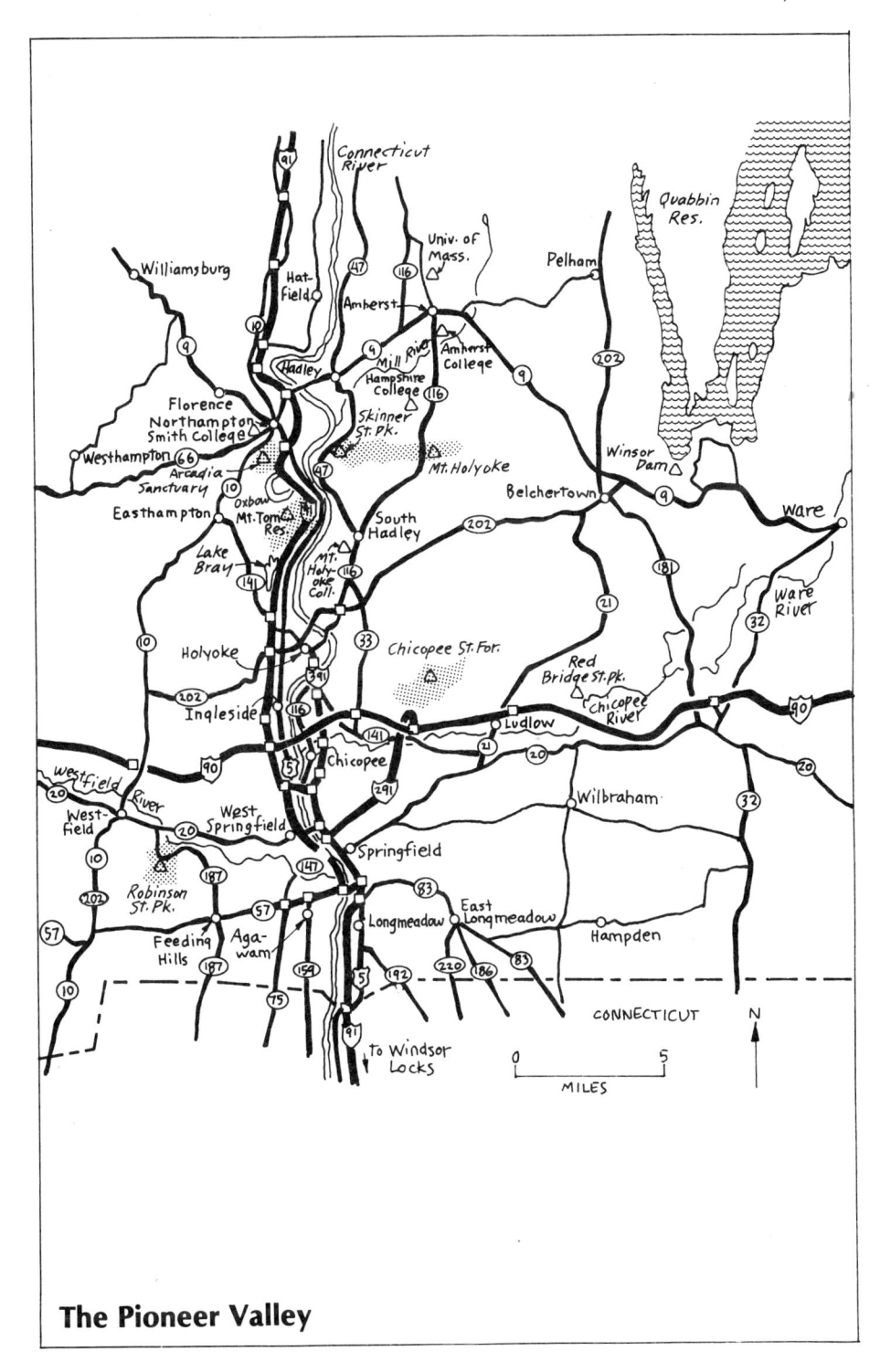

The Pioneer Valley

and its institutions designed in every revival style. All these are gifts of the nineteenth-century philanthropists, who refused to be forgotten; each bears the donor's name. Mt. Holyoke stands in vast Skinner Park, given by a family who made their fortune producing satin. Northampton's 200-acre Look and 22-acre Child's Park were both donated by the industrialists whose names they bear. If you have a chance stop by the George Walter Vincent Smith Art Museum in Springfield; note the wall hung with portraits of the valley's pioneer industrialists, a formidable group.

The Five College Area

A fire and brimstone brand of Calvinism, trumpeted as it was by Jonathan Edwards from his Northampton pulpit, lingered on in the valley into the early nineteenth century, long after Boston had forgotten its Puritan horror of sin and embraced a more permissive Unitarianism.

It bred a concern for proper schooling. Amherst College was founded in 1821 by stern town patriarchs, and in 1837 an earnest, Buckland-bred teacher, named Mary Lyon, opened an Amherst Female Seminary in South Hadley. Amherst College and Mount Holyoke (as the female seminary became known) contributed more than their share of souls to the Protestant missionary cause. Young Emily Dickinson retreated home after a brief dose of Mary Lyon's regime to spend the remainder of her life a recluse, penning the powerful verses for which she is world-celebrated today, most of them puzzlings on the themes of death and eternity.

Subtly but surely education became a religion in its own right, and today it represents the area's leading industry. Amherst, Mount Holyoke, and Smith (founded in 1871, now the largest women's college in the world) stand easily among the country's top private colleges, and the town of Amherst is now dominated by the 1,200-acre campus of the University of Massachusetts, which enrolls 26,000. Its high-rise buildings form a startling contrast to the cows pasturing in its shadow. And, as if four educational giants were not enough for this small patch of valley floor, coeducational and experimental Hampshire College was opened in 1970.

Under a unique "Five College Plan" students at each of the institutions now enjoy access to courses, special lectures, and performances at the others. The buses that serve the five campuses last year carried 1.3 million passengers. The Northampton–Amherst–South Hadley area has become one lively campus for a student body of nearly 33,000.

In the past decade Northampton has emerged as the area's dining and shopping center and also as a showcase for one of the country's largest concentrations of craftspeople. It's also an antiques center.

Holyoke is a very different place, a planned brick mill city, which peaked in the late nineteenth century and bottomed out in the '50s–'70s. It is now coming back. The Holyoke Heritage State Park

Visitors Center dramatizes the history of the town and is a starting point for exploring what is offered—from weekend excursion trains to laser shows—in the city. There's also the adjacent new Children's Museum complex, shopping in old mills, and the recreation—from Alpine skiing to some spectacular hiking—on Mt. Tom above the city.

There was once a summit house on Mt. Tom, and there is still one atop Mt. Holyoke. At this writing there is talk of turning it into a restaurant or bed & breakfast and of restoring the cog- and cable-driven railway by which guests used to ascend. Some day soon this area may even be considered as much of a destination as it was in the 1880s, an era in which the rich and famous stayed at Holyoke's elegant Hotel Monat, attended its opera house, and then traveled upriver by steamboat, taking the perpendicular ride to the top to enjoy the expansive vista of the Connecticut Oxbow and the file of mountains that parade across the valley like so many dinosaurs.

AREA CODE 413

GUIDANCE **Pioneer Valley Convention and Visitors Bureau** (787-1548), 1500 Main Street, Springfield 01115, publishes a handy, annual booklet *Visitors Guide*.

Amherst Chamber of Commerce (253-9666), 11 Spring Street, Amherst 01002, maintains a brochure-packed year-round office in the basement of the Lord Jeffrey Inn (open weekdays 9–4) and an information booth on the Common, open May–October daily 10–4, except Sunday mornings.

Greater Northampton Chamber of Commerce (584-1900), 62 State Street, Northampton 01060. The chamber's office is a brick-box of a building that welcomes visitors year-round. It maintains a walk-in information booth across from the Hotel Northampton (Route 5 North) from Memorial to Labor Day, open daily 9–5.

Holyoke Heritage State Park (534-1723), 221 Appleton Street, Holyoke 01040, open daily 9–4:30, until 9 PM on Thursdays; closed Mondays off-season. Uniformed staff have information on the city as well as the park.

GETTING THERE By air: **Bradley Field,** see Springfield.

By train: **Amtrak** (1-800-272-7245) trains from New York stop in Northampton at 2:45 AM.

By bus: **Peter Pan Bus Lines** connects Amherst, South Hadley, and Northampton with Boston and Springfield; also Bradley Airport. It also connects Holyoke with Springfield and Boston. The local departure points are: in Amherst (586-0431) 79 South Pleasant Street; in Northampton (586-1030) Old South Street; in Holyoke (536-5330) 1607 Northampton Street.

GETTING AROUND **The Pioneer Valley Transit Authority,** better known as the PVTA (781-7882), offers frequent service between Springfield–Holyoke and Northampton–Amherst (586-5806).

Peter Pan Bus (see above) connects Northampton with Holyoke.

Limobility (584-0058), in Northampton, will chauffeur you around in a stretch-limo.

THE COLLEGES **Amherst College** (542-2328), Amherst 01002. Founded in 1821 to educate "promising but needy youths who wished to enter the ministry," Amherst is today one of the country's most selective colleges (enrolling 1,500 men and women), offering a B.A. and, in cooperation with the four other colleges, a Ph.D. Campus tours depart from the Admissions Office in Converse Hall, next to the parking area off College Street, weekdays year-round.

Sites to see include: **Mead Art Building** (542-2335), open weekdays 10–4:30, weekends 1–5, displays outstanding nineteenth-century paintings, Assyrian carvings, representative pieces from most periods, and a reassembled medieval dining hall.

Pratt Museum of Natural History (542-2233), open September through May, weekdays 9–3:30, Saturday 10–4, Sunday 2–4. Houses the skeletons of a number of dinosaurs, including "the world's largest mastodon"; also a collection of meteorites, dinosaur tracks, and fossils.

Emily Dickinson's Home (542-2321). Open only by previous appointment and then only for tours scheduled at 3:00, 3:45, and 4:30 on Tuesdays; also on Fridays between May and October (same hours). The "Mansion" at 280 Main Street was the first brick house to be built in Amherst. Emily Dickinson was born here and it formed the self-imposed confines of her world during the years (1855–1886) when she wrote her finest verse. Her bedroom has been restored to look as it did then (for more on the poet, see Jones Library).

Hampshire College (549-4600) is south of Amherst on Route 116, 893 West Street, Amherst 01002. Opened in 1970, this is a liberal arts college predicated on cooperative programming with the other four colleges. The 800-acre campus accommodates 1,600 students. Campus tours are geared to prospective students; other interested persons should contact the public relations office, ext. 780. The Art Gallery–Library Center is worth a visit: open Monday–Thursday 9–4:30.

Mount Holyoke College (538-2000), South Hadley 01075. Founded in 1837, Mount Holyoke is generally agreed to be the country's oldest women's college. The present enrollment is 1,850 women. The 800-acre campus, its center designed by Frederick Law Olmsted, contains ivied buildings in a number of revival styles, including an

Mount Holyoke College, the country's oldest institution of higher learning for women

outstanding library (walk in to get the full effect of the stained-glass windows). There are also Upper and Lower Lakes to walk around. Tours of the campus are offered by students frequently (daily September–May and weekdays May–August). Most leave from the Harriet Newhall Center across Route 116 from the campus, but Saturday afternoon they depart from Mary Lyon Hall (right inside the gates with the clock tower), also a source of walk-in campus information. The surrounding village is gap-toothed at present due to a fire that destroyed the valley's largest bookstore, among other things. The Odyssey Bookstore is the first occupant of the new village center, a new complex that will eventually include an inn and restaurant as well as shops.

Mount Holyoke College Art Museum (538-2245), open daily year-round, longer hours during the academic year, closed Thanksgiving, Christmas, and spring vacations. The modern building houses a solid permanent collection, which has been evolving since 1876. It includes some outstanding nineteenth-century landscapes and changing special exhibits.

Skinner Museum (538-2085), on Route 116, is open June–August, Wednesday–Sunday 2–5; also May, September, and October on Wednesday and Sunday 2–5. Housed in the 1846 church that once stood in the town of Prescott (flooded to help form the Quabbin Reservoir), this is a treasure trove: 4,000 items ranging from Indian artifacts to medieval sets of armor.

The Talcott Arboretum (538-2116) is a Victorian-style greenhouse crammed with exotic flora.

Also note **Mount Holyoke College Summer Theatre** under Entertainment.

Smith College (584-2700), Northampton 01063. Founded in 1875 for "the education of the intelligent gentlewoman," it currently enrolls some 2,660 women and also a small number of undergraduate men for two semesters as visitors under the Twelve College Exchange. The 125-acre campus includes 97 buildings, an eclectic mix of ages and styles. Don't miss Paradise Pond or the Lyman Plant House, known for its spring and fall flower shows. Tours are available through the Office of the Secretary of the College (584-0515), in College Hall (just inside the main gate), regularly Monday–Saturday in the academic year; weekdays in June, July, and August.

Museum of Art (548-2700, ext. 2760), Elm Street. Open daily except Monday, September–May; by appointment in June; and Tuesday–Saturday in July and August. An outstanding collection, including paintings by Picasso, Degas, Winslow Homer, and Whistler; sculpture by Rodin and Leonard Baskin.

University of Massachusetts (545-3017), Amherst 01002. Sited on the northern edge of town. The university now includes eight undergraduate schools and colleges, also graduate schools, in more than 150 buildings on a 1,200-acre campus. Some 5,500 courses are offered by 1,300 faculty members to 26,000 students. Hour-long tours (phone: 545-2621) leave the campus center concourse twice daily, except holidays during the school year and weekdays June–August (when they depart from the Whitmore Administration Building). The number listed above is the Whitmore Information Desk, open 10–3.

Fine Arts Center and Gallery (545-1945). A wide variety of top performances in theater, music, and dance are offered September–May. There are changing exhibits in the gallery here and in summer the theater is home for a resident company.

TO SEE AND DO In Amherst: **The Jones Library** (256-0246), 43 Amity Street. Special Collections. Open Monday–Friday 9–5, Saturday 10–5. One of New England's most welcoming libraries, this stone, hip-roofed building was purposely built to resemble a home (its construction was funded entirely through the bequest of a former Amherst resident who made his fortune in the Chicago lumber business). It's known for collections of works by two former Amherst residents: Emily Dickinson and Robert Frost. Because Emily Dickinson's home is so difficult to gain access to (see Amherst College), the room devoted to the poet—which always displays the hand penciled originals of several of her poems as well as portraits and a miniature of her room—is a popular pilgrimage point. The collection itself includes 6,000 items, and the Robert Frost Room houses 11,000 items, including signed editions, manuscripts, the woodcut prints and blocks created for Frost's books, and photographs of the poet.

The Strong House (253-2678), 67 Amity Street. Open June through September, Tuesday and Saturday. This high, hip-roofed house was built in 1744 and houses the Amherst Historical Society's collection of toys, tools, and artifacts from two centuries. The fine eighteenth-century garden is maintained by the Amherst Garden Club. $1 admission, children free.

In Hadley: **Forty Acres** (584-4699), 130 River Drive. Its proper name is the Porter-Phelps-Huntington House Museum and it is on Route 47, two miles north of the junction of Routes 9 and 47. Open for one-hour tours Saturday–Wednesday 1–4:30. One of the most beautiful historic houses in New England, this aristocratic old farm was built right on the banks of the Connecticut River in 1752, and there have been no structural changes since 1799. The furnishings have accumulated over ten generations, conveying a vivid sense of how its owners lived. Each Saturday in July and August from 2:30 to 4:30 tea and pastries are served on the veranda while musicians play ($3.50). On summer Sunday afternoons at 3:00 there are concerts in the sunken garden (picnickers are welcome before and after), which is also the scene of Wednesday evening storytelling and folk music (7 PM). There are also monthly exhibits in the Corn Barn. $2 per adult, $.75 for children.

The Farm Museum, junction Routes 9 and 7. Open May through October 12, 10–4:30; Sundays 1:30–4:30. The 1782 barn from Forty Acres was moved in 1930 to its present site near the 1808 First Congregational Church and white pillared Town Hall. It houses old broom-making machines (broom corn was once the town's chief crop), hay tedders and other old farm implements, pottery, an old stagecoach from Hardwick, and other assorted mementoes of life in the valley. Free.

In Granby: **Dino Land** (467-9566), Aldrich Street off Route 116, 3 miles north of the village of South Hadley but technically in Granby. Open mid-April until snow. Locally found dinosaur tracks are on exhibit. $2, adult; $1, child.

In Northampton: **Northampton Historical Society** (584-6011), 46–66 Bridge Street, Route 9. Open for tours Wednesdays, Fridays, and Sundays 2–4:30, also by appointment. There are three houses, two of them maintained as house museums: the **Parsons House,** which dates in part from 1658 but has a nineteenth-century parlor with memorabilia from the Prospect House hotel on top of Mount Holyoke (currently under restoration), and the **Shepherd House,** a mid-nineteenth-century home reflecting life-styles over three generations. The barn behind displays trade signs and weathervanes, among other things. $1.75 for two houses, $.50 for the barn; children $.50 per building.

Forbes Library (584-8399), 20 West Street. The Calvin Coolidge Room is open Monday, Tuesday, and Thursday 9–6; Wednesday 9–9; Friday and Saturday 9–5. This is a fascinating trove of memorabilia about the Amherst graduate who lived in Northampton for 38 years before becoming Massachusetts' governor and eventually president. There is also an art gallery with changing exhibits.

In Holyoke: **Holyoke Heritage State Park** (534-1723), 221 Appleton Street (follow signs for downtown). Open daily 9–4:30, until 9 PM on Thursdays, closed Mondays in winter. The imposing, round, brick Visitors Center is set on a five-acre urban plaza with restored 1920s rail cars parked on the tracks that happen to run through. Inside exhibits tell a remarkable story: In 1847 Boston investors formed the Hadley Falls Company, buying 1,000 acres here on the Connecticut, envisioning 54 cotton mills utilizing the power of the 60-foot falls. The company and its dam went bust but was soon replaced by the Holyoke Water Power Company, until very recently the city's major force. You learn that Holyoke is a classic, planned mill city. Its four and a half miles of canals rise in tiers past what seems to be a like number of brick mills. The commercial area is set in a neat grid above the mills. Housing changes with the altitude, from handsome 1840s brick workers' housing (most of it now restored) near the river, through hundreds of more hastily built late nineteenth- and early twentieth-century tenements, to the mill owners' mansions above, and above that the delights of the mountaintop park on Mount Tom. There are exhibits about Holyoke's industries: paper, cotton, silk, machinery, wire, thread, and more. A short film conveys a sense of the city's late nineteenth-century vitality, of the era in which immigrants turned neighborhoods into "Little" Ireland, Poland, France, and a half dozen more bastions. The multi-level exhibits demand roughly an hour. Frequent events range from guided walking tours (throughout the city) and Sunday films to train excursions.

The Children's Museum at Holyoke (536-KIDS), open daily, is set to occupy the brick mill building adjacent to the park in 1987. The volunteer-staffed museum includes a wide variety of exhibits, a recycling center, and store. $2 admission. A cafe and a Volleyball Hall of Fame, with exhibits depicting the invention of the sport in Holyoke, will also be part of this complex.

Wistariahurst Museum (534-2216), 238 Cabot Street. Open Tuesday–Saturday 1–5. This elegant Victorian mansion was moved, in part, from its original site on the Mill River north of Northampton. In 1874 the Haydenville Dam collapsed, destroying Joseph Skinner's silk mill. The developing city of Holyoke invited him to rebuild what became the world's largest silk mill. For many decades the mansion has served as a cultural center for the city, its Tiffany glass windows, inlaid floors, and music room serving as a backdrop for frequent concerts and workshops.

Holyoke Water Power Company (536-5520), canals and fish viewing station. Holyoke still has its original four and one-half miles of working canals, still controlled by the company that has owned them since 1859. Holyoke Water Power still furnishes most of the electricity for the city's industries. In summer months it maintains a series of 50-foot-high fountains on the second level canal (Lyman Street), and a new fish viewing station at the dam is open in April when you can watch shad and salmon making their way upriver to spawn.

PARKS AND RESERVATIONS **The Holyoke Range State Park** (253-2885), Route 116, Amherst. This dramatic, east–west range rises abruptly from the valley floor. It is the most striking feature of the area, visible everywhere from Belchertown to Northampton. But until the 1980s, it was only something to look at. Mount Holyoke at its western tip (see Skinner State Park) was the only accessible summit. In recent years the Department of Environmental Management has been systematically acquiring ownership of the entire nine-mile-long ridge line and to date has roughly 3,000 acres. From the Visitors Center at "the Notch" on Route 116 (open daily in season), trails lead to Bare Mountain, Round Top, Mt. Norwottuck, and connect with trails to Mt. Toby in Sunderland and Mt. Monadnock in New Hampshire. Ask about the Horse Caves in which Daniel Shays and his men are said to have sheltered after raiding the Springfield Armory (they are actually so shallow that two boy scouts and a pony would have trouble fitting in).

Skinner State Park (586-0350), Route 47, Hadley. In 1938 Joseph Skinner donated the Summit House and accompanying 375 acres to the state. The reservation's hiking paths and road all lead to a spectacular view out across the Connecticut River Oxbow. The Summit House (also known as Prospect House) dates back to 1821 and is the last survivor among dozens of similar inns that once stood atop New England mountains. Feasibility plans for its restoration are presently under study.

Quabbin Reservation (323-7221), 485 Ware Road, off Route 9 between Ware and Belchertown; follow signs for Winsor Dam. The Visitors Center, just founded in 1984 by Friends of Quabbin, is housed in the brick administration building, open 7:30–4 on weekdays, 10–4 on weekends. This is the source of maps ($3.15 to $5, depending on the finish) that detail the hiking paths within the 87-square-mile reservation, which rims the reservoir's 181 miles of shoreline. The Visitors Center offers the best approach to this wilderness, telling the story of one of the world's largest reservoirs. Boston's Metropolitan District Commission (MDC) created it in the '30s by flooding four towns (Enfield, Greenwich, Prescott, and Dana), displacing 2,500 residents from their 650 homes. It is now a wildlife preserve, famed for its unusual number of wild turkeys and bald eagles. Since the '50s fishermen have been permitted to use motor boats on the upper reaches of Quabbin, but none are permitted near the southern end. Gazing out from the Winsor Dam you are struck by the silence of this vast, hill-rimmed lake. The 12-square-mile Quabbin Reservoir Park, adjoining the Administration Center, offers 20 miles of hiking trails and a paved road to Quabbin Hill. The Quabbin Cemetery is also here, final resting place for the 7,500 bodies that were once buried in the Swift River Valley's 34 cemeteries. Also see Fishing and the North of Quabbin section of Upcountry Massachusetts.

The Amherst Conservation Commission (256-1413), Amherst Town Hall, maintains more than 500 acres for walking, birding, and ski-touring. These include the Mill River Conservation Area (State Street off Pine), good for swimming and picnicking. Pick up a copy of *Around and About Amherst* ($1.50) from the Chamber or local bookstores.

Northampton Conservation Areas include **Robert's Hill** in Florence (overlooking the Lower Leeds reservoir); **Fitzgerald Lake** in Florence; and **Childs Park** (30 acres off Elm and Prospect Street).

Look Memorial Park (584-5457), Route 9 in Florence, offers 150 acres with picnicking, swimming and wading pools, pedal boating and canoeing on Willow Lake, a playground, the Longwoods Zoo, the Pines Outdoor Theater (summer concerts and theater), and the Pancake Cabin Restaurant; open Memorial through Labor Day.

Dinosaur Tracks, in Holyoke. Thousands of these tracks were uncovered along the riverbank during construction of I-91; the Trustees of Reservations now protect an eight-acre stretch of these Triassic beds off Route 5 north of Holyoke. Look for the Trustees sign.

Mt. Tom State Reservation (527-4805). Access from Route 5 in Holyoke or Route 141, Easthampton. This 1,800-acre mountaintop woodland contains 30 miles of trails, picnic tables, a lookout tower, and the Robert Cole Museum (open May 30–Labor Day), with nature exhibits. Goat Peak has a spectacular view across the valley. In winter the road isn't plowed, but you can ski or snowshoe in. Lake Bray offers fishing in summer.

WILDLIFE SANCTUARIES **Arcadia Wildlife Sanctuary** (584-3009). Grounds open dawn to dusk except Mondays (unless a holiday); the office is staffed from 9–3 Tuesday–Friday; 1–4 on Saturday. Accessible from Northampton (take Lovefield to Clapp Street) and Route 10 (off Route 5) in Easthampton. This Massachusetts Audubon Sanctuary owns more than 500 acres of field, woodland, and marsh on the Connecticut River Oxbow. Walk out the Cedar Trail and along the Mill River to look out over the Arcadia Marsh from the observation tower. Duckling Trail is a short loop for children. The Conservation Center offers a full program of guided walks, canoe trips, and camp-outs; also an August week of family camping on the Mount Holyoke College campus across the river. $1.50 per person, $.75 for children aged 6–16.

Hitchcock Center for the Environment (256-6006) at the Larch Hill Conservation Area, one mile south of Amherst center on Route 116. The 25 acres include hiking trails and the center offers a variety of lectures and workshops; also exhibits local artwork.

AMUSEMENT PARKS **Mountain Park** (532-4418), Route 5 in Holyoke, open mid-June to Labor Day, then weekends through October. This is a great old-fashioned amusement area with a small roller coaster, 14 "major" and 14 kiddie rides, also space for picnicking. No admission.

Alpine Slide at Mt. Tom Ski Area (536-0416), Route 5, Holyoke. Open daily 10–10 in July and August; weekends noon–8 mid-May to late June and after Labor Day to mid-October. Take the chair lift to the top and coast down. $3.25 per ride, $6.95 for three rides; $3.25 for a half hour on the water slide. Snacks and light meals in the base lodge cafe.

BALLOONING   **Silver Eagle Balloon** (549-2660), in North Amherst, takes paying passengers.

BICYCLING   Bike rentals are available from **Peloton Sports** in Amherst (549-6904) at 1 East Pleasant Street, and in Northampton (584-1016) at 15 State Street. The shop keeps a current schedule of rides led by the Franklin-Hampshire Freewheelers Cycling Club. A pamphlet guide to six local rides is available from the Pioneer Valley Convention and Visitors Bureau. *Bicycle Touring in the Pioneer Valley* by Nancy Jane (University of Massachusetts Press) is available at local bookstores.

BOATING   See Canoeing for description of the Connecticut. **Mitch's Marina** (584-7932) and the **Oxbow Marina** (584-2775; rentals, instruction) in Northampton; and **Brunelle's Marina** (536-3232) in South Hadley all charge for use of their launch areas. There is also a state access ramp 1.4 miles north of Hatfield Center, another off Route 5 at the Oxbow in Easthampton.

CANOEING   The 16-mile stretch of the Connecticut River above the Holyoke Dam is heavily used on summer weekends by water skiers, fishermen, and power boat owners as well as canoeists. Canoes can be rented from **Sportsman's Marina** (584-7141) in Hadley and guided tours are available both from **Arcadia Wildlife Sanctuary** (see Wildlife Sanctuaries) and from the **Connecticut River Wa-**

Belchertown Common

tershed Council (584-0057), 125 Combs Road, Easthampton, source of a pamphlet *It's Your River*, showing the river access points at Sportsman's and Mitch's Marinas in Hadley, at Oxbow Marina in Northampton, at the Oxbow off Route 5 in Northampton, and at Brunelle's Marina in South Hadley.

HIKING In addition to the trails described above (see Parks and Reservations, Wildlife Sanctuaries), there is the long-distance Metacomet–Monadnock Trail, which traverses the ridge of the Mt. Holyoke range, continuing north through Warwick to Mt. Monadnock in New Hampshire and south (the logistics of getting across the Connecticut and I-91 are a bit fuzzy) to Mt. Tom and on into Connecticut. A copy of the trail guide is available for $3 from: Walter Banfield, Pratts Corner Road, Amherst 01002. For a pamphlet guide contact the Trails Program, DEM, Division of Planning, 725 Friends Street, Boston 02914. The chief stretches of the M&M trail in the valley are the **Holyoke Range Trail,** the **Mount Tom Range Trail, Holland Glen** (a steep-sided ravine with cascades tumbling through hemlock forests), **Mount Lincoln,** and **Mount Orient** in Pelham.

HORSEBACK RIDING See Upper Pioneer Valley in Upcountry Massachusetts chapter. Note that U Mass, Mount Holyoke College, and Smith College all have excellent riding programs that permit limited public access.

FISHING **Quabbin Reservoir** (see Parks and Reservations) is the area's prime fishing hole. Both shore and boat fishing seasons run from the third Saturday in April to the third Saturday in October (fly fishing in the catch-and-release area below Winsor Dam is open all year); boat rentals are available at Gate 8 (between Pelham and Belchertown). Landlocked salmon and lake trout are the big catch, but smallmouth bass, white perch, and bullheads can be found later in the season. In late May and early June salmon shad can be found in the Connecticut River, especially below the Holyoke bridge. Salmon fishing is forbidden in the Connecticut; each spring they return in larger numbers to spawn (a fish ladder helps them up over Holyoke Falls: for details about the underwater facility where you can view them at Turners Falls see the Upper Pioneer Valley). For advice about local fishing contact the **Fish and Wildlife Office** in Hadley (586-4416).

GOLF In Amherst: **Amherst Golf Club** (256-6894), nine holes. **Hickory Ridge Country Club** (256-6638), an 18-hole, championship course with a clubhouse and snack bar. **Cherry Hill** (253-9935), a public 9-hole course in North Amherst.

In South Hadley: **The Orchards** (538-2543), an 18-hole golf course.

In Belchertown: **Mill Valley Golf Course** (323-4079).

In Northampton: **Northampton Country Club** (584-0106); **Pine Grove Golf Club** (584-4750), 18 holes.

In Holyoke: **Holyoke Country Club** (534-1933), 18 holes, clubhouse.

SWIMMING In Amherst the unofficial swimming hole is **Factory Hollow Pond** (also known as Puffers Pond) in the Upper Mill River Conservation Area. Also check **Look Park** in Northampton under Parks and Reservations and **Lake Wyola** under Upper Pioneer Valley.

ALPINE SKIING **Mt. Tom** (536-0416/0516), Route 5, Holyoke. This is a teaching and, frankly, locally geared mountain, with Christmas and February vacation ski camps for area youngsters.

> Vertical drop: 680 feet
> Terrain: 17 trails and slopes
> Lifts: 3 chairs, 5 tows, 3 bars
> Night Skiing: nightly
> Facilities: base lodge, ski shop, large ski school
> Snowmaking: 100%
> Rates: $21 per adult, $19 per child weekends; $2 less midweek.

CROSS-COUNTRY SKIING Check Mt. Tom and Holyoke Range under Parks and Reservations.

HOTELS AND INNS **Yankee Pedlar Inn** (532-9494), 1866 Northampton Street (Route 5), Holyoke 01040. A Victorian house, now a large, popular restaurant, serves as centerpiece for a complex of clapboard buildings containing 47 rooms, each with private bath and individually furnished with a mix of antiques and reproductions, including a number of canopied, queen-size beds. $48–$53 double, $53–$61 for suites.

Hotel Northampton (584-3100), 36 King Street, Northampton 01060. This is one of New England's few surviving, locally owned, in-town hotels, a five-story brick building that has evolved over the years from Wiggins Tavern (still a popular restaurant in its bowels) through a variety of nineteenth- and early twentieth-century additions. The 75 guest rooms, all with private bath, TV, radio, phones, and air conditioning, have been recently refurbished with flowery wallpaper and reproduction antiques; a few have canopied beds and fireplaces. $52–$75 double occupancy.

Note that the 47-room **Lord Jeffery Inn** on the Common in Amherst is closed at this writing but will, we assume, reopen within the life of this book.

BED & BREAKFASTS **Amity House** (549-6446), 194 Amity Street, Amherst 01002. Molly Turner welcomes guests in her spacious Queen Anne-style house near the middle of town. There are four guest rooms, all bright, roomy, and nicely furnished; also an inviting living and dining room for guests. The morning croissants come by UPS from Vie de France in Boston. $35 single, $45 double, $10 per extra person.

The Beeches (586-9288), Hampton Terrace, Northampton 01060.

Built in 1914, this mansion was the home of Calvin Coolidge in the 1930s. Stockbroker Tudor with many very modern, clean-lined touches, this is an unusually bright house high on a knoll with views across the extensive acreage of the Holyoke Range. Local ordinance permits them to rent only three rooms, two with fireplaces and one with an immense bathroom. $50–$60 double includes a gourmet breakfast, maybe Eggs Benedict with whole wheat muffins and asparagus. Daisy Mathias loves to cook but, because she works and mothers, accepts guests only on weekends and on 26 weekdays scattered through the year.

The Knoll (584-8164), 230 North Main Street, Florence 01060. This large, attractive home is set on a knoll overlooking 17 acres of farmland and forest. Look Park is a few minutes' walk. Lee and Ed Lesko welcome guests and have three rooms, two with double beds, one with twins. No smoking please. $30 single, $40 double.

Wildwood Inn (967-7798), 121 Church Street, Ware 01082. Margaret Lobenstine shares her enthusiasm and her Victorian house with its five guest rooms, nicely furnished with antiques, no private baths. Breakfasts of homemade breads and peach butter are included in the $31–$54 double, range depends on the room and season.

Outlook Farm (527-0633), Westhampton 01060. Built in 1781 as a tavern, now a working farm set in apple, peach, and pear orchards. There are two guest rooms (sharing one bath), living room with TV, a pool, and hiking and ski trails on 200 acres. $35–$40 includes a full breakfast.

Bed & Breakfast Reservation Services with hosts in this area include: **Pineapple Hospitality** (617-990-1696), 384 Rodney French Boulevard, New Bedford 02744.

Berkshire Bed & Breakfast (268-7925), 106 South Street, Williamsburg 01096.

MOTELS **Autumn Inn** (584-7660), 259 Elm Street, Northampton 01060. This is a splendidly built and maintained 30-room motel, built for and geared to parents of Smith students. Rooms are large with double and single beds, TV, phones, and private baths. Breakfast and lunch are served in an attractive coffee shop with a huge hearth, and there is a landscaped pool out back. $50–$58 for rooms, $72–$80 for suites.

Hilton Inn (586-1211), junction Routes 5 and I-91, Northampton. A resort motel with 125 rooms, an indoor and outdoor pool, sauna, game room, and lighted tennis court; also a locally popular restaurant (Page's Loft). $58–$64 double, $48–$58 for studio rooms, $116–$148 for suites.

Campus Center Hotel (549-6000), Murray D. Lincoln Campus Center, University of Massachusetts 01003. A high-rise building with 160 rooms (each has a double and single bed, color TV), $48 double.

DINING OUT   **Beardsley's Cafe** (586-2699), 140 Main Street, Northampton. Open for lunch, dinner, and Sunday brunch. White linen and an Edwardian decor; prints by Beardsley create the right ambiance for grilled salmon, delicate veal dishes, and fresh game birds. Entrees average $12 at dinner.

Hot Tomato's (584-0010), 12 Crafts Street. This is a small, informal place decorated with tomato prints. Pasta is the specialty, made daily along with all the sauces, and surprisingly light. Pasta Pomidor, for instance, includes artichoke hearts, broccoli, and prosciutto, sauteed in a fresh dill cream sauce over tomato fettucini ($9.25). The menu is large, including rabbit and veal dishes. Dinner runs $7.25–$12.95, and lighter fare like fried mozzarella and antipasto is served in the Cafe Pomidoro up front.

Sze's (586-5708), 50 Main Street, Northampton. Open for lunch, dinner, and Sunday brunch buffet. The decor is soothing and the fare is Chinese: shredded pork with Peking sauce, crispy fish and shredded pork with Peking sauce. Entrees in the $6–$10 range at dinner.

Carbur's Restaurant (586-1978), Route 9 in Hadley. Open for lunch and dinner. Prime rib, steaks, and seafood (including southern-style fried frogs legs) head the menu and the decor is nostalgia: brass, eclectic antiques. There is also an extensive sandwich menu. Dinner runs $7.25–$12.95.

Plumbley's (253-9586), 30 Boltwood Walk (just off the Common), Amherst. This is a high Victorian mansion geared to splurging students, with dishes like Baked Halibut Marucca and Veal Provencale under $10; Sunday brunch is big.

Log Cabin (536-7700), Easthampton Road, Holyoke. Open for lunch and dinner. This is a large old dining landmark set near the top of the Mt. Tom range with a spectacular view and an all American menu, the kind of place where you take your mother or have an office party; moderately expensive.

Fitzwilly's (584-8666), 23 Main Street, Northampton. Open daily for lunch, dinner, and Sunday brunch. This is one of New England's original fern bars: brick walls, plenty of copper, antiques, and hanging plants. It all works, including the great deli sandwiches and salads; moderate.

Yankee Pedlar (532-9494), 1866 Northampton Street, Holyoke. Breakfast, lunch, and dinner. The decor is an eclectic mix of antiques and local nostalgia, varying with the bars and dining rooms. The new owner, a CIA-trained chef, has broadened the traditional American menu to include continental dishes, including a dozen different kinds of crepes and quiches; moderate.

Page's Loft (586-1211), Northampton Hilton Inn, junction Routes 5 and 91. Open for all three meals. Dinners attract a large local following. The specialties are beef and seafood, $7.95–$15.95.

North Star Seafood Bar (586-9409), corner of Green and West Street, Northampton. Open for lunch and dinner except Monday; dinner only on Monday. Sushi is the specialty, along with a wide variety of seafood and vegetarian dishes, but you can also get a 10-ounce steak or apricot-glazed chicken, even a burger deluxe. $3.25–$9.25.

Top of the Campus (549-6000, ext. 639), Murray D. Lincoln Campus Center, U Mass, Amherst. Closed Sunday and for lunch on Saturday, otherwise open for lunch and dinner. On the 11th floor (the only 11th floor in this area) a pleasant dining room with a moderately priced ho-hum menu; commands a spectacular view.

Paul and Elizabeth's (584-4832), 150 Main Street in Thorne's Market, Northampton. Open for lunch and dinner except Sunday. An attractive brick-walled dining room features fresh seafood and tempura, vegetarian plates, salads, and fresh baked breads and desserts.

Wiggins Tavern (586-5000), 36 King Street, Northampton. Low-beamed and ancient looking, this restaurant in the Hotel Northampton is open for three meals and has a loyal following among locals as well as visitors; moderate.

India House (586-6344), 45 State Street, Northampton. Authentic, well-prepared Indian food, informal dining, Sunday brunch, under $10.

Jack August's (584-1197), 5 Bridge Street, Northampton. Closed Mondays, otherwise open for lunch and dinner. A long-standing, no frills fish restaurant featuring chowders, stews, and fish: fried, broiled, and baked; lobster too, $5–$10.

Golden Lemon (536-2751), 260 Appleton Street, Holyoke. Open for lunch and dinner, closed Sundays. A Victorian atmosphere, fine dining, continental menu, $10 average.

EATING OUT **Jakes** (584-9613), 17 King Street, Northampton. Open from 5:30 AM weekdays, 7 AM weekends, closes at 3 PM, but also open 11 PM–3 AM Friday and Saturday nights. Two storefronts, brick-walled, upbeat, popular.

Miss Florence Diner (584-3137), 99 Main Street (Route 9), Florence. Open 4 AM–10 PM daily. Known locally as "Miss Flo," great diner food, blue plate specials.

Judie's (253-3491), 51 North Pleasant Street. Open for lunch and dinner daily. The atmosphere (including a greenhouse area) and food is light: salads, quiche, popovers; also full course dinners.

La Cazuela (586-0400), 7 Old South Street, Northampton. Billed as "the Mexican Restaurant at Rahar's" this informal place occupies the rambling old hotel known as a semi-legal watering hole to generations of students. Nachos and tortillas are the specialty, also soups and salads. $1.85–$6.75.

The Bus and American Grill in Thorne's Marketplace (586-8104), 150 Main Street, Northampton. You order from the counter and then take your pick of seats at round tables in an adjoining dining space or downstairs in the bar. Pizza, salads, homemade soups, and the valley's best burgers. The chowder is in Styrofoam cups and the salad in plastic, but it tastes great (soup and salad come to $2.50), both served with speed.

Woodbridge Cafe (536-7341), junction Routes 116 and 47, South Hadley. Open daily for lunch and dinner, light meals, bar.

Classe Cafe (253-2291), 168 North Pleasant Street, Amherst. The atmosphere is upbeat and the fare runs from omelets through burgers to cheesecake, $1.85–$2.90.

Newman Center, U Mass. Just inside the main university entrance. If you are pressed for time and money, or want a full dose of student atmosphere, this is the place to lunch: a classic cafeteria with a wide variety of specials from the grill.

Sylvesters (586-5343), 111 Pleasant Street, Northampton. Homemade muffins, breads, coffee cakes. Great omelets. Open for breakfast and lunch.

Taco Villa (584-0673), 21 Center Street in Northampton, and (256-8217) off North Pleasant, through a well-marked alleyway, in Amherst. Open daily for lunch and dinner. Nachos, enchiladas, tostadas, and chili with atmosphere, prices in the $1.95 to $5 range.

ENTERTAINMENT The Five College Scene: Throughout the academic year The Five College Calendar (available from each of the colleges) is crammed with live theater, lectures, and films, most of them free.

The Fine Arts Center Concert Hall (545-2511), University of Massachusetts, Amherst, is the prime stage for area theater, music, dance, and special performances.

Mount Holyoke College Summer Theatre (538-2406/2118), at Mount Holyoke College, July through August, stages a lively mix of comedies and classics, also a children's theater and special children's events.

Beyond the Colleges: Northampton has its own community theater that performs, along with a variety of local dance groups, at the **Old School Common** (584-2310), 17 New South Street, Northampton.

The Iron Horse Cafe (584-0610), 20 Center Street, Northampton, is the action center for the area's '20s–'30s crowd: jazz, folk music, Nu-Wave music.

Pearl Street Cafe (584-7771), 10 Pearl Street. A popular disco, open evenings. Sophisticated atmosphere, live music or DJs.

Cinema: The local movie houses include **Amherst Cinema** (253-5426), 30 Amity Street; **Calvin Theater** (584-7327) has 99-cent Wednesday specials, 19 King Street, Northampton. **The Pleasant Street Theater** (586-0935), 27 Pleasant Street, Northampton, shows an outstanding selection of art, lesser known and regional films in its main theater and in the downstairs **Little Theater. Academy of Music** (584-8435), 274 Main Street, Northampton. Billed as the oldest continually operating movie theater in America. Built in 1890 as a theater, it retains its balconies and plush, foreign and American films.

SELECTIVE SHOPPING   Antiques: **The Pioneer Valley Antiques Dealers Association**, PO Box 244, Westfield 01086 (or from the Pioneer Valley Association) publishes a pamphlet guide to its 32 members. Northampton is a particularly rich hunting ground with a half dozen shops within a few blocks of each other along Bridge and Market streets.

Crafts: Some 1,500 craftspeople are said to work in Western Massachusetts, exhibiting at local fairs and at the American Craft Council's annual June fair in West Springfield. Northampton is the major showcase for craftspeople from throughout the region. Galleries include **Pinch Pottery** (586-4509), Thornes Marketplace, 150 Main Street, Northampton, exhibiting art quality pottery (and only pottery); **Celebrations: An Artisans Collective** (584-2750), Old School Commons, representing more than 20 local craftspeople; **Skera** (586-4563), Old School Commons, sells quality craft work from throughout the country, as does the **Artisan Gallery** (586-1942) in Thorne's Marketplace. Individual galleries include **Don Muller** (586-1119), 16 Main Street, Northampton (glass, ceramics, jewelry); **Abraxis** (253-7401), 199 North Pleasant Street, Amherst; and **HoHo's**, 380 Dwight Street, Holyoke. The **Leverett Craftsmen and Artists**, one of the state's major crafts galleries, is just north of Amherst (see Upper Pioneer Valley). Local craftspeople who open their studios by appointment are listed in the *Western Massachusetts Craft Directory*, available from the Arts Extension Service (545-2360), Division of Continuing Education, University of Massachusetts, Amherst 01003.

Books: Book browsing is a major pastime in this area. In Amherst check out **Albion Bookshop,** 91 Main Street; **Food for Thought** (a worker-run cooperative, focusing on New Age subjects), 67 North Pleasant Street; the **Jeffery Amherst Bookshop,** 55 South Pleasant Street; and **Laos Religious Book Center,** 16 Spring Street. In Northampton the **Beyond Words Bookshop** occupies two separate spaces in Thornes Market; the **Bridge St. Bookshop,** 4 Bridge Street, does out of print searches as well as carrying new and used books; and the **Globe Bookshop,** 38 Pleasant Street, has a wide selection. The valley's outstanding bookshop, the **Odyssey** (534-7307), in South Hadley, occupies the first building in the new village Center. Note that this listing represents roughly one-third of the bookstores in the area.

Shopping Areas: **Thornes Marketplace,** 150 Main Street, Northampton has gone farther with the gallery-style shopping complex than any town we are aware of in New England. There are five stories, almost 40 stores, restaurants, galleries, and studios. You can buy a health-food cookie, towel rack, flowers, T-shirts, and one-of-a-kind tea pots. You can dine for $1 or $10 and feel like a prince. It's a magical place, open daily except Sunday, Thursdays until 9 PM. Note that if you can't find what you want, there is still a Woolworths five and dime a few doors down Main Street.

In Amherst there's more to North Pleasant Street than meets the driver's eye. Interesting stores like **Faces** (a student-geared combo of clothes and furnishings) and a dozen carriage shops like **The Mercantile** (Indian prints and Chinese gimcracks) fill two stories of a former motel (facing away from the street).

Holyoke Mall (536-1440), at Ingleside, Whiting Farms Road, off I-91. More than 100 stores are gathered in this immense, two-story mall, and 30 food booths line the sides of an atrium, filled with tables.

Hadley Village Barn Shops (584-6760), Route 9, Hadley. A shopping mall with oldie New England facades, geared to tourists.

Factory outlets are listed in a pamphlet available from the Pioneer Valley Convention and Visitors Bureau. Our favorites include **Elco Dress** (534-3767), 532 Main Street, Holyoke, and the half-dozen shops grouped in the Ware's old mill yard. These include: **Ware Sportswear** (967-5965), great for traditional women's clothing, and **Ware Knitters** (967-6261), good for sportswear.

Other: **Atkins Farms Fruit Bowl** (253-3243), open daily, except major holidays, 8 AM–6 PM. "The farms aren't all gone from the valley," says Howard Atkins, the entrepreneur who has put his grandfather's orchards to good use, harvesting the fruit from 25,000 trees (at least) on 290 acres. A few years ago he opened the fanciest fruit stand in New England: a handsome redwood-style building, housing aisles of vegetables and fruit, as much of it locally grown as possible. There is also a deli, bakery, gourmet corner, and tables where you can lunch well. In '87 there will be blueberry, raspberry, and peach picking across the road, on a slope overlooking Amherst. The Fruit Bowl is the scene of seasonal events like sleigh rides in January and February and pony rides in July.

SPECIAL EVENTS   February: **Northampton Winter Festival,** snow sculpture, fireworks.

March: **St. Patrick's Day Parade,** Holyoke.

May: **Western Massachusetts Appaloosa Horse Show** (584-2237), Three-County Fairgrounds, Northampton.

June: **"Le Festival,"** two-day celebration of French culture in the Pioneer Valley; **Crafts Night,** Northampton, open house and special exhibits throughout town.

July and August: Sunday afternoon concerts in Look Park, Northampton.

August: **Amherst's Teddy Bear Rally** (253-9666), a meeting of Teddy Bear dealers and lovers on the Amherst Common; **Train excursions** from Holyoke Heritage State Park; **Three County Fair** (584-2237), at the Three-County Fairground, Northampton.

December: **Celebration of Emily Dickinson's Birthday,** Amherst.

MEDICAL EMERGENCY Northampton: **Cooley Dickinson Hospital** (584-4090), 30 Locust Street.

Ware: **Mary Lane Hospital** (967-6211), 85 South Street.

Westfield: **Noble Hospital** (568-2811), 115 West Silver Street.

Springfield

Springfield's high-rises, shops, and major museums are all within a few blocks of each other, nicely set (if you forget I-91) by the Connecticut River.

Many visitors are drawn to the area by extravaganzas like the American Craft Council's Fair in June or the Eastern States Exposition in September, both staged in West Springfield near the museum village of Storrowtown. Others come to see the Basketball Hall of Fame or just to ride the Cyclone at Riverside.

Springfield itself rewards everyone who stops long enough to find her stately old Common and the museum-packed Quadrangle or explore the downtown shops and the Springfield Armory, now a campus.

The Armory Museum, founded as a research library in 1871, now houses the world's largest collection of small arms. The handsome brick complex, which occupies more than 15 acres of bluff above the city, was demilitarized in 1968 and is now Springfield Technical Community College. During the War of 1812 the armory turned Springfield into a boom town, and the nearer to the armory you lived, the more fashionable the address. On Sunday afternoons couples gathered to stroll the gardens and to admire the glitter of the stacked guns.

The armory's technicians (and their sons) went on to invent an impressive array of things: the first gas-powered car and steel-bladed ice skates, for instance. Ironically, while nineteenth-century industrialists bequeathed the Quadrangle Museums (which include outstanding art, science, and historical collections) and grand public spaces (Forest Park in Springfield and Stanley Park in Westfield), they never did establish a museum to dramatize all those industrial inventions. So the only thing anyone remembers is basketball.

AREA CODE 413

GUIDANCE Greater Springfield Convention and Visitors Bureau (787-1548), 600 Baystate Plaza, Springfield 01115.

Also see the Pioneer Valley introduction.

GETTING THERE By air: **Bradley International Airport** (203-627-3940) is just 18 miles south of Springfield in Windsor Locks, Connecticut. It is served by most national and regional carriers. Most major car rentals are represented here.

By train: AMTRAK (1-800-872-7245) connects Springfield with Hartford; New Haven; New York City; Philadelphia; Baltimore; Washington, DC; Montreal; and Chicago. There is frequent service from New York (change in New Haven) and one afternoon train a day (departing 5:15, arriving 7:40) from Boston. The bus depot is right around the corner from the train station.

By bus: **Peter Pan Bus** (781-3320), based in Springfield (with its own terminal at 1776 Main Street), connects with the airport, with Boston, Hartford, Cape Cod, Albany, and New York City.

Greyhound (781-1500) stops en route to Burlington, VT, New York City, and Albany.

Trailways (781-3320) stops en route to Hartford and New York City.

Vermont Transit (781-1500) stops en route to Vermont, New Hampshire, and Montreal.

GETTING AROUND Pioneer Valley Transit Authority (781-7882) serves Springfield–Holyoke; **Longeuil Transportation Company** (525-4571) connects Springfield with Longmeadow and Wilbraham; **Western Massachusetts Bus Company** (584-6481) serves Agawam and Riverside Park.

Taxis: **Airport Service of Springfield** (732-1101), **Diamond Cab** (732-1101), **Yellow Cab of Springfield** (732-2151).

PARKING Because downtown Springfield is such a relatively small, congested area of one-way streets, it's best to park as quickly as possible and walk around. Reasonably priced parking lots can be found under I-91, in the **Baystate West** complex (Worthington Street off Main), and in the **Civic Center Garage** (enter from East Court or Harrison Streets).

TO SEE AND DO The **Quadrangle** (739-3871), corner of State and Chestnut streets. A unique cultural Common: four museums and the city's main library assembled around a Green; the museums are all open noon until 5, free. The **Quadrangle Cafe** is open summers and there are frequent special events. The bronze Puritan by Augustus Saint-Gaudens stands at the entrance, welcoming visitors to each of the following:

The Museum of Fine Arts (732-6092). A 1930s Art Deco building with a courtyard, the museum houses a collection which touches the usual bases (ancient, medieval, modern) with paintings by Winslow Homer, John Singleton Copley, and a few by Erastus Field, a Leverett portrait painter, whose "Historic Monument of the American Republic" is a huge, absorbing fantasy. There are also changing exhibits.

George Walter Vincent Smith Art Museum (733-4214). The first museum on the Quadrangle (1899), this is a one-man collection housed in a magnificent palazzo. G. W. V. Smith (always called by his full name locally) amassed his fortune early enough to devote most of his life to spending it on ancient Japanese swords, armor, and art; on Islamic rugs; and on contemporary paintings, some of them depicting the Connecticut Valley. Italy, however, seems to have been a more popular subject, just as it was the inspiration for the city's architecture.

Connecticut Valley Historical Museum (732-3080). A dignified stone mansion houses collections devoted to the history of the entire Connecticut River Valley from 1635 to the present. Furnishings, paintings, and artifacts tell of hunters, farmers, merchants, craftsmen, and mills.

Science Museum (733-1194). Collections are geared to children, with exhibits on dinosaurs, Indians, and the cosmos. There is a "Discovery Place," a Bird Hall, a big freshwater aquarium, and an observatory.

Court Square, bounded by Court, Main, and State Streets. This imposing seventeenth-century square is still the center of the twentieth-century city. The most striking buildings are the "municipal group," the columned city and symphony halls, which flank the campanile (modeled after the bell tower in the Piazza San Marco in Venice). The observation tower is open weekdays 2:30–3:45; an antique, water-powered elevator hoists you to the top.

The white, columned **Old First Church** (737-1411 for tours, open weekdays 8:30–4:30 and weekends 8–2) was built in 1819; it's topped with a rooster, shipped from England in 1749. As the core of Springfield's Heritage State Park, the Square has had a facelift in recent years and is now the scene of a July 4th festival, which includes an open-air concert by the Springfield Symphony, an arts festival, and fireworks.

Springfield Armory National Historic Site (734-8551). One Armory Square, off Federal Street. Open daily 8:30–4:30. Federal Street is off State, an easy walk from the Quadrangle in good weather. Billed as the world's largest military collection, exhibits include an array of weapons used in every war since the Revolution. The 55-acre grounds, now a college campus, command a great view above the city. Aside from the Main Arsenal (built 1847), the site includes the palatial Commanding Officer's Quarters and the Master Armorer's House.

Basketball Hall of Fame (781-6500), 1150 West Columbus Avenue. Open daily 9–5 in summer, 10–5 September–June. The new three-story building located by I-91 right downtown (it's the one thing that's well marked from the interstate) tells the story of how Dr. James Naismith first threw a soccer ball into a peach basket in 1891. There is a basketball court, multi-image presentations of the game, and a hall depicting its greats down through the ages. New-

The Springfield Amory stands on a bluff, high above Springfield

comers are inaugurated each spring. $5 adults, $3 senior citizens and children aged 5–15.

Storrowtown Village (736-0632), in West Springfield at Eastern States Exposition Park, 1305 Memorial Avenue (Route 147). Open June–Labor Day, Monday–Saturday 11:30–4:30; the rest of the year by appointment; the gift shop and Old Storrowtown Tavern are open year-round (closed Sundays). Donated to the Exposition in 1929 by the late Mrs. James Storrow of Boston (the same family for whom Storrow Drive is named), this is a grouping of 13 restored, eighteenth-century buildings, one of the first museum villages in the country. All buildings were moved here from their original locations. $1.50 adult, $.75 per child over age six.

Springfield Indian Motorcycle Museum (737-2624), 33 Hendee Street. Open daily 1–5 and by appointment. From downtown Springfield take Route 291 to the St. James Avenue exit, then right onto Page Boulevard until you see the Historic Springfield sign. The museum is a brick garage-like building in an industrial complex. The collection includes a wide variety of vehicles, from old Columbia bikes to motorized toboggans. $2 adults, $1 children.

GREEN SPACE   **Forest Park** (787-6440). Three miles south from the center of town, just east of I-91, also off Route 21 (Sumner Street). The 750 acres includes a Kiddieland Zoo (open mid-April to mid-November, 10–4 daily; until 5 on Sundays and holidays), paddle boats ($4 per half hour), pony rides (on weekends), 21 miles of nature trails, tennis courts, picnic groves, swimming pools, and summer concerts at Barney Amphitheatre.

Stanley Park (568-9312), open mid-May to mid-October, 8–dusk. Endowed by the founder of Stanley Home Products, the 100-acre park is known for its extensive rose garden (over 50 varieties), mini-New England village, 96-foot-high carillon tower, Japanese Garden with Tea House, arboretum, and large fountain. Sunday evening concerts range from singing groups to the Springfield Symphony's Pops.

Laughing Brook Education Center & Wildlife Sanctuary (566-8034), 789 Main Street, Hampden (from I-91 in Springfield, take exit 4, Route 83, to Sumner Avenue for 3.6 miles). Off any main route to anywhere, this is a popular destination for families drawn by the one-time home of storyteller Thornton Burgess. It is now part of a 259-acre preserve owned by the Massachusetts Audubon Society, which includes hiking trails, fields, streams and a pond, caged local animals, a picnic pavillion, and a "touch and see" trail.

Chicopee Memorial State Park (594-9416), Burnett Road, Chicopee. A 574-acre park with two man-made lakes and the Chicopee and Morton Brook reservoirs. There is a beach and bathhouse at

Chicopee Reservoir, also four separate picnic areas and a two-mile, paved bicycle path. $3 day use fee in summer.

Blunt Park, Roosevelt Avenue, Springfield. A fitness trail with 10 stations fitted with equipment and signs indicating what exercise should be done and how often.

Riverfront Park, foot of State Street, Springfield. A six-acre, riverfront park offers a view of the Connecticut, otherwise walled from public access. This is the site of summer concerts, a viewing spot for regattas.

AMUSEMENT PARK   Riverside (786-9300), 1623 Main Street (Route 159), Agawam. Open weekends April–May; daily June through Labor Day; weekends in September; 10:30 AM–11 PM. Largest amusement park in New England: over 50 rides, including the Cyclonne roller coaster and three more coasters, a flume ride, midway, arcades, 35 food outlets, live entertainment. $10.95 per adult, $7.95 per child aged 3–8, for all rides, all days. No pets allowed. Stock car races on NASCAR speedway, Saturdays: $5.95 adults, $3.95 children.

BOATING   The Connecticut River is accessible from a state ramp on Medina Street, Chicopee; from **Bondi's Island,** off Route 5 in Agawam; and from **Pynchon Point,** off River Road in Agawam. **Red Bridge State Park** (594-9416), Plumley Street, Ludlow, offers boat access to the Chicopee River.

GOLF   In Springfield: the **Franconia Municipal Golf Club** (734-9334) and **Veterans Municipal Golf Course** (787-6449).

In Agawam: the **Agawam Country Club** (786-2194).

In Chicopee: the **Chicopee Country Club** (592-4156).

In East Longmeadow: the **Pine Knoll Executive Par 3 Course** (525-7647).

In Feeding Hills: the **Oak Ridge Golf Course** (786-9693) and **Saint Anne Country Club** (786-2088).

In Westfield: the **East Mountain Country Club** (568-1539) and the **Tekoa Country Club** (562-9858).

HIKING   See Green Space.

SWIMMING   See **Forest Park** and **Chicopee Memorial State Forest** under Green Space. **J. C. Robinson State Park** (786-2877), North Street, Agawam also offers swimming and picnicking.

LODGING   This is a convention city with a downtown high-rise **Mariott Hotel** (781-1777; 800-228-9290) and **Skyline Inn** (731-0900), both with indoor pools. A **Holiday Inn** (800-238-8000) and a half-dozen more chain motels, including a **Sheraton Tara** are due to open the summer of '87.

Greater Springfield Bed & Breakfast (739-7400), 25 Bellevue Avenue, Springfield 01108, is a reservation service for a number of homes in the Springfield area. $28–$35 single, $42–$48 double.

Gnome Crossing (739-3133), 11 Ingersoll Grove, Springfield. A fifteen-room mansion, convenient to downtown but with an in-ground pool, rooms with fireplaces, antiques. $42.50 for a single with private bath.

Berkshire Bed & Breakfast (268-7244) host in Longmeadow. A 1920s English country-style home in a residential area offers one double and one single antiques-furnished room, $30–$40; $5 extra for private bath.

DINING OUT **Chestnut Tree** (736-3637), 2 Matoon Street, Springfield. Open for lunch and dinner weekdays, dinner only on Saturday, brunch on Sunday. This is the current chic downtown dining spot: seafood and veal specials; expensive.

The Fort Restaurant (734-7475), 8 Fort Street (off Main), Springfield. Open daily for lunch and dinner, sandwiches served until midnight. A grand old downtown restaurant, hung with beer steins, serving imported wine and draft beers and a large menu of German specialties: Kassler Ripchen, Hasenpfeffer, and Wiener Schnitzel; also honeycomb tripe, fresh lobster, and Hungarian goulash. Seasonal specialties include a February wild game menu (where else can you try young bear or buffalo in wine sauce with spaetzle). Dinner runs $5–$15, lunch $2.95–$5.

Old Storrowtown Tavern (732-4188), Eastern State Fair Grounds, West Springfield (on Route 147). Open for lunch and dinner except Sundays. Built as the John Atkinson Tavern in Prescott (one of the towns drowned by the Quabbin Reservoir), it has a continental menu and a local following. Seafood, veal, and beef dishes are the specialty, $2.85–$10 for lunch, $7–$16 for dinner.

Twelve Pynchon (736-5036), 12 Pynchon Place, Springfield. In a restored 19th century hotel building across from City Hall, busy at lunch serving pastas, salads, specials; for dinner a continental menu.

Monte Carlo (734-6431), 1020 Memorial Avenue, West Springfield, opposite the Exposition grounds. Family-owned since 1934, a dining landmark; specialties include Beef Marsala, Veal Francaise, Zuppa de Pesce with Linguine; moderately expensive.

Orient Express (734-2318), 1441 Main Street (Center Square Mall). Open daily for lunch and dinner, on Sunday from 4 PM. Authentic Vietnamese cuisine prepared and served with traditional flare; moderate.

Bernadino's (592-2111), 17 Market Square, Chicopee. Open daily for lunch and dinner. Portuguese food in three elegant dining rooms, $10 average for entrees.

EATING OUT **Tilly's** (732-3613), 1390 Main Street, Springfield. Open 11:30

AM–12:00 PM daily, full dinners Wednesday–Saturday, closed Sunday. Homemade soups, quiches, breads, and desserts; daily specials, full dinners.

Ann Fields Country Pie Restaurant (739-4103), 337 East Columbus Avenue, Springfield. Open 7 AM–10 PM daily, featuring over 30 varieties of pies for dessert and takeout, full menu.

Ichabod's (739-7557), 80 Worthington Street. Open daily, lunch and dinner; weekends for dinner. A deli restaurant with a lively bar, reasonable prices.

Mr. C. Magoo's (736-4090), 84–90 Worthington Street, Springfield. Open 11 AM–11 PM daily except Sunday when there's brunch. Nineteenth-century saloon decor, food and spirits.

Schneider's Delicatessen (732-8664), 53 State Street. Open weekdays 7 AM–3 PM; closed weekends. A dependable, cafeteria-style delicatessen.

Berni's Dining Depot (539-9238), 749 James Street, Chicopee. Open weekdays from 6:30 AM, Saturday from 7:30; Sunday brunch. A restored dining car features seafood and home cooking; has beer and wine.

La Fiorentia (732-3151), 883 Main Street, Springfield. Open daily from 8 AM except Sunday, 7–3 PM. A genuine coffee house in the Italian South End. Real Cappucino, Cannoli.

Millie's Pierogi (594-4991), 129 Broadway, Chicopee Falls. Open daily except Sunday, 5–5 PM. A diner specializing in authentic pierogi (dumplings stuffed with a mix of meat, potato, cabbage, and cheese).

ENTERTAINMENT   **Stage West** (781-4470), 1 Columbus Center, Springfield; professional theater, November–May.

Springfield Civic Center and Symphony Hall (787-6610, Box Office: 787-6600), 1277 Main Street, Springfield. This complex, across from Court Square, stands on the site of the courthouse that Daniel Shays and his friends beseiged after the Revolution. It includes a 7,500-seat Grand Arena, which doubles as a theater, a basketball court for the NCAA Division II Championship Playoffs, and (with a coat of ice) as the home of the Springfield Indians hockey team and scene of annual Ice Capades. There is also a Little Arena, scene of a variety of live presentations.

Symphony Hall, the classic, columned music hall on Court Square itself, is the home of the Springfield Symphony Orchestra (733-2291). It also stages top name performers, Broadway shows, children's theater, and travelogues.

Nightspots: **Juke Box** (737-5317), 57 Taylor Street, Springfield. Nostalgia and music. Saturday night music of the '50s and '60s played out of a '57 Chevy.

Jazberry's (732-4606), 405 Dwight Street. Comedy on Wednesday evenings; Disco Thursday–Sunday.

Zone Center for the Arts (732-1995), 395 Dwight Street, Springfield. A gallery on the second floor of an industrial building, displays sculpture, paintings and photography by respected contemporary artists; also stages theater, music, poetry, and film.

SELECTIVE SHOPPING   **Steigers** (781-4211), 1477 Main Street. This is the home store of the Western Massachusetts chain, "in fashion since 1896." It's an old-fashioned department store complete with a men's shop, restaurant, and beauty salon.

Baystate West, 1500 Main Street, dwarfing Steigers, is a high-rise, indoor mall, harboring 70 shops and restaurants.

Johnson's (732-6222), 1379 Main Street. A two-floor bookstore that's got whatever you are looking for.

SPECIAL EVENTS   February: **Spring Flower Show** at the Civic Center.

May: **Peach Basket Festival,** includes enshrinement of newcomers to the Basketball Hall of Fame.

June: **The American Crafts Council's Fair** at the exposition grounds in West Springfield; **Laurel Week** in the Westfield River Valley.

June–August: **Summer Sounds,** free outdoor concerts Saturday evenings in Riverfront Park.

July–August: Sunday performances by the **Springfield Pops** in Stanley Park, Westfield; theatrical and musical performances in Forest Park, Sunday evenings. **Fourth of July Celebration**—the Symphony Orchestra performs, there's an arts festival, and fireworks in Court Square.

Mid-August: **Harambee Festival of Black Culture,** Winchester Square, Springfield.

September: **Glendi** (Greek festival), folk dances, crafts, and food at the Greek Cultural Center, Springfield; **Kielbassa Festival,** Polish music, dance, and food at Fairfield Mall, Chicopee; **Eastern States Exposition** ("The Big E": 732-2361), biggest annual fair in the East, livestock shows, horse shows, giant midway, entertainment, avenue of states, always runs 12 days including the third week in September; **Quadrangle Weekend** (737-1750), outdoor festivities, films, lectures, crafts demonstrations; **Mattoon Arts Festival,** an outdoor fair on a downtown street lined with brownstones and gas lights.

October: **Chicopee Octoberfest; Tip-Off Classic,** first official college basketball game of the season.

November: **Fall Color Festival** in Springfield, day after Thanksgiving.

December: **First Night,** the New Year's Eve Celebration, centered in the Quadrangle.

MEDICAL EMERGENCY   **Springfield: Mercy Hospital** (781-9100), 271 Carew Street. **Springfield Hospital Unit,** Baystate Medical Center (787-3233), 759 Chestnut Street. **Wesson Memorial Hospital Unit,** Baystate Medical Center (787-2500), 140 High Street.

Central Massachusetts

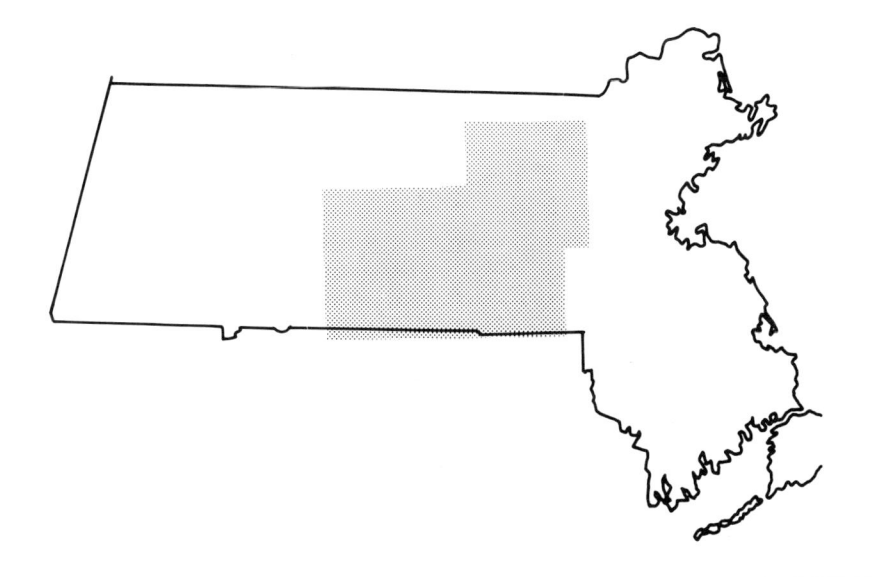

Old Sturbridge Village Country

Most Worcester County towns evolved their center villages between 1790 and 1830, an era in which churches, taverns, stores, and farms still clustered around the Common, and each community was a self-sufficient and self-contained entity. Today most of these towns still retain their steepled old church and Common, much as a family preserves its formal head-and-shoulders portrait of a nineteenth-century forebearer. At Old Sturbridge Village you explore the mills, shops, humbler homes, and farms that formed the body for that 1830s face. Based on thorough and ongoing research, the museum village offers vivid insights into life during this heavily romanticized era. Buildings straggle out from the Green along dirt roads. The carefully backbred farm animals are skinnier and shaggier than the current norm, and it is difficult to believe that a family of ten once crowded into the small house on the working farm. There is just one mansion in town—a square, Federal era home, where the local member of the rural gentry lived among his Boston-bought furnishings and passed city ideas on to his neighbors.

Although the more than 40 buildings in the village have been gathered from throughout New England, the story they tell is that of the surrounding countryside. We suggest that you allow a few days for the area: one day for Old Sturbridge Village (OSV) and its accretion of Route 20 shops; more days to find local swimming holes, orchards, antiques stores, and to explore the back roads of the Brookfields, Spencer, Hardwick, New Braintree, and Barre. This is rewarding countryside (almost) any time of year. We actually prefer the village in winter when there are far fewer people and the Publick House stages its Yankee Winter Weekends. Sturbridge represents the greatest concentration of lodging places (ranging from small classic inns and bed & breakfasts to large resort motels) between Boston and the Berkshires.

AREA CODE 617

GUIDANCE Sturbridge Area Tourist Association Information Center (347-7594), Route 20, opposite the entrance to Old Sturbridge Village. Open daily 10–5:30 in winter, 9:30–6 May–October. Staff answer mail inquiries (the zip is 01566) and help walk-ins. This is an unusually welcoming information center with wing chairs and racks of brochures. Staff make lodging and restaurant reservations on request, sell bus tickets, and offer a wide range of advice about the entire area.

GETTING THERE By bus: **Peter Pan Bus** (752-1717 for Sturbridge area) offers frequent service between Boston and Sturbridge. **Bonanza Bus** (800-556-3815) ties Sturbridge in with Lee; Springfield; Providence, RI; and Albany, NY; with connections to Cape Cod and New York City.

Sturbridge is at the junction of the Massachusetts Turnpike, I-84 to Hartford (and NYC) and Route 20.

GETTING AROUND A trackless trolley circulates between Sturbridge motels, Old Sturbridge Village, and the Route 20 shops, June–September; $1.

King Courier (832-5365) offers 24-hour limousine service to Bradley and Logan airports and also tours (reservations through the Sturbridge Information Center) to Quabbin Reservation and other local sites and to Sturbridge museums and restaurants.

TO SEE AND DO **Old Sturbridge Village** (347-3362), Route 20, Sturbridge. Open daily year-round except winter Mondays, Christmas, and New Year's Day. $8.50 per adult, $4 for children ages 6–15. Special rates for groups of more than 20. Leashed pets welcome, but strollers not allowed in museum buildings.

A non-profit museum, Old Sturbridge Village is one of the top attractions in New England. Expect to spend most of a day strolling the unpaved roads that wind around the Common and down to the Freeman Farm or through the covered bridge to the Mill Neighborhood. A film sets the tone. Be sure to talk with the costumed "interpreters": the shoemaker and printer are delighted to describe their daily lives (in the 1830s) and the minister's wife will tell you why she'd like a cookstove like her neighbor Mrs. Towne. Three water-powered mills are important features, as well as the cider mill, which operates for six weeks in the fall.

Notice the care with which the Knight Store has been stocked: English china, foreign fabrics, West Indian ginger and rum, tooth powder, and 2,000 more items drawn from throughout the world. You learn that the storekeeper was the town's link with seaboard cities, the trusted middleman who exchanged his neighbor's produce for manufactured staples and the luxuries of life. There are countless such discoveries.

In addition to the village buildings there is a Visitors Center, the adjacent Clock Gallery, and seasonal displays of glass, textiles, militia equipment, and lighting devices. There is both a cafeteria and more formal dining in the Tavern and an extensive gift shop. Frequent special events are staged and there are a variety of special crafts and theme programs, including hearthside cooking and dining in the homes (in winter only).

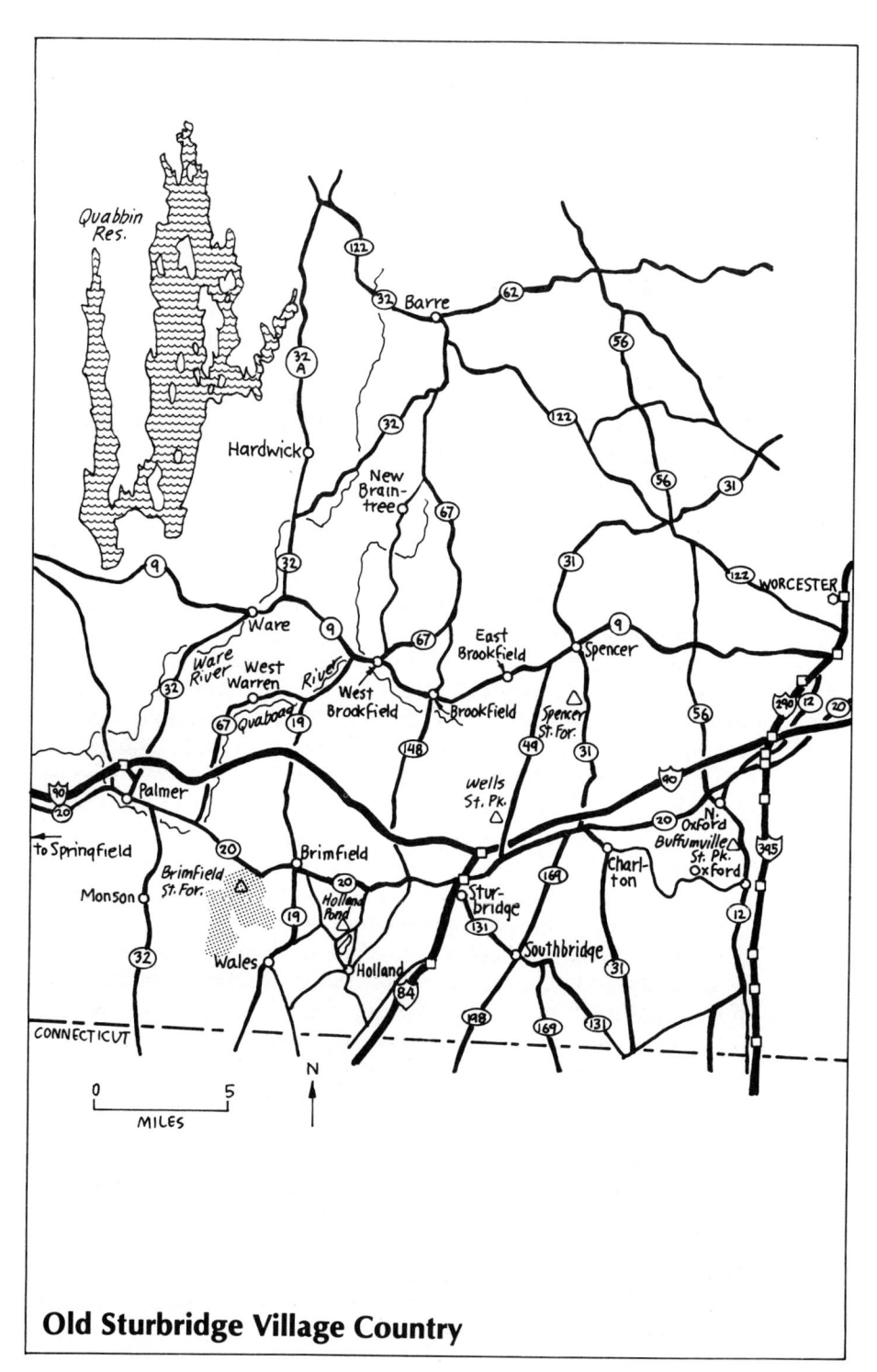

Old Sturbridge Village Country

The story of how Old Sturbridge Village came to be is a typical Massachusetts tale. It was founded through the philanthropy of brothers Albert Wells and J. Cheney Wells, Southbridge optics magnates. Their enthusiasm for antiques set them to collecting in such quantities that they eventually outgrew their home. So the family bought this 200-acre tract of meadow and woodlot on the Quenebaug River. Since its 1946 opening the museum has changed substantially, acquiring, through dedication to authenticity (its research library includes 20,000 books and manuscripts on early nineteenth-century life in New England rural towns), a life of its own. You come away with a genuine sense of how this area not only looked but also how it smelled and felt in the nineteenth century.

Other Sturbridge Museums: **Fairbanks Doll Museum** (347-9690), Hall Road (off Route 131) one-half mile south of the Public House. Open Tuesday–Sunday and Monday holidays, 1–5 and 7–9 PM; $1 ages 12 and up, 50 cents over age six. Some 2,500 dolls are displayed in a barn-like addition to the home of Kay and Philip Fairbanks. The dolls come from around the world and range in age from the 1830s to Cabbage Patch vintage.

Bethlehem in Sturbridge (347-3013), Stallion Hill. Continue on the road that runs off Route 20 to OSV. Open daily, year-round, 10–4. George Duquette has painstakingly crafted some 600 figures and buildings to re-create the Bethlehem nativity scene. Call before coming to make sure your visit doesn't coincide with a big bus group. From November to January there are two free shows daily (2 PM and 7 PM): thousands of tiny lights and a recorded narrative dramatize the Christmas story. No fee.

Sturbridge Auto Museum (867-2217), Route 20. In summer 10:30–9:30; September–November 10:30–5:30; closed December to late May. $2.50 per adult, $1 per child. There are some 30 steam, gas, and even electric cars here, including Pierce Arrows, Packards, and a classic 16-cylinder Cadillac.

St. Anne's Shrine (347-7338). There are two century-old churches just off Route 20, St. Anne's and St. Patrick's. The latter houses a collection of 60 Russian icons, some more than 200 years old. There is also a picnic ground and an open-air pavillion in which mass is celebrated on summer weekends.

Beyond Sturbridge: **American Optical Museum** (765-9711), off Route 131, Southbridge, in the American Optical Company's castle-like factory (use Mechanic Street entrance). Open weekdays 12–1 and Saturdays 12–4. Displays include eyeglass frames from four centuries (including a diamond-studded pair) and artifacts related to the town's industrial history.

Clara Barton's Birthplace (987-0498), 68 Clara Barton Road, off Route 12, North Oxford. Open June through mid-October, Tuesday, Thursday, Saturday, Sunday; the rest of the year by appointment. A charming house on a back road tells the story of the founder of the American Red Cross and of her work during and after the Civil War. Note that the clapboard house is just up the road from North Oxford Mills (great for braided rugs, see Selective Shopping) and handy to Buffumville Pond State Park (see State Parks and Swimming).

St. Joseph Abbey (885-3901), Route 31, Spencer. This is a Trappist monastery, famed for the beauty of its Gregorian chant (available on tapes and records), for its jams, and as a place to find peace. Visitors are welcome to hear daily mass in the side chapel at 7:05 AM; also for evening vespers. For details about staying here in the guest house, phone 885-3010.

STATE PARKS   **Brimfield State Forest** (245-9966), Dirth Hill Road, Brimfield. This is a 4,033-acre forest, but most visitors are interested only in the Dean Pond Recreation Area with its 100-foot beach and picnic facilities. Fishing, swimming, and boating are permitted and the Woodman Pond Group Camping Area has three bunk-room buildings.

Buffumville State Park (248-6348), Charlton Street, Oxford (from the center of Charlton, left onto Muggett Hill Road, 4 miles right on to Oxford Road, 2 miles on left). There is a beach here, open 10 AM–8 PM in season; swimming in Buffumville Reservoir. There are wildflowers under the White Pine Observatory, lady's slippers and lilies of the valley; also picnic facilities and a self-guided nature trail.

Holland Pond (245-3935). From Sturbridge west on Route 20 to Holland. East Brimfield Road south, 4 miles to Day Hill Road. There is swimming, a beach, and no less than 71 picnic tables, 21 grills, and a volleyball court. The pond is stocked with pike and is suitable for canoeing.

Streeter Point Recreation Area (347-9316), Sturbridge. There is swimming, a beach, picnicking, and a boat launch area. It's pleasant but marshy.

Spencer State Forest (885-2320), Howe Pond Road, Spencer. Swimming and picnicking at Howe Pond, trails used for hiking and horseback riding (note local stables under Recreation).

Wells State Park (347-9257), Route 49, Sturbridge. There are 55 campsites (first come, first serve, $5 per night) with a swimming beach and picnic facilities for campers.

GREEN SPACE   **Tantiusques Reservation,** Sturbridge, one mile west of Route 15. This 55-acre preserve includes a graphite or black lead mine, granted by the Indians to John Winthrop in 1644. Several open cuts that followed the original veins are still visible. Owned by the Trustees of Reservations.

The Asa Knight store in Old Sturbridge is stocked with the same items that it carried in the 1830s when it stood in Dummerston, Vermont

Old Sturbridge Village photo by Donald F. Easton

Norcross Wildlife Sanctuary (267-9654), Peck Road, Wales. Open year-round, Monday–Saturday 8–4; closed Sundays and holidays; free. An exceptional visitors center displays pictures of flowers, ferns, and trees native to the Eastern Seaboard, and the sanctuary itself has been planted to represent 80 percent of this continent's vegetation, including rare wildflowers. Birds and animals, needless to say, are protected within the area. The 3,000-acre preserve is a gift of Arthur D. Norcross, a Wales native who founded Norcross Greeting Cards.

Quabbin Reservation. See Five College Area and North of Quabbin in the Upcountry Massachusetts chapter.

BALLOONING The **Balloon School of Massachusetts** (413-245-7013), Brimfield, offers year-round rides, usually at daybreak. The $135 fee includes breakfast and the whole adventure takes under three hours with one hour in the air.

BICYCLING This is a relatively flat, rural area with many little-trafficked back roads. *Short Bike Rides in Greater Boston and Central Massachusetts* by Howard Stone (Globe Pequot Press) suggests some specific routes in the area. Westville Recreation Area offers good pedaling.

BOATING Two flood-control dams have turned the Quinebaug River into a chain of ponds and reservoirs, ideal for canoeing and sailboarding. A Quinebaugh River canoe trail map is available from the local state parks. On the Quaboad River a canoe launch (and fishing) spot can be found in Brookfield, just before the railroad bridge on Route 148.

GOLF **Bay Path Golf Club** (867-8161), East Brookfield, 9 holes.
Hemlock Ridge (347-9935), Sturbridge, 9 holes.
Heritage Country Club (248-5111), Charlton, 18 holes.
Oxford Golf and Racquet Club (892-9186), North Oxford, 18 holes.

HIKING The **Mid-State Trail** passes through Charlton and Oxford. This long-distance trail is described in the *Massachusetts and Rhode Island Trail Guide* published by the Applachian Mountain Club, 5 Joy Street, Boston 02108. A Mid-State Trail map is also available (indicated on USGS sheets) by writing to The Mid-State Trail Committee, PO Box 155, Clinton 01510. Also see State Parks and Green Space.

HORSEBACK RIDING **Rocking M. Ranch** (248-7075), Charlton, offers trail rides, also country music shows and clam bakes.
Wildaire Equine Center (764-7725), Southbridge.
Gold Nugget Farm Riding Academy (885-4852), Spencer.

MINIATURE GOLF Behind the Sturbridge Sheraton (Route 20, Sturbridge) check out the mini Old Sturbridge Village course.

SWIMMING Note under State Parks that Brimfield State Forest, Buffumville State Park, Holland Pond, and Spencer State Forest all have swimming areas. Other local swimming holes include: the **East Brimfield Dam** area at Long Pond, under Route 20 in Sturbridge; the **Cedar Lake Recreation Area** in Sturbridge; and **South Pond** in Brookfield (small but free, with shade trees, off New Boston Road).

CROSS-COUNTRY SKIING The **Sheraton Village Ski-Touring Center** (347-9824), Route 20, Sturbridge, is open mid-December to mid-March (snow permitting) weekdays 1–4, and weekends 12–4. Rental equipment, lessons, eight miles of groomed trails. The local state parks also offer many miles of trails.

INNS AND BED & BREAKFASTS **Publick House** (347-3313), PO Box 187, Sturbridge 01566. This proud white tavern was built in 1771 by

Ebenezer Crafts (Yale, class of 1740), who gave his all to the Revolution. Impoverished by 1791 (a year after planting the elms that still grace the inn), he was forced to move north (150 neighbors went with him), founding the northern Vermont town of Craftsbury. Positioned at the junction of Boston and New York highroads, the inn prospered and was lucky enough to be restored in the 1930s, offering an extension of the Old Sturbridge Village atmosphere (even before OSV opened). While shops, restaurants, and motels have proliferated to form a "strip" outside the museum village entrance along Route 20, the old inn has remained secure in its pristine setting on the original Sturbridge Village Common, complete with town hall and meetinghouse. Behind the inn stretch 60 acres of meadow. While the Publick House is now known primarily for its dining rooms (see Restaurants) there are 18 rooms upstairs and four suites plus one room in neighboring Chamberlain House. All rooms are furnished with antiques, including wing chairs, four-posters and canopy beds. There is also an adjacent 100-room motor lodge, nicely furnished with colonial reproductions and small-print wallpaper. There is a pool, tennis, and rental bicycles. $76–$79 per room, $98–$104 per suite, $54–$64 per room in the motor lodge. Inquire about Yankee Winter Weekends (offered January to March), weekend packages that include eighteenth-century-style feasting, entertainment, and special tours of Old Sturbridge Village.

Colonel Ebenezer Crafts Inn (347-3313), Fiske Hill, Sturbridge 01566. While it is owned by the Publick House, this eighteenth-century home is off by itself, up on a hill instead of in the middle of the village. There are gracious living and sun rooms, inviting spaces to linger, and tea or sherry are served in the afternoon. Rooms are beautifully paneled, furnished with antiques, and there is a secret panel downstairs behind which runaway slaves were once hidden. There is a pool here and guests have access to the Publick House tennis court. $84–$87 double, $109 for a suite, less off-season.

Oliver Wight House and Old Sturbridge Village Motor Lodge (347-3327), Sturbridge 01566. The Oliver Wight House is the only building on Old Sturbridge Village property that stands on its original site. In recent years the 1789 mansion has formed the centerpiece for a motel complex and has been restored, offering a genuine inn atmosphere in its ten rooms (furnished with reproduction antiques from the period). The remaining 50 units are a chock above standard motel design (furnished in colonial reproductions and Hitchcock chairs, bright chintz), scattered in clapboard-sheathed buildings. A continental breakfast is laid out mornings in the office. The inn and hotel (formerly the Liberty Cap) are owned by Old

Sturbridge Village. $75 double in the Oliver Wight House, $58 double in the motel units; less off-season.

Brookfield House Inn (867-6589), Route 9, West Brookfield 01585. A high Victorian mansion with a public dining room and two large, antiques-furnished guest rooms; $85 double includes a full English breakfast.

Hotel Barre (355-4405), Barre 01005. Built in 1889, this country hotel has recently been restored and furnished throughout with antiques. It now offers 38 rooms (double beds, a few singles) with "cluster commodes" (six full baths for the 19 rooms per floor). The restaurant serves three meals. The ambiance is high Victorian. $35–$50 per room.

Deer Meadow Farm (436-7129), RFD #1, Bragg Road, West Brookfield 01585. Carol and Ed Perron welcome guests during summer months (he teaches on Cape Cod during the academic year), also weekends in May, September, and October. The authentic post and beam 1780s home stands on an open rise, commanding views of fields and orchards. Blueberries and raspberries (late July, early August) are available for the picking and are served with the continental breakfast. $40 double.

Misty Meadows (245-7466), Allen Hill Road, Box 31, Holland 01550. A deceptively small-looking home, which Ron Croke built 24 years ago, truly delightful within, offering three rooms nicely furnished with Dot's family antiques—which include an iron bedstead and classic cottage furniture. $38 double includes a full breakfast.

Spencer Country Inn (885-9036), 500 Main Street, Spencer 01562 is an early country mansion that is now primarily a restaurant with four rooms upstairs, $35 double with private bath.

Avondo's Bed & Breakfast (267-5829), 26 East Hill Road, Monson. There are four guest rooms (sharing one bath) in this pleasant, gambrel-roofed home, handy to Brimfield's antiques markets and to the Brimfield State Forest. $45 double.

Commonwealth Inn (347-7603), 11 Summit Street, Sturbridge 01566. Just far enough off Route 20 to distance it from the noise of the strip. Kevin MacConnell, the young bachelor who owns and runs this bed & breakfast, is still in the process of restoring the 16-room mansion. When we visited decor was still spotty but the six rooms were comfortable, one with a black marble fireplace. $40 includes a full breakfast.

Alpine Haus (245-9082), Box 782, Mashapaug Road, Holland 01550. When we visited this modern chalet-style house was being emptied for new owners, but the advantages of the location were obvious: right across from a private beach on Lake Hamilton. A full breakfast is included in the $40 price.

Lake Shore Bed & Breakfast (347-9495), 94 South Shore Drive, Sturbridge 01566. This modest but comfortable home is down a dirt road, one in a lineup of summer-geared places in Lake Quacumquasit. There are three clean, comfortable rooms with lake views. Breakfast is served on the terrace. Guests have use of a gas grill, picnic area, canoes, and are (of course) welcome to jump in the lake. $45 double, full breakfast included.

Lake View House (867-7807), PO Box 531, East Brookfield 01515. Bill and Jill Compton welcome guests to their large, late eighteenth-century home across from a lake, complete with sandy beach. $35, breakfast included.

Insight Meditation Society Center, "Metta," Barre 01005. This brick, former Catholic retreat house, now serves the same purpose for practitioners of the Southeast Asian school of Theavadin Buddhism. The emphasis is on simplicity of life-style and personal insights: the latter often gained by long medative walks.

Also see Five College Area (Upcountry Massachusetts) for the **Wildwood Inn,** Ware; and see Worcester for the **Capt. Samuel Eddy House.**

MOTELS   In Sturbridge 01566: **Sheraton Sturbridge Inn** (347-7393), Route 20. This 245-unit motor inn is nicely sited on Cedar Lake but just back from the main drag. There is an inside pool, whirlpool, tennis and racquetball courts, boating, cross-country skiing. This is a convention facility with standard motel rooms, a VIP floor with its private lounge and quasi-colonial furnishings. $78–$110 double, $135–$185 for suites, $95–$110 for VIP floor rooms.

Best Western American Motor Lodge (347-9121), Route 20. Located on Cedar Lake, indoor pool, saunas, game room, boating, standard motel rooms with two double beds and TV, large restaurant. $65 double.

Sturbridge Motor Inn (347-3391), PO Box 185. A nicely built inn with 34 brightly furnished rooms and a "pool in the woods," back away from it all. $46–$59.

Green Acres Motel (347-3496), off Route 131. A family owned and geared place with 12 big rooms, each walled in knotty pine with two double beds. There is a pool, picnic area, basketball hoop, and choice of lawn games. $44 double.

DINING OUT   **Salem Cross Inn** (867-2345 or 8337), Route 9, West Brookfield. Open Tuesday–Friday 12–9, Saturday 5–9, Sunday and holidays 12–8, closed Mondays. The original part of this handsome, four-square house was built in 1705 by the grandson of Peregrine White (the baby born of the Mayflower), and it still stands alone, surrounded by its 600 acres. Hosts Richard and his niece Nancy describe the sorry condition in which their family found this landmark in the '50s and tell how the family threw themselves into the work of scraping away centuries of paint, restoring the eighteenth- and nineteenth-century woodwork. The menu is traditional New England: entrees include baked stuffed scallops ($12.50) and broiled, herbed lamb steak ($9.50). In winter special Friday Hearthside Traditions include mulled wine, chowder, prime ribs, breads, and pies all cooked on the hearth ($32.50 per person). Sleigh rides are part of these Friday evening and Sunday (brunch) rituals. There are also outdoor hayrides and drovers' roasts in summer. The inn is worth stopping by just to see the clutter of old tools, sleds, butter churns, and assorted antiques in the barn; also the collection of photos on the "Lost Towns" drowned to form the Quabbin Reservoir. "Salem Cross" refers to a traditional design on the inn's front door.

Publick House (347-3313), Sturbridge. The original, low-beamed eighteenth-century tavern is now but one of six dining rooms in this grand old inn. While 400 patrons can sit down to dine in these various spaces, the service is remarkably personal. There are cranberry muffins and pecan rolls at all meals and hearty all-American fare, from deep dish apple pie for breakfast to Yankee Pot Roast ($13.95) and Individual Baked Lobster Pie ($14.95) for dinner. Child's plates. Special Yule Log dinners in Christmas season ($37).

The Whistling Swan (347-2321), 502 Main Street, Sturbridge. Closed Mondays, otherwise open for lunch and dinner. Three formal dining rooms in a Greek revival mansion are the setting for enjoying Mussels Marinières or Frogs Legs followed by Medallions of Veal in Three Mustard Sauce or Duckling au Poivre, topped off by Russian Cream with Strawberries Romanoff or Chocolate Almond Pie. Light meals are served in the Ugly Duckling Loft. Lunch: $4.25–$8.95; dinner: $8.95–$18.95.

Brookfield House Restaurant and Inn (867-6589), Route 9, West Brookfield. Open for lunch Tuesday–Friday, for dinner Wednesday–Saturday, and for Sunday brunch. Very Victorian. Specialties include Beef Wellington. $5.95–$11.95 for lunch; dinner, $15.50–$20.

The Olde Village Inn (347-7933), corner of Route 20 and Cedar Street, Sturbridge. Open daily (except Tuesday) for lunch and dinner. The constantly changing menu is French Nouveau: specialties include Duck a l'Orange and stuffed sole but the menu changes constantly. This is a relatively small, locally popular place. Dinner entrees average $12.95.

Spencer Country Inn (885-9036), 500 East Main Street (Route 9), Spencer. Closed Mondays, otherwise open for lunch, dinner, and Sunday brunch. A nineteenth-century country mansion with five dining rooms including the Hogshead Tavern, live music Thursday–Saturday evenings. Dinners run $8.95–$16.95.

Crab Apple's Eating and Drinking Place (347-9555). Open daily for lunch, dinner, and late supper; also Sunday brunch; children's menu available. In the rear of the Publick House complex, actually in its orchard, sits this gem of a family restaurant. The decor is zany (chicken coops, stained glass, farm implements), and there's a reasonably priced menu to match. We recommend the "Pirates Popcorn" (deep fried tiny shrimp) $7.95, but you can dine for $3.50.

Rom's (347-3349), Route 131, Sturbridge. Open daily for lunch and dinner, Wednesday night buffet; Italian specialties: Gnocci, Lasagna, Chicken Cacciatore, seafood dinners. Lunch $2.95–$4.95. Dinner $4.35–$9.50.

Tanners' Restaurant (867-8186), Barre Hiller Airport, Route 67 off Route 32, Barre. Open April–December, gourmet caliber food at lunch-counter prices; open weekdays for lunch and dinner, weekends for three meals. Specials, $5.95–$10.95 for full dinners. Watch the gliders and small planes between courses.

Hotel Barre (355-4405). Three daily meals are served in this newly restored Victorian-style inn on a classic New England Common. The Hunt Club bar is off the main Barre dining room, and there is also a Sidecar Saloon nightclub. Lunch runs $3–$6, dinner $8–$13.

Flatiron Mexican Cafe (764-7003), 218 Hamilton Street, Southbridge. Off Route 131. Closed Mondays. Outstanding Mexican food, including regional specialties, homemade desserts, and complementary appetizers. American dishes and children's menu available. Live entertainment Thursday–Saturday nights.

Broken Wheel (764-3181), 856 Eastford Road (Route 198), Southbridge. Owned by the Prince family for 24 years, hearty, reasonably priced fare, specializing in seafood.

C.J.'s (283-2196), Route 20, Palmer. Locals swear by this unpretentious place. A full lobster dinner is $6.95.

"Dinner in a Country Village," at Old Sturbridge Village (357-3362), is offered Saturday nights, December–March by reservation; $25 per person. Guests arrive at 5 and are ushered into one of the village homes where they help prepare the dinner that they then consume. Recipes and atmosphere are as authentically 1830s as possible; limited to 15 per evening.

EATING OUT The Sunburst (347-3097), 484 Main Street, Sturbridge (corner of Route 20 and Arnold Road). Home-baked muffins are the breakfast specialty and for lunch there are homemade soups, quiche and salads, smoothies, and more muffins.

Woodbine Country Store and Restaurant (413-245-3552), Route 20, Brimfield. A friendly, reasonably priced eatery in the middle of this classic New England village.

Kozy Corner, Holland, middle of the village. Open daily from

6 AM, a country store with a neat little restaurant, counter and tables, grinders, chili, full breakfasts.

Kozy Cabin (355-6264), Route 122, Barre. A roadhouse exterior but comfortable interior, serving seafood and an extensive menu (including cream pies). Patrons will journey from Worcester to eat here.

SELECTIVE SHOPPING **Sturbridge Yankee Workshop** (347-7176), Route 20, Sturbridge 01566. Billing itself as "New England's largest store specializing in early American furniture, home furnishings, gifts," this is an immense space in an old wooden factory: a trove of reproduction wing and ladder-back chairs, banjo and grandfather clocks, harvest tables and hutches, pewter and brass, bric'a'brac and old hardware.

The Shaker Shop (347-7564), Route 20 across from Cumberland Farms, Sturbridge. A shop devoted entirely to Shaker-style furniture and accessories.

Old Sturbridge Village Gift Shop (347-3362). Strategically positioned at the entrance to the museum village so that you do not have to pay the entry fee, this is an extensive emporium selling early nineteenth-century furniture, furnishings, a variety of gifts, and books.

Hartman's Herb Farm (355-2015), Old Dana Road off Routes 32 and 122, Barre. Open Thursday–Sunday. Reasonably priced herb plants (175 varieties), dried herbs, and teas packaged on the spot; also herb wreaths, potpourri, dried flowers, and raffia dolls. You can walk through the gardens and browse in the barn where products drip-dry on rafters and walls.

FACTORY OUTLETS **Millyard Marketplace,** Route 20, Sturbridge, houses the following outlets: **Sturbridge Lace Company** (bedspreads, table linens); **Van Heusen** (clothing); **Piano Factory Outlet and Sturbridge Furniture Warehouse** (pianos, clocks, a range of furniture).

Hyde Factory Shoe Outlet (885-5740), East Brookfield, is the area's sneaker source, also good for roller skates (made on the premises).

Wright's Mill Store (436-7737), Route 67, West Warren: a genuine old outlet in an old mill; trims, tapes, braids, lace, ribbon, and notions; penny sales in March and September.

North Oxford Mills (987-8521), Route 12, North Oxford. THE place to buy braided rugs, all sizes, all shapes; also carpets, remnants.

Ivy Products (867-8311), New Braintree. This little broom factory makes the witch's-style hearth brooms used in OSV and sold at their gift store. You can watch them being shaped from natural broom straw here, buy them for far less than in Sturbridge. Open weekdays 7–3, a beautiful ride.

Maurice The Pants Man (347-7859), Route 20, Sturbridge. A discount store rather than a factory outlet, this is a great place to shop for Woolrich and other name brand sportswear for the whole family. (Note the outstanding outlets in the Ware Millyard under the Five College Area.)

ORCHARDS This is apple country and the orchards are in some of its most beautiful corners. Call ahead to make sure the following are open and set up for visitors.

Brookfield Orchards (867-6858), Orchard Road, off Route 9, East Brookfield. High on a hill, with picnic tables, children's play equipment, and a country store selling jellies, gifts, and apple dumplings (each with an apple baked into it). Owned by the Lincoln family since 1918.

Cheney's Apple Barn (245-9223). Open daily in season: cider, fruit stand.

Cheney Orchards (436-7688), marked off Route 148 between Sturbridge and Brimfield. In the family since 1911, an 80-acre orchard and a country store selling 35 varieties of apples, peaches, pears (10 varieties), eight varieties of honey, frozen apple pies, and more. This is also a place to cut your own Christmas tree in December.

Fay Mountain Farm (248-7237), Stafford Street, Charlton. In the Gilmore family since 1910. Apples, fresh cider in season.

Hyland Orchards (347-3416), Arnold Road, Sturbridge. Apples and cider in season.

Breezeland Orchards (413-436-7100), Southbridge Road, Warren. Apples and cider in season.

Baxter Echo Hill Orchard (413-267-3303), Wilbraham Road, Monson.

ANTIQUES Brimfield, just seven miles west of Sturbridge, is one of the antiques centers of America. Three times a year—in May, July, and September—some 2,500 dealers gather in the open spaces along Route 20 just west of Brimfield's Common. Over the years this massive influx of sellers and buyers has developed its own organization with a 24-hour taped information number: 413-245-7479. It tells you when the next Antiques Market will occur (in May of '86 it was a 10-day extravaganza, culminating with Mother's Day on May 11; in July it is usually the week after Independence Day, and in September the week after Labor Day). The shows are divided into more than a dozen different markets, each 50 to 500 dealers. It's a scene. The crowd usually tops 100,000. Stands serving surprisingly good finger food mushroom around the markets. For details about the next market send a self-addressed, stamped envelope (8 by 10 inches) to The Brimfielder, Worcester County Newspapers, 25 Elm Street, Southbridge 01550 (764-4325).

Sturbridge Antiques Shops (347-9848), east on Route 20, houses 75 dealers year-round, open daily.

Sturbridge House Antique Center (347-9338), second and third floors above Yesterday's Restaurant, Route 20; 50 dealers year-round.

A pamphlet guide to 17 smaller dealers is available from the Quaboag Valley Antique Center, 10 Knox Street, Palmer 01069.

Sunday Flea Markets: Every Sunday look for: **Auburn Antique & Flea Market** on Route 12; **Ye Old Brookfield Mill** (just over the Quaboag River in Brookfield); and the **Spencer Flea Market** on Route 9.

Auctions: **Gouvin's** (413-283-6197), 29 Palmer Road, Palmer 01069 (Auctioneers and Appraisers). **Pioneer Auctioneers and Appraisers** (867-8967), 10 Knox Street, Palmer 01069 (specializes in estates). Auctions in the area are held almost every week. Inquire about the next one.

SPECIAL EVENTS Old Sturbridge Village (OSV) publishes its own calendar, filled with events dictated by the seasons. The following notes only some of the highlights.

February: **George Washington's Birthday** is celebrated at OSV as it would have been in the 1830s. Maple sugaring at OSV.

March: **Hog butchering** at OSV.

April: **Spring Town Meeting** at OSV.

May: **Brimfield Flea Market. Militia Day** and **Wool Days** at OSV.

July: **Brimfield Flea Market. Independence Day celebrations** at OSV.

August: **Wales County Fair,** local exhibits and livestock, Main Street, Wales. **Hardwick Fair,** just off the Common.

September: **Brimfield Flea Market. Spencer Fair** (Labor Day weekend). **Antiquarian Book Fair** at OSV. Apple picking and cider pressing at local orchards.

November: **Thanksgiving** at OSV.

December: **Yule Log celebrations** at the Publick House. **Christmas shows** at Bethlehem in Sturbridge.

MEDICAL EMERGENCY **Harrington Memorial Hospital** (765-9771), 100 South Street, Southbridge, marked from Route 131.

Worcester

Worcester, with a population of 161,000, is the metropolis of Central Massachusetts and also the second largest city in both the state and New England. Because of its strategic location—roughly in the center of the region—Worcester can and does boast that it is "The Heart of New England."

Geography has shaped Worcester's character, assured its growth as a diversified manufacturing center, and is the factor on which future prosperity will likely depend: some six million people now live within a 50-mile radius of the city.

The municipal emblem is the heart, prominently displayed on city seal and flag and on the signs directing traffic into the downtown shopping district. This logo is particularly appropriate since urban development projects over the past 20 years have given Worcester's urban core what amounts to a heart transplant.

The area around the historic old Common was totally transformed in the early 1970s by the creation of Worcester Center, an office and shopping complex that is the focus and pride of the "New" Worcester. The center contains some 100 shops, theaters, and restaurants, along with two bank buildings and a 4,300-car parking garage. The Worcester Center's own center is called The Galleria, a three-story indoor mall splashed by fountains, graced by greenery, and covered with an all-weather Plexiglas canopy that lets sunshine through but keeps unpredictable Massachusetts weather out.

A recent addition to downtown is The Centrum, a multi-purpose civic auditorium on Foster Street, a block north of The Galleria. Initially controversial, Centrum has proven to be a great success and is much used for meetings, conventions, and pop music concerts: in fact, Worcester is now the rock concert capital of New England. A private development near Centrum, One Exchange Place, recycled the former municipal courthouse and police and fire department complex into an attractive commercial center.

With its sophisticated year-around amenities, The Galleria has taken over the traditional function of the Common as communal loitering, lounging, and gossiping place. But the real Common still exists directly across from The Center, and (although modishly redesigned and given a reflecting pool that mirrors City Hall) still contains the graves of early settlers, the Civil War monument, a decorative horse trough, and a few stately survivors of the Dutch Elm disease plague.

The present city hall building, inspired by that of Siena, Italy, stands on the site of the simple eighteenth-century South Meetinghouse, which was the cradle of local government. It was here on July 17, 1776, that the patriot printer Isaiah Thomas—whose *Massachusetts Spy* is considered the the country's first newspaper—read the Declaration of Independence to a large crowd assembled on the Common. This was the first such reading in New England and one of the very first in the nation.

Thomas remained in Worcester after the American Revolution, expanding his print shop until for a period it was the largest in the United States. He also founded the American Antiquarian Society, which today occupies a handsome neo-federal building at 185 Salisbury Street. The society's magnificent library contains an estimated two-thirds of all the material printed in the country before 1820.

Worcester was first settled in 1670 but was abandoned several times because of Indian raids. Even after permanent settlement was effected in the eighteenth century, the community grew very slowly, largely because of poor communications. Worcester is the only major manufacturing city east of the Mississippi not located on a navigable body of water. Early in the nineteenth century, town fathers tried to solve the vexing problem of Worcester's lack of a river by digging a canal to connect Worchester with Providence, RI. The Blackstone Canal opened in 1828 but ceased operation 20 years later, rendered obsolete by the arrival of the railroad. The year the canal closed, 1848, was also the year that Worcester became a city.

Short-lived as it was, the canal launched Worcester as a manufacturing city and brought the first wave of foreign immigrants to the city: the Irish laborers who dug it. As the Irish moved up the economic ladder, other ethnic groups moved into their old neighborhood. Shrewsbury Street, which follows the canal route, became Worcester's Little Italy and still retains an Italian flavor with several long-established Italian restaurants and pizzarias.

The middle years of the nineteenth century constitute New England's Golden Age, a sunburst of Yankee ingenuity and creativity. Nowhere was that legendary race of inspired tinkerers busier than in Worcester. Within three years of each other in the mid-1850s, for example, Russell Hawes invented the first practical envelope folding machine; George Crompton designed a revolutionary power loom; Thomas Blanchard developed a lathe for turning irregular forms; and Erastus B. Bigelow produced the carpet loom. Descendants of these devices and other products of Worcester's fertile industrial imagination—unlike most New England manufacturing centers, it has never been a one-industry town—are still hard at work in the city's factories, mills, and machine shops.

Each factory became the center of a little world of its own, usually complete with bands, choral groups, sports teams, and social clubs. Worcester in its early years was a collection of loosely related industrial villages that only gradually grew together.

The mills had voracious appetites for labor, sucking in workers from around the world to give Worcester an ethnic diversity unusual even by the polyglot standards of New England mill towns. Grafton Hill, where the French Canadians first settled, remains "French Hill." Wall Street was the center of the Middle Eastern community—Lebanese, Syrian, Assyrian, and Armenian—many attracted to Worcester by the carpet industry, as were Yorkshiremen, Greeks, Albanians, and Romanians.

Swedes, not a major group elsewhere in the state, once made up about 20 percent of the city's population. They started arriving in the 1860s, most going to work for the American Steel and Wire Co. and the Norton Co., one of the world's largest manufacturers of grinding wheels and abrasives. Irish bars and sports organizations and French, Italian, and Polish social clubs still remain the backbone of Worcester blue-collar neighborhoods; churches are the focal point of national groups.

Proximity to Boston has certainly had an inhibiting effect on social and cultural life, but Worcester tries hard to cultivate the arts. The Worcester Art Museum is one of the country's leading medium-size museums, and the Worcester Music Festival, held annually in autumn since 1858, attracts nationally and internationally known performers and ensembles. Concerts by local classical groups are often held in Mechanics Hall.

AREA CODE 617
GUIDANCE **Visitors and Cultural Information Center,** a restored antique horse-drawn diner of a pioneering type once made in Worcester, this information center is parked on the Common during the tourist season.

Worcester Area Chamber of Commerce and Worcester County Convention & Visitors Bureau (753-2924), both at 350 Mechanics Tower, Worcester 01608.

The Cultural Connection (757-3500). Call for daily cultural events and programs.

Books: *In and About Worcester,* by Beverly H. Osborn (Commonwealth Press, Worcester).

The Artist's Directory, Worcester Cultural Commission, 41 Elm Street, Worcester.

Magazines: *Worcestersights,* Worcester County News, 475 Washington Street, Auburn 01501. Distributed free.

Worcester County Illustrated, 167 Pleasant Street, Worcester 01609.

GETTING THERE By car: Worcester is 40 miles from Boston via Route 9 or the Massachusetts Turnpike. If coming from Boston, take Exit 11 off the turnpike, Exit 10 if approaching the city from the south or west.

By train: AMTRAK service (755-0356) from Boston and Chicago; the passenger depot is on Shrewsbury Street, just east of the I-290 overpass; free parking.

By bus: National service by **Trailways** (754-2611), Seven Hills Plaza (75 Madison Street). **The Worcester Bus Co.** (791-8106) serves the hilltowns east and west of the city, while **ABC Bus Lines** and **Bonanza** (from the Greyhound Terminal) serve the Blackstone Valley and South County towns. **Peter Pan Bus Lines** (754-2611) runs west out of Route 9 to towns in that area.

GETTING AROUND Worcester's attractions are widely scattered and a car is necessary to see the city properly.

Parking: There is a 4,300-car garage in Worcester Center and several large municipal parking lots downtown.

TO SEE AND DO **Higgins Armory Museum** (853-6015), 100 Barber Avenue off Gold Star Boulevard. Tuesday–Friday 9–5, weekends and holidays noon–5 PM; $2.50. Located in an industrial section, this unusual museum is the result of an industrialist's research into ancient metallurgy. While looking for the secrets that produced fine steel in the Middle Ages, John Woodman Higgins collected suits of armor—more than 100 of them. The collection includes very rare and beautiful armor, such as the tournament armor of kings and special suits for children and dogs. Most of the "steel knights" are lined up in the Great Hall, designed to resemble a medieval banqueting hall, and make an impressive sight. Also displayed are banners, swords, shields, battle axes, maces, and crossbows along with period paintings, stained glass, wood carvings, tapestries, and a replica of an armorer's workshop.

Worcester Art Museum (799-4406), 55 Salisbury Street. Tuesday–Saturday 10–5, 1–5 Sunday; free. Founded in 1896, the museum has the second largest permanent collection in New England and ranks among the best medium-sized museums in the country. The collection includes fine examples of Greek, Roman, Mexican, Asian, Persian, European, and American art. The early American paintings displayed are outstanding. There is also a complete room from a twelfth-century French monastery and a collection of Roman mosaics from Antioch. The museum has a gift shop, restaurant, and in summer a garden cafe.

Worcester Historical Museum (753-8278), 39 Salisbury Street.

Tuesday–Saturday 10–4. Free. Devoted to local history, this handsome brick building is the headquarters of the **Worcester Historical Society** and has interesting exhibits tracing the city's evolution from frontier town to industrial city. Frequent special exhibitions. The library has more than 10,000 volumes. A block away from the museum, at 40 Highland Street is the **Salisbury Mansion** (the residence of the prominent Salisbury Family from 1772 to 1852), one of Worcester's few surviving eighteenth-century buildings, which has been restored by the Historical Society to re-create the home life of the Salisburys circa 1830.

Massachusetts Avenue Historic District, a parkway off Salisbury Street, laid out in the late nineteenth century and lined with stately Victorian and Edwardian homes of various styles, built by local professional men and industrialists. Teddy Roosevelt paraded down it in an open carriage in 1902.

American Antiquarian Society (755-5221), 185 Salisbury Street, Monday–Friday 9–5. Founded by Isaiah Thomas in 1812, the society specializes in American printed material—literature, newspapers, broadsides, sheet music—between 1670 and 1876. Thomas' original flatbed press and selections of the society's vast collection of Americana are displayed. The magnificent library is open only to qualified scholars and researchers.

Worcester Science Center (791-9211), 222 Harrington Way, Wednesday–Saturday 10–5, Sunday noon–5; $3.50 adult, $2.75 child. A modern three-story building, the Science Center is set in a 50-acre park that includes a zoo—complete with wolves, mountain lions, and polar bears—and a miniature railroad. Visitors are encouraged to touch and experiment with the exhibits. There is a planetarium and also a gift shop, restaurant, and picnic areas.

Providence and Worcester Railroad (755-4000), PO Box 1188, Worcester 01601. A working railroad offering frequent train excursions. $4.95–$39.95.

GREEN SPACE **Elm Park,** off Park Avenue, established in 1854, is the oldest public park—as distinguished from Green or Common—in the nation. The ornate Victorian bridge over the ornamental pond is a popular spot for wedding photos.

Green Hill Park, off Lincoln Street, covers nearly 500 acres and has a barnyard zoo and 18-hole municipal golf course.

Regatta Point State Park, off Lake Avenue on Lake Quinsigamond. Swimming beach, changing facilities, rental sailboats, tennis, and picnic areas. Frequently the site of regional and national rowing competitions.

Moore State Park (792-3969). This unusual, 324-acre park is the site of a (still standing) early nineteenth-century mill and blacksmith shop on Turkey Brook. There is also a country mansion (not open to the public) from its days as a private estate. It's a great place to picnic and hike.

Rutland State Park (886-6333). A 1920-acre wooded area with a swim beach and picnic area at Whitehall Pond and a boat launch ramp on Long Pond, one of the few DEM facilities where water skiing is permitted.

HOTELS **Marriott** (791-1600), 10 Lincoln Square, at junction of I-290 and Route 9. A 250-room motor inn with indoor and outdoor pool, health club, and restaurant. Single $88–$94, double $100–$106.

Sheraton-Lincoln Inn (852-4000), 500 Lincoln St. A 143-room motor inn with an indoor pool and restaurant. Double $81–$86.

For other places to stay in the Worcester vicinity see Lodging in the chapter on Sturbridge.

BED & BREAKFASTS There are no bed & breakfasts in Worcester proper, but there are a number in surrounding towns:

Captain Eddy House (832-3149), 609 Oxford Street, South Auburn 01501. A vintage 1740 house offers two guest rooms, both with private bath. This is also an herb farm. $38–$48.

Folkstone Bed & Breakfast (869-2687), PO Box 131, Station 1, Boylston 01505. A reservation service representing half a dozen bed & breakfasts in the Worcester area.

DINING OUT **El Morocco** (756-7117), 100 Wall Street. Monday–Thursday 11:30 AM–10 PM; Friday 11:30 AM–11 PM; Saturday 4–11 PM; Sunday 4–10 PM (closed Sundays in summer). A Worcester landmark, "the El" specializes in Middle Eastern food, such as lamb shish kebab ($9.75 dinner, $4.95 lunch) and babaganoosh ($3.50).

Maxwell Silverman's Toolhouse (755-1200), 25 Union Street. Lunch daily 11:30–2:30, except Sunday. Sunday brunch served 11 AM–2 PM in Club Maxine. Dinner: Sunday 4–9 PM; Monday–Tuesday 5–9 PM; Wednesday 5–9:30 PM; Friday–Saturday 5–10 PM. Located in an old factory building. The Toolhouse has an industrial ambience: the dessert menu is even delivered in a toolcase. The specialty is prime rib offered in "tap and die" cuts. The "tap" is $14.25 and the "die" $17.25.

Legal Seafoods (792-1600), One Exchange Place. Monday–Thursday 11 AM–10 PM; Friday 11 AM–11 PM; Saturday noon–11 PM; Sunday 1–10 PM. Obviously seafood of all kinds is the house specialty, but this restaurant also serves Cajun dishes, such as gumbo. Dinner prices range from $8.95 for a basic fish dish to $25.95 for the three-lobster special.

Firehouse Cafe, (753-7899), One Exchange Place. Monday–Thursday 11:30 AM–9:30 PM; Friday–Saturday 11 AM–11 PM; Sunday 5 PM–12:30 AM. A popular spot in a former firehouse: the bar incorporates a 1921 Mack fire truck. Dinner specialties include baked stuffed shrimp ($9.95) and chicken con pesto ($8.85).

EATING OUT **Heo's** (753-4367), 245 Summer Street. Luncheon buffet, Monday–Friday 11:30 AM–2 PM; dinner Monday–Saturday 4:30–9:40 PM. Famous for its all-you-can-eat buffet—which includes baked fish, roast beef, and an elaborate salad—for $6.95. Dinner prices are also reasonable.

La Patisserie (756-1454), 252 Commercial Street. Weekdays 7:30 AM–3:30 PM; Sunday 8 AM–2 PM. This restaurant features homemade soups and sandwiches served on croissants or French bread. The daily luncheon special consists of a cup of soup and half a sandwich for $2.95.

ENTERTAINMENT **Centrum** (798-8888), 50 Foster Street, a multi-purpose, 13,500-seat, centrally located auditorium that hosts more big name rock and popular music concerts than any other facility in New England.

Mechanics Hall (752-5608), 321 Main Street. Built in 1857 primarily for lectures—Charles Dickens was a speaker—the hall fell on evil days in this century and was long used for wrestling matches and roller skating. Restored as a Bicentennial project, Mechanics Hall's acoustically superb auditorium is now used for concerts, balls, and theatrical presentations.

SELECTIVE SHOPPING Main Street has a variety of shops and the 100 or so in the **Galleria** on Front Street include **Jordan Marsh, Filene's,** and **Filene's Basement.** There are about 50 factory and outlet discount stores in the Worcester area, many specializing in Massachusetts-made clothing and fabrics and housed in old mill factory complexes.

Spag's, 193 Boston Turnpike, Shrewsbury, just over the Worcester line on Route 9. For more than half a century, both a unique business enterprise and a local landmark, selling everything from housewares and clothing to foods, toys, and hardware at discount prices; often as much as 60 percent less than the same item would sell for at a conventional retail store. Stored in trucks parked out back, most of the merchandise is brand name and first quality. Always crowded. Cash only. Monday–Friday 9–9, Saturday 8–9.

For a brochure listing more than 101 bargain outlets in Central Massachusetts write to: Worcester County Convention and Visitors Bureau, 350 Mechanics Tower, Worcester 01608.

Craft Center (753-8183), 25 Sagamore Road. One of the country's oldest craft complexes, includes quality exhibits.

SPECIAL EVENTS May: **Eastern Sprints Regatta,** intercollegiate rowing competition at Regatta Point on Lake Quinsigamond.

July–August: **Summer's World,** city-wide cultural celebration in public parks and neighborhoods.

August: **New England Mime Festival** in Institute Park.

October–November: **Worcester County Music Association An-**

Mechanics Hall, 1857, outstanding both architecturally and acoustically, is the scene of frequent concerts

nual Music Festival. Held every year since 1858, the festival features major ensembles and internationally known artists.

December: Handel's *Messiah*, performed in Mechanics Hall by the Worcester Chorus and Orchestra.

First Night, a community-wide cultural New Year's Eve celebration featuring mime, poetry readings, theater, dance, and music.

MEDICAL EMERGENCY **Worcester City Hospital** (799-8016), 26 Queen Street.

Worcester Hahnemann Hospital (792-8555), 281 Lincoln Street.

Blackstone River Valley

The Blackstone Canal, completed in 1828, linked Worcester to Providence, RI. Already there were dozens of small textile mills and some of New England's first mill villages along the river. The canal turned the villages into boom towns during the following two decades. Route 122 now hugs the river, the canal route, and the rail line, which put the canal out of business in the 1840s. The evolving Blackstone River and Canal Heritage State Park, a mix of waterside green space and historic sites in a half-dozen villages, is intended to lure travelers off the road and onto snatches of tow path and waterway, into old mills and "interpretive centers." What sets this area apart is its abundance of water—millponds, reservoirs, and natural lakes as well as the river—and tower-topped old textile mills. The picturesque Stanley Woolen Mill in Uxbridge, built in 1851 and managed by the Wheelock family for seven generations, still produces quality yarns and fabric. With completion of the Heritage State Park it will be possible to take a canal barge from the mill to the Voss farm and from there to hike through the thousand-acre nature preserve around Rice City Pond. Towns around Uxbridge already offer a variety of surprises: New England's largest collection of animals and Purgatory Chasm for starters. And there are some exceptional places to stay.

AREA CODE 617

GUIDANCE **Blackstone Valley Chamber of Commerce** (753-2924), 350 Mechanics Tower, Worcester 01608.

Blackstone River and Canal Heritage State Park (278-7336), 21 Mendon Street, PO Box 405, Uxbridge 01569.

Blackstone Valley Tribune (234-5686), Whitinsville 01588.

GETTING THERE By train: The Providence & Worcester RR (755-4000), PO Box 1188, Worcester 01601, offers frequent weekend excursions through the Valley.

By car: Although Heritage State Park plans call for a transportation network (including shuttle buses and mule-drawn barges) linking park segments, car is the only way to go at present. From Boston the quickest access to Uxbridge is Route 495 to Milford, then Route 16. To follow the canal from Grafton to Blackstone, exit off the Massachusetts Turnpike at Route 122 in North Grafton; follow it south (be sure to detour the mile up Route 140 to Grafton

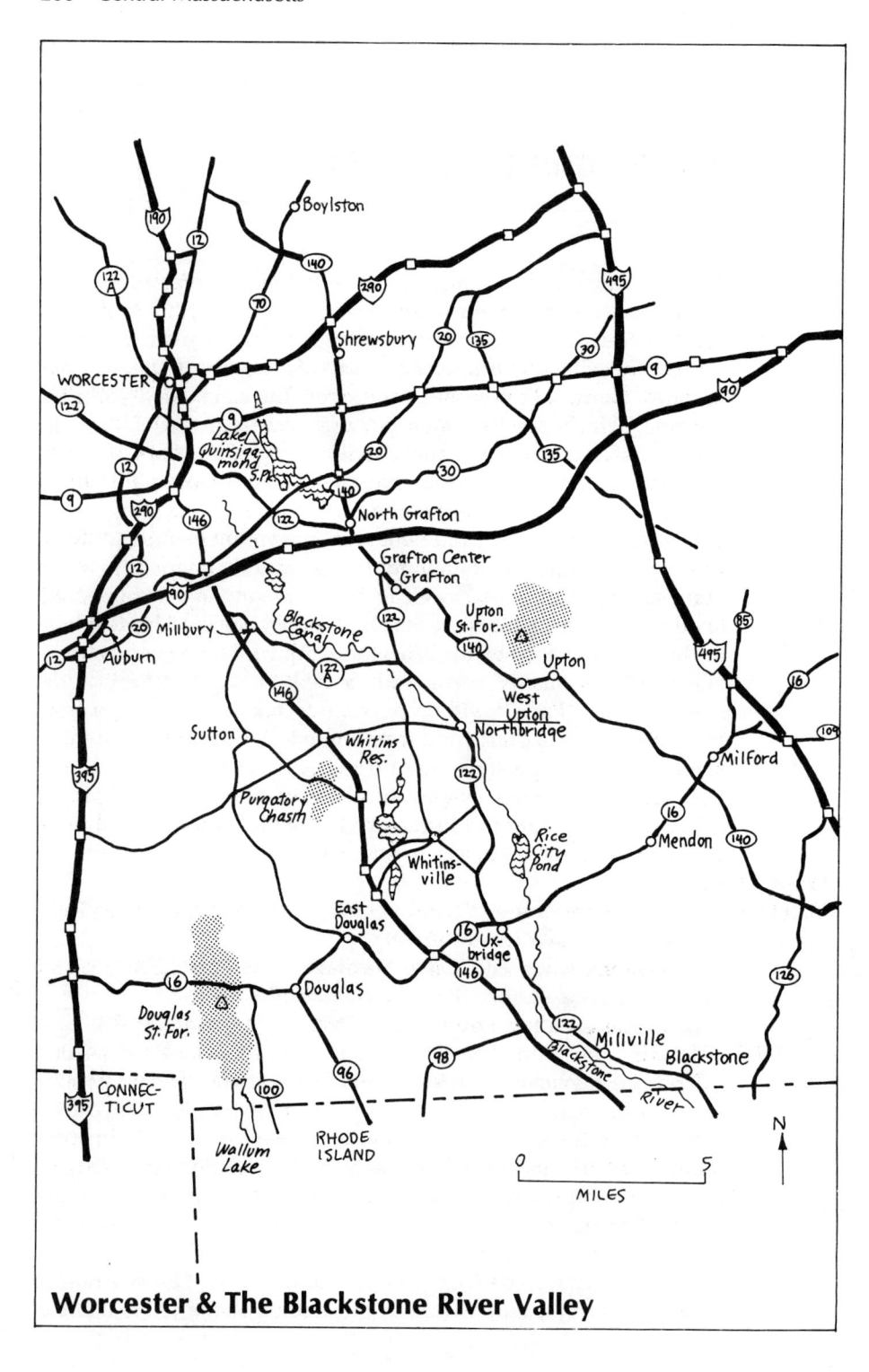

Worcester & The Blackstone River Valley

Center) through Whitinsville and Uxbridge. Route 146, a Mass. Pike exit at Millbury, is a major north-south highway, the quickest access to Sutton's Purgatory Chasm.

TO SEE AND DO **Blackstone River and Canal Heritage State Park** (278-7336), 21 Mendon Street, PO Box 405, Uxbridge 01569. The first segments of the park will be completed over 3 years, starting in 1986: Capron Park, just one-third of an acre but offering access to the Mumford River (a tributary of the Blackstone River) in the center of Uxbridge; the Visitor Center in Uxbridge, with interpretive exhibits; a 1000-acre nature preserve (canoe access, birding, and hiking) at Rice City Pond in Uxbridge; and canal ride with mule-drawn barge. Other major park segments to be developed later will include Blackstone Square (Blackstone), the Millville Lock and industrial ruins (also an island whose sycamore trees provided wood for buttons), and, finally, the Riverdale and Rockdale mills in Northbridge, Farnumsville and Fisherville mills in Grafton, and Singing Dam in Sutton.

Stanley Woolen Mill (278-2451), 140 Mendon Street (Route 16), Uxbridge. This is New England's oldest textile mill, still operated by its founding family. The mauve-colored brick and clapboard mill is a beauty, and tours of the plant (in which raw wool is converted to yard and to bolts of soft, durable wool fabrics) are offered twice daily on weekdays, 11 AM and 2 PM. $2.50 charge for tour. (See Selective Shopping for details about the Mill Store.)

Willard House & Clock Museum (839-3500), 11 Willard Street, Grafton, sign-posted from Routes 22 and 140 (the way back isn't posted so note turns). Open Tuesday–Saturday 10–4, Sunday 1–5. This classic saltbox was built in 1716 by the grandfather of four clock-making brothers who made some 5,000 timepieces in the early nineteenth century, many of them now gracing Federal-era churches. Some 40 magnificent clocks are displayed. $1.50 per adult, $.75 per child.

Grafton Center. Founded in 1654 as "Hassanisco," one of John Eliot's Praying Indian villages, it is now known for its oval Common, one of the most handsome in all New England. Complete with bandstand, it is surrounded by handsome nineteenth-century buildings, which include an inn and an outstanding country store. A sleepy Worcester bedroom town, the village is now stirring with new life; it has recently become the new home of Tuft's School of Veterinary Medicine.

Southwick's Wild Animal Farm (883-9182), off Route 16, Mendon. Open May–October, daily 10–6. Given the lack of a first-rate public zoo in New England, this is the next best thing: the largest collection of animals in the region—some 1,000 plus of them—exotic creatures: tigers, baboons, and antelopes. There is a petting zoo, a choice of animal rides (pony, camel, and elephant), a snack bar, and picnic tables. Adults, $4; children aged 3–12, $3.

Meetinghouses. Many of the valley's first settlers were Quakers and two of their eighteenth-century buildings survive. In Uxbridge on Route 146 (south of town; across from the Quaker Motor Lodge, from which you can secure details and the key) stands a 1770 meetinghouse with its interior unchanged—a wooden curtain once divided men and women. The space is still used by a Worcester Society of Friends. The second is a simple, restored eighteenth-century building on Elm Street in East Blackstone. For open times and directions check with the Mobil Station in the center of Blackstone. **Chestnut Hill Meetinghouse** (883-8466), built in 1769, is on Chestnut Hill Road, one mile south of Southwick's Wild Animal farm or north of Route 122 in Millville, built in 1769 with an unusually beautiful interior.

GREEN SPACE **Purgatory Chasm State Reservation** (234-3733), Purgatory Road (exit off Route 146), Sutton. The chasm itself is awesome, actually comprising three ravines one after another. A trail takes you along the rim and then to the floor, 65 feet below—heaven for small boys aged 7 to 70. The 188-acre Purgatory Reservation includes a playground and picnic tables scattered in the pines.

Sutton State Forest (234-3733). Adjacent to Purgatory Chasm Reservation, undeveloped except for a few miles of hiking trail.

Douglas State Forest (476-7872), Wallum Lake Road, Douglas. Badly marked from Route 16, just west of the old village of Douglas. Wallum Lake (see Swimming) is one of the state's outstanding swimming and fishing lakes. The recreation area includes a boat ramp, picnic tables and grills, changing rooms, and hiking trails. $3 day-use fee (no one was collecting on a summer Friday at 5 PM.)

Upton State Forest (529-6923), Westboro Road, Upton. A 2,660-acre spread with hiking, snowmobiling, and biking trails; fishing in Dean Pond.

Blackstone State Forest (278-6486), off Route 122, Northbridge, offers canoeing and hiking.

West Hill Dam and Recreation Area, West Hill Road, Uxbridge. This is an Army Corps of Engineers project and includes the dam at the end of one road and a recreation area with swimming, picnicking, and hiking trails at the end of the other. Well posted from Route 16.

CANOEING There are dozens of put-in places in valley ponds and rivers. Check with the Blackstone Watershed Association for sites along the Blackstone. Rentals are available from **Fin'n'Feather Sports** (529-3901), Route 140, Upton: $7 per hour if you want to canoe right there on Mill Pond, $18 per 24-hour day to take away (deposit required).

GOLF **Pleasant Valley Country Club** (865-4441). A highly rated 18-hole course, frequent site of tournaments.

Pine Ridge Golf Club (839-5093), Upton. A nine-hole, par-33 course.

HORSEBACK RIDING **Eagle Rock Riding Center** (839-5784), Route 122, Grafton. Trail rides are offered daily, $10 per hour.

ROCK CLIMBING Purgatory Chasm is one of the state's premier climbing places, but a permit is needed (see Green Space).

SWIMMING **Wallum State Park,** Douglas (see Green Space), is exceptionally clear, sandy-bottomed with a beach large enough to absorb the weekend crowd; relatively empty midweek. Changing rooms, picnic tables, $3.

West Hill Recreation Area, Uxbridge, is a glorified mud puddle, great for children (older kids can swim right across the pond to the opposite beach). Changing rooms, picnic tables.

Breezy Picnic Grounds and Waterslide (476-2664), West Street (off Route 16), Douglas. Open daily in season, 9 AM–7 PM. On Whitins Reservoir, a landscaped waterslide and beach. The charge for use of the beach and changing facilities is $2 per adult, $1.50 per child; for the water slide it is $6.50 per adult, $5.50 per child, good for all day.

INNS AND BED & BREAKFASTS **Charles Capron House** (278-2214), 2 Capron Street, Uxbridge 01569. Built for a local mill owner in 1865, this grand Victorian house has been the Taft's home for more than 20 years. With their seven children launched, Ken and Mary now offer four rooms, all with private bath. All are spacious, nicely decorated with comfortable antiques (our favorite features a sleigh bed with a beautiful quilt). Guests feel welcome in the airy, high-ceilinged downstairs rooms and on the screened sun porch. Grounds extend back past a carriage house to the Blackstone River. $55–$60 double, full breakfast included.

Heritage House (839-5063), 28 North Street, Grafton 01519. Built in 1795, a classic Federal-era mansion on a maple-lined street, now the gracious home in which Peg and John Koomey have raised their seven children. The four guest rooms share one large, inviting bath and so Peg offers her guests terry-cloth robes (also alarm clocks and hair driers). Each room is exquisitely furnished with antique beds and coverlets. Guests are welcome to relax in the comfortable, low-beamed living room and music and sitting rooms and to enjoy a full breakfast either in the dining room or pleasant garden. $35 and up.

The Grafton Inn (839-5931), Route 140, Grafton Center. This handsome old inn dates from 1805 but just nine guest rooms (all on the third floor, accessible by elevator) are presently in use. Refurbished in 1985, each room has private bath and TV. The inn's

Ploughboy Restaurant serves lunch and dinner but no breakfast, $39.50–$69.50.

The Victorian (234-2500), 585 Linwood Avenue, Whitinsville 01588. In 1826 Paul Whitin built a mill, then another, and soon an entire village. The graceful stone Cotton Mill (1845), heart of the community, is now housing for the elderly. The Victorian, a Whitin mansion built in 1871, with high ceilings and etched glass, offers guest rooms; over-priced from $82–$108.

MOTELS **Quaker Motor Lodge** (278-2445), Route 146, two miles south of Uxbridge. Two dozen units with a small pool, clean and friendly, $37 for a double bed, $42 for twin beds.

Pleasant View Motor Lodge & Pub (865-5222), Route 146, Sutton. Geared to groups and business travelers, 55 rooms. Facilities include a dining room serving all three meals, an 18-hole golf course, swimming pool, and tennis courts to which guests have access. $35–$40 single, $40–$47 double.

DINING OUT **The Victorian** (234-2500), 585 Linwood Ave., Whitinsville, open for dinner only, Wednesday–Saturday. The menu is divided into a choice of $3.50 soups (Creme d'asperges for instance), $6.75 "Entrees" (like salmon mousse garnished with truffles), and $22.50 "Plats" (our choice would be shelled lobster in a Mousseline sauce with brandy and tomato essence, accompanied by a puff pastry and a julienne of fresh vegetables).

Cock 'n' Kettle (278-5517), Route 122 south of Uxbridge. Open for dinner nightly. An imposing Georgian mansion featuring large servings. THE local place to dine on Veal "Cordon Bleu" ($10.45) or broiled Cape Scallops ($9.95); $5 minimum.

New England Steak and Seafood (473-9787), Route 16, Mendon. Closed Tuesdays, otherwise dinner from 5 PM nightly, lunch on weekdays. A dependable dining spot; try the California Cream Scampi ($13.95) or Fish'n'Chips ($8.95); broiled pork chops are $7.95.

Ploughboy Restaurant in the Grafton Inn (839-5931), 25 Central Square, Grafton. Open daily 11 AM–9 PM, until 11 PM on Saturday, from 5 PM on summer Sundays. A pleasant dining room with a full menu but a reputation for inconsistent quality, $10 entree range.

EATING OUT **Lowell's Restaurant** (473-1073), Route 16, Mendon. Open daily from 6:30 AM through dinner. A great family find, good for all three meals, real crab salad rolls for less than $3.00.

Milly Mitchell (473-4230), Route 16, Mendon. Open Tuesday–Friday for lunch, Tuesday–Saturday for dinner. Overlooking Lake Nipmuc, a pleasant place for fried clams, sandwiches.

The Elmwood Club (476-2535), East Douglas. Open daily 7 AM–10 PM, good for fried seafood, sandwiches, Hershey ice cream.

SELECTIVE SHOPPING Factory Outlets: **The Mill Store,** Stanley Woolen Mill (278-2451), 140 Mendon Street (Route 16), Uxbridge. Open Monday–Saturday 9–5. Knitters come from throughout the country to buy the Beroco line yarn, and the bolts of coat and suit material have an equal following. Soft wool animals, rag rugs, blankets, and a limited but tempting line of coats and suits are also carried.

Uxbridge Yarn Outlet (278-5611), 29 Mendon Street, Uxbridge. Open daily 9–5. Bernat Yarns also draw fans from afar; rug, stitchery, and needlepoint kits are also carried.

Curtain Factory Outlet (234-2944), 2400 Providence Road (Route 122), Northbridge. Open daily 9–5, good for shades, rods, curtains, bedspreads, tie backs, towels, and quilts.

Ladies Hats Factory Outlet Store (839-9011), 308 Providence Road (Route 122), Grafton. Open weekdays 9–5, a great assortment of hats.

Mr. Christmas (476-7482), just off Route 16, Douglas. Call to check changing hours, an outlet for Chinese-made artificial flowers and trees, Christmas lights, and decorations.

Other: **Grafton Country Store** (839-4898), Grafton Common. Open Tuesday–Saturday 10–5; Sunday 10–4. Gifts, cards, penny candy, herbs, and spices.

Village Crafters (478-0870), Lowell's Plaza, Route 16, Mendon. Open Tuesday–Saturday 9:30–5:30; Friday until 9; Sunday, Monday 1–5. An artisans cooperative representing local artists.

Mendon Country Gift Barn (473-1820), Route 16, Mendon. Open daily. A source of gifts, dinnerware, candies, good for rainy day browsing.

SPECIAL EVENTS May: **Blackstone River Canoe Race,** Uxbridge.

July: The Common in Grafton Center is THE place to be July 4th—the Worcester Symphony plays at the bandstand and there are fireworks.

October: **Blackstone Valley Heritage Homecoming Days** around the Heritage State Park: launching of Capron Park by the Department of Environmental Management, tours, dinners, concerts, parades, fireworks, special events in all communities along the river.

MEDICAL EMERGENCY Milford-Whitinsville Regional Hospital (473-1190), Route 16, Milford.

The Nashoba Valley

The orginal Nashaway Plantation included only the towns of Lancaster, Sterling, Bolton, West Boylston, and Clinton, but its descendant, the Nashoba Valley, has come to designate all the rolling apple country west and northwest of Boston. To see apple blossoms in spring, Bostonians drive out Route 2 to Harvard, then follow country roads (great for bicycling) south along the Nashua River to the Wachusett Reservoir or north to Croton. They follow the same routes in fall to pick apples and in winter to cut Christmas trees and to ski. Few major cities have as handy access to such genuinely rural and beautiful countryside. Thanks to the recent rash of bed & breakfasts, the Nashoba Valley is also now a convenient weekend getaway.

AREA CODE 617
GUIDANCE North Central Massachusetts Chamber of Commerce (343-6487), 344 Main Street, PO Box 7330, Fitchburg 01420, publishes a seasonal guide that covers part of this area; the other part simply isn't covered.
TO SEE AND DO In Harvard: Harvard has a classic Common surrounded by white steepled churches, a fine old library, and a general store; its rolling, rural roads are lined with gentleman's farms and orchards.

Fruitlands Museums (456-3924), Prospect Hill, Harvard 01451. Open May 30 to September 30, Tuesday–Sunday 1–5. Nakamachekamuck was changed to "Prospect" Hill around 1800, but the memory of Indians who once camped here is perpetuated in a fine collection of Indian artifacts (including an interesting account of recent New England Indian history). Fruitlands is actually a complex of museums, centered around the eighteenth-century farmhouse in which Bronson Alcott and his fellow communards established a "New Eden" in 1843. The group wished to exploit neither man nor beast, and so practiced vegetarianism and refused to use cotton (raised by slaves), silk, or wool. The lack of the latter during a severe winter helped do the commune in. The farmhouse is now a museum of the Transcendental Movement, with pictures, books, and relics of Emerson, Alcott, and other movement leaders. A picture gallery up the path contains some outstanding early nineteenth-century portraits by itinerant artists and late nineteenth-

The Nashoba Valley and North

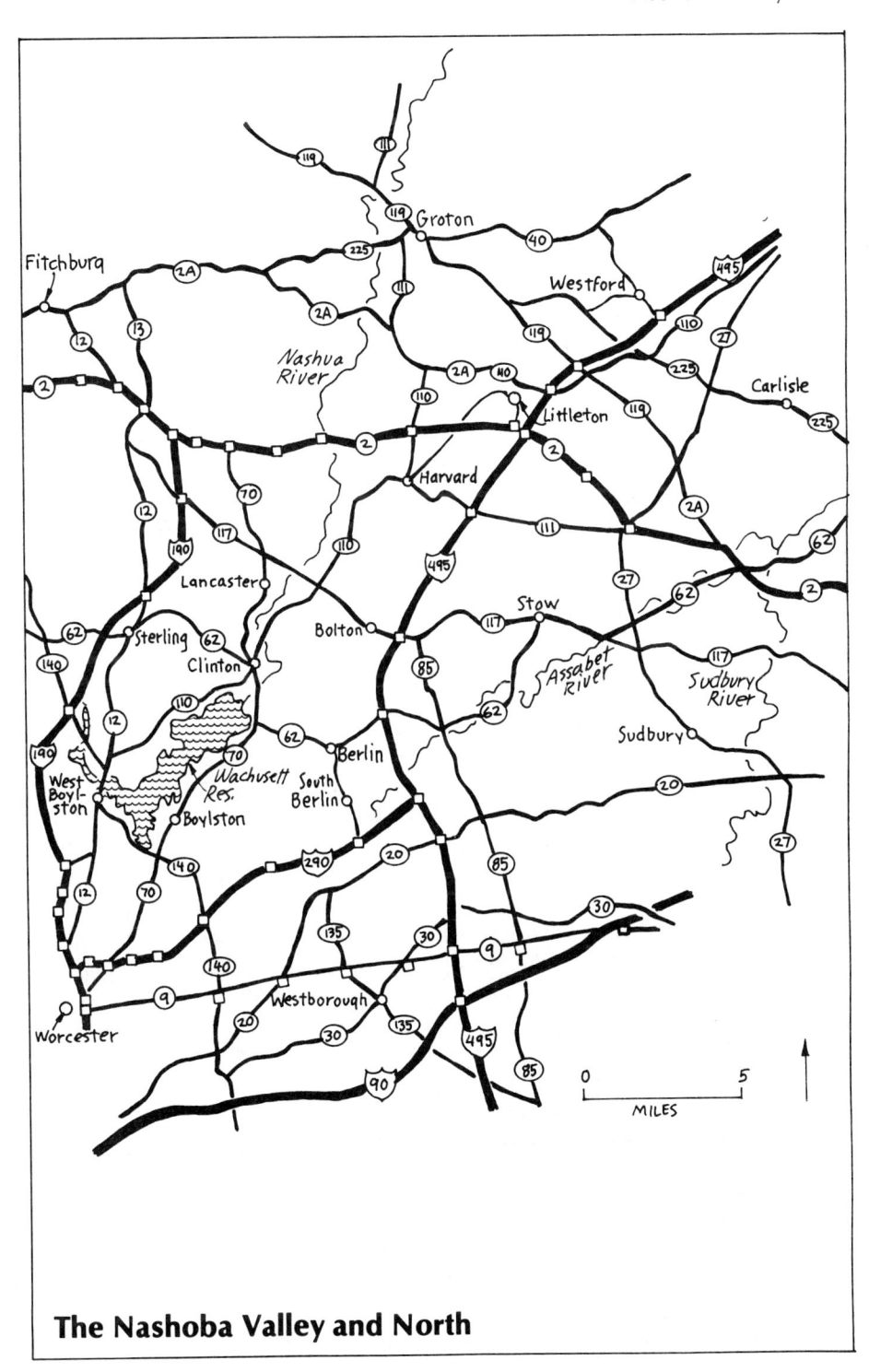

century New England landscapes by Thomas Cole, Albert Bierstadt, F. E. Church, and others. There is also a 1790s Shaker House displaying Shaker furnishings and crafts, moved here from the Shaker Village of which vestiges can still be seen elsewhere in town (ask directions). This unusual collection was put together by Boston blue blood Clara Endicott Sears in the early twentieth century. Sited high on a hill, it overlooks a spread of hill and valley, a view which can be enjoyed from the Tea Room, open for lunch, 1–3. There is also a reception center with changing exhibits. Nominal admission charge.

In Lancaster: Lancaster was the first town in Worcester County, founded in 1642 when a man named Thomas King established a trading post on what is now George Hill Road. In 1676 the town was sacked by Indians, and a number of prisoners were carried off, including Mary Rowlandson, the minister's wife. She wrote a vivid account of her ordeal and described her first night of captivity, spent under the boulder on George Hill, now "Rowlandson's Rock." Lancaster is peaceful now. Many of the handsome buildings on its wide Main Street are occupied by the Atlantic Union College, operated by the Seventh Day Adventists.

The First Church of Christ (Unitarian), Town Green, is one of New England's outstanding church buildings, complete with a Paul Revere bell and handsome horse sheds. It was designed by Charles Bulfinch in 1816 and built of local brick. The interior retains its box pews, fluted columns, and box stoves (lighting has been discreetly added). Open for Sunday services and by appointment: 365-2427.

The Lancaster Library (365-2008), also on the Green, was built as a Civil War memorial with a dome above its octagonal center and a luxurious 1920s children's room designed to look like a gentleman's study. Note the Audubon prints in the rare book room.

Toy Cupboard Theater and Museums (365-9519), 57 East George Hill Road (just off Main Street). Puppet performances year-round: September–June, the first and last Saturday of every month at 11 AM; in July and August, Wednesdays and Thursdays at 2 PM. The museums are also open Sunday afternoons (please call ahead) and by appointment anytime. 1986 marked the 45th anniversary of the remarkable puppet shows, which Herbert Hosmer orchestrates in his delightful theater, a converted 200-year-old woodshed. The **John Greene Chandler Museum**—with an extraordinary collection of toys, puppets, doll houses, and antique children's books, including *The Remarkable Story of Chicken Little* (written by John Greene Chandler who lived in Lancaster)—is next to the theater and included in the 75 cents per person puppet show fee.

APPLES In Harvard: Pick-your-own apples are available in season at the following: **Carlson Orchards** (456-3916), Oak Hill Road and also at

Carlson's roadside stand, with a cider press just north of Route 2; **A&M Orchards** (456-8408), 282 Eldridge Road; **Giskes Orchard** (456-3560), St. Johns Lane; **Pick-A-Peck Apples** (456-8521), Westcott Road; **Wade Orchard** (456-3926), on Westcott Road and 11 Ayer Road; **Hammerhead Farm** (456-8592), Westcott Road; **West Orchard Farm Stand** (456-8363), Route 111; **Windy Ridge Farm** (456-8334), 448 Bolton Road; and **Doe Orchards** (772-4139), Ayer Road.

In Bolton: **Nashoba Valley Winery and Orchards** (779-5521), 100 Wattaquadoc Hill Road, off Route 117. Open year-round, Friday, Saturday, and Sunday 11–6 for tours; weekdays for tastings. The yield of this 50-acre orchard is processed into a variety of wines; peach, cranberry, and blueberry wines are also produced on the premises, all of them piquant rather than sweet. Few tasters go away without a bottle or three. New England cheeses are also sold. Pick-your-own in season, picnic tables, touing trails in ski season.

Bolton Orchards (779-2733), junction of Routes 110 and 117. Open year-round, daily 9–6. A landmark roadside stand with its own brand name canned baked bean supper, chowders, jams; also sells syrup, fruit baskets, honey, cheese, and its own apples (250 acres), peaches (15 acres), pears (9 acres), and vegetables (60 acres); cider mill in season. At **Bolton Spring Farm** (779-2898), East Main Street, Bolton, you can pick-your-own in season.

In Sterling: **Meadowbrook Orchards** (365-7617), Chase Hill Road, off Route 62, just west of the Lancaster town line, open early August through Christmas, 9–5. A complete farm stand geared to ship apples, syrup, jams, jellies, fruitcake. Also fresh-baked muffins, turnovers, deep-dish apple pie.

Sterling Cider Co. (422-6622). Waschaum and School Streets, pick-your-own in season.

Sterling Orchards (422-6170), 60 Kendall Hill Road, farm stand (open August until the Sunday before Christmas), Apple Seed Tea Room, cross-country trails, and lodging (see Bed & Breakfasts).

In Lancaster: **Deershorn Farm Orchard** (365-3691), Chase Hill Road, off Route 62. Pick-your-own, trailer rides through the orchards, picnic area; farm stand sells native corn, pumpkins, vegetables, and cider as well as apples.

George Hill Orchards (365-4331), George Hill Road, South Lancaster. Open Sunday through Friday in season: wagon rides, music, cider press.

In Groton: **Hillbrook Orchards** (448-3248), 170 Old Ayer Road, off Route 119. Open daily in season, pick-your-own.

In Littleton: **Chase Farm** (486-3893), 509 Great Road; pick-your-own in season.

Nagog Hill Farm (486-3264), Nagog Hill Road. Open daily in season.

In Stow: **Honey Pot Hill Orchards** (562-5666), 144 Sudbury Road. Mid-September to mid-October, daily for pick-your-own; also **Carver Hill Orchards** (897-8200).

GREEN SPACE   J. **Harry Rich State Forest** (597-8802), Route 119, Groton. An undeveloped, 508-acre park with more than six miles of dirt woods roads and trails, canoeing.

New England Forestry Foundation properties in Groton include the 54-acre, former estate **Groton Place** (Route 225), notable for its avenues of trees and good for ski touring; and **Sabine Woods,** 146 acres adjoining Groton School and harboring a swimming hole (from Groton village drive east on Route 40, roughly six miles).

Wachusett Reservoir (365-4756), Clinton and Boylston. Just one-tenth the size of the Quabbin, with a 37-mile shoreline and maximum depth of 120 feet, Wachusett was created in 1906 by building a 205-foot-high dam on a ledge across the south branch of the Nashua River. Look for the access point off Route 70 for South Dike, extending two miles out into the reservoir, good for strolling.

Most of these towns have also set aside conservation land, available for walking and ski touring. Inquire locally about public land along the Nashua and Assabet rivers.

BICYCLING   Boston bikers have discovered the beauty of the area's narrow, rural roads, some with sweeping views. There is even a hostel (see Bed & Breakfasts) in Littleton, a source of suggestions for precise routes. You might also want to consider the 17-mile loop around Wachusett Reservoir: country roads circle the water and Route 70 takes you through Boylston, notable for its diamond-shaped Green, with a small but handsome fieldstone town hall built in 1830.

FISHING   At Wachusett Reservoir shore fishing is permitted at gates 3–20, 21–27, and 28–37. A state fishing license is required.

HANG GLIDING   **Aeolus Hang Glider** (448-5214), Martin's Road, Groton. Certified instructors offer lessons year-round.

HORSEBACK RIDING   **Bobby's Ranch** (263-7165), off Route 2A in Littleton (behind the Acton Mall). Open Wednesday–Sunday 9–6; $10 per hour weekdays, $15 on weekends. Trails are through a 2,000-acre conservation area.

ALPINE SKIING   **Nashoba Valley** (692-3033), Power Road, Westford (between Routes 2A-119 and 110). Open December 1–March 15; daily and night skiing. This is a learning hill with just a 240-foot vertical drop but considerable uphill capacity.

Lifts: 2 chairs, 5 tows, 1 bar
Snowmaking: 90% of area
Rates: $11 adult, $9 children on weekends, holidays.
Other: a strong children's ski school

CROSS-COUNTRY SKIING   **Great Brook Farm State Park** (369-6312), Lowell Road in Carlisle; marked trails and winter rentals, instruction.

Nashoba Valley 211

Trails also available at **Nashoba Winery** in Bolton and **Sterling Orchards** in Sterling (see Apples), also available on conservation land, inquire locally.

INNS **The Sterling Inn** (422-6592), Route 12, Sterling 01564. This tudor-style, 1920s inn has eight upstairs rooms. This is primarily a restaurant and the rooms are small, tidy but uninspired; $40 double with private bath includes breakfast.

Longfellow's Wayside Inn (443-8846), Sudbury 01776, just off Route 20. Although really east of the Nashoba Valley, we include the inn because it is so handy to this area and serves as a rural roost from which to explore Boston as well. Better known as a restaurant, and surrounded by a mini-New England village assembled on the grounds by Henry Ford in the 1920s, it has ten rooms beautifully furnished with authentic antiques. The tavern dates back to the 1680s but was so creaky by 1861, when Henry Wadsworth Longfellow visited it on weekends, that he dubbed it "Hobgoblin Hall." He grouped a half-dozen characters around the hearth and gave each a story to tell, like Chaucer's Canterbury pilgrims. The hit from these "Tales of a Wayside Inn" was, and still is, the landlord's:

Listen my children and you shall hear
Of the midnight ride of Paul Revere

Restored by Henry Ford, the inn has since survived a major fire. Rates are $50 double plus tax; breakfast is served to houseguests only.

BED & BREAKFASTS **Folkstone Bed & Breakfast** (869-2687; live, 8 AM– 1 PM), PO Box 121, Station 1, Boylston 01505. This service places guests in more than a dozen homes, most of them historic, throughout Worcester County. $30–$65 per room including breakfast.

Pineapple Hospitality (990-1696), 384 Rodney French Boulevard, New Bedford 02744. This reservation service has two inviting local listings. One is within the Boylston historic district and is known for its breakfasts, which can include scones with strawberry butter, popovers, sausages, and, in the fall, cranberry buttermilk pancakes. Another in South Berlin is an early nineteenth-century farmhouse on five acres with woodland and ponds. $40 double including full breakfast at both.

Olde Rose Cottage (835-4034), 24 Worcester Street (Route 12), West Boylston 01583. A Gothic-revival (1850) house within sight of Wachusett Reservoir. The Carriage House (which now has a three-room, skylit apartment upstairs and meeting space, down) was actually moved from the drowned area before it was flooded. The five guest rooms are furnished in country and elegant antiques (Michael and Loretta Kittredge also have a two-floor antiques store in their barn), $65 for a double room with bath, $55 with shared bath, full breakfast included; $350 per week for the apartment.

Heywood House (366-2161), 207 West Main Street, Westborough 01581. Built in 1729 and in the Heywood family since 1850, this gracious home offers four bedrooms and a pleasant common room with TV and two acres, good for strolling. $40 double with private bath, $25 with shared bath.

Carter-Washburn House (365-2188), 46 Seven Bridge Road, Lancaster 01523. A classic federal-style mansion has been nicely restored and furnished with antiques brought from Scotland by its young proprietors; guests can enjoy the beamed library and try their skill on the rosewood piano in the living room. There are five guest rooms sharing three baths. $35 double, $30 single.

Sterling Orchards (422-6170), 60 Kendall Hill Road, Sterling 01564. Shirley Smiley offers two suites, each with a sitting room and private bath, at the 1720 homestead, which is also a 100-acre orchard with a seasonal farm stand, cross-country ski trails, and an Apple Seed Tea Room, open August through mid-December.

Stonehedge Bed & Breakfast (838-2574), 119 Sawyer Road, Berlin 01503. A 1785 home with 30 acres, a swimming pool, and tennis court offers one suite with its own living room and bathroom; $40 double with full breakfast.

Friendly Crossways Youth Hostel (456-3649), Whitcomb Avenue, Littleton 01460 (but the house is actually in the town of Harvard). A farmhouse set on a country road with a big barn on 60 acres. This has been an American Youth Hostel since 1945 and still caters to hostelers ($8.50 per night) and groups ($15 per night with meals, can accommodate up to 75 comfortably) but now also offers cushier lodging for bed & breakfast guests ($25 including breakfast).

DINING OUT **The Sterling Inn** (422-6592), Route 12, Sterling. Closed Mondays, otherwise open for lunch and dinner, which ranges from $9 for dishes like Chicken Paprikash, to $14 for Broiled Filet Mignon with mushroom caps. This is the popular local eating spot and has an authentic 1920s atmosphere. There are daily lunch and dinner specials, daily baked desserts like Midnight Chocolate Cake and Indian Pudding.

Longfellow's Wayside Inn (443-8846), Route 20, Sudbury. Open daily for lunch and dinner. Just east of the Nashoba Valley but too special (and near) to omit. Lunch is in the $6–$12 range, and dinner $10–$20, but there are child's plates. Roast duckling, deep-dish apple pie, and Indian pudding; traditional New England cooking. See Inns above.

Arturo's Ristorante (835-6000), Route 12, West Boylston (at the Fair Shopping Plaza). Closed Sundays otherwise open daily for lunch and dinner. Italian menu featuring Fettucini and Linguini ($4.25–$6.95) and veal dishes ($9.75–$12.50).

EATING OUT **Johnson's Drive-in** (448-6840), Route 119, open from 6 AM daily, year-round, until 10 PM in summer; until 8 PM in spring and fall; until 3 PM in winter except Thursday, Friday, and Saturday when it's until 8 PM. This is a handy place to eat breakfast if you are setting out for a day's cross-country skiing or exploring; anytime for a basic burger or homemade ice cream.

4 Corners Restaurant (448-3358/59), junction Routes 119 and 225, Groton. Open daily for lunch and dinner. We will never forget the evening that a seven-year-old son said he felt like eating Chinese food and we all laughed. There we were driving through a classic Yankee landscape. But lo and behold, the next road sign had Chinese lettering. The menu at the 4 Corners features Chop Suey, Chow Mein, and Egg Foo Yong. There are Pu-Pu platters, sweet and sour shrimp, and a variety of shrimp and sea food dishes, $5–$10.

Fruitlands Museums Tea Room (456-3924), Prospect Hill, Harvard. Open May 30–September 30, lunch served 1–3. The dining area, both inside and out, is one of the most pleasant spots around; the menu features Shaker recipes, nothing over $6.

Apple Seed Tea Room at Sterling Orchards (422-6170), Kendall Hill Road, Sterling. Open daily in summer, weekends in fall, serving English-style tea 1–4:40, then high tea through December (soup and sandwiches) in an early eighteenth-century farmhouse set in its 100-acre orchard.

ENTERTAINMENT **Thayer Conservatory Orchestra** (365-4561, ext. 363), Main Street, Lancaster, stages frequent concerts at the handsome old conservatory, adjacent to Atlantic Union College.

Also see the **Toy Cupboard Theatre** puppet shows under To See and Do.

Groton Center for the Arts (448-3001), Willowdale and Main Streets, Groton, is an information source about frequent free children's and adult performances and special events.

SPECIAL EVENTS January: **First Night** in Groton, sponsored by Groton Center for the Arts (see Entertainment).

May: **Spring Apple Blossom Festival,** held sporadically in Harvard; even when it isn't, this is a beautiful time to tour the area.

October: **Horse Sheds Crafts Festival,** Bulfinch Church, Lancaster, first weekend.

MEDICAL EMERGENCY **The Clinton Hospital** (365-4531), 201 Highland Street, Clinton; emergency room open daily, 24-hours.

The Merrimack Valley

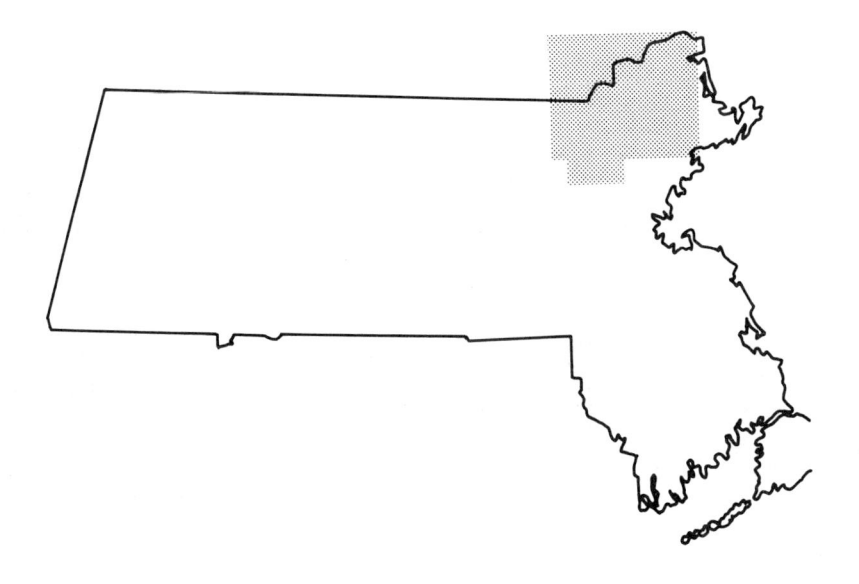

INTRODUCTION

The Merrimack River is one of New England's grand waterways. For three centuries its lower reaches have formed both a highway and a boundary between New Hampshire and Massachusetts.

For more than a century the river itself was badly polluted by mill cities which harnessed the power from its mighty falls. But in recent decades the beauty of both the river and brick mills has been recognized—and improved.

The Merrimack is now rated "Class B," safe for fish and swimmers. The Merrimack River Watershed Council has published a fine map of the entire river, pinpointing canoe access spots and parks, also noting prime fishing areas. The state's Department of Environmental Management is presently creating beaches in both Lowell and Lawrence.

Lowell, the country's first important, planned industrial city, can now be toured by canal boat and trolley. Thanks to National and Heritage State Park programs, many industrial and commercial buildings have been restored. Dramatic exhibits and guided tours now tell Lowell's remarkable story.

Lawrence, not many miles downriver, is on the verge of the kind of renaissance that has transformed Lowell. Its Heritage State Park opened just this fall and major canal-side restorations are under way. Even now it is well worth a visit, rich in reasonably priced ethnic restaurants and in factory outlets.

Beyond these two mill cities in the Merrimack Valley lie peaceful old clapboard towns like Andover and North Andover. Route 113, hugging the south bank, draws you through the old river towns. Don't miss Rocks Village, Haverhill's original 1640 settlement.

We have included Newburyport in the North Shore because that's the way most people think of it. But the old port city is as much a part of the valley as Lowell and Lawrence, and some of the most beautiful public river frontage is found in West Newbury.

AREA CODE 617

GUIDANCE **Merrimack River Watershed Council, Inc.** (363-5777), 694 Main Street, West Newbury 01985. The detailed map/guide to the river costs $3.95. Also inquire about guided trips, special events.

North of Boston Tourist Council (532-1449), PO Box 3031, Peabody 01960, publishes a Visitors Guide that includes sights to see in this area.

Also see Guidance under Lowell and Lawrence.

Lowell

This brick mill city is enjoying a rebirth as dramatic as its 1820s birth. Because Lowell was the country's first important, planned, industrial city, its canals and many of its mills now form a unique National and Heritage State Park.

Tourists are nothing new in Lowell. Davy Crockett and Charles Dickens were among the mid-nineteenth-century visitors who came here to see one of the world's wonders: an attractive, even cultured, industrial city.

The idea of an industrial utopia was conceived by Francis Cabot Lowell, a Boston merchant who was permitted to view British power looms in 1810, a time when only cotton yarn—not cloth— was being manufactured in the United States. Lowell managed to memorize enough about the process to reproduce the English machinery in a factory on the Charles River. With his "Boston Associates," he searched for a site with enough space and water power to build an entire mill city, unfortunately dying before the 1821 selection of 400 acres by the Merrimack River in East Chelmsford.

In 1836 Lowell became the third city (population: 17,000) incorporated in Massachusetts. It already included eight major textile mills, employing 7,500 workers. Most of these workers were the daughters of Yankee farmers who lived together in tidy boarding houses and spent their limited free time attending lectures, reading, and writing.

This industrial utopia was, however, short-lived. Competition from other mill cities forced longer hours and lower wages. Yankee mill girls were replaced at the looms by immigrant families, willing to accept work at any pay and to live in the flimsy wooden tenements that mushroomed around town. By the turn of the century, mill-hands were working a 72-hour week for $5 or less. The city's population, with its 40 nationalities, peaked in the 1920s at 126,000. When the textile mills moved south many workers moved away too, and the immense brick buildings, built to withstand the throb of the power looms, stood vacant for decades. From the end of World War I until the mid-70s, Lowell stagnated. It lost one third of its people to the suburbs. In 1975 Lowell's unemployment was the highest in the state. Its enterprising young people, writer Jack Kerouac among them, had fled.

It was a school principal named Patrick J. Mogan who first rallied residents to the idea that Lowell had a history so special that it deserved a state park. The rest is now already history. Merrimack Street is bustling again and the new Parks Visitors Center is surrounded by shops and restaurants. A variety of light industries (led by Wang computers) now fill the old mills and more than 80 downtown buildings have been rehabilitated in recent years. The University of Lowell (formed in 1975 when Lowell State College and Lowell Technological Institute merged) is a source of outstanding theater and music.

In 1988 the Boott Mill, one of the largest and most handsome complexes, will become the showcase of the new Lowell. In the meantime the 1828 Market Mills remain the focal point for visitors, housing the National Park Visitors Center and also a dining area, shops, and galleries. The Heritage State Park's lively exhibit (focusing on waterpower and the story behind the city's 5.6 miles of canals) is next door in a former stove and pipe factory. Free tours—which include transport by trolley (year-round) and canal boat (warm weather)—are offered by uniformed rangers, and there are frequent special events. There is also some fine dining and luxurious lodging. Dickens and Crockett would have approved.

AREA CODE 617

GUIDANCE　**The National and State Parks Visitor Center** (459-1000), 246 Market Street, open daily 8:30–5. The place to phone before you come and check into as soon as you arrive for an idea of the day's tour and events schedule. There's also a courtesy phone for the Hilton and major motels.

　　Chambers of Commerce, Northern Middlesex (454-5633), 45 Palmer Street (in the old firehouse), dispenses information about dining, lodging, social events.

GETTING THERE　By train and bus: MBTA Commuter Service, operated by the Boston & Maine Railroad, offers frequent daily service from Boston's North Station (227-5070) to the Charles A. Gallagher Transportation Terminal (459-7101) on Thorndike Street. This is also the local depot for Trailways and Vermont Transit. Shuttle service to the Parks Visitor Center runs every 10 minutes.

　　By car from Boston: Either Route 128 to Route 3 or I-93 to Route 495; either way exit onto the Lowell Connector and follow signs for the Parks Visitor Center at Market Mills; free parking in back.

GETTING AROUND　Beginning in the fall of '87 enclosed, vintage 1901 trolleys (powered by an electric overhead line) will shuttle between the visitors center and other points of interest like the Boott and Suffolk Mills and Lower Locks. Until then the open-sided trolley cars operate Memorial Day Weekend through Columbus Day, also the season for the canal boats (see Tours under To See and Do).

TO SEE AND DO **National and State Parks Visitor Center and Tours** (459-1000), 246 Market Street, in the former Lowell Manufacturing Company Mill Complex, now called "Market Mills." A multi-image slide show, "Lowell: The Industrial Revelation" (presented twice each hour), glosses nicely over the dramatic rise of Lowell and its factory system, its turn-of-the-century excesses and rich ethnic life, also its subsequent decline. Here you also sign up for one of the day's tours (it's best to call ahead to reserve a spot); fill the time before the tour starts by ambling over to the Melting Pot (see Restaurants) or A Brush with History galleries (see Selective Shopping), or by examining an assortment of exhibits in the center itself and/or up the street at the Lowell Heritage State Park.

Lowell Heritage State Park (453-1950), Waterpower Exhibit in the Mack Building, 25 Shattuck Street, open daily 9–4, Thursdays until 9 PM. Audiovisuals, working water models, and life-sized sculptures tell the story of how Lowell's canals, waterwheels, and turbines worked. Children can move a log raft through locks and speed the revolutions of a waterwheel; press buttons to hear the eerily lifelike clothed grey sculptures tell their stories; and clamber on the giant waterwheel out front.

TOURS October through May the National and State parks offer daily walking tours (60 to 90-minutes long) that vary, some focusing on general Lowell history, others focusing on the mill girls and immigrants or on the power canals. All tours are free until summer, 1987, after which there will be a nominal charge. It is best to make advance reservations. Memorial through Columbus Day the tours are undeniably more interesting, including:

The Mill and Canal Tour (two and one-quarter hours). You ride the open-sided trolley to the Suffolk Mill to view turbine restoration and worker housing, then ease through the newly reconstructed transportation locks on the Pawtucket and Northern Canals. Children tend to hold up well on this.

Waterpower Tour. Travel by barge along the Pawtucket Canal, also take the trolley to experience nineteenth-century high tech; sites include the Lower Locks and Appleton Mills.

Mill and Trolley. By trolley and foot you tour the Boott Mills to learn about the technology of cotton textile production and the living and working conditions of the factory "operatives."

Knapsack Tours. Offered Fridays at 6 PM in June, July, and August. Bring your own bike and a picnic to explore Lowell's canals and rivers, mills, mansions, and neighborhoods.

OTHER ATTRACTIONS **Whistler House** (452-7641), 243 Worthen Street. Open Tuesday–Friday 1–4, also Saturday 1–4 in summer. Built in

1823 to house the agent of Lowell's machine shops. Later it was home for George Whistler, father of the artist James McNeil Whistler whose etchings now fill the first floor. The Historical Society collection occupies the upper floors.

St. Anne's Church, corner of Merrimack and Kirk streets, built in 1825, is said to be haunted by the first minister who sided with the rebellious mill girls (who refused to pay tithes to the church as they were ordered). It's also said to be built from stone excavated during the construction of the Merrimack Canal.

Pawtucket Falls. This 30-foot drop is still impressive; best viewed from the Pawtucket Canal Gatehouse, School Street.

For the **Museum of American Textile History** in North Andover and the **Phillips/Andover Museums,** see Lawrence.

STILL TO COME Summer of '87: **The Patrick J. Mogan Cultural Center,** a restored 1836 boardinghouse with exhibits depicting the working people of Lowell, from mill girls through a variety of immigrants. It is named for the former Superintendent of Schools who first suggested changing Lowell's image, creating a National Park.

Sometime in '88: **Mill 6** in the Boott complex, a five-story museum with an entire weave room (100 working looms). There will also be exhibits on the rise and fall of the cotton industry, an art gallery, and shops.

GREEN SPACE In Lowell: **Vandenberg Esplanade River Front Park,** Pawtucket Boulevard (north bank of the Merrimack River), includes the Sampas Pavilion performance stage, the new boat dock, community sailing and rowing programs, and a mile of paved walkway with flower gardens, trees, and benches adjacent to the river.

Lucy Larcom Park, adjacent to St. Anne's Church by the Merrimack Canal.

Victorian Garden, adjacent to the Mack Building, part of the Heritage State Park.

Beyond Lowell: **Lowell Dracut State Forest** (452-7191), Trotting Park Road off Varnum Avenue. This 997-acre park has a 30-acre lake for skating and fishing; picnicking; also scenic trails for hiking, cross-country skiing, and bicycling. There is an Indian spring and the springhouse for a former bottling works. Granite from the forest's quarries was used for mill foundations and canal embankments.

Great Brook Farm State Park (369-6312), Lowell Road, Carlisle. Open meadows, wooded trails, and a scenic pond; also a ski-touring center in winter. From Lowell, take Route 110 to Route 4 through Chelmsford to Carlisle. The park is on the left just over the Carlisle line.

Carlisle State Forest (369-6312), Forest Road, Carlisle, a 22-acre

Rangers offer frequent historical tours of Lowell's Canal System

area. This former estate is webbed with hiking and touring trails. Also see Cross-country Skiing.

Warren Manning State Park (369-6312), Chelmsford Road, Billerica, Route 129. A 380-acre wooded spread with picnic tables, a children's spray pool, bridle paths, hiking trails.

GOLF **Trull Brook Golf Course** (851-6731), Tewksbury, 18 holes.

HIKING Note description of trails under Green Space.

CROSS-COUNTRY SKIING **Great Brook Farm Ski Touring Center** (369-7486), 96 Pleasant Hill Lane, Carlisle. Open in ski season daily from 9 AM to 4:40, until 9 PM Tuesday and Thursday; nine miles of trails, instruction, rental equipment, night skiing on a 1.5 kilometer loop.

North Country Ski Touring (369-7486), Carlisle State Forest, Lowell Road. Ten miles of trails, instruction, rentals, snack bar at Hart Barn. Open daily from 9 AM to 4:40, until 9 PM Tuesday and Thursday.

SUNSET CRUISE In addition to its sight-seeing cruises, the National Park sponsors a purely recreational canal cruise departing Saturday and Sunday evenings from Bellegrade Boathouse, offering an hour's ride up to Ting's Island, passing through restored transportation locks. Fee.

SWIMMING Privately operated **Wyman's Beach** (692-6287) in Westford offers swimming, camping, and picnicking.

A public beach on the Merrimack at the **Bellegrade Boathouse** is due to open within two years.

Also see Harold Parker State Forest under Lawrence.

LODGING **Lowell Hilton** (452-1200), 50 Warren Street, Lowell 01852, at the Lower Locks. A new, 251-room hotel overlooking the Pawtucket Canal, within walking distance of all the Heritage State Park sites and downtown shops. Facilities include a swim and fitness club, two restaurants, and two lounges. Packages begin at $62 per couple; rack rates at $92 single, $107 double.

Westford Regency (692-8200), 219 Littleton Road, Westford 01886. A four-story, 193-room motel just off Route 495. Facilities include a health club with swimming pool, racquetball court, and two restaurants. From $80 single to $225 for a suite. For Sheraton Rolling Green Inn, Andover, see Lawrence.

Town House Inn (454-5606), 850 Chelmsford Street, Lowell 01851. A 75-room motel with restaurant, outdoor pool, and landscaped grounds. $62 double.

Commonwealth House (454-5663), 87 Nesmith Street—but inquiries should be addressed to COMFED Savings Bank, 45 Central Street, Lowell 01852, attention: Marketing Department. This aristocratic mansion, built in 1843, has been restored by the COMFED Savings Bank and is used for a variety of community functions. It is furnished with antiques and has four homey guest rooms, sharing two baths. $35 per room.

Bed & Breakfast (454-4949), 29 Burton Street. Nothing fancy but two rooms in a private home, $25 including a full breakfast; strong repeat business.

The Bed & Breakfast Folks (692-3232), 73 Providence Road, Westford 01886. A reservation service for a dozen homes in Pepperell, Chelmsford, and Westford as well as Lowell; $45 double, breakfast included.

Also see Lawrence.

DINING OUT **The Speare House** (452-7191), 525 Pawtucket Boulevard, is one of the city's leading Greek restaurants. Closed Mondays, otherwise open for lunch and dinner ($8.45–$14.95).

A.G. Pollard and Son's (459-4632), 98 Middle Street, around the corner from the Parks Visitors Center. Open for lunch weekdays, dinner daily. Walled-in brick and old books, specializing in seafood and steaks ($12.95 for New York sirloin). The Boston schrod is $5.75 at lunchtime; dinners are two for one Sunday–Thursday.

Oliver's Restaurant (459-3755), 91 Dutton Street, near the Merrimack Gatehouse and St. Anne's Church. A former agent's mansion is now a pleasant restaurant with specialties like Seafood Fettucini and Fisherman's Platter. Lunch daily except Sunday, dinner daily (on Sunday from noon). The lunch buffet is $4.99, otherwise ranges from $3–$5; dinner from $6.99–$14.99.

Prince Grotto Restaurant (458-0621), Carter Street. This is the big Italian restaurant in town, owned by Prince Marconi. Marble statues and strolling minstrels set the tone.

Athenian Corner (458-7052), 207 Market Street. Boasting the "largest variety of fine Greek food in New England," handy to the Park Visitors Center. Daily luncheon specials, dinners from $4.25, music and belly dancing Thursday through Sunday nights.

Windsor Mills Restaurant (459-2331), Lowell-Lawrence Boulevard, Route 110, Dracut. Open daily for lunch and dinner. Decorated with textile-mill artifacts, this is a locally popular dining place with a conplimentary soup bar for lunch, salad bar for dinner. Luncheon runs $4.25–$5.95; dinner $7.95–$14.95.

Manning Manse (663-4282), 56 Chelmsford Road, Route 129, North Billerica. Closed Monday, open at 4 PM Saturdays, and otherwise for lunch and dinner. This 1696 house is a landmark dining place, serving lunch and dinner, closed Mondays, traditional New England fare, children's menu. Lunch: $3.50–$7.95. Dinner: $7.95–$13.50.

EATING OUT **Southeast Asian Restaurant** (452-3182), 351 Market Street, corner of O'Connel Parkway. Open daily 8 AM–7:30 PM, Thai, Laotian, Cambodian, and Vietnamese specialties all made from scratch; $1.50–$4.50; cafeteria-style. The adjacent store sells a wide selection of Southeast Asian food specialities, both imported and fresh (meat cut Asian style, fresh vegetables).

The Dubliner (459-9831), 197 Market Street. Open daily except Sunday for lunch and dinner; around the corner from the Parks Visitors Center. An Irish pub atmosphere featuring the same menu—sandwiches, steaks, and seafood—all day. Plates average $5.75.

Derby Park (459-8882), 82 Middle Street. Best in summer when its outdoor cafe is the place to lunch on quiche or gourmet burgers, also open for dinner in summer. Otherwise this turns into a college-age geared nightspot with a DJ, live entertainment on Sundays; the salad bar is $3.95; soup and salad is $4.85. Same menu all day.

The Himalaya (937-9355), 45 Middle Street. Open Sunday–Friday for lunch, daily for dinner. North Indian cuisine ranging from mild to spicy, moderately priced. $2.95–$3.50 for lunch, $4.50–$6 for dinner.

The Melting Pot, 246 Market Street, in the Market Mills complex, adjacent to the Visitors Center. Mall-type counters selling Greek, American, Italian, and Mexican foods, which you consume at tables if you are lucky enough to find one, otherwise outside in the courtyard.

The Old Worthern Tavern (458-3132), 147 Worthern Street. Open Monday–Saturday for lunch, the city's oldest tavern and bar; luncheon specials from Chucky's kitchen.

Palmer Restaurant (452-8458), 50 Palmer Street. Good for spinach pie and soup or fried chicken fingers ($3.50). Open for breakfast, lunch, and dinner; no frills but fast service and good food.

Mill-Town Deli (937-3876), corner of Middle and Palmer Streets. Open from 6:30 AM–4:30 PM Monday–Saturday. Daily specials, homey, busy.

ENTERTAINMENT   **Park Offerings** (Call 454-5633 for updates): **Market Mills Summer Stage.** June through August, free concerts and dramatic presentations, Thursdays at 7 PM. **Tunes and Tales.** Alex Demas presents anecdotes and songs drawn from Lowell lore, year-round at the National Park Visitors Center; Tuesday, Wednesday, and Thursdays at 10:30 AM.

Merrimack Repertory Theatre (454-3926), Liberty Hall, East Merrimack Street. A professional equity theater presenting a full program of plays October–May, also special summer events.

Merrimack Lyric Opera Company (453-4560), PO Box 8633, operas are staged in spring at the Durgin Performing Arts Center, South Campus of the University of Lowell.

University of Lowell Foundation (459-0350). Performing arts program with artists of international repute, also music and happenings for children.

Lowell Memorial Auditorium (454-2854), East Merrimack Street, Lowell. The theater seats 1,200 and is the frequent stage for nationally known groups and Broadway shows.

SELECTIVE SHOPPING Galleries: **A Brush with History** (459-7819), 246 Market Street, across the courtyard from the Parks Visitor Center, includes twelve studios and a gallery. Open Tuesday–Sunday 11–5, Thursday until 9 PM. We especially liked the Lowell paintings by James McGowan.

Parker Gallery (452-7641), 243 Worthern Street. Open Tuesday–Friday 1–4; Saturdays during summer. Adjacent to the Whistler House, home of the Lowell Art Association; the Parker Gallery features changing exhibits.

Factory Outlet Stores: **Hub Mills Factory Outlet** (937-0320), 12 Perkins Street (off Cabot Street). Wool, mohair, cotton and silk yarns; wool sweaters, blankets, and lingerie.

Shoe Inn Factory Outlet (459-4119), 200 Market Street, across from Market Mills.

Other: Lowell's main shopping drag, Merrimack Street, is lined with shops, among them **Jordan Marsh Company** (a Boston department store), **Margaret's Needhearts of Lowell** (a large, friendly sewing source), and **Prince's Bookstore** (an old-fashioned bookstore and adjacent stationery shop). Don't miss **Parrot Hatters,** around the corner on Middlesex Street. Billing themselves as New England's hatters, this great shop has been in business since 1923.

SPECIAL EVENTS March: **Irish Cultural Heritage Week**—lectures, concerts, and special exhibits in the week that includes St. Patrick's Day.

May: **Spring Festival,** the week before and including Memorial Day—a multi-ethnic festival in JFK Plaza, sidewalk sales, parade.

June: **Bastille Day,** French celebrations.

July: **July 4th Celebration**—concert in the Sampas Pavilion, fireworks on Pawtucket Boulevard.

September: **Labor Day Weekends Kids Fair** (Sunday before Labor Day), games and free pony rides at Market Mills and Lucy Larcom Park. **Banjo and Fiddle Contest** at Market Mills (Saturday after Labor Day).

October: **Octoberfest** (Columbus Day Weekend), multi-ethnic festival and car show.

MEDICAL EMERGENCY **Saint Joseph's Hospital** (453-1761), 220 Pawtucket Street (west end of Merrimack Street), 24-hour emergency service.

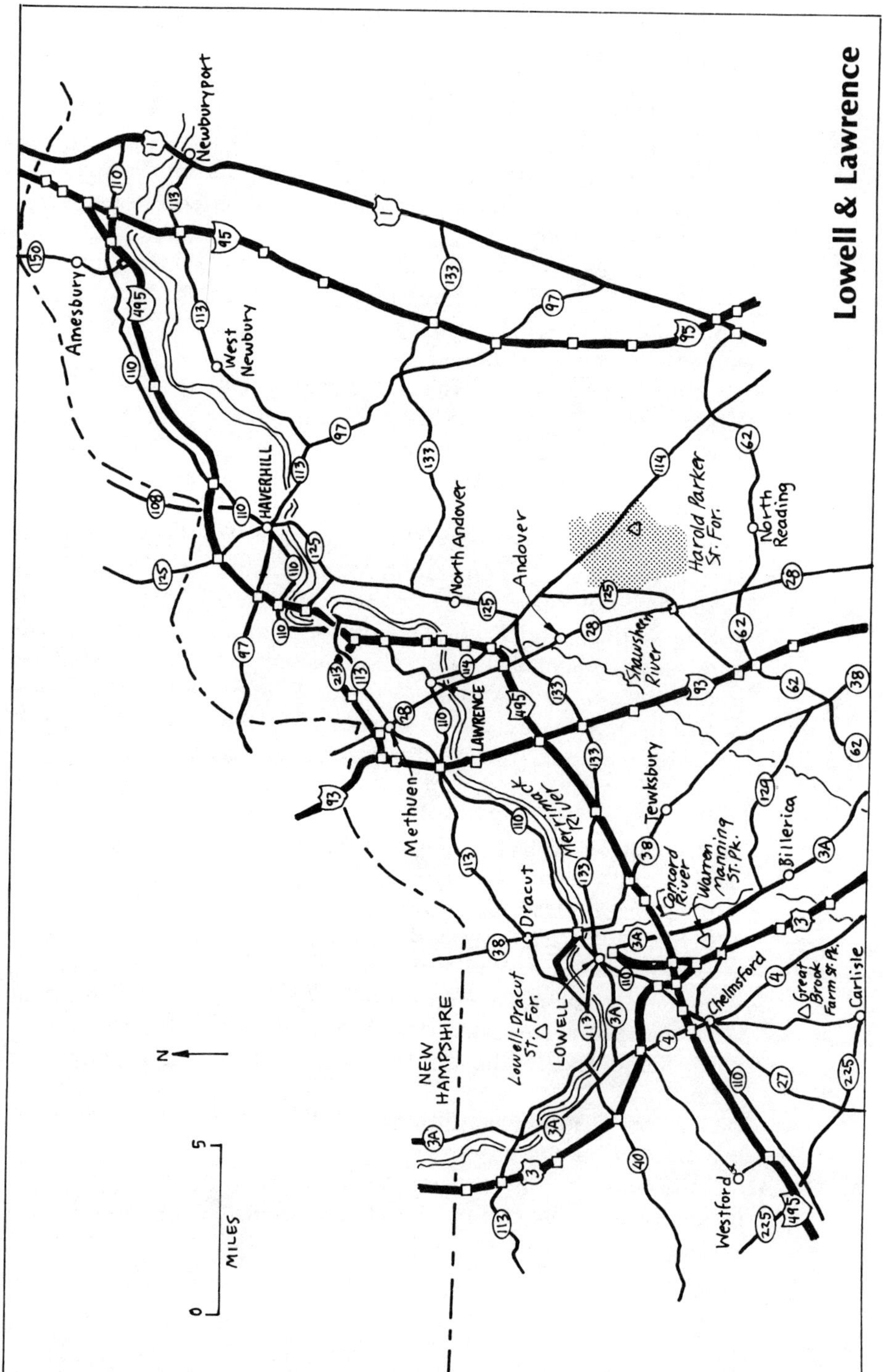
Lowell & Lawrence
Newburyport
Amesbury
West Newbury
HAVERHILL
North Andover
Andover
Harold Parker St. For.
North Reading
LAWRENCE
Methuen
Shawsheen River
Merrimack River
Tewksbury
Concord River
Warren Manning St. Pk.
Billerica
Dracut
Lowell-Dracut St. For.
LOWELL
Chelmsford
Great Brook Farm St. Pk.
Carlisle
Westford
NEW HAMPSHIRE
N
0
5
MILES

Middlesex Canal

This area includes the towns of Chelmsford, Billerica, Wilmington, and Winchester. The Middlesex Canal, approved by Governor John Hancock in 1793, was the first major canal in this country. It was 27 miles long, linking Boston with the Merrimack River at East Chelmsford (now Lowell). At the time it was begun, America had neither the engineers nor the tools necessary to cross so many rocks, swamps, and rivers while adjusting to varying elevations. It took 10 years to complete the twenty aqueducts (the means by which the bathtub-shaped channel crossed over small rivers) and 49 bridges. And the process entailed a number of engineering breakthroughs, like the invention of the dump cart and the floating towpath.

Opened in 1803, the Middlesex became a prototype for other canals, including the Erie. Its heyday came in the 1820s, when a barge could pass, via interconnecting waterways, the entire way from Boston Harbor to Concord, New Hampshire.

The glory was short-lived. A railroad to Lowell put the canal out of business. The train could get to Boston from Lowell in a half hour while the barge took all day. By the 1850s life-styles had also changed; passengers no longer seemed to enjoy gliding all day in the summertime, picking the blackberries that hung along the "berm" (opposite side of the canal from the towpath), or listening for hours to the band in the Pavilion at Horn Pond.

Less than half the canal can now be easily traced. Roughly six miles still hold water, another three miles of canal can be driven by or walked along. Glimpses of an aqueduct here, a lock there, and a tavern or tollhouse somewhere else compose the remaining evidence. The distance from the Merrimack River to the Mystic Lakes is 37 miles.

To trace the route of the canal for yourself you should begin in Lowell at Hadley Field, where the canal met the Merrimack River. Take Middlesex Street to Wood Street, then your first right onto Westford Road, where you pick up Route 3 to Route 110, and follow Route 3 south under Route 495 to Chelmsford. Note the tollhouse that still stands on Chelmsford's attractive Green and the Old Chelmsford Garrison House (105 Garrison Road, Route 110, open mid-June to mid-September, Wednesdays 2–5, free), a saltbox built in the late seventeenth century as an Indian defense.

Take Route 129 south and then left on Route 3A into Billerica and look for the Talbott Mills on the Concord River. This was the highest point and water source of the canal, which crossed at a right angle to the river. Horses and boatmen crossed the pond on a floating bridge (the towpath), which could be opened to permit through traffic on the Concord. The anchor block to the towpath remains, along with the traces of the canal's guard lock.

Return to Route 3A and on to Route 129. At the Billerica line note the abutments of the biggest and best-preserved canal aqueduct, standing in the Shawsheen River.

Routes 129 and 38 merge as you cross the canal; follow Route 38 south until you see the sign and parking area for the Wilmington Town Forest on your right. Walk in here past the ballpark, following the path into the woods; it leads to the old canal bed. Turn right and you come to the stone abutments of a small aqueduct; slightly farther along two boulders still bear the mark of two ropes straining against them.

Continue south on Route 38 to Rumford House (933-0781), 90 Elm Street, Woburn; open Wednesday–Sunday 1–4:30. This 1714 farmhouse has nothing to do with the canal, but it tells the interesting story of Benjamin Thompson. A friend of a British general, he fled to England during the Revolution, where he became a famous scientist. He later was privy counselor of Bavaria and eventually became a Count of the Holy Roman Empire. The house contains working models of his early experiments. This is said to be the first house in the country to be preserved by a historical society.

Continue down Route 38 until you see a three-story, boxlike mansion that sits incongruously behind a Route 128 interchange. The mansion belonged to Loammi Baldwin, the first sheriff of Middlesex County and the engineer and construction superintendent of the canal. Saved from demolition by the Woburn Historical Commission, it is now the Baldwin Landing Restaurant. Rides are available aboard the "Colonel Baldwin" packet boat, moored at its door (Sundays in July and August, 1–4).

Route 38 becomes Woburn's Main Street. At the Winn Memorial Library (designed by Henry Hobson Richardson in 1877) pick up a leaflet "Towpath Trail," showing the route of the old towpath, preserved now for hiking and jogging from the Baldwin Mansion to Winn Street and from Pleasant Street to Horn Path, which, unfortunately, bears no trace of its old island pavilion, nor of the four taverns that once stood handy to the three sets of double locks.

The Middlesex Canal

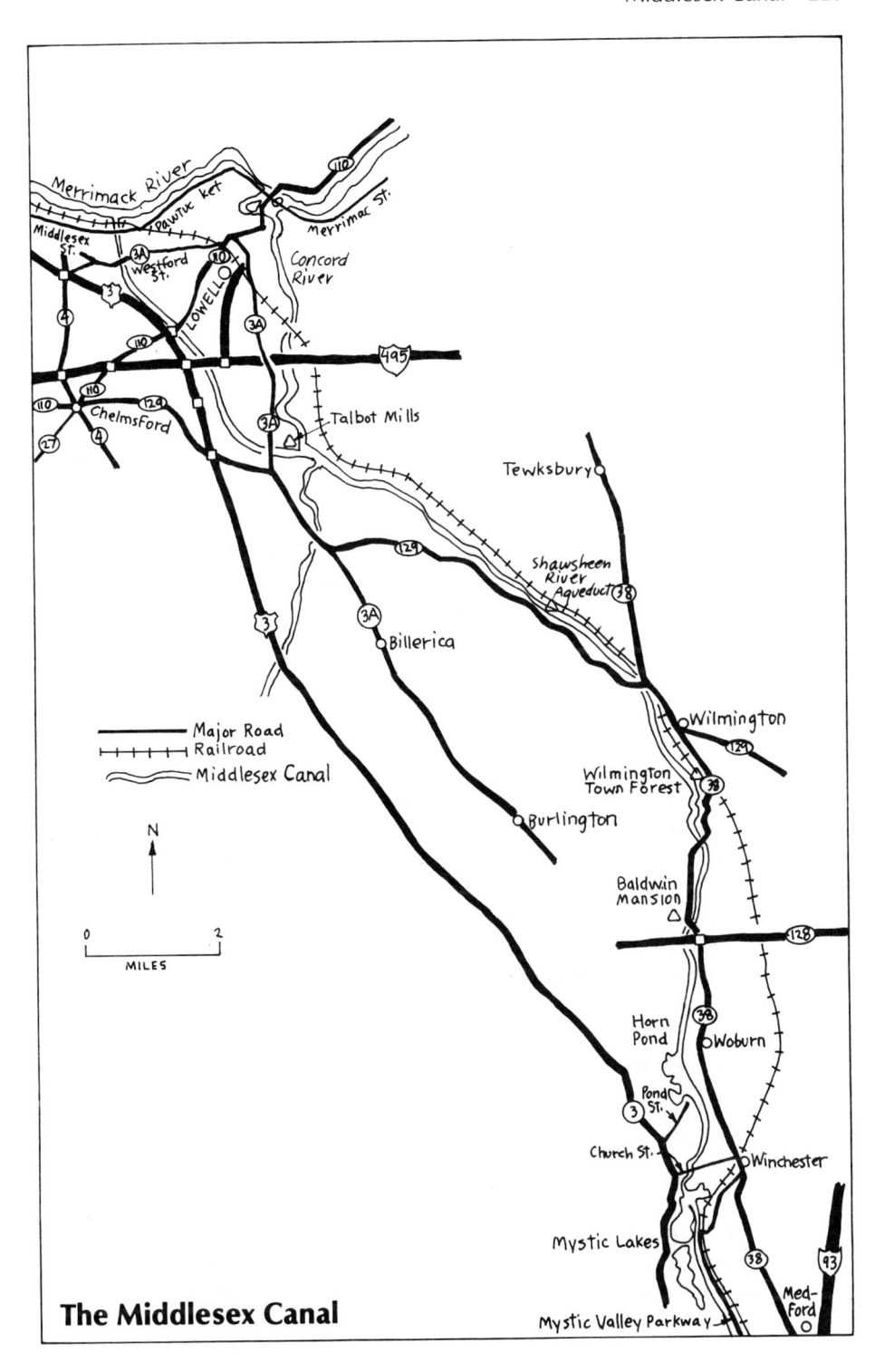

Lawrence

In 1845 when the Essex Company first selected this site, it was still a rural stretch of the Merrimack River known for its great falls. In 1847 Lawrence (named for Abbot Lawrence, a partner in the company) was incorporated and within six months its population grew from 200 to 2,500. By 1848 the Essex Company had already built the Great Dam (which still stands), two canals, a machine shop to build locomotives, the Prospect Hill Reservoir, 50 brick buildings, a large boardinghouse, and the Atlantic Cotton, Pemberton, Upper Pacific, and Duck mills. They conscientiously planted elms, laid out a Common and parks, and built their mills and workers' boardinghouses solidly. By 1850 the town boasted 11 schools and a lecture series which drew Emerson and Melville.

This was the Lawrence that attracted trainloads of Bostonians to breathe its clean air and stroll its handsome streets—and it vanished quickly. In 1860 the five-story Pemberton Mill collapsed, killing 88 and seriously injuring 116 more, an ominous sign of things to come as the town doubled and redoubled its size. Close-cramped, wooden four-deckers soon housed immigrants from Italy, Germany, Britain, Russia, Austria, Poland, and Syria, among other places. Those born in the city rarely lived beyond 40, if they survived infancy. The whole sorry scene became one of national concern with the "Bread and Roses Strike" of 1912. At the time the city was the "worsted center of the world," a city of 86,000 in which 74,000 were foreign born or of foreign parentage.

In the wake of the strike wages increased slightly and immigration dropped off, largely because an investigation of conditions in Lawrence led to the passage of a federal quota law. The city's population today is 63,175 but it continues to attract new arrivals, with Hispanics now representing more than 16 percent. It remains one of the country's most vividly ethnic cities with numerous Middle-Eastern, Southeast Asian, Italian, and Hispanic restaurants; also Italian bakeries and shops within an easy walk of the city's new sites.

A decade behind Lowell in its restoration, as it was in its birth, Lawrence hovers on the edge of a major renaissance. Exhibits in the Lawrence Heritage State Park Visitors Center, housed in a former canal-side mill boardinghouse, depict working life in this city. The surrounding canal area is undergoing a major restoration. A four-square-block Museum Square (due in '87) will include the Museum of American Textile History (still in North Andover at this writing) and a substantial number of apartments (this was the city's original boardinghouse area). Most of the mills themselves were on the island where many still stand, including the solidly rebuilt Pemberton Mill, noteworthy for its cathedral-like windows.

Across the river, adjacent to the old American Woolen Company buildings (incomplete now, but the largest woolen mill in the US when it was completed in 1848), the former Lawrence Print Works are now Riverwalk, a complex that includes a convention center and a dramatic Marriott Hotel (probably the only one in the world with both a central atrium and two tall smokestacks).

The Lawrence Heritage State Park has upgraded the city's Campagnone Common, a grand expanse just off Essex Street, the genuinely appealing main drag. Shopping has, in fact, drawn Bostonians to Lawrence for some years now, at least as far as the Polo/Ralph Lauren factory store.

AREA CODE 617

GUIDANCE **Lawrence Heritage State Park Visitor's Center** (794-1655), One Jackson Street, corner of Canal Street.

GETTING THERE By train: Lawrence is on the Boston and Maine (227-5070) commuter line; the terminal is a reasonable walk across the Casey Bridge from the canal area sites; check to see if a shuttle is operating.

By car: Access is a breeze. Take the "downtown" exit off Route 495, just north of I-93.

By bus: Check with **Merrimack Lines** (686-2777) for commuter bus service from Boston's South Station and Park Square to Lawrence and the Andovers.

GETTING AROUND Parking: From 495 take Canal Street to the end and look for the lot below the Casey Bridge, 50 cents per day. A trackless trolley is due to begin shuttling visitors around downtown sites by '87.

TO SEE AND DO **Lawrence Heritage State Park** (794-1655), The Visitors Center, One Jackson Street. The 1847 brick boardinghouse contains two full floors of exhibits depicting life from the point of view of the various immigrant groups (who are said to total more than 50) who came to work in the mills. A video depicts the 1912 Bread and Roses strike. On the third floor there are changing exhibits and regularly scheduled shows presented by the "Three Trees Puppet Theater" (park staff built the stage, made the puppets, and write the scripts) on environmental and historical themes.

Museum of American Textile Industry (686-0191), currently at

800 Massachusetts Avenue, North Andover, due to move sometime in '88 to Museum Square (Canal and Appleton Streets) in Lawrence. Open Tuesday–Friday 10–5; weekends 1–5. $2 per adult, $1 children and senior citizens. Established and endowed by the Stevens (mill-owning) family in 1960 as the Merrimack Valley Textile Museum, this institution includes a large research library and has become the museum of record for the American Textile Museum. In its present shape exhibits include working looms dating from the early nineteenth to twentieth centuries, also changing exhibits. The new premises will include three floors depicting the evolution of the factory system from small village enterprises to the cities that Lawrence still exemplifies. The present site is a ten-minute drive from downtown Lawrence; phone for directions and details about guided tours and special events.

Great Stone Dam, the largest in the world when completed in 1848 (35 feet high). Descend below the John W. Casey Bridge to Pemberton Park; drive or walk beyond the parking lot to the viewing platform.

ANDOVER AND NORTH ANDOVER Visitors to Lowell and/or Lawrence should side step to the classic old New England towns of **Andover** and **North Andover** for a sense of the pre-Industrial Merrimack Valley. These towns continue to thrive as bedroom communities.

Phillips Academy Museums, Main Street (Route 28). Phillips Academy, founded in 1778, is one of the country's leading prep schools with a college-sized (450 acres) and quality campus.

Addison Gallery of American Art (475-7515). Closed August, otherwise open daily except Monday 10–5, from 2:30 on Saturday. The permanent collection includes a striking portrait by Thomas Eakins and a superb painting of Fifth Avenue by Childe Hassam. Don't miss the collection of ship models in the basement.

Robert S. Peabody Foundation of Archeology (475-0248), Phillips and Main streets. Open Monday–Friday 8:30–4, closed most holidays. Collections of shards, bones, and Indian implements unearthed in digs around the region, including 9,000-year-old implements found in an Ipswich sand bank; also general exhibits on the evolution of man.

Shawsheen Village, junction of Routes 28 and 133 in Andover. A classic, mid-nineteenth-century mill village built by the American Woolen Company. The attractive mills still stand, housing diverse businesses.

Historic Houses: **Andover Historical Society** (475-2236), 97 Main Street. Open Wednesday–Sunday 2–4 or by appointment. An early nineteenth-century house is furnished to different periods.

North Andover Historical Society (686-4035), 153 Academy Road (next to the Textile Museum). Both the **Johnson Cottage** and the **Parson Barnard House** (1715) are open Sundays 1–5.

Stevens-Coolidge Place (927-1391). Open mid-April through October, Sunday 1–5 and by appointment: $2 adult, 50 cents child. Grounds are open daily in warm-weather months; free. Owned by the Trustees of Reservations, this is a colonial-revival country mansion with collections of Chinese export porcelain, landscaped grounds and gardens, and a pasture with a small herd of Hereford cattle.

GREEN SPACE   In Lawrence: **Campagnone Common.** An unusually large Common just off Essex Street, contains the Leonard Bernstein Stage and Robert Frost Fountain (both named for former Lawrence residents).

Pemberton Park, a four-acre area (presently half complete) on the Casey Bridge end of the island between North Canal and Merrimack streets; accessible from the bridge near the dam.

Den Rock Park on the Shawsheen River, known as a practice ground for technical rock climbers.

Riverwalk Park, developed by the Department of Environmental Management, below the Riverwalk and Marriott Hotel, will offer stone seats and a view of the massive river wall of mills (due to be completed in '87).

Eventually a tow path walk is planned to stretch the length of Canal Street.

Beyond Lawrence: **Harold Parker State Forest** (686-3391), Middleton Road, North Reading. A 3,000-acre preserve with a total 135 campsites, eleven ponds (nine man-made) with swimming, picnic grills, 35 miles of trails and woods roads. $3 per car day use, $5 per night camping.

Charles W. Ward Reservation. Prospect Road, east of Route 125, North Andover. A self-guided interpretive trail explores a typical northern bog; hiking and cross-country ski trails traverse woodland; includes Holt Hill, highest hilltop (just 420 feet) in Essex County.

BOATING   **Merrimack River Watershed Council** (363-5777), 694 Main Street, West Newbury 01985, has published a detailed map ($3.95) showing launch areas along the river. It is also the source of a pamphlet guide to canoeing, fishing, and bicycling along the river and of guided canoe trips and special events.

The Greater Lawrence Community Boating Program (681-8675), PO Box 955, Lawrence 01840, charges a flat fee of $35 per adult, $15 per youth for a season's use of sloops, sunfish, Force 5's, wind surfers, canoes, dories, rowboats, and rowing shells. The boat house and an adjacent bathhouse (the water is Class B, swimmable) plus a sand beach will eventually be completed by the state. This property abuts the evolving Emerson College Campus.

Moore & Mountain (475-3665), Park Street, Andover. Rents canoes. $18 for first day plus $300 security deposit (credit card acceptable).

FISHING   **The Shawheen River** is stocked with trout. For details about the Merrimack see the Merrimack River Watershed Council's guide (under Boating).

GOLF   **Chemawa Country Club** (761-8754), 9 holes; and **Rolling Green** (475-4066), 9 holes, both in Andover.

HORSEBACK RIDING   **Andover Riding Academy** (683-6552), instruction, trail rides.

SWIMMING   See **Harold Parker State Park.** There is also swimming at **Pomps Pond** in Andover and at the town beaches on **Fall Pond** in North Andover.

ALPINE SKIING   **Boston Hills** (683-2733), open daily and for night skiing in season. From I-93, Route 125 to Route 114 East. Vertical drop of 240 feet, alpine and cross-country rentals, a real learning hill.

CROSS-COUNTRY SKIING   **Rolling Green** (475-4066), 311 Lowell Street, Andover, at the Sheraton Rolling Green. A touring center with rental equipment, instruction, three miles of trails including a lighted loop. Also see **Ward Reservation** and **Harold Parker State Forest** under Green Space.

LODGING   **Andover Inn** (475-5903), Chapel Avenue, Andover 01810. One of the most elegant and formal country inns in New England, this columned brick establishment caters to the parents of Phillips Academy students. Three inn-owned, stretch Cadillac limousines were parked outside the day we stopped by, all available for airport runs ($50 to $60). There are 33 rooms, an elegant dining room (serving a Rijsttafel Sunday evenings), and bar. $47–$68 double, $105 for a suite; all rooms have phones, color TV, radio, and air-conditioning. Closed the last two weeks in August.

Sheraton Rolling Green Inn and Conference Center (475-5400), 311 Lowell Street, Andover. See Lowell.

Koala Inn (685-6200), 131 River Road, Andover. A 124-room motel with an indoor pool, whirlpool, complimentary continental breakfast, cafe. $68–$76 double.

Lawrence Marriott (Marriott Hotels information: 800-228-9290). Due to open fall of '87. A 300-room hotel designed within the walls of two buildings in the former Lawrence Print Works, retaining two tall smokestacks. Each room will have two large, arched windows and there will be a seven-story atrium and a two-level health club, including a swimming pool with a retractable roof that can be opened in summer.

DINING OUT   **Bishop's** (683-7143), 99 Hampshire at Lowell Street. Open weekdays for lunch and dinner, weekends from 4 PM. The atmosphere and menu is Middle Eastern, but lobster and roast beef are also specialties. Whatever our Arabic dish was, it was delicious. Dancing (Tuesday–Saturday evenings), bar until 1 AM. $4.50–$7.50 for lunch, $7.75–$16 for dinner.

Metamorphosis (681-8315), 210 Essex Street. Pleasant ambiance;

they make their own bread, butter, and vanilla ice cream. New American cooking: fruit with chicken; daily specials; Bouillabaisse ($12.95) or Rack of Lamb (from $6.95). Open Tuesday–Saturday, lunch and dinner.

Cedar Crest Restaurant (685-5722), 187 Broadway (Route 28), Lawrence. Open for breakfast, lunch, dinner. Family restaurant, reasonable prices, daily specials.

Top of the Scales (681-8848), 4 Johnson Street, North Andover, center of the village just up from the Textile Museum. A downstairs crafts center, upstairs dining (inside and on the sun porch): fresh baked croissants, quiches, soups, salads. Open for all three meals, Sunday brunch; moderately priced.

Fishing Well (689-9191), 131 Broadway, South Lawrence. Korean food, popular locally; moderately priced.

The Courtyard Restaurant (475-8389), 349 North Main Street, Andover. Open for lunch and dinner, a Victorian mansion, fairly formal, popular locally.

The Den (687-9888), Turnpike Road (Route 114), North Andover. No atmosphere but good Italian fare at reasonable prices.

EATING OUT **Lawton's Hot Dog Stand,** corner of Broadway and Canal streets, features unique hot dogs fried in oil; highly rated.

China Chef (682-4838), 129–129-A South Broadway, Lawrence. Reasonably priced, good.

Tally Ho (682-8681), 74 Swan Street, Methuen (just off the continuation of Jackson). One of the best places for Lawrence's unique chicken barbecue sandwich (pressure cooked, spiced chicken [white meat] served on a bun with lettuce and mayonnaise).

Ellie's Arabic Food (682-6676), 76 South Broadway, Lawrence, locally respected.

La Oasis (687-9244), 191 Essex Street, Lawrence. Open daily, Spanish food, fast service, take-out.

Hanagasa (686-6632), Essex Street. Japanese, Okinawan specialties, Sushi bar.

What's Cooking (470-3333), 93 Rear Main Street, Andover (next to the Municipal parking lot). A lunch place with great sandwiches, daily specials.

Raspberry's, Main Street, Andover. A small sub shop with four tables, specials, loyal following.

SELECTIVE SHOPPING Factory Outlets: A directory, listing some 30 outlets, is available from the Greater Lawrence Chamber of Commerce (686-7075), 225 Essex Street 01843. The outstanding ones include:

Blotner Woodworks (682-9412), 599 Canal Street. Open Monday–Friday 1–4. A long-established pilgrimage point for mothers and nursery school teachers: piles of wooden balls, beads, tubes, rings, cubes, and pegs for creating.

Cardinal Shoes (686-9706), 468 Canal Street. Tuesday–Saturday

Amesbury on the Merrimack River

10–5. Great savings on women's shoes (sizes 6–10, medium width only) made here.

Creations Unlimited (686-7911), 599 Canal Street (third floor), silk, dried, and plastic flowers; other materials for arranging centerpieces.

Huntington Fabrics (686-9531), 21 Glenn Street, Lawrence Industrial Park, open Tuesday–Friday 10–4, Saturday 10–1. Great upholstery fabrics and substantial savings.

KGR (683-5999), 300 Canal Street. Classic women's suits and separates. Open only four times a year, at the end of each manufacturing season. Ask to be put on the mailing list and you get alerted to sale dates, savings of up to 50 percent below retail.

Polo, Ralph Lauren (794-0594), 15 Union Street in the Everett Mills (take the downtown exit off Route 495, turn left on Canal Street, and then take first right), weekdays 9:30–9, Saturday 9:30–5, Sunday 1–5. Thousands of polo ponies gallop across everything from bathing suits and designer jeans to bath towels and pillows. Prices range, but the savings in the clearance corner are great. This is a large, sophisticated shopping space: bright "polo" shirts, jackets, a large selection of men's suits, also good for children.

New Balance (682-8960), Union Street, at the Duck Bridge. Sneakers and jogging clothes.

Plycraft (686-9571), 39 South Canal. Open weekdays 9–5, Saturday 9–12. Contemporary office furniture but much of it suitable for homes, including Eames-style chairs.

Essex Street Stores: The main shopping drag is worth a stroll, a pleasant mix of mid- and late nineteenth-century buildings with some noteworthy stores. **Kaps** (at 381) has upscale clothing; **Macartney's** (at 356) and **Gentry** (at 343) are also worth a look, and there are two outstanding sporting goods stores: **Whitworths** (at 487) and **Mickey's** (at 500).

Ethnic Food Stores: Common Street is lined with Italian bakeries and delis. A complete list of local stores, which include Arab, Hispanic, and Southeast Asian, is available from **Lawrence Community Development** (686-7075), 225 Essex Street.

Main Street, Andover: A number of small specialty stores add up to interesting shopping. **The Andover Bookstore** is exceptionally well stocked and offers a crackling fire in winter.

SPECIAL EVENTS June: (Last Sunday) **Pedal, Paddle, Portage, Pedestrian Race,** a four-person relay that includes a 10K road race, 10-mile bike race, and a five-mile canoe race, sponsored by Greater Lawrence Community Boating (see Boating).

July: **River Monster Week,** sponsored by Heritage State Park.

September: (Labor Day Weekend) **Feast of the Three Saints** on Common Street, Italian food, dancing, music. **Folk Festival** in Lawrence.

October: **Octoberfest,** Lawrence. **Middle Eastern Festival** in Methuen.

MEDICAL EMERGENCY **Lawrence General Hospital** (685-2151), 1 General Street.

North Shore

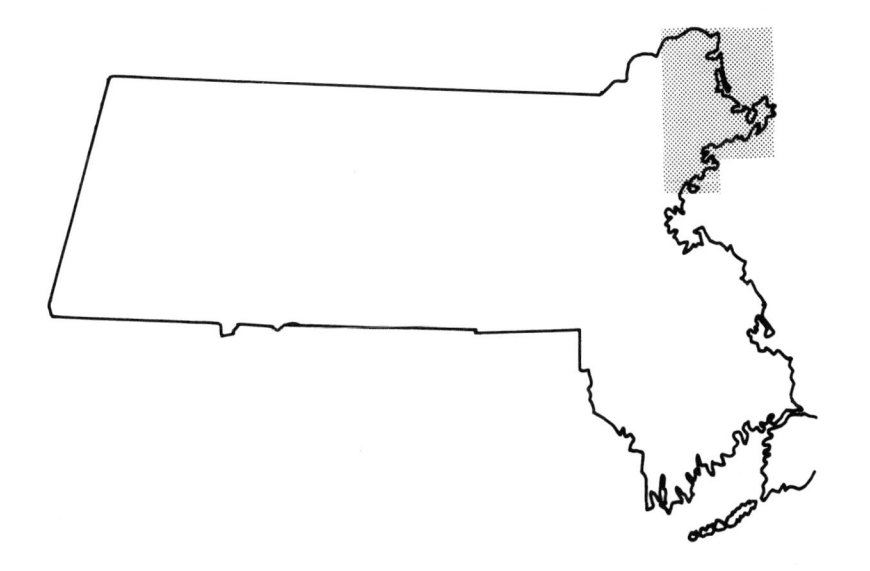

INTRODUCTION

The North Shore begins less than 20 miles north of Boston and runs on 30 miles or so, tacking and jibing around Cape Ann, along the ragged edge of Ipswich Bay to Newburyport, and on to Salisbury just below the New Hampshire line.

On the North Shore, old families, old money, and the purest of Massachusetts accents prevail. What strikes visitors is the way old seaports remain much the way they did in their heyday—a day which varies: for Ipswich it was the seventeenth century; for Marblehead, the decades just prior to the Revolution; for Salem and Newburyport, the Federal era; and for Gloucester, the late nineteenth century. Always pleasant places to visit, these towns are now also great places to stay. In the past few years dozens of small inns and bed & breakfasts have opened in Newburyport, Salem, and Marblehead to complement the choice of lodging places on Cape Ann. More and more visitors are discovering the beauty (and savings) of bedding down on the North Shore instead of in Boston (easily accessible by commuter trains and buses).

AREA CODE 617

GUIDANCE North of Boston Tourist Council (532-1449), PO Box 3031, Peabody 01960, publishes an annual guide to Essex sights and facilities and distributes *Along the Coast of Essex Country*, produced by the Junior League of Boston ('84 edition, $9.95), an excellent guide to sights.

Also note Guidance sources under Salem/Marblehead, Cape Ann, Newburyport.

North Shore Life, a bimonthly magazine ($2.50 at newsstands, $3.75 by mail from Cape Ann Publishing, PO Box 6, Gloucester 01930) covers the scene nicely.

The Salem and Marblehead Area

Salem is older than Boston and it looks it. When Nathaniel Hawthorne lived here, mesmerism and old wives' tales were rampant. Salem had lapsed into listless decay. Now another century has passed and the city is reshaping its image from "witch" to "China Trade" city.

Marblehead's glory days came just prior to the Revolution when its fleet reaped their share of the Triangle Trade. There are splendid merchants' mansions, but most of the early homes are modest, clustering around the Old Town House (1727), their token gardens recalling that only fishermen, not farmers, were permitted to live downtown. Today the town is still synonymous with sailing vessels, but fishermen have long since been upstaged by yachtsmen.

Beverly (just north of Salem) and Swampscott (just south of Marblehead) remain primarily suburban places but with amenities that round this corner of the North Shore into an inviting destination and also a comfortable roost from which to explore Boston.

AREA CODE 617

GUIDANCE **Salem Chamber of Commerce** (744-0004), Old Town Hall, 32 Derby Square, Salem 01970; open weekdays, 9–5. Information booths at **Riley Plaza** (open daily, 9–5) and **Central Wharf Warehouse** (Derby Wharf), also open daily but hours vary according to available funding. The chamber's *Best of Salem* map/guide and booklet are handy.

Marblehead Chamber of Commerce (631-9000), PO Box 76, Marblehead 01945. The office is open weekdays 9–3 at 62 Pleasant Street, dispensing a guide and maps (essential for getting around Old Town on foot as well as by car).

GETTING THERE By train: MBTA (1-800-392-6100 or 722-3200) commuter trains connect Salem's Riley Plaza with Boston's North Station, departing daily 6:55 AM to 11:59 PM

By bus: MBTA (1-800-392-6100 or 722-3200) buses from Boston's Haymarket Square (daily, at least once every half hour).

Airport shuttle: North Shore Shuttle (631-8660) connects the Salem/Marblehead area with Logan Airport.

GETTING AROUND **Salem Trolley** runs April through September, offering guided tours of Salem; tickets are good for one day and permit

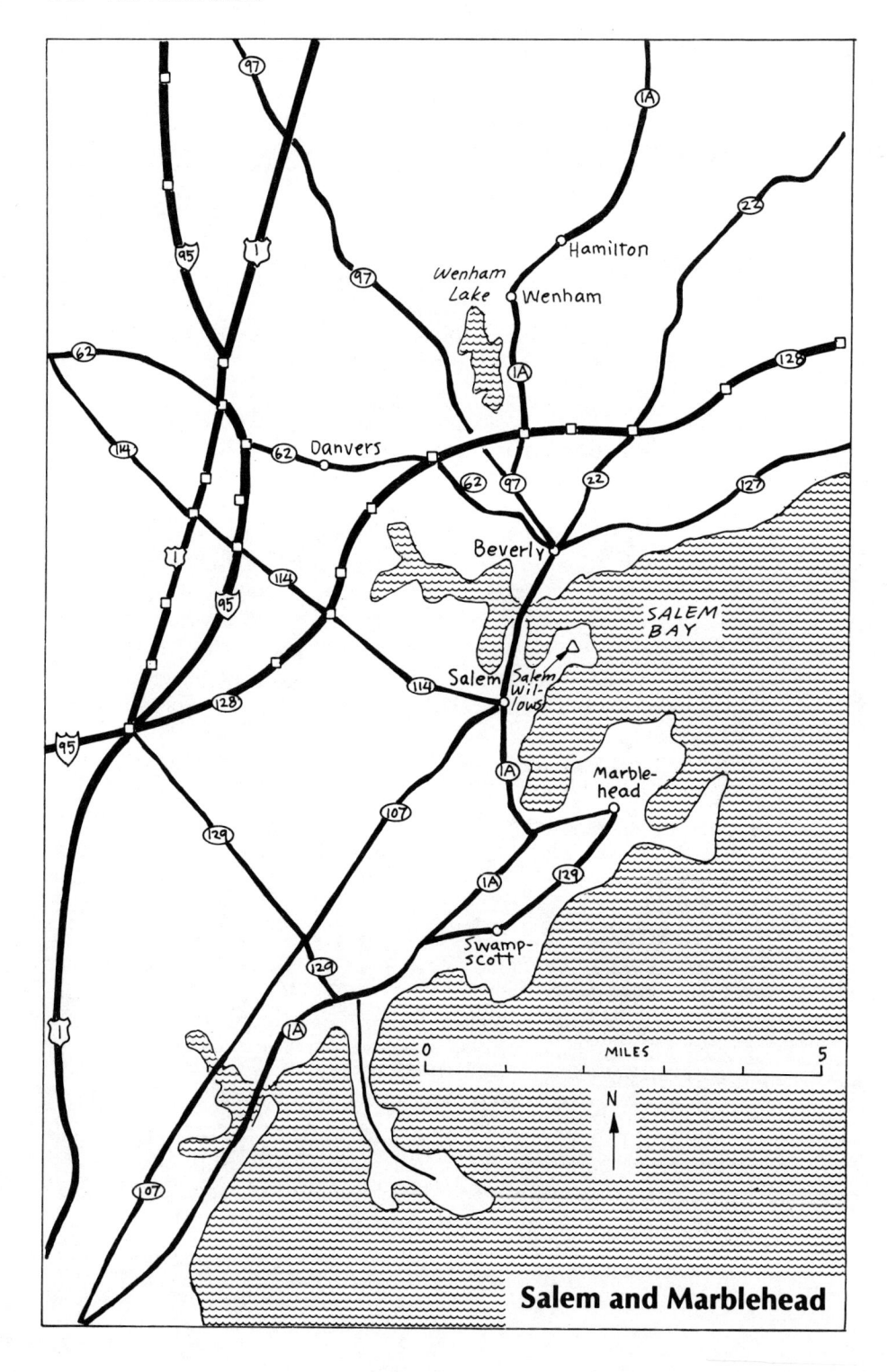

Salem and Marblehead

you to board and reboard at a dozen stops spaced between Riley Plaza and Salem Willows. $4 adult, $2 children aged 5–12.

PARKING   In Marblehead: In crunch times you simply have to walk farther. Parking is free throughout town, but watch the two-hour limit because there is ticketing.

In Salem: **The East India Square Garage** (off Essex Street) offers nominally priced space if the Derby Street lot at the **Salem National Maritime Historic Site** (free) is filled.

TO SEE AND DO   In Salem: Begin by exploring Salem's China Trade treasures. If possible, park in the free waterside lot maintained at the waterside Custom House and look into the neighboring brick mansion that was built in 1762 for Elias Hasket Derby. "King Derby," who pioneered a new sailing route around the Cape of Good Hope, is said to be America's first millionaire. The trade he initiated with India and the Orient was soon vastly expanded by other Salem merchants.

Cabinetmaker Samuel McIntire designed the four-square mansions, which resemble those of Charles Bulfinch in Boston, but the Salem versions are airier, more graceful, and garnished throughout with delicately carved detailing, arches, and stairways. The lineup of these homes make Chestnut one of the handsomest streets in America. Other mansions cluster around the Essex Institute.

The **Peabody Museum** is Salem's (and New England's) ultimate treasure chest of exotica. It was founded as the East Indian Marine Society in 1799 by the city's captains and "supercargoes" to encourage the collection and display of "natural and artificial curiosities" gathered from the globe's far corners. The museum is currently expanding to include the collection of the former Museum of the American China Trade.

It's a short walk from the Custom House up to the Peabody Museum and in good weather you will want to linger outside on a bench in East India Square, then stroll past the Essex Street shops down to the Old Town Hall, given in 1816 by "King Derby" (it now houses the Chamber of Commerce).

Of course most visitors come to see Salem's witches, and they are not disappointed. From the vivid presentation in the Salem Witch Museum to the paintings and relics in the Essex Institute, there is plenty to see and there are even some witches in residence (see Selective Shopping).

Peabody Museum (745-9500 and 745-1876), 161 Essex Street. Open Monday–Saturday 10–5, Sunday and holidays 1–5. A guided tour is offered daily at 2 PM. The museum is named for George Peabody, the philanthropist who saved it in 1860 when the East India Marine Society seemed doomed to sell the collection of South Pacific and Far Eastern souvenirs. Billed as "the oldest continuously operating museum in the country," the museum's collection now includes 300,000 items, not counting the 12,000 pieces acquired through its recent merger with the Museum of the American China Trade (formerly located in Milton). Items on exhibit change frequently. Admission (not necessary for the gift shop) is $3 per adult, $2 seniors and students, $1.50 children aged 6–16.

Salem Maritime National Historic Site (744-4323), 178 Derby Street. Open daily 8:30–5. The waterfront property includes a long, grassy wharf (completed in 1806) with a small lighthouse, a Bonded Warehouse (selling appropriate wares), and the West India Goods Store, as well as the Custom House (built 1819) and Derby Mansion (see Salem introduction above).

House of Seven Gables (744-0991), 54 Turner Street. Open year-round, daily 9:30-5:30 in summer, 10:30–4:30 otherwise. Continuous audio-visual introduction and guided tours of the famous house, built in 1668, complete with hidden staircase; also tours of Nathaniel Hawthorne's birthplace. $3.75 adults, $1.50 children.

Essex Institute (744-3390), 132 Essex Street. Open June 1–November 1, Monday–Saturday, 9–5, Sundays and holidays 1–5. Closed Mondays in winter. The museum was founded in 1848 and houses a collection of portraits, period rooms, local silver, and memorabilia. The bulk of the collection fills a two-story, balconied hall, one of the most amazing rooms in New England. Admission to the main building is $2 per adult, $1.50 seniors, and $1 children aged 6–16. Combination tickets ($5 per adult, $2.50 per child) are available for the museum and three of the following houses owned by the Institute (admission fee not necessary for gift shop):

The John Ward House (1684 & later), with its attached shop (the kind Salem wives kept while their husbands were away at sea), stands on the museum grounds (open June-October 31, Tuesday-Saturday 10–4, Sunday 1–4:30), also the hours for the neighboring **Crowninshield–Bentley House** (1727). The **Gardner–Pingree House** (1804), also on the museum grounds, is a 14-room mansion generally believed to represent Samuel McIntyre's work at its best: airy, yet filled with exquisite detail. Open year-round, Tuesday–Saturday 10–5, Sundays 1–5. **Andrew Spafford House** (1818–19), 13 Washington Square West. An outstanding Federal-era mansion. **Peirce–Nichols House** (1782, 1801), 80 Federal Street. An early McIntyre beauty. Open by appointment only. **Cotting–Smith Assemble House** (1782 and later), 138 Federal Street, remodeled by McIntyre so cleverly that no one can tell where the grand ballroom stood (by appointment only).

Ropes Mansion and Garden (744-0718), 318 Essex Street. Open June–October, Tuesday–Saturday 10–4, Sunday 1–4:30. A mid-1720s home furnished with imports collected by four generations of a Salem merchant family. $1.50 per adult, $1 seniors, $.75 children.

Stephen Phillips Memorial Trust House (744-0440), 34 Chestnut Street. Open Memorial Day to mid-October, Monday–Saturday 10–4:30. The only house open to the public on Chestnut Street, it displays paintings, Chinese porcelain, and Oriental rugs. There is also a carriage house with antique cars and carriages. $1.50 adults, $1 seniors, $.75 children.

Pickering House (744-1647), 18 Broad Street. Open Mondays (year-round) 10–3; also Sundays 2–4:30, mid-May to mid-October, and by appointment. Built in 1651, the oldest house in America to be continually occupied by the same family. $1.50 adults.

Pioneer Village (744-0180), Forest River Park (off Route 114 and West Avenue). Open June–Labor Day. Ducks nest in the reeds beside replicas of crude English wigwams and more pretentious thatched cabins. You read about the "four classes of emigrants," most of whom were unable to pay the five pound passage to *Naumkeag*, or "fishing place," as Salem was originally known. $2 adults, $.75 children aged 5–12.

Salem Witch Museum (744-1692), 19½ Washington Square North. Open year-round, daily 10–5 (until 7 PM in July and August). In "computerized sound and light" this so-called museum tells the whole lurid tale of the fourteen women and five men who were executed in 1692, the four who died in jail, and the 55 more who saved their necks by accusing others. $2.75 per adult, $2.25 seniors, $1.50 aged 6–14 (under six should not be admitted).

The Witch House (744-0180), corner of Essex and North Streets. Open March–June, 10–5; June–December, 10–6. Nicely restored and furnished, this 1642 house is now owned by the city; the witches are only a part of the spiel. $2 adults, $.75 children aged 5–12.

The Witch Dungeon Museum (744-9812), 16 Lynde Street. Open May–October, 10–5. Yet another dramatization of the witch trials, this one with mannequins. $2.50 adults, $1.50 children aged 5–12.

In Beverly: Beverly claims to have seen the birth of the American Navy (a claim disputed by Marblehead and Whitehall, New York). It also claims America's oldest house (disputed by Dedham) and says it put a stop to Salem's witch hysteria. The town itself was transformed in the nineteenth century by the shoe industry, but Prides Crossing and Beverly Farms still harbor a number of estates, many of them now private schools. The summertime North Shore Music Theater and the year-round magic of Le Grand David (whose troop has restored two vintage Cabot Street theaters) draw large audiences.

The Beverly Historical Society (922-1186), 117 Cabot Street, maintains three outstanding houses, open May 20–October 15, Wednesday–Saturday 10–4, Sunday 1–4. The Cabot House is also open mid-October to mid-May, Thursday through Saturday 10–4. Guided tours are offered of all three houses, $1.50 per adult, $.50 per child per house, or $3 per adult, $1 per child for all three.

Balch House, 448 Cabot Street. A Tudor-style clapboard house built in 1636, now within sight of the mammoth United Shoe factory. It is said to be the home of the first male born in Massachusetts Bay Colony and tells its own witchcraft story.

John Hale House, 39 Hale Street, off Route 22. Built partially in 1694 by a minister who was involved in the Salem witch trials until his own wife was accused of being a witch; Reverend Hale quickly helped to end the trials.

Cabot House, 110 Cabot Street. A handsome brick Federal-style home built for John Cabot, ship owner and co-founder of America's first cotton mill. There are relics from the city's privateering and Far Eastern trade, antique toys, and special exhibits.

Long Hill (921-1944), 572 Essex Street. From Route 128, Exit 18, take Route 22 (Essex Street) north one mile (bear left at fork) to brick gate posts and a sign on the left. Open office hours; gardens open daylight hours. The brick mansion, built as summer home for Ellery Sedgwick, author, editor, and publisher of *The Atlantic Monthly* from 1909 to 1938, is now headquarters for the Trustees of Reservations. There are 114 acres of grounds, including Sedgwick Gardens. A remarkable collection of trees, shrubs, and flowers, including Japanese maple, weeping cherry, rhododendron, and azaleas. Walking trails thread fields, forest, and wetland.

In Marblehead: Half the size of Salem and untouched by the Industrial Revolution, Marblehead is a delightfully walkable tangle of crooked streets, with old houses perched like so many sea birds above the harbor. On summer weekends the streets can be bumper-to-bumper traffic, all headed for the harbor's buoy-to-buoy sailing yachts. But Marblehead is actually less touristed than Cape Ann and Salem and offers some fine places to stay, dine, and shop. It's a place to sit for a spell (my favorite spots are at State Street Landing and Crocker Park), to breathe in the salt air and eyeball the yachting scene. It's also a great place to learn to sail. Don't miss Marblehead Neck across the causeway. The first summer residents here camped in tents and the first summer "cottage" wasn't built until 1867. Today the spacious homes are all winterized, but there is still space to sun and stroll.

Jeremiah Lee Mansion (631-1069), 161 Washington Street. Open mid-May to mid-October, 10–4. Lee was a ship owner who could import his own building materials: mahogany from Santo Domingo for the grand staircase and wallpaper from England. Today the

Old Town Hall (1816) and Derby Square, Salem, the center for a colorful marketplace

striking building is headquarters for the Marblehead Historical Society, whose third-floor exhibits include bright early twentieth-century primitives of Marblehead scenes by J. O. J. Frost; also early nineteenth-century portraits by William Bartoll. $2.25 per adult, $1.25 per student aged 10–16, free under ten.

King Hooper Mansion (631-2608), 8 Hooper Street, open Tuesday–Sunday 1–4. The rare five-story section of this remarkable house dates from 1728; the three-story block-front facade and front rooms were added in 1745. The building now serves as headquarters for the Marblehead Arts Association; changing exhibits are in the former third-floor ballroom. Nominal fee.

Abbott Hall, Washington Square. Open year-round, weekdays 9–5; in summer until 9 PM weekdays, 9–6 Saturdays and 11–6 Sundays. A brick, Victorian town hall that stands on the highest point of land and literally towers over the town; the famous (and not disappointing) "Spirit of 76" painting commissioned for the 1876 centennial is in the Selectman's Room. In the lobby is the seventeenth-century deed to the town, complete with totem signatures of the sachems.

Old North Church, 41 Washington Street. Open weekdays and for Sunday services. Built of stone with a graceful steeple and a golden fish for a weathervane.

St. Michael's Church, 11 Summer Street. Open Monday–Saturday 9–5 and for Sunday services. Built in 1714 by resident Anglicans, simple and quite beautiful, now Episcopalian.

Old Town House, Market Square. No longer open to the public, this bright yellow building was built in 1727, designed (like Faneuil Hall) to house butcher and produce stalls on its ground floor and a meeting hall on its second floor (it was here that General Glover organized his Essex Regiment). It is an unusually graceful building, but compromised by the heavy granite first floor added in 1830.

In Danvers: Danvers evokes an image either of the spooky, Victorian State Mental Hospital (the view from I-95), or of the sprawling Liberty Tree Shopping Mall (seen from Route 128). Beyond these strips, however, the town is worth exploring. It was here back in 1692 that the slave Tituba fired the imagination of two young girls by telling them ghost stories. The girls then accused village women of witchcraft, sparking the "Salem Witch Hunt." Danvers was part of Salem at the time.

Rebecca Nurse Homestead (774-8799), 149 Pine Street. Open mid-June to mid-October, Tuesday–Saturday 1–4, Sunday 2–4:30, and by appointment year-round. The vintage 1678 house is starkly silhouetted against its old pastureland, and Rebecca's body lies buried on the grounds, only because her family risked their own necks to retrieve it by night from Gallows Hill in Salem. The 72-

year-old mother of eight stoutly refused to say that she was a witch.

In Wenham: Wenham Historical Association and Museum (468-2377), Route 1A, 132 Main Street, next to Town Hall. Open late May–Labor Day, Monday–Friday 1–4, Sunday 2–5. An unusually interesting collection in an unusually handsome town. The Clafin Richards House (1664) is furnished to period, and there is a major collection of nineteenth-century dolls; also toys, games, an exhibit of tools once used to harvest ice in Wenham Lake (the ice was exported by clipper ship to India), a nineteenth-century shoe shop, changing exhibits, and an herb garden. $1.50 per adult, $.50 children aged 6–14.

GREEN SPACE **Salem Willows** (745-8713), Salem. Follow signs out along Derby Street to Fort Avenue. The amusement area and food stands are open in summer months only but the park is a beauty anytime, occupying a point of land overlooking the Beverly waterfront on one side, Salem Sound and the coast to Cape Ann on the other. The willows were planted in 1801 to form a shaded walk for smallpox victims. Old-style wooden pavilions and gazebos enforce the nostalgia look.

Derby Wharf, Derby Street, in front of the Custom House, Salem. The wharf itself extends some 2,000 feet into Salem harbor and, now grassed over, forms a great picnic and relaxing spot. It is now part of the Salem Maritime National Historic Park.

Crocker Park, Front Street, Marblehead. A grassy rise with a harbor view and old-fashioned stone seats, up beyond the house designed to look like a Viking castle. Bring a sketch pad.

Massachusetts Wildlife Sanctuary, Risley Road, Marblehead Neck. Massachusetts Audubon maintains $15\frac{1}{4}$ acres here; the pond is used for winter skating.

Chandler Hovey Park and **Lighthouse Point,** tip of Marblehead Neck, a great spot to picnic, to get your bearings, and to watch summer boat races.

Old Burial Hill and **Fountain Park,** Pond Street. The gravestones tell a moving story of early Marblehead. They surround the site of the town's 1638 meetinghouse and include 600 Revolutionary War soldiers. There is a great view of the town and harbor, and you can picnic just up the way (turn right) at Fountain Park, site of a Revolutionary-era fort. Below Fountain Park (access off Orne Street) is a small, sandy beach and at low tide you can walk out to a little island. Redd's Pond, nearby on Norman Street, is also a place to picnic in summer and to watch skaters in winter.

Fort Sewall, Marblehead, at the eastern end of Front Street. Begun as an earthworks during the seventeenth century, improved as the Revolutionary-era fortification that still stands, now a pleasant park with a great view of all the moored boats in the harbor.

Hospital Point, Beverly. Driving north from the city on Hale Street (toward Route 127) turn right on East Corning Street for a short detour to an 1871 lighthouse overlooking Salem and Marblehead. This was also the site of a revolutionary fort and later of a smallpox hospital.

Lynch Park, Ober Street off Route 127, Beverly. Once part of a grand estate, this extensive park includes a beach as well as a grassy expanse for sunning, rest rooms, picnic tables, and parking at $5 per car on weekends, $3 weekdays (there's also a great sledding hill).

Appleton Farms Grass Rides, Route 1A, Hamilton. A portion of this fine old 123-acre estate, which has been in the Appleton family since 1638, is open for hiking and ski touring, five miles of mowed paths, maintained by the Trustees of Reservations.

Misery Islands Reservation, Salem Bay. Accessible only by boat, the second largest island between Boston Harbor and Cape Porpoise, Maine. Once the site of summer cottages, a clubhouse, and golf course; now rolling field and a favorite destination for weekend sailors.

Glen Magna Farms (774-9165), Ingersoll Street, Danvers (two miles north of town on Route 1, East on Centre Street to Ingersoll). Open June through September, Tuesday–Thursday 10–4. A 20-room mansion and a summer house with carving by Samuel McIntyre and 11-acre grounds designed by Frederick Law Olmsted. $1 adults, $.50 per child.

Also see under To See and Do: Pioneer Village in Salem's Forest Park; Long Hill in Beverly.

SPECIAL SPACES **Salem Common** (Washington Square). Set aside for public use early in the 1700s, this was a swampy, hilly space, but in the early nineteenth century it was leveled into the classic Common that survives, complete with benches and bandstand.

Derby Square and Essex Street, Salem. From Washington Square you now walk down Essex Street, lined with museums and shops, on a pedestrian way from East India Square (stone benches surround a large fountain) to Derby Square (the original market area around the Old Town Hall).

State Street Landing, Marblehead (officially called Philip T. Clark Landing). A landing since 1662, this is a place to people and boat watch (some 3,000 sailing craft summer in the sheltered inner harbor).

AMUSEMENT AREA At **Salem Willows** (see Green Space) a small collection of rides is geared to young children; the carousel is said to be more than a century old.

GOLF **Beverly Golf Club** (922-9072), Beverly, 18 holes.
Salem Municipal Golf Course (744-9747), 9 holes.

HARBOR TOUR **Pier Transit** offers one-hour tours of Salem Harbor, Memorial Day weekend to Labor Day, departing daily from Salem Willows pier (see Green Space) every hour from noon until 4. $4 per adult, $3 per child and senior.

BOATING **Marblehead Boat Rental Co.** (631-2259), 81 Front Street. From $15 for one hour for a four-passenger, 15-foot craft to $100 a day for a six-passenger Rhodes 18; weekend afternoon rentals range $50–$75. Management say the boats always come back (credit card required as a deposit).

Coastal Sailing School (639-0553), PO Box 1001. Over the past 14 years Bert Williams has taught more than 3,000 people to sail. The 20-hour course, conducted entirely on a 30-foot sailboat, can be spread over five weeks or compressed into five days, $200. Sailboats can also be rented and yachts chartered.

The Marblehead Sailing Club (639-1867), 83 Front Street. Learn to sail with week-long and weekend programs. The $220 weekend can be booked with lodging (extra) at a bed & breakfast a short walk from the landing. If participants pass the course they can use the club's boats, gratis, for the remainder of the week.

SCUBA DIVING **New England Divers** (922-6951), 131 Rantoul Street, Beverly. Certification Course offered year-round.

SWIMMING **Devereux Beach,** Ocean Avenue, at the causeway to Marblehead Neck, rest rooms; $3 weekdays, $5 weekends in season.

Forest River Park, off Route 114 and West Avenue, Salem. Two small beaches and "the largest outdoor swimming pool in the state." City-owned, nominal fee.

In Beverly swimming is permitted at **Lynch** (entrance on Oceanside Drive) and **Dane Street Beach** (Route 127).

Fisherman's Beach, Swampscott. This is a fine beach adjacent to the Fish House (built 1896) and town pier. Parking is a challenge, but the beach is free.

WHALE WATCHING **Barnegat Transportation Company** (745-6070), Pickering Wharf, Salem, offers whale watching Tuesday–Sunday, 10 AM departure.

The Queen (639-0151), Commercial Wharf, Marblehead. Whale watch, Tuesday–Sunday, Memorial Day weekend through September, departing 8:45, four-hour cruises, twice daily on weekends; inquire about sunset cruises.

Pier Transit (744-6311), Salem Willows, Memorial Day to Labor Day, Thursday, Friday, Saturday, twice daily departures: 10 and 2.

INNS AND BED & BREAKFASTS **Bed & Breakfast in Marblehead and the North Shore** (921-1336), 54 Amherst Road, Beverly 01915. Helena Champion's reservation service places guests in more than four dozen Salem, Marblehead, Beverly, and other nearby homes, among them many of the places listed below. Prices range from $36 single to $75 double.

Bed & Breakfast Associates, Bay Colony Ltd. (449-5302 or 449-5588), PO Box 166, Babson Park Branch, Boston 02157, have more than 20 listings in private homes in the Marblehead, Salem, Beverly, and Danvers area.

Suzannah Flint House (744-5281), 98 Essex Street, Salem 01970. A Federal-style home just off Washington Square offers two downstairs bedrooms, one with a double and single bed (and parlor stove), the other with cottage-style furnishings, both with private bath, TVs, and inviting books. Breakfast is included in $60 double in summer, $50 in winter, less without breakfast.

Spray Cliff, Marblehead (reserve through B&B in Marblehead [921-1336] or through the Salem Inn [741-0680], see below). This Tudor-style mansion offers five rooms, each with private bath; nicely furnished with superb views, use of the living room and dining room. $65–$75 per couple, including continental breakfast.

The Salem Inn (741-0680), 7 Summer Street, Salem 01970. This is a four-story, 23-room inn. All rooms are furnished in antiques and have private baths (although some baths are across the hall from the room); 12 have kitchenettes, 12 have fireplaces, and one penthouse suite has both. There is no common space; a restaurant occupies much of the ground floor: $65–$90 double, including continental breakfast.

The Coach House Inn (744-4092), 284 Lafayette Street, Salem 01970. In business more than 20 years, a friendly Victorian-style place with 11 rooms: nine doubles with private baths, two downstairs sharing one bath (down the hall from the front door); also one suite. Rooms are pleasant with coffee machines, no breakfast. In summer, $53–$66; off-season, $41–$50 double.

Cap'n Jacks (595-7910 or 595-9734), 253 Humphrey Street, Swampscott 01907. Built as a rooming house in 1835, this unpretentious 16-room inn has a lot going for it: bright, clean rooms with views of the water, a pool and jacuzzi, harbor-side patio, and a fine beach within a short walk. All rooms in the main house have private bath, some have balconies; all have TVs and fridge. Two oceanside apartments are available by the week or month. $42–$68 double in summer, 10 percent less November through April.

Lindsey's Garret (631-2653 or 631-7214), 38 High Street, Marblehead 01945. One studio apartment with a working fireplace, private entrance, Pullman kitchen, queen-size bed, TV, air-conditioning, and deck under the eaves of an eighteenth-century mansion; $50 year-round, includes a full breakfast.

10 Mugford Street (639-0343), 10 Mugford Street, Marblehead 01945. Just off Market Square, built in 1837, with five double guest rooms (sharing three baths), a parlor, and flower garden. A continental breakfast is served in the dining room. $50 double, year-round.

The Stephen Daniels House (744-5709), 1 Daniels Street, corner of Essex Street, Salem 01970. Built in 1667 by a sea captain, enlarged by his great-grandson in 1756, it remained in the same family until 1931. There are four rooms, all with private bath and genuine antique furnishings, some canopy beds. A shaded, flowery terrace; complimentary coffee and tea, full breakfast extra. $50 double.

Nathaniel Bowditch Guest House (745-7755), 2 Kimball Court, Salem 01970. Just behind the Salem Witch Museum, handy to shops and museums. This is the birthplace of Salem's famous navigator and it's a fine old house (despite accounts of Bowditch's childhood poverty) with wide pine floors and fine woodwork. There are two guest rooms, both with private bath; $50 including continental breakfast, which is served on the porch, weather permitting.

The Turner Inn (745-2156), 19 Washington Square North, Salem 01970. A yellow, mid-nineteenth-century house located right next to the Salem Witch Museum. There are eight guest rooms and a common room and living room. Continental breakfast is served in the dining room; handy to shops and museums. $65–$70 double in summer, $50–$55 in winter.

Tidecrest (631-4515), Spray Avenue, off Route 129 (Atlantic Avenue), Marblehead 01945, overlooking the ocean. A mansion with three guest rooms, all with ocean views, sharing two baths; use of a huge sun porch and beach. $60 per room, continental breakfast included.

Pleasant Manor Inn (631-5843), 264 Pleasant Street (Route 114), Marblehead 01945. This classic, Victorian house, set in grounds that include a tennis court, has been welcoming guests for 12 years. There are 11 rooms with private baths; $56 double plus tax.

The Amelia Payson Guest House (744-8304), 16 Winter Street, Salem 01970. A Greek Revival home within a short walk of shops and museums; three rooms at $45 double (including a light breakfast), use of the handsome living room.

State Street Pilot House (631-0601), 4 State Street, Marblehead 01945. Brothers Phil and Daniel Devan have renovated a nineteenth-century home just up from the State Street Landing. At present two ground-floor rooms are offered, both with fireplaces (nonworking), wood paneling, and private baths, $55 double.

Samuel Legro House (774-1860), 78 Centre Street, Danvers 01923. Built in 1854, a gracious house with beamed ceilings and fireplaces in the kitchen and living room, two guest rooms upstairs sharing a bath; pool for summer use; $50 includes breakfast.

The Nautilus (631-1703), 68 Front Street, Marblehead 01945. Just steps from the State Street Public Landing, Mrs. Dermody offers four rooms in a typical Old Town house; $50 double, without breakfast (but just across the street from the Driftwood Restaurant).

HOTELS AND MOTELS Hawthorne Inn (744-4080), 18 Washington Square West, Salem 01970. A fine, 89-room hotel that has managed to keep its standards high in an era in which few small city hotels have survived. All rooms have private baths; facilities include the Tavern on the Green (an oak-paneled bar) and the Maine Brace restaurant. The lobby is furnished in oriental rugs and Victorian reproductions. $64–$86 double; $120 for a one-bedroom suite.

The **Hotel Lafayette** (745-5503), 116 Lafayette Street, Salem 01970. Just 15 of the 55 rooms are available for "transients." The rest are reserved for businessmen and other regulars, but this is a clean, recently renovated hotel just a short walk from Pickering Wharf; also handy to buses and trains. $45 double.

King's Grant Inn (774-6800), Route 128, Danvers 01922. A 125-room resort motel with indoor pool, restaurant, $63–$77 double, free under age 18.

Sheraton Tara Hotel & Resort (777-2500), Ferncroft Village, Danvers 01922. Overlooking I-95 (formerly the Radisson Ferncroft), an eight-story, 300-room hotel with two pools (one indoor), whirlpool, lighted tennis courts, 18-hole golf course, and restaurant, $90–$104.

DINING OUT In Salem: **Lyceum Restaurant** (745-7665), 43 Church Street. Open daily for lunch and dinner. Housed in the city's nineteenth-century Lyceum, the forum for a number of celebrities, including Alexander Graham Bell, who gave his first public demonstration here of the telephone. There are now a number of different dining rooms, ranging in atmosphere from the living room to an outdoor patio and brick-walled pub; same menu all day, $2.95–$16.95; specialties include Veal and Chicken Lyceum.

Stromberg's Restaurant, 2 Bridge Street. Open daily, except Monday, from 11–8:30 (open Monday holidays). Claiming to be the oldest restaurant on the North Shore, Stromberg's proudly displays its 1935 menu. There is a water view and fresh fish is featured, but the nightly special can be broiled lamb dinner, or prime ribs. Dinner runs $4.50 to $10.50 for steak; the fried fisherman's platter is $9.50.

Topsides (744-8500), Pickering Wharf. Open daily for lunch and dinner. The upstairs Seafood Grill, with its deck-dining overlooking the water, is open May through October, specializing in seafood and lobster ($10.95 average for dinner includes salad). The Bull Finch Pub downstairs is less formal: chicken fingers, burgers, steamers, fish & chips, and sandwiches in a pub atmosphere.

China Clipper Restaurant (744-4328), 143 Washington Street. Open daily 11:30–1 AM, luncheon specials 11:30–3 PM. An attractive Chinese restaurant with a good local reputation. Mandarin and Szechuan dishes like Moo Shi and Peking Duck; from $3.75 for meatless Chow Mein to $12 for "Jewels of the Sea" (lobster, shrimp, crab, and scallops sauteed with mushrooms, pea pods, water chestnuts, and vegetables).

Victoria Station (745-3400), Pickering Wharf. Open daily for lunch and dinner, Sunday brunch. It's difficult to beat the tip-of-the-wharf location, especially in warm weather when you can dine *al fresco*. Lunch on Acapulco Salad (beef and guacamole) for $3.79 or Scampi Victoria, $6.99. Dinner in the $10–$12 range.

In Marblehead: **Rosalie's** (631-5353), 18 Sewall Street. Open daily for lunch and dinner. Housed in a skillfully decorated (upscale Victorian) factory space. The northern Italian menu includes creative pastas (like angel hair with a cream sauce, peas, and prosciutto) and nightly specials like grilled swordfish with a wine and butter sauce. Lunch is $5.50–$8.50, dinner is $11.95–$16.95.

Giancarlo's Italian Restaurant (639-2156), 261 Washington Street. Open daily 4–10 for dinner. The chef is from Florence and the menu is northern Italian, featuring seafood and pasta, $6.95–$15.50; a small rather formal place with rave reviews.

The Barnacle (631-4236), 141 Front Street. Open daily for lunch and dinner, right on the water. Seafood of course: broiled scallops ($7.95) and Jumbo Shrimp Scampi (sauteed in butter, herbs, and white wine, $7.95) or maybe just steamers served with drawn butter and natural broth ($8.95) or fresh water smelts ($3.95). This place is so popular that it's wise to come early in the lunch and dinner hours. At lunch it's possible to get away with just a bowl of chowder ($2.95) in the bar.

Sneakers (639-1560), 9 Atlantic Avenue. Open daily 11:30–10:30, brunch both Saturday and Sunday. Unprepossessing from the outside (set at the back of its parking lot) but a bright, upbeat atmosphere within (brass, with-it prints, sky lights, plants); lunch on a sausage pocket ($5.95) or a French dip croissant ($6.95); nightly specials are under $10.

Michael's House (631-5255), 26 Atlantic Avenue. Open for lunch and dinner daily. Eat in the informal Pancho Crowley's Cantina on the bar side—a tuna melt or Mexican basics (under $5)—or in the more formal dining rooms; Cajun specialties served in both: Chicken Jambalaya ($9.95 at dinner) and Cajun Steak ($11.95).

EATING OUT **Sail Loft** (Maddie's) (631-9824), 15 State Street, Marblehead. Closed Sundays. Open downstairs for lunch, upstairs too for dinner: an unvarnished, all-American place with the most famous bar on the North Shore (drinks are big). A favorite local dining spot.

Driftwood Restaurant (631-1145), 63 Front Street, Marblehead.

Open daily 5:30 AM–2 PM, until 5 PM in summer. Next to the landing, a narrow, weathered eatery with formica counter and eight, red-check-clothed tables; this is the fishermen's breakfast gathering place; the town coffee stop, crowded in summer but worth the wait. You can take out (there are seats and public washrooms on the landing). A superb cup of clam chowder with a salmon salad on whole wheat is $2.65.

Soup du Jour (744-9608), 7 Central Street, Salem. Open daily in summer (closed Sundays off-season) for lunch and dinner. A great lunch place just off the Essex Street mall. Soup of the day is $1.60, spinach pie is $2.85, and broccoli strudel, $2.95; the five-page menu also good for dinner but there are evening specials and entrees that go up to $9.95 (Beef Wellington).

Dill's Restaurant (631-9820), 141 Pleasant Street, Marblehead. Open daily for lunch and dinner. Where the 'Headers come to eat seafood. Lunch is $3–$6, dinner is $5–$12.

Jacob Marley's (631-5594), 28 Atlantic Avenue, Marblehead. Open daily except Monday lunch. Family oriented, family geared, blackboard specials like Oriental Meatball Soup. Same menu all day: burgers, Mexican specialties, great frozen drinks, $4 lunch, $7 dinner average.

King's Rook Coffee House (631-9838), 12 State Street, Marblehead. Open 7 PM nightly, serves coffees, hot sandwiches, wines, a true European coffeehouse atmosphere in a historic 1747 building.

In Swampscott: **Dale's "On Nahant Bay"** (595-9339), Route 129 (at the only light), open year-round 11 AM–11 PM, take out in warm weather months. There is a pleasant waterside dining room, also a sidewalk cafe in the summer; or you can take out and enjoy on benches overlooking the beach. Clam rolls, $3.95; try the Seafood Reuben.

In Wenham: **Wenham Tea House** (468-1498), on the village Green (Route 1A). Lunch daily until 1:30, tea from 3:15–4:30, reservations recommended. A charming old house (which also has a gift and bookshop, Gourmet Food Room) serves soups, salads, and a luncheon buffet ($5.25 for entree, salad bar, and desserts); tea includes home-baked cakes and cinnamon sticks.

ENTERTAINMENT "Le Grand David and his own Spectacular Magic Company" (927-3677), based at Cabot St. Cinema Theatre, 268 Cabot Street, Beverly 01915. Billed as the world's largest resident magic company: 65 performers, 500 costumes, two dozen sets, and backdrops are part of a 2½-hour production featuring three generations of stage magicians (Marco, David, and Seth) performing incredible feats on weekends, year-round. Must be seen to be believed; additional two-hour morning and early afternoon performances (mostly weekday productions) are staged at the Lacrom Theatre, 13 Wallis

Street. Both theaters have been restored by the company (which builds its own props); the Cabot St. Cinema features art films on nights when Le Grand David doesn't perform. Reservations a must.

North Shore Music Theatre (922-8500), PO Box 62, Beverly 01915 (Exit 19 off Route 128, Dunham Road). A summer theater, June through September: popular name concerts, big name performers, musicals. Weekend matinees 2 PM, otherwise 8 PM curtain time; Thursday children's productions; restaurant; patio with snack bar; tickets $11–$28 depending on performance.

Polo at the Myopia Polo Club (468-1402), Route 1A, Hamilton. A great spectator sport, every Sunday, 3 PM Memorial Day weekend through Columbus Day. Admission $5 per adult, children free age 12 and under.

SELECTIVE SHOPPING **Pickering Wharf,** Derby Street, Salem. I counted two dozen shops in this attractive waterside complex, all specialty places that change frequently or are based elsewhere, but fun to browse.

Marblehead's **Old Town** has a good variety of quality gift and gourmet shops. They start on Front Street around the Public Landing, go along State Street, then spread out in both directions on Washington Street, and continue along Pleasant Street.

Antiques: The Marblehead Antiques Association publishes a pamphlet guide available at most village shops. Don't miss **We Three Antiques,** 7 Pleasant Street, good for Victorian pieces; **Cargo Unlimited,** 82 Washington Street, which features Scandinavian yellow pine; and **Old Town Antique Coop,** 108 Washington Street, representing ten dealers. **The Old General Store,** 121 Washington Street (open weekends only), furnishes props for TV shows. **Sacks Antiques,** 4 State Street, is known for its English antique furniture; **Brass 'N' Bounty,** 68 Front Street, specializes in nautical brass.

Salem Witches: **Crow Haven Corner** (745-8763), 125 Essex Street. Laurie Cabot, "Official witch of Salem," offers Tarot Card readings, psychic consultations, and love readings.

BOOKSTORES **Spirit of '76 Bookstore** (631-7199), 107 Pleasant Street, Marblehead, features nautical, children's, regional books, and an extensive selection of cards.

Derby Square Book Store (745-8804), 215 Essex Street, Salem. A family-run, well-stocked, and inviting store.

Much Ado (639-0400), 1 Pleasant Street, Marblehead. Used, rare, and out-of-print books; specializing in children's books, local history, and literature. A wonderful place to browse, talk books, and perhaps share a cookie or a glass of wine with owners Cate and Nash.

Pyramid Books (745-7171), Derby Street, across from Pickering Wharf. A metaphysical book store owned and operated by two astrologers; tarot card reading offered, a center for psychic self-development.

CANDY **Stowaway Sweets** (631-0303), 154 Atlantic Avenue, Marblehead. Open daily. Housed in an ancient mansion, this is a name known to candy connoisseurs: 87 varieties of candy, much of it hand-dipped chocolate. They have been in business since 1929 and ship throughout the country.

Harbor Sweets (745-7648), 85 Leavitt Street, Salem. Open weekdays 8:30–4:30, Saturdays 10–3. Handmade chocolates like Sweet Sloops (chocolate, almond, butter crunch sailboats) and Marblehead Mints made here; distributed throughout the country. Factory tours on request.

Ye Olde Pepper Companie, 122 Derby Street, Salem. Open daily. Established 1806, billed as America's oldest candy company, specializing in blackjacks, gibralters, and other nineteenth-century treats.

CRAFTS **O'Flaherty's** (744-0194), 3 Central Street, Salem. Open daily; a trove of unusual jewelry, pottery, and a range of things crafted.

Marblehead Handprints (631-7921), 111 Washington Street. An attractive shop selling locally designed, handprinted fabric, canvas bags, quilts, and pillows.

Marblehead Kite Company (631-7166), 1 Pleasant Street, Marblehead (second floor). Open daily. Bright, nicely designed kites and wind socks, ties, pot holders, all handmade.

Quaigh Designs, 24 Atlantic Avenue, Marblehead. Open daily. A branch of the Wilmington, Vermont store, specializing in Scottish woolens, New England crafted pottery, jewelry, etc.

The Rusty Rudder (631-6318), 134 Washington Street, Marblehead. A local craftsmen's cooperative that has been going for more than 20 years.

SPECIAL EVENTS April: **Historic Salem Annual Auction** at Old Town Hall.

July: **Independence Day** celebrations in Marblehead (fireworks and harbor illumination); also **Marblehead Festival of the Arts** in Crocker Park.

Late July: **Marblehead Race Week** draws thousands of boats to compete; related special events.

August: **Beverly Homecoming Week**, (first week) Sunday pancake breakfast, road race, food, fireworks, concerts; **Heritage Week in Salem,** city-wide festival includes concerts, exhibits, sidewalk sales, fireworks, parade.

October: **Haunted Happenings** in Salem, events during week preceding and climaxing with Halloween—special slide shows, dances, costume parties, candlelight tour with music at the House of Seven Gables.

December: **Marblehead Christmas Walk**—Santa arrives by boat, sailboats are decorated with lights, caroling, tree lighting, special shopping days; **Caroling and Wassail Party** at Assembly House in Salem.

MEDICAL EMERGENCY **Salem Hospital** (741-1200), Highland Avenue, Salem; for ambulance: 744-4414.

Cape Ann Region

Cape Ann is a knobby fist of land thrust into the Atlantic. Its interior, "Dogtown," was virtually abandoned by 1830 and still remains an offbeat outing. But the coastline is one of the most varied and inviting in all New England. Circled by a 15-mile road, which I challenge anyone to drive in less than a day, it is impossible not to be snared by the Cape's beaches, art galleries, shops, restaurants, and those smooth oceanside rocks made for sunning.

In the 1980s Cape Ann began to call itself "Whale Watching Capital of the World." According to the Chamber of Commerce, more than 100,000 people a year come here to watch the more than 400 whales who congregate in the course of the season, a dozen miles offshore (but on a typical whale watch you see a half-dozen whales and a few other boats). Cape Ann also continues to be what it has always been: one of New England's chief departure points for fishing, sailing, and sight-seeing boats.

Cape Ann has a personality that is split between the very different towns of Gloucester and Rockport. Founded by fishermen back in 1623, Gloucester remains home port for some 200 draggers and trawlers, which land more than 300 million tons of fish a year. This city's brightest colors are still the fishing boats, not the spinnakers or boutique signs, and the new benches on Main Street tend to be occupied by old salts.

Rockport, with two-thirds of the Cape's inns and bed & breakfasts, is the North Shore's resort town. Named for its mid-nineteenth-century granite quarrying, it has been primarily an artists' colony and summer haven. The town is "dry," meaning that you must buy your liquor in Gloucester but can have it served to you in most Rockport inns and restaurants.

The Cape Ann area is accessible without a car. From Boston you can come by train to Gloucester, Rockport, Manchester (it's an easy walk to Singing Beach), and to Ipswich, which boasts more seventeenth-century homes than any town its size in the country. In summer you can also bring your bike from Boston to Gloucester's Rocky Neck by boat.

Despite its proximity to Boston (just 32 miles) the area—which includes the old shipbuilding village of Essex as well as Ipswich and Manchester—is far less crowded and cluttered than the state's more famous cape. What summer crowds there are converge on Rockport's Bearskin Neck shops and on the half-dozen major beaches. But there is much, much more. Few other corners of the country pack as much varied beauty into such small space.

AREA CODE   617

GUIDANCE   Cape Ann Chamber of Commerce (283-1601), 128 Main Street, Gloucester 01930, maintains two seasonal information centers, a booth on Stacy Boulevard (open daily in summer 10–6), near Blynman Bridge, and the hard-to-miss Fitz Hugh Lane House, a gabled stone house on the waterfront (Rogers Street), just beyond the lineup of boats and restaurants. It has bathrooms and is open in summer: weekdays, 10–4; weekends 10–5; also on spring and fall weekends.

The Rockport Chamber of Commerce (546-6575), Box 67, Rockport 01966, maintains a year-round information center (seasonal bathrooms) on Route 127, just south of town. It's open daily 9–7, June to mid-October; otherwise 10–12 and 1–4; Sundays from noon year-round.

GETTING THERE   By train: Commuter trains serve both Gloucester and Rockport from North Station (227-5070 and 1-800-392-6099), and CATA (283-7916) shuttles meet the commuter trains. Inquire about summer buses from Gloucester to the beaches. There is also a fleet of Gloucester-based taxis: **A Touch of Class** (281-4203), **Broadway Taxi** (283-7222), **Jim's West End Taxi** (283-3200), **Cape Ann Cab** (283-2008), and in Rockport **Horton's Taxi Service** (546-6233). All serve Boston's Logan International Airport as well as local destinations.

By car: There is free parking in St. Peter's Park in Gloucester's West End, right on the waterfront. In Rockport on summer days you are asked to park out on Route 127, south of the village, and take the shuttle ($3.75), which connects with Dock Square at 15-minute intervals. Parking is less of a problem in Ipswich and Essex, but it is impossible during the summer in Manchester.

GETTING AROUND   The Cape Ann Transportation Authority (283-7916) offers frequent daytime bus service around Cape Ann itself. Also see taxis listed above. Inquire about beach buses that may meet trains.

TO SEE AND DO   In Gloucester: Cape Ann Historical Association (283-0455), 27 Pleasant Street, Gloucester. Open Tuesday–Saturday 10–5; $2 per adult, $1 children and retirees, free age 12 and under. This is an elegant little museum with fine china from China and silver pieces by Paul Revere. It has a fine collection of seascapes by American luminist Fitz Hugh Lane (1804–65) and a variety of other interesting paintings, including a 1931 view of Dogtown by Marsden Hartley and sketches by Winslow Homer. In the Fisheries

Room there are more paintings and photo blowups of nineteenth-century life in Gloucester depicting, among other things, waterfront acres filled with drying fish ("flake yards"). Inquire about the walking tours of downtown Gloucester that the museum sponsors regularly in summer.

Gloucester Fishermen's Museum (283-1940), Rogers and Porter streets. Open daily 10–4, from noon on Sundays. $2 adults, $1 per child, $5.50 per family. Over the past half-dozen years we have watched this amazing museum grow to fill a windowless warehouse with a wild and wonderful collection of relics from the sea (like the cranium and nostrum of a 60-foot whale). Exhibits tell the story of the Gloucester fishing industry from schooner days to current life at sea (a short film depicts life aboard the 72-foot dragger *Debbie Rose*). This is a hands-on place where you can salt cod and try your hand at the crank fog horn. There is also a short sequence on whale watching. The museum houses the Cetacean Research Unit, a source of naturalist guides for the excursion boats. There are special summer workshops for children and also whale-watching and boat tours.

Beauport (283-0800), Eastern Point in East Gloucester, off Route 127A. Open for guided tours on the hour from mid-May to mid-October, weekdays 10–4; also on weekends in foliage season, 1–4. $4 per adult, $2 per child. Even historic-house-haters shouldn't pass up this one: an overgrown cottage of some 40 rooms, all filled with decorating ideas, most of them representing a period in American history. "Beauport," incidentally, is the name that Samuel de Champlain gave to Gloucester Harbor when he chartered it in 1604. This Beauport was the home of the famous interior decorator Henry Davis Sleeper between 1907 and 1934. It is maintained by the Society for the Preservation of New England Antiquities. To get there you must ignore the "private" signs at the entrance to Eastern Point.

Hammond Castle Museum (283-2080/2081), 80 Hesperus Avenue, Magnolia (five miles south of Gloucester, off Route 127). Open daily spring through fall, 10–4. $3.50 per adult, $3 for seniors and students, $1.50 for children ages 6–12. It is best to come for one of the special events, staged year-round, ranging from the annual (late June) Medieval Festival, to art films and concerts (on the 8,200-pipe organ). The castle-like mansion was built by John Hays Hammond, the inventor of remote control radio, among other things. Hammond collected medieval artifacts: armor, tapestries and portions of buildings, which he incorporated into his home. From the grounds you can see the pile of offshore rocks known as Norman's Woe, immortalized by Longfellow in his poem, "Wreck of the

Hammond Castle, Gloucester, is the scene of frequent happenings

Hesperus." Light lunches are served in the rooftop cafe, and evening concertgoers are invited to picnic here beforehand.

The Sargent House Museum (281-2432), 49 Middle Street, Gloucester. Open June through October on Tuesday, Thursday, Saturday 1–5, and by appointment other times of the year. $1.50 per adult, $1 per child and senior citizen. Built in 1768 this is a late Georgian house, with a fascinating story about Judith Sargent and her marriage to John Murray, the founder of Universalism in this country. Locally crafted highboys, lowboys, and a wealth of period furnishings.

In Rockport: **Sewall-Scripture House,** 40 King Street (corner of Granite, near the railroad station). July–Labor Day, open daily 2–5. Free. This unusual Federal-style granite house was built in 1832 and has an extensive exhibit of town memorabilia.

Old Castle. Set back from Route 127, north of Rockport, at the corner of Granite Street. Open July and August, Saturday and Sunday 2–5. Free. This garrison-style house dates from the 1700s and houses local historical collections.

Paper House (546-2629), Pigeon Hill Street, Rockport. Open July and August: daily 10–5. Age ten and over, $.50. North of Rockport on Route 127, turn up Curtis Street. At first you think that this is just a modest summer cottage set in a rock garden. On closer inspection you find that even the exterior walls are made of newspaper: 215 layers of paper, pressed under two tons of pressure. Inside a fireplace, piano (the casing), a grandfather clock, chairs, tables, a desk, and more are all made of "newspaper mache." The creator was Elis F. Stedman, a Swedish immigrant who read a half-dozen newspapers a day. He began the project in 1920, worked on it steadily for 20 years.

In Ipswich: **The John Whipple House,** 53 South Main Street, on South Village Green. Open April through mid-October, Tuesday–Saturday 10–5, Sunday 1–5. $2 per adult, $3 for joint admission to the John Heard House, (see below). One of the oldest buildings in New England, the major part of this weathered, double-gabled house was built in 1640 by "clothiers of good estate." It remained in the family for two centuries and in 1898 became one of the country's first houses to be restored. It is well furnished and the herb garden contains 60 varieties of medicinal plants.

John Heard House, 40 South Main Street. Built in 1795, this is a stately Federal mansion crowned with four corner chimneys. Maintained, like the Whipple House, by the Ipswich Historical Society, it is filled with China Trade treasures; there is also a collection of carriages, from a doctor's surrey to a funeral rig. For hours and admission see Whipple House listing above. Also see the village of Essex below.

VILLAGES   No one should limit a Cape Ann visit simply to Gloucester and Rockport. The villages of Magnolia and Manchester to the south and Essex and Ipswich to the north all invite exploration.

Essex. Most of the "Gloucester schooners" were built in this tidy white village. The Causeway, site of most of the boat-building yards, is now top heavy with seafood restaurants, but the **Essex Shipbuilding Museum** (768-7541), housed in an 1820s schoolhouse in the center of town (Route 133), tells the story well with old photographs, ship models, and tools (open May through October, Thursday and Friday 1–5, Saturday and Sunday 12–5). Note the eighteenth-century graveyard (also see Green Space, Dining, and Antiques).

Ipswich must have been a glad sight to settlers in 1633: a broad, winding river giving shelter from the sea, falls to power a mill, a convenient landing area (now Town Wharf), and salt marshes protected by gently sloping, wooded hills. No wonder it was one of America's first important ports. Much of the early town remains, including more seventeenth-century homes than any American town its size, and two town Greens. The present Congregational Church on Meeting House Green is the sixth to occupy the site, but the devil's footprint is still outlined on one of the rocky outcroppings below it. Legend has it that Satan was chased right up the steeple and sent running down the hill by fiery eighteenth-century evangelist George Whitefield.

Nineteenth-century industry—which began with two small lace-making factories in the 1820s and included tanning, shoemaking, and the country's first hosiery factory (the picturesque Ipswich Mills are now owned by Sylvania)—changed the town's Yankee face, adding Greeks, Poles, and Frenchmen. The shore here is mostly salt marsh but includes the stunning Crane Reservation (see Green Space and Swimming) with the North Shore's best beach. Lineal homesteads are tucked away in the sea and sky-cupped world of salt marsh off Argilla Road. The Feoffees, a group of town property trustees who have been perpetuating themselves since 1642, manage Little Neck, thickly covered with summer cottages. Most of the town's late seventeenth- and eighteenth-century houses are grouped around Meeting House Green (the meetinghouse itself burned and has been replaced by a modernistic church). The Old Burying Ground on High Street contains stones dating from 1634, and the carvings on many gravestones are outstanding. Also note the Choate Bridge in the middle of the village, said to be the oldest stone arched bridge (1764) in English-speaking America (see Museums, Green Space, and Swimming). The **Ipswich Chamber of Commerce** (356-3231), PO Box 456, Ipswich 01938, publishes a pamphlet guide and maintains a seasonal information center, open Memorial Day–Labor Day, daily 10–4.

Manchester. This seaside town (separated from Salem in 1645) traded with Europe and the West Indies in the eighteenth century and became the first North Shore summer resort in the 1840s. Splendid Singing Beach remains open to those willing to walk more than a mile from the train station. The **Trask House** (526-7230), open in summer, Tuesday–Friday 2–5, is a curb-side, Federal-style home that houses the town's historical collection. It was owned originally by Abigail Trask, the wife of a sea captain who traded with Russian Czar Nicholas I (Abigail was happily married but insisted that the house remain officially hers). Along Union Street note the Congregation Church, a graceful 1809 classic. The Manchester Memorial Library next door was designed by Charles McKim. Masconomo Park, on Beach Street, is the site of periodic concerts and is a good picnicking spot with a view of Manchester's largely hidden harbor and two yacht clubs. Also note the Old Burial Ground on Summer Street (Route 127), a beautiful plot with seventeenth- and eighteenth-century headstones.

Annisquam. This village's narrow streets and crooked old homes date from its improbable eighteenth- and early nineteenth-century status as a thriving port. The Annisquam Village Church dates from 1830 and the Village Hall was built as a Baptist meetinghouse in 1828. On the Green there is also an old firehouse, now the historical society (open June–September, Monday 3–5, Thursday 7 PM–9 PM, with a stagecoach display), and the Leonard School, now the Annisquam Exchange and Art Gallery. Also note the Lobster Cove Bridge, built in 1847.

ART CENTERS   Since the mid-nineteenth-century artists have gathered on Cape Ann to paint its fishing boats, beaches, rocky shores, and narrow lanes. Fitz Hugh Lane was Gloucester's famous painter (his gabled granite house is now a summer information center and his works hang in the Cape Ann Historical Society). Winslow Homer came here to paint in the 1870s, and in recent years many nationally known artists have gathered in East Gloucester's Rocky Neck and in Rockport. The Cape's special, luminous light, as well as its land and seascape, continues to draw them.

Rocky Neck, off Route 127A. There is a parking lot at the entrance to this picturesque peninsula, which is traversed by a narrow, one-way (no parking anywhere in summer) road. One of the country's oldest art colonies, it is also the place where Rudyard Kipling wrote *Captains Courageous*. Fairly quiet these days, the neck is a colorful jumble of art galleries and restaurants. It's accessible directly from Boston via the excursion boat *Virginia-C* (see Excursions).

The North Shore Art Association (283-1857), 197 East Main Street (near the entrance to Rocky Neck), is open daily early June through late September, with demonstrations and changing exhibits. It sponsors a midsummer festival with musical and theatrical performances.

Rockport Art Association (546-6604), 12 Main Street, Rockport. Open daily 9:30–5, Sundays 1–5. This is an eighteenth-century tavern with galleries meandering off into the skylit barn out back. The pictures on display are by association members. Art classes and concerts are also held here, and a small gift shop sells cards and prints.

LOCAL LANDMARKS   In Gloucester: **Gloucester Fishermen's Statue,** on Western Avenue, or Stacy Boulevard, as Route 127 is doubly known at this point near Bynman Bridge. This stalwart seaman at the wheel honors the more than 10,000 Gloucester fishermen who have died at sea and all "Who Go Down to the Sea in Ships." The nearby drawbridge spans an eighteenth-century canal between Gloucester Harbor and the Annisquam River.

Stage Fort Park, Western Avenue. This is the site of the fish flakes set up by the Dorchester Company in 1623. If you can avoid the broken bottles the park is a delight: winding pathways climb the smooth rocks overlooking the harbor.

Gloucester Waterfront. Park and stroll by the boats tied up here;

there's a Hidden Park behind the Gloucester House Restaurant where you can take in the scene.

Independent Christian Church (283-2410), Middle and Church streets. Now Unitarian-Universalist, this is the mother church of Universalism in this country. Built in 1804, it is a graceful building with a Wren-style steeple, a Paul Revere bell, a Willard Clock, and a Sandwich glass chandelier.

Our Lady of Good Voyage Church (283-1490), 124 Prospect Street. A church of unusual warmth and grace, modeled on the cathedral of San Miguel in the Azores, the origin of much of its congregation.

Eastern Point Lighthouse and **Dog Bar Breakwater** off Route 127A. Marking the entrance to Gloucester Harbor, the lighthouse (owned by the United States Coast Guard and open for tours 9:30–3:30 daily) dates from 1890, and the breakwater marks the presence of a treacherous sandbar beneath. This is a great spot to clear your lungs and head. The view is of Boston's skyscrapers hovering improbably above the horizon.

Thatcher's Island and **Twin Lights.** Visible from Route 127A between Eastern Point and Good Harbor, this small island, marked by twin granite lighthouses, is named for a couple who survived the 1625 shipwreck in which they lost four children.

Babson Museum, on Route 127 midway between Gloucester and Rockport. Open July and August, Tuesday–Sunday 2–5. This small shedlike building is a restored cooperage shop, displaying early tools. The museum is also good for local information.

In Rockport: **Bearskin Neck.** This rocky natural neck extends off of Dock Square, the commercial center of Rockport. It is lined with fishermen's shacks, converted decades ago into artists' studios, and now is an enclave of shops and restaurants that have become a tourist magnet.

Motif #1, a much-painted red fish shed on Tuna Wharf, Bearskin Neck, best viewed from T-Wharf. It has become a symbol of Cape Ann.

Granite Quarry, Granite Street, Route 127 north of Rockport. A water-filled granite quarry, now a local beauty spot.

Granite Pier, Route 127 north of Rockport. Across from the quarry, accessible by car, this is a great spot from which to enjoy the view of Rockport Harbor.

Pigeon Cove, farther along Route 127, is hidden behind Cape Ann Forge. It's a quiet inlet where fishing boats tie up. The New England Lobster Co. at the end of the pier has a reasonably priced selection of fish and lobster.

Castle Hill (356-4070), Argilla Road, Ipswich. The 59-room Great House was built as a summer residence for Chicago plumbing magnate Richard T. Crane, Jr. It overlooks 2,000 acres of preservation land, Crane's Beach, and the Atlantic Ocean. The property, which includes 165 acres of grounds landscaped by the Olmsted brothers and Arthur Shurcliff, is owned by the Trustees of Reservations and administered by the Castle Hill Foundation. The formal gardens are the setting for the late June through mid-August Castle Hill Festival, a series of weekend concerts, plays, and happenings before which guests picnic. Inquire about tours. The house is also available for weddings and functions.

GREEN SPACE In a world of flux Rockport traditions abide. Anyone wishing to take a long, guided walk (the destination varies each week, but most of the following are included) should come to the parking lot behind Rockport Town Hall, Sunday (year-round) at 10 AM. Just one-quarter of Cape Ann is settled, leaving ample public space. Two source books offer detailed information about these areas: *The Wilds of Cape Ann* (1981) available for $5.95 in many local stores, and the *Passport* booklet ($2.00 plus $.75 for postage) published by Essex County Greenbelt (768-7241), 82 Eastern Avenue, Essex 01929. Greenbelt owns and maintains some 3,000 acres in the county and conducts monthly Sunday walks.

Ravenswood Park, off Western Avenue (Route 127) south of Gloucester, look for the Ravenswood Community Chapel. The 300-acre park next door was laid out in 1889 and contains miles of wide wooded paths, good for jogging and cross-country skiing. This is said to be the northernmost point that the wild magnolia grows.

Dogtown. Accessible from Cherry Street in Riverdale, from the Cape Ann Industrial Park off Blackburn Circle, and from Summit Avenue in Rockport. A map of this 3,000 acre tract is available from area information booths. No houses survive, but there are a few dozen cellar holes, traces of the 80 families who lived here between the early 1700s and 1830s. Over the past few years Essex County Greenbelt has been instrumental in acquiring land, removing trash, and improving directional signs to this area. It's a superb place for birding in spring and fall and for blueberrying in July, but it can be confusing. There are also occasional muggings. Visitors are advised not to come alone. A detailed map is available from Essex County Greenbelt (see Green Space introduction).

Eastern Point Sanctuary, at the tip of Eastern Point. A 26-acre Massachusetts Audubon Sanctuary with a pebbly beach, rocky shore, salt marsh, and woods with a spectacular view of Boston. Persevere past all the "Private" and "For Eastern Point Residents Only" signs.

Halibut Point, Gott Avenue, off Route 127 north of Rockport. A narrow path leads down to one of the most dramatic sites on the Eastern seaboard. First there is the 12-acre Halibut Point property, maintained by the Trustees of Reservations ($2 weekends, $1 weekdays in summer), where a path leads through low scrub to flat rocks and a fine view across Ipswich Bay. The adjoining 54-acre state park (369-3350) section commands the same view (on a clear day Mt. Agamenticus in York, Maine looms at the end of the sweep of coastline) and includes deep granite quarries (a sign says no swimming). This rocky headland forms the northern tip of the Cape, a spot where sailing vessels have always had to tack ("Haul-About"). This is a great picnic spot and there are tidal pools to explore.

Mt. Ann Park, New Way Lane, off Route 133, east of Route 128. These 87 acres are maintained by the Trustees of Reservations. It's forested land, representing the highest elevation on Cape Ann and commands views as far as Blue Hill (south of Boston) to the south and Mt. Agamenticus in Maine to the north.

The Cox Reservation, 82 Eastern Avenue, Essex, is headquarters for the Essex County Greenbelt Association, which is housed in the old farmhouse that was once the home of muralist Allyn Cox (his paintings grace Grant's tomb and the capitol dome in Washington, D.C.). A path leads down past the gardens and orchard, through marsh, to a landing on the Essex River with a fine view of Hog Island and Crane's beach in the distance. Bring paper and paints.

Ipswich River Wildlife Sanctuary (887-9264), Topsfield. From Route 1 turn east on Route 97 at the lights, and go left at the first intersection (Perkins Row) $2 per adult, $1 per child. This is the largest sanctuary maintained by Massachusetts Audubon: 2,000 acres of marsh, pond, and upland along the Ipswich River. There are 10 miles of paths, marked for skiing in winter (also see Canoeing).

Bradley-Palmer State Forest (887-5931) in Topsfield (from Route 1 turn right at second light north of the Topsfield Fairgrounds, then onto Hamilton Road) offers picnic areas, fishing, and canoeing on the Ipswich River, and 35 miles of hiking and ski trails.

Willowdale State Forest (887-5931), Linebrook Road in Ipswich, is 2,400 acres with 40 miles of trails; canoeing and fishing.

Stony Cove and Presson Reservation, Exit 13 off Route 128, near the confluence of the Annisquam and Little rivers. This 45-acre property includes a granite pier, tidal inlet, salt marsh, and uplands of white pine, oak, and sweet birch. Detailed directions and descriptions are in the Essex County Greenbelt's *Passport* booklet (see Green Space introduction).

Pigeon Hill. Take Landmark Lane off Route 127 near Pigeon Cove (north of the village). A vantage and picnic spot above Sandy Bay in Rockport.

Agassiz Rock in Manchester (east side of School Street, one-half mile north of Route 128, Exit 15). This 104-acre property is wooded upland with two glacial boulders said to have been discovered by Harvard naturalist Louis Agassiz. A great spot for a picnic.

Whittemore Marsh. Open only October through May, this is 75 acres of salt marsh and barrier beach owned by Essex County Greenbelt. Access is from Wingaersheek Road in West Gloucester.

EXCURSIONS Whale Watching: Whales fast all winter in the Caribbean and feast here during the months that conveniently coincide with tourist season. They feed on small sand eels that thrive on Stellwagen Bank, a dozen miles off of Cape Ann. A total of more than 400 whales—humpbacks, minkes, finbacks, and right whales—feed here from April through October. They add up to the world's greatest concentration of whales, not only in numbers but in species. The fact is, however, that on most trips passengers see four to ten whales, mostly humpbacks, who often come within 50 feet of the boat, responding to an audience by breaching (flinging their entire 50-foot, 40-ton bodies out of the water). They also "spy-ho" (shove their massive snouts out of the water) and "lob-tail" (wave their huge tails in the air). All the Cape Ann boats have naturalists aboard to narrate the whale story. See the "What's Where" section for advice on how to choose your boat and what to wear.

Cape Ann Whale Watch (283-5110), Rose's Wharf at the eastern end of the Gloucester waterfront. Captain Fred Douglas was the first (in 1979) to take whale watchers out from Gloucester. His 55-foot *Daunty II* and 70-foot *Daunty V* offer twice daily trips, May through October. The average price of the four-hour excursions is $15.

Gloucester Whale Watch at the Yankee Fleet (283-0313 or 800-322-0013), Cape Ann Marina, 79 Essex Avenue, Gloucester. The five boats in the fleet range in size from the 36-foot *Nautibuoys* to the 100-foot *Yankee Freedom*. Twice daily trips, three on summer weekends.

Seven Seas Whale Watch (283-1776), Gloucester, departs from the wharf behind the Gloucester House Restaurant. Three boats, two of them sleek 90-foot long vessels, offer four daily trips, also 6 PM sunset trips on summer weekends.

Whale Safari (281-4163), Gateway Marina, Gloucester, off Route 128, offers three daily runs aboard the 75-foot *Capt. Joseph II*.

Capt. Bill's Deep Sea Fishing and Whale Watch (283-6995), Gloucester. The 70-foot *Island Queen* and 60-foot *Miss Gloucester II* sail from Cape Ann Marina, and the 60-foot *Miss Cape Ann* departs from St. Peter's Park two or three times a day in season.

Capt. Ted's "Rockport" Whale Watching (546-2889), from T-Wharf in Rockport, Tuesday–Sunday; the *Lady Dianne* sails late June to Labor Day. Captain Ted claims that he is a half hour nearer the banks than the Gloucester boats.

Fishing Party Boats: **The Yankee Fleet** (283-0313), Cape Ann Marina, 75 Essex Street, Gloucester, offers all-day, half-day, and overnight deep-sea fishing trips. All-day trips leave at 6 and 7 AM, return at 3 and 4 PM. Bait is supplied and tackle can be rented.

Lady Dianne (546-2889), T-Wharf, Rockport. Tuesday–Sunday. Five-hour, deep-sea fishing trips, from late June–Labor Day, leaving 7:30 AM, returning 12:30.

Winner III (546-6752 and 283-5457), T-Wharf, Rockport. Bob Anderson and Brett Clayton offer all-day, deep-sea fishing trips departing at 7 AM, returning at 3:30 PM; tackle rental available.

Other boat excursions: *The Dixie Belle* (283-5110), Rose's Wharf, 415 Main Street, Gloucester, leaves hourly on summer days and offers a one-hour tour around the harbor. Tickets are $3.50 per adult, $2.50 per child under 12. It makes a pick-up stop at Rocky Neck.

The Virginia C. (426-8419) offers Sunday–Wednesday runs from Boston to Rocky Neck, departing Boston's Northern Avenue Bridge at 10 AM and Rocky Neck at 3 PM; $16.50 round-trip adult.

Bev (546-2889) leaves T-Wharf, Rockport, daily late June through Labor Day; four hour-long cruises per day. $5 per adult, $4 per child.

BICYCLING   Although the roads are heavily trafficked, they border the water in many places, and you can park (in places you cannot park a car) and clamber onto the rocks or browse in shops and pay far less at beaches. Bikes can be rented from **Smith Hardware** (546-6518), at the Whistlestop Mall in Rockport; from **Seaside Cycle** (526-1200), Manchester; and from the **Skol Shop** (356-5872), in Ipswich.

BOAT RENTALS   **Capt. Hook's Boat Rentals** (281-4114), 138 Main Street, Gloucester.

CANOEING   The Annisquam River lends itself to saltwater canoeing. Rentals available from **Annisquam Canoes** (283-2112), at the Cape Ann Marina. The Ipswich River is eminently canoeable. A "Canoeing Map of the Ipswich River" ($3.50) is available by writing to the Ipswich River Watershed Association, 262 Maple Street, Danvers 01937. Canoes can be rented from **Foote's Canoes** (356-9771), on Topsfield Road in Ipswich; and from **Nabor Canoes** (887-8626), on Ipswich Road in Topsfield. The **Ipswich River Wildlife Sanctuary** (887-9264) rents canoes (by reservation) and is a source of advice and a popular put-in place; it also offers overnight camping on Perkins Island (see Green Space).

GOLF   **Rockport Golf Club** (546-3340), South Street, Rockport. Nine-hole course; closed to nonmembers on weekends.

Candlewood Golf Club (356-5377), Route 133, Ipswich. Nine-hole public course.

Cape Ann Golf Course (768-7544), Route 133, Essex. Public nine-hole course.

HORSEBACK RIDING **King of the Hill Farm** (283-7016), 44 Bennett Street, Gloucester, offers trail riding and semi-private lessons on gentle horses; $10 per hour.

Ponderosa Pines (768-6669), in Essex, also offers trail rides.

Meadow Ridge Farm (768-7842), 105 Southern Avenue, Essex. Private and semi-private lessons, summer riding camp.

Silver Star Stables (526-1104), off School Street, Manchester, offers year-round instruction and trail rides ($10 per hour), reservations required. There is also a riding camp, late June–Labor Day.

Ascot Riding Center (356-5932), Argilla Road, Ipswich. Not a livery stable but riding lessons are available at $15 per hour, children and adults.

SAILBOARDING **Performance Sailboarding** (283-1161), in Magnolia, rents boards by the hour, day, and week (also see Manchester).

SAILING **The Sailing School** (281-4441), 77 Rocky Neck Avenue, Gloucester, offers a basic, 20-hour course aboard a 20-foot sloop.

Schooner Morning Star (768-7630 or 281-1047), offers half-day and full-day courses. Also cocktail cruises from the Gateway Marina in Gloucester.

Racing yacht *Sweetwater* (contact Captain Brad Sweet, 546-7543, of the Addison Choate Inn) offers two daily trips from Gloucester; $30 per person.

Seaport Yachts (281-4441), 77 Rocky Neck, Gloucester, rents sailboats by the week: $695 for a 26-foot boat to $1,650 for a 40-foot boat.

SWIMMING Gloucester beaches all forbid the use of inflated tubes and the like. Green flies are a serious problem on all area beaches from July through early August. Lifeguards are on duty from 9 AM–5 PM and the non-resident fee is $6 on weekends; $5 midweek. All have bathhouses and snack bars. On weekends it's best to be there before 10 to insure a spot. **Good Harbor Beach,** Thatcher Road, is the most popular and **Wingaersheek Beach,** on Atlantic Street (Exit 13 off Route 128), is favored by families with small children (great climbing rocks and relatively small surf). **Half Moon Beach** and **Cressy Beach,** at Stage Fort Park, (see Local Landmarks) are city beaches.

Rockport beaches include **Long Beach** (lined with cottages) and **Cape Hedge Beach** (one parking area serves both); also **Old Garden Beach,** accessible by foot from many Rockport inns; **Front Beach** and **Back Beach,** on the other side of the village; and well-named **Pebble Beach** on Penzance Road. There are rest rooms at Front Beach, which, along with Back Beach, is accessible to anyone who can find a legal parking space. Most people come on foot. Visitors need a parking sticker (available from the Town Office Building) for Long and Cape Hedge beaches.

Crane's Beach, technically the Richard T. Crane, Jr. Memorial Reservation (356-4354), Argilla Road, Ipswich. $8 per car weekends, $5.50 weekdays, $1 on foot. This 1,352-acre property, maintained by the Trustees of Reservations, includes more than four miles of shoreline on Ipswich Bay. The superb, dune-backed beach never quite fills, but the 1,500-car parking lot frequently does (by 11 AM on weekends), despite the stiff fee. Overflow parking is at **Steep Hill Beach** (use Castle Hill entrance), entailing a fair walk down a steep hill, not ideal if you are trying to manage both gear and small children. Both sides of the beach are also plagued by green flies in late July and early August. There is a snack bar and bathhouse (check Local Landmarks and Entertainment for more on Castle Hill). In the off-season leashed dogs and horseback riders are welcome.

Singing Beach, Manchester. A wide, smooth beach now backed by mansions. There is an elegant little beach house with a weather vane and fanlight. Anyone can use the snack bar and rest rooms, but changing rooms are for Manchester residents only.

TENNIS In Gloucester: **O'Malley School,** Cherry Street, has three lighted outdoor, four indoor courts (reserve: 281-2480).

Gloucester High School has four outdoor courts, and **Swinson's Farm,** off Mt. Pleasant Avenue, has two courts.

In Rockport: **Sandy Bay Motor Inn,** Route 127, has courts available by the hour (reserve: 546-7155).

INNS AND BED & BREAKFASTS In Rockport 01966: **Addison Choate Inn** (546-7543), 49 Broadway. Margot Sweet obviously enjoys creating "ambiance." Although the 1850s house is right downtown on Broadway, it offers peace: a deep garden with a nicely landscaped swimming pool; rooms artfully decorated with family antiques, fresh fabrics and quilts, watercolors, and flowers. There's a small library with a TV and luxuriant built-in reading nooks; a cheery dining room; and a third-floor guest room with an ocean view and a skylit, stained-glass ceiling. Breakfast in bed is available, but most guests prefer to socialize over the homemade pastries in the dining room. $62–$72 per room for two, breakfast included, $105 for the suite (sleeps four).

Beach Knoll Inn (546-6939), 30 Beach Street. The core clapboard house was one of the first on Sandy Bay, and it has a wide old hearth with a hidden passage from its back to the beach. Rooms all have a private bath, some have fireplaces and refrigerators. Back Beach is just across the street. $60–$70 for standard rooms, $75–$85 for two-room apartments, $95–$105 for three-room apartments, also weekly rates; cheaper off-season.

The Captain's House (546-3825), 109 Marmion Way. This is a large, white stucco, black-shuttered house sited on the ocean, a mile and a half from the center of town. Open April through November. There are five bedrooms, three with private baths. The feel here is that of a traditional guest house, but a continental breakfast is laid out in the seaside sun room. $42–$65 in season; $40–$60 off-season.

Chicatabut Inn (546-3342), a rambling, old, reasonably priced, wooden summer inn, right on Long Beach. Open mid-May through mid-October. The 16 units all have private baths and small fridges for drinks and snacks; morning coffee or tea is included in the $67 waterfront (double) room; $63 for a rear room; three-day minimum in July and August; cheaper in May, June, September, and October.

Inn on Cove Hill (546-2701), 37 Mount Pleasant Street. Built in 1791, this classic Federal-style house has a curving staircase with 13 steps, representing the 13 colonies. Legend has it that it was built with pirate gold found at nearby Gully Point. There are 11 guest rooms, most of them doubles, two with an extra bed. There's also a bright little single on the third floor. The wide-planked floors and the detailing on moldings and doors have been preserved. Rooms are papered in designer prints, furnished with family antiques, comforters, and canopies. $30–$65, including continental breakfast.

Eden Pines Inn (546-2502), Eden Road. A turn-of-the-century mansion set right on the water two miles south of the village. It offers six upstairs bedrooms, all with private baths and most with ocean views (several are large enough to accommodate four people). There is a paneled living room with a stone hearth and a bright breakfast room overlooking the ocean. There is plenty of lounging space on the sea side of the house, and the smooth rocks below are great for sunning. $76–$82 per double room, breakfast included. Also inquire about three Bearskin Neck harbor-side apartments.

Linden Tree Inn (546-2494), 26 King Street. This is a friendly, Victorian home on a quiet street, within easy walking distance of both the railroad station and beaches. There are 18 nicely decorated rooms, a spacious living room, and sun porch. There are also four new motel rooms (each sleeping four) in the Carriage House. Continental breakfast is included in the $39–$53 per room rates, $12 less off-season.

Old Farm Inn (546-3237), Pigeon Cove. This 1799 saltwater farm, better known for its restaurant, offers three pleasant rooms in the inn itself (one with a canopy bed and two with fireplaces) and four in The Barn Guest House (one with a kitchenette, the others with fridge and hotpot). All have private bath and TV. There is a comfortable sitting room for guests in the inn, and continental breakfast is provided in the sun room. It's a bit far from the village but set on five acres of lawn and meadow adjacent to Halibut Point (see Green Space). $60–$110 (for a two-room suite) in summer; $50–$90 off-season.

Pleasant Street Inn (546-3915), 17 Pleasant Street. Set high on a knoll above the town, this large Victorian house has been recently renovated by Roger and Lynn Norris. It offers seven rooms, all with private baths, $45–$55 per room including continental breakfast.

Ralph Waldo Emerson House (546-6321), Green Street. Open mid-April through November. The interior doesn't measure up to the wonderful facade of this 1850s summer hotel. The public rooms are vast and pleasant but nothing special, and there is a sub-lobby recreation area (ping-pong, whirlpool, and sauna). There is also an outdoor pool. The 37 rooms all have private baths and many have ocean views. $49–$70 per room (no meals), $85–$115 per couple per day. Less before July and after Labor Day.

Rocky Shores (546-2823), Eden Road. Open mid-April through October. A shingled, 1905 mansion forms the centerpiece for a clutch of two- and three-bedroom efficiency cottages. The view from the main house (in which there are 10 rooms, each with private bath) is wonderful but the atmosphere is a shade stiff. On the other hand it's a beautiful spot for older guests who want a view and peace and quiet. $51–$67 per room including full breakfast, $430–$530 per week for the cottages, less off-season.

Seacrest Manor (546-2211), 131 Marmion Way. A large old mansion with eight large guest rooms, all with private bath, some with deck space and ocean views. There's a friendly clutter to the public rooms and guest rooms, and, although not furnished in antiques, they are pleasant. The deck (good for tanning) and two acres of grounds are appealing. $54–$72 in summer, less in winter, full breakfast included.

Seafarer Inn (546-6248), 86 Marmion Way. Open April through November. A homey, gambrel-roofed inn with a great water view. There are ten airy guest rooms filled with paintings by local artists. The best views are from the two third-floor rooms, with breakfast nooks and efficiency kitchenettes (rented on a weekly basis). Most rooms have their own bath. A continental breakfast is included in $42–$58 in summer.

Seaward Inn (546-3471), Marmion Way. Open mid-May to mid-October. For more than 40 years Roger and Anne Cameron have welcomed guests to their brown-shingled inn overlooking Sandy Bay. Roger tends the beautifully landscaped grounds and the gardens that supply the greens, flowers, and herbs for the dining room. The 31 rooms (all with private bath) are scattered among the main house, the Breakers (directly on the bay), and assorted small cottages. All have night-lights and writing tables but no phones. A few have TVs and three cottages have fireplaces. Behind the inn is a sheltered, spring-fed pond with a small sandy beach. A path winds along the shore and through high-bush blueberries into a small wood. Rustic benches are scattered along the way. Old Garden Beach is a five-minute walk and the village is a mile away. All three meals are served, breakfast and dinner are included in the rates: $104–$138 per couple, $57 single, $25 under age six, $42 for an additional person in the room. Special rates for three and four in a suite.

Sea Ledges (546-2366). This attractive seaside building is divided into apartments available by the day and week; $60 per day for a one-bedroom unit right on the ocean. It is at the tip of Marmion Way, within walking distance of Old Garden Beach.

Seven South Street (546-6708). This eighteenth-century house packs some surprises. There are rooms in the house; more rooms, four efficiencies, two one-bedroom suites, two two-bedroom suites, and one cottage scattered in a mix of garden buildings. In all, the seemingly snug little inn has 20 units, sleeping 50. The second surprise is a basement studio, used by the week-long art workshops that fill the inn in the spring and again in September and October (each is led by an accomplished artist). There is a small pool out back; Old Garden Beach is a short walk, and the rest of the village is just up South Street (Route 127A). In summer, rooms are $20–$28 single, $38–$63 double; efficiencies are $380–$495, less off-season.

Tuck Inn (546-6252), 17 High Street. An early nineteenth-century home on a quiet corner with nicely furnished rooms (some with working fireplaces) and a pool. There is also a fireplace in the dining room where a continental breakfast is served ($2.50 extra); $50–$60 double.

Yankee Clipper (546-3407), PO Box 2399, Route 127 north of the village. The main inn is hedged off below the road, facing Sandy Bay and, across it, the village. The living room is carpeted in orientals, richly paneled, and decorated with ginger jars, ships models, and the portrait of Mehitable Lamon, great-grandmother of innkeeper Barbara Wemyss Ellis. Barbara's parents opened the Yankee Clipper in 1946. A total of 28 rooms are scattered between the inn, its annex, and the Bulfinch House (named for its architect), which caters to more transient guests across the road. Grounds are terraced in flowers and rocky promontories overlook the water. There is an outdoor pool and a small excursion boat. A buffet lunch is served on the inn terrace. The dining room is open to the public only by reservation. $117–$174 per couple all meals, less off-season.

Rockport Lodge (742-8681), 61 South Street. Open late May to mid-September. Just a 15-minute walk from Dock Square, this is a unique old inn specifically for women. Founded in 1906 for working women "of low or moderate income," it continues to be a haven for women who want to get away by themselves; it's also open to groups. The house dates from the 1750s and the Annex, completed in the 1920s, includes a large screened-in porch. Each building accommodates 22–25 people. The rooms are simple, clean, and sparsely furnished with one, two, or three single metal beds, a chair, and dresser. Bathrooms are dorm-style with showers in one room, toilets in another. There are organized activities like whale watching, films, and lectures. Rates range from $35–$42 for a night with three meals, $127–$210 for a full week.

In Gloucester 01930: **Anchorage Inn** (283-4788). Under new ownership, now surrounded by condominiums on a small peninsula off Route 127. The site is lovely, overlooking the harbor. Rooms are $45–$70 double, $80–$90 for two rooms sharing a bath; continental breakfast included.

Blue Shutters (281-2706), 1 Nautilus Road. Open May through October. This gracious old home faces a tranquil stretch of sea, just up the road from Good Harbor Beach. Colors within the house reflect the blue without, and seascapes on the walls mirror the view. Pat Earl makes you feel at home. There are 10 rooms and three apartments, all with ocean views. All guests have access to the refrigerator and the patio grill and help themselves to the buffet-style breakfast, which usually includes yogurt in warm weather. High season: $35–$67 per night, $225–$410 (four in a suite) per week, $375 per apartment; less off-season.

Gray Manor (283-5409), 14 Atlantic Road. This is a comfortable, unpretentious old home within walking distance of Good Harbor Beach. Mrs. Madeline Gray has three guest rooms and six efficiencies. No breakfast, but Charlie's Place (see Dining) is a short walk; $40–$50 a night, $300 per week for the efficiency.

Best Western Twin Light Manor (283-7500), Atlantic Road. This is a complex of two inns (one bought out the other), each flanked by their motel annexes; a total of 75 rooms. Located just across the road from the ocean, this complex includes two pools and conference facilities. It's geared to groups. $103–$140 double in summer, less off-season (no meals included).

Williams Guest House (283-4931), 136 Bass Avenue, is Betty and Ted Williams' home. Four guest rooms (two with private baths, two sharing) are available with a light breakfast for $35–$45 per room. A small cottage next door is $375 per week, and there are two apartments, $300 and $375 per week. The house overlooks the ocean and is a short walk from Good Harbor Beach.

In Manchester 01944: **Old Corner Inn** (526-4996), 2 Harbor Street. There are nine rooms in this spacious Victorian house, for 30 years the Danish summer embassy. There is a very attractive living room with a hearth, and just a short walk away is Tuck's Point with a beach and picnicking. The Manchester train station is a mile's walk. In summer a continental breakfast is served and the dining room is open to the public for Friday and Saturday dinner, also Sunday brunch. $40–$60 in season, cheaper off-season.

In Magnolia 01930: **The White House** (525-3521), 18 Norman Avenue. This gracious old house has six rooms, also 10 in an adjacent motel (open all year). It is within walking distance of Magnolia shops and offers access to a private beach. Continental breakfast included in the $60–$70 summer rates, cheaper off-season.

MOTELS In Rockport 01966: **Captain's Bounty** (546-9557). This multi-story facility has 25 basic units, some of them with kitchenettes. Its appeal

Gloucester remains a serious fishing port

is the location: right on Front Beach on the edge of the village. $65–$80 (for the efficiency suite) in summer; $5 for each person above two.

Sandy Bay Motor Inn (546-7155), 173 Main Street. The rooms are basic: two double beds, a phone, and TV, but facilities include an attractive indoor pool, whirlpool, and outside tennis courts. There is also a pleasant coffee shop where breakfast and lunch are served daily. When we stopped by two guests were, however, complaining about the thin walls and noisy neighbors; $56 double, $52 single.

Turk's Head Motor Inn (546-3436), 283 South Street, open mid-June to mid-October. A two-story, 28-unit motel with a pool, coffee shop, and within walking distance of Land's End and beaches. $72 double, mid-June through Labor Day, otherwise $52 double.

In Gloucester 01930: **Cape Ann Marina Motor Inn** (283-2116), 75 Essex Avenue. Right at the marina, geared to those who are setting out on 7 AM fishing expeditions or morning whale watches but a nice, sea-geared atmosphere. The complex also includes good eating. $60 per day in summer, less off-season.

Cape Ann Motor Inn (281-2900), 33 Rockport Road. This is a three-story, basic motel that stands right on Long Beach. Open year-round. $66 double in summer, $6 for each extra person, $6 for kitchenette.

Gloucester Traveler (283-2502), 612 Essex Avenue. An unusually attractive motor lodge set high above Route 133 (the quiet, windy road to Essex) on its own 14 acres. A full breakfast is served in the central house, which belonged to 1940s movie queen Jessie Ralph. The units, walled in knotty pine (some with fireplaces), range from $45–$50 double to $375–$400 for housekeeping units, $5 for each additional person. The grounds include wooded paths, an attractive rock garden, and a pool.

Good Harbor Beach Inn (283-1489), Salt Island Road. Open spring–fall. This place has charm. The check-in desk is in a pine-paneled living room with oriental rugs and a fireplace. The 17 rooms are pine-walled too, furnished in traditional beach-cottage style, and each has two double beds and full bath. There are also efficiency apartments. Good Harbor Beach is just over a hedge. Breakfast and lunch are served in an oceanfront dining room; $60–$70 per night.

Sea Lantern Inn (283-1198), Atlantic Road. This is a fairly attractive motel in the Bass Rocks section of Gloucester, near the ocean. Rooms are basic, with floor-to-ceiling sliding doors. There's a pool and a continental breakfast. $90 plus in summer (same ownership as Twin Light Manor).

In Essex 01929: **Essex River House** (768-6800), Route 133 in Essex, overlooks the marshes and lobster boats. It's a tidy, quiet place with rooms named for sea captains. Double rooms for $48–$65, two doubles for $64–$68, and efficiencies for $72 in season, cheaper off-season. Rooms have cable TV.

CAMPGROUND **Cape Ann Campsite** (283-8683), 80 Atlantic Street, West Gloucester 01930. Within walking distance of Wingaersheek Beach, sites for tents and trailers, groceries, wood; $9 double.

DINING OUT In Gloucester: **The Rudder** (283-7967), 73 Rocky Neck Avenue. Seasonal waterfront restaurant on Smith Cove (Bostonians drive here for dinner). Specialties include roast leg of lamb, shrimp, clams, and Scallop Farcie. Piano music and after-dinner sing-a-longs. Open daily for lunch and dinner, $3–$25.

The White Rainbow (281-0017), 65 Main Street. Upstairs in an 1800s commercial building. Dine by candlelight on Lobster Monte Carlo or Seafood Capellini ($13–$20) or on lighter fare in the cafe and outdoor garden ($3–$13). Open for dinner only, closed Mondays.

The Studio (283-4123), 51 Rocky Neck. Seasonal. Open daily for lunch and dinner. Airy space with an open hearth, paintings, windows on Smith Cove; the *Virginia C* from Boston docks here (see Excursions), piano bar in the evening, moderate prices.

Howard's (283-9108), 2 Main Street. Housed in a square brick building at the head of Main Street, open daily except Tuesday for lunch and dinner, Sunday brunch. Formerly the Blackburn Tavern, so recently changed at this writing that we have not had a chance to try the rather formal dining room ($5.95 average for lunch, $13.95 for dinner) or the upstairs lounge, scene of live jazz and theatre.

Captain Courageous (283-0007), 25 Rogers Street. A large waterfront landmark geared to groups and tourists but with a solid local reputation. Open for lunch and dinner, with a menu ranging from sandwiches to full dinners; $4.95 to $11.75.

DaiGo (281-1578), Main Street. Open for dinner nightly except Sunday. A locally well-received Japanese restaurant.

Gloucester House Restaurant (283-1812), Seven Seas Wharf on Rogers Street. A large waterfront fish restaurant with views of the boats out the windows. The open-air Cafe Seven Seas on the back deck is as near as you can get to the water. Geared to groups and tourists but locally respected. Open daily for lunch and dinner, $6.95–$17.

The Raven (281-3951), 197 East Main Street. A traditional candlelight menu: Roast Duckling à L'Orange, Veal Marsala, and Baked Scrod; $10–$13 entrees, à la carte.

In Rockport: (no liquor served but set-ups usually provided) **Blacksmith Shop** (546-6301), 23 Mt. Pleasant Street. Overlooks Rockport Harbor; a long-established place in an old Dock Square home. Open daily for lunch and dinner, $3–$17.

Old Farm Inn (546-3237), 291 Granite Street (Route 127), Pigeon Cove (at Halibut Point). Open nightly for dinner. A 1799 farm house in which you dine by candlelight on traditional American fare like roast duck and broiled seafood: $9–$15.

Oleana by the Sea (546-2049), 27 Main Street. A cheerful old restaurant with picture windows overlooking Sandy Bay, featuring fresh seafood in sauces (Seafood Newburg, Haddock Au Gratin). Open daily for lunch and dinner, $3–$13; children's menu available.

Peg Leg Restaurant (546-3038), 18 Beach Street. Open April through October, Monday–Saturday for three meals, Sunday from noon. A long-established place with views over Front Beach through large windows and a converted greenhouse. The traditional menu features broiled scrod, baked stuffed shrimp, and lamb chops. $6.25 and up.

The Hannah Jumper (546-3600), Tuna Wharf off Bearskin Neck. Great view of Rockport Harbor from the dining room and deck above. A big, moderately priced, tourist-oriented place; open daily for lunch and dinner, $4–$8.

My Place Restaurant (546-9667), 72 Bearskin Neck. Open daily mid-May through October for lunch and dinner. Near the tip of Bearskin Neck. Breakfast all day ($1.95–$4.95), lunch ($2.45–$6.95), dinner ($13 tops); specializing in fresh seafoods and homemade pastries.

In Essex: **Tom Shea's Restaurant** (768-6931), on the Causeway. Open for dinner from 4 PM daily, brunch on weekends. The atmosphere is casual with antique decor and a view of the marshes. Generally rated as the best of the more expensive seafood places on the Causeway. $9.95–$14.95.

Dexter's Hearthside (768-6002), Route 133. Open for lunch and dinner, closed Sundays. You dine in the loft of a converted barn or in the fireplaced dining areas of this farmhouse that overlooks the marshes. Lunch from $4.50–$7.50, dinner from $7.25–$11.95. Luncheon specials until 9 PM

Village Restaurant (768-6400). Closed Mondays, otherwise open for lunch and dinner, $5.95–$6.95. The Riccis began with five booths and seven counter stools 30 years ago, and they now seat 225. They specialize in local seafood: an Essex River Sampler includes sauteed haddock, shrimp, and clams.

In Manchester: **J.P.'s Harbour Side** (526-1941), 37 Beach Street. Open daily for dinner (from 4 PM on Sundays). Candlelight and a view of the harbor. Traditional menu featuring lobster, steak, and continental specials, $8–$20.

Seven Central Publick House (526-4533), 7 Central Street. Open daily for lunch and dinner. Housed in a former Farmer's Market dating from 1753, with patio dining overlooking Mill Brook. A lobster salad roll at lunch is $6.75 and a hot turkey sandwich, $3.95; lobster pie for dinner is $10.75.

In Ipswich: **Chippers River Cafe** (356-7956), at the Choate Bridge. Open daily for breakfast (from 6 AM on weekdays), lunch, and dinner; seasonal deck. Omelets, Belgian waffles, interesting sandwiches, salads, dinner entrees like Mustard Lemon Chicken ($7.95) and Cipper's Cioppino (seafood simmered in marinara sauce) $9.95.

Apple Orchard (356-5969), 24 Essex Road (behind Bruni's Market), on Route 133. Closed Mondays; lunch weekdays; dinner Tuesday–Sunday (open from 3 PM). Set behind (and operated by) the area's big fruit, vegetable, and gourmet food center (see Shopping). A pleasant dining room with homemade pasta (Fusili Pugliesi and Fettuccine ai Frutti di Mare), as well as fresh fish, Norwegian Shellfish Chowder (with scallops, shrimp, and lobster), and northern Italian meat dishes. $7.50 to $14.95 for dinner entrees.

EATING OUT In Gloucester: **Charlie's Place** (283-0303), 83 Bass Avenue, near Good Harbor Beach. Open daily year-round, 6:30 AM–8:30 PM. A bright, formica place with a counter and tables, Styrofoam cups and paper plates. A huge fried shrimp roll is $3.99, luscious crabmeat $3.95, a haddock plate $4.50; breakfasts are a specialty (fresh squeezed orange juice). We like this much better than Charlie's Other Place in Rockport.

The Gull Restaurant (283-1812), 75 Essex Avenue, at the Cape Ann Marina. Open seasonally from 4:30 AM to 10 PM, geared to the owners of the motor yachts tied up here and passengers on the Yankee Fleet's fishing and whale-watching expeditions. A great old standby on the Annisquam River, $4–$13.

Halibut Point (281-1900), 289 Main Street. A serious fish restaurant open daily for lunch and dinner until 1 AM on weekends. It has a pub atmosphere, and the specialties include spicy Italian fish chowder, clam chowder, halibut steaks, oysters, and little necks on the half shell; $1.50 to $8.95 for full dinners.

Harbor Front Restaurant (283-4412), 374 Main Street (across from the head of the harbor). Open daily from 5 AM weekdays (6 AM weekends) to 8 PM. Lobster and clams are the specialty, $1.95–$14.

Old Fire House (283-5004), 1072 Washington Street, Lanesville (a village in Gloucester). Housed in the old fire house, open daily for breakfast and lunch: blueberry blintzes, peach-walnut crepes, omelets; moderately priced.

Main Street Cafe (281-2936), 151 Main Street. Open Monday–Saturday 7–3. A cheerful, popular storefront with a counter and small tables squeezed back to back. With artsy prints on the walls, fresh flowers, and Dijon mustard on the tables, it has a salad bar, great deli sandwiches (Romanian pastrami), soup of the day; moderately priced.

Union Hill Coffee House (283-0333), 284 Main Street. Open 6–3 Tuesday–Saturday, breakfast served all day: omelets, sandwiches, salad plates, $3 to $5.

Sailor Stan, off Route 127A at the entrance to Rocky Neck. Open for breakfast and lunch: counter and tables, good chowder, local gossip center, bargain priced.

The Hungry Wolf, on Rocky Neck. Open daily 9–9 (closes January and February). A friendly spot near the top of Rocky Neck, it is four tables wide with geraniums, a blackboard menu, and picnic tables outside. Hamburgers to steaks, moderately priced.

Gleason's (283-4414), 42 Eastern Avenue. Open daily year-round, 8–8. "Lobster-in-the-ruf" is the specialty, crab roll for $2.99, lobster roll for $3.99, boiled lobster from $4.99.

Rooftop Cafe at Hammond Castle (283-7673), 80 Hesperus Avenue, open for breakfast and lunch (10–4) in warm weather months. The open-air deck overlooks Gloucester Harbor; the fare includes salads, sandwiches, soups, and "Midsummer Knight's Dream" pastries.

In Rockport: **Ellen's Harborside** (546-2429), T-Wharf. THE place for budget dining in Rockport, right on the harbor, open daily from 5:30 AM for breakfast, lunch, and dinner. Counter and tables, authentic atmosphere, seafood specialties but hamburgers too. Dinner $3–$9.75 for adults, $1.95–$4 for children, no credit cards.

Folly Cove Pier Restaurant (546-6568), 325 Granite Street, at Folly Cove. Open seasonally, daily for lunch and dinner. The dining room is right on Ipswich Bay, and the specialty is moderately priced seafood. There is also take-out. Clam fritters for lunch or a seafood roll with salad are under $4. It's the kind of place that you expect, but have difficulty finding, in Maine.

Greenery Creamery (546-9593), 15 Dock Square. Open daily 9–9. A bright, casual place with a harbor view: salad bar, gourmet sandwiches, fresh fruits, lobster; $2.95 to $12.95.

The Lobster Pool (546-7808), Route 127 at Folly Cove. Informal dining room and outdoor tables on Ipswich Bay. Open daily in season for lunch and dinner, specializing in clams and fried fish.

Claws Restaurant (546-2429/2627), 229 Main Street. Open year-round, closed Mondays in winter. No view but a great local reputation; specializing in lobsters, steamers, homemade chowders, fresh seafood, daily blackboard specials, children's menu ($3.49 for fried clams, $2.49 for chicken fingers). Dinners $4.95 (for sirloin Teriyaki of all things) to $7.95 for fried (!) lobster and broiled scallops.

In Essex: **Farnham's** (768-6643), Route 133. Open seasonally, daily from 5 AM until 10 PM This is my favorite: wooden booths, windows overlooking the Essex marshes, chowder, fried clams, dinners from $4–$6. No credit cards.

Woodman's (768-6451), Route 133. The most famous clam house on the North Shore. Open daily for lunch and dinner. Fried seafood by the plate and bucket, picnic tables in the rough. As with most legendary places, you hear it's too crowded and not as good as it used to be, but everyone has to try it at least once. $4.50–$8.50. No credit cards.

Ship Ahoy Restaurant (768-7711), on the Causeway. Open daily for lunch and dinner. Family-style and -priced dining featuring seafood, also pizza and sandwiches in the lounge. $3.50–$10.

Misty Acres (768-6613), Route 22. Family restaurant, closed Mondays, open for lunch ($2.95–$5.95) and dinner ($4.25 to $9.99).

In Manchester: **The Coffee Cup** (526-4558), 25 Union Street. Open daily 6 AM to 9 PM Greek specialties, homemade soups, grinders, and pizza. $3.25–$4.95.

The Edgewater Cafe (526-4668), 69 Raymond Street. Daily 5 to 9 PM Specializing in Mexican food; casual atmosphere, $2 to $9. Reservations. BYOB.

In Ipswich: **The Clam Box,** High Street, on Route 1A just north of the village. This landmark dates back to the '30s and derives its name from its original shape: a 15-foot × 15-foot × 30-foot clam box. There is now space for eating in as well as taking out. Current owners Ted and Marina Aggelakis charge $4.95 for a small box of clams; you can also have a clam plate. Open March–Memorial Day daily except Monday, then daily until Labor Day. Closed Mondays again until Columbus Day, then open Wednesday–Sunday through December 15.

Robinson's Ice Cream, Argilla Road. Seasonal. Strategically sited on the way to the beach, homemade ice cream in many, many flavors.

ENTERTAINMENT Theater: **Gloucester Stage Company** (281-4099) has been performing mostly original American plays at Howard's Restaurant (alias Blackburn Tavern), 2 Main Street, in the past few years.

Cape Ann Theatre Company (check current listings) also performs at Howard's.

Movies: **Little Art Cinema** (546-2973), 18 Broadway, Rockport, shows a variety of classic and popular films in summer.

Cape Ann Twin Cinema (281-1990), 283 Main Street, Gloucester, shows current hits.

Special series: Check **Hammond Castle's** (283-7363) lively year-round calendar of happenings, concerts, and films.

The Castle Hill Festival (356-4070) offers a summer series of plays and concerts.

The Cape Ann Symphony (283-5200) performs off-season in various locations.

The **Rockport Music Festival** (546-2825) is a series of chamber concerts in June.

SELECTIVE SHOPPING Bearskin Neck, Rockport, harbors some two dozen shops, which change from year to year. Among our current favorites are: **Rockport Clothing Works** (open year-round) with traditional clothing at "discount prices" (featuring Woolrich), and **House of Glass** (a variety of things made from glass).

Pierce & Company (356-3755), 30 Brownville Avenue, Ipswich. Open Monday–Saturday 9–5. Design oak furniture made on the premises, outlet store.

Hills, Ipswich and Rockport. Quality, informal clothing and pleasant staff attract residents from throughout Cape Ann.

Glass Sail Boat, 3 Duncan Street (off Main), Gloucester. An eclectic combo of natural foods, audio equipment, and women's clothing: natural fiber, nicely styled skirts, dresses, jumpers, sweaters, and things woven.

The Boundard Turkey Farm (768-7718), Chebacco Road, Essex. Frozen turkey pies and fresh turkey meat.

Alprilla Farm (768-7804), 94 John Wise Avenue, Essex, sells its own naturally raised (no hormones, additives, tenderizers, etc.) lamb and beef: steaks, stew meat, hamburger, liver, tongue, in packages ranging from one to 40 pounds.

Goodale Orchards (356-5366), Argilla Road, Ipswich. Open 9–6 daily from June 15th to December 24th, featuring pick-your-own strawberries in June, raspberries in July, blueberries in August, and apples and tomatoes in September. The Russell family has an Orchard Store in their eighteenth-century barn, specializing in the fruit, vegetables, and flowers all grown on the farm; also in cider donuts (made from scratch using a special family recipe), pies, old-fashioned candies, cheese, and honey. Hayrides are also offered, and there are animals to see and pet; also picnic tables.

ANTIQUES Essex styles itself the "Antiques Center of New England" and is the scene of the annual late October Antiques Show and Sale. You might check out the **Essex Antiques Co-op** at Bruni's Marketplace on Route 133; **Hotel Essex Antiques** (768-7716), 67 Main Street; **Main Street Antiques** (768-7039); and the **Rowley Antique Center** (948-2591), with more than 40 dealers at the junction of Routes 1A and 133.

Cape Ann dealers include **Gloucester Used Furniture & Antiques** (281-3116), 53 Main Street, and **Ye Olde Lantern Antiques** (546-6754), across from the Rockport depot. Others are scattered along Route 127 and along Route 127A in East Gloucester.

ART GALLERIES At the entrance to Rocky Neck a roster lists more than a dozen seasonal galleries, and another clutch are found on Bearskin Neck. Other galleries include **The Yankee General Gallery,**

275–79 East Main Street, Gloucester; **Ken Gore,** 186 East Main Street, Gloucester; **Geraci Galleries** (traditional landscapes), 6 South Street, Rockport; **Paul Striski,** open summer, 10 Main Street, Rockport; and **Doris Glasso's Studio and Gallery,** 15–17 Langsford Street in Lanesville (see Art Centers).

CRAFTS   **Ten Hands,** at 8 Dock Square, Rockport, is a showcase for many local craftspeople.

New England Pottery, Bearskin Neck, Rockport.

Warp & Woof Shop, 209 Granite Street, Rockport.

Lion & Harp, 1 Main Street, Rockport.

Mahri's, 11 Beach Street, Manchester: gold and gold-filled jewelry, also a variety of imported handcrafted gifts.

Port o'Call Exchange, 67 Main Street, Gloucester. A non-profit outlet for a variety of things made by local artisans.

BOOKSTORES   **Toad Hall Bookstore** (546-7323), 51 Main Street, Rockport, is exceptional, housed in an old granite bank building and walled with inviting titles. It sponsors Sunday morning children's reading hours in summer and donates its net profits to cultural and ecological projects; open daily, evenings in summer.

The Bookstore (281-1548), 61 Main Street, Gloucester. Open daily. A pleasant store with a rear view on the harbor.

Libertas Bookshop (356-9240), Central Street, Ipswich. Books and lithographs.

SEAFOOD OUTLETS   On Bearskin Neck: **Eddie Donovan's Lobster Pool** and **Roy Moore Lobster Company** both sell cooked lobster at one-third of the price you pay in most restaurants; also lobster in tanks, fresh fish.

J.A.H. Seafood, 10 Railroad Avenue, Gloucester, sells the catch of the day, Essex clams, lobster meat.

Northeast Seafood, 2 East Street, Gloucester, features a "clambake special": two lobsters, steamers, also fresh fish, scallops, shrimp.

New England Lobster Company, in Pigeon Cove (north of Rockport, hidden behind Cape Ann Forge), offers flapping fresh fish, shrimp, and lobsters. The boats dock a few feet away.

SPECIAL EVENTS   April: **Panic Day Sale,** Ipswich, community-wide yard sale by Town Hall.

May: **Prince of Whales Ball** (283-1601), to celebrate the return of the whales; **Five-mile road race; Motif No.1 Day Celebration** (546-6575), in Rockport.

June: **Annual Medieval Festival at Hammond Castle** (283-7673), arms and armor demonstrations, crafts, costumed troubadours, damsels, jesters, dancing, games, grog, and victuals; **Rockport Chamber Music Festival** (546-2825), series of concerts by prominent performers in varying sites; **Rocky Neck (studios) Open House** (283-4319); **St. Peter's Fiesta** (283-1601), biggest event of the year in Gloucester (a week of music, sporting events, parade, blessing of the fishing fleet); **Swedish Festival** of Swedish dances, foods, in Rockport.

July: **Independence Day** parades in Gloucester, Rockport, and Manchester (information: 283-1601); also at Castle Hill where events include skydiving, fireworks, and music on the Grand Allee overlooking Crane's Beach; **Strawberry Festival** at the Baptist Church, Meetinghouse Green, Ipswich; **North Shore Art Association Festival** (283-1857),

August: **Olde Ipswich Days** includes a block dance, marathon, public dinners; **Gloucester Waterfront Festival** (283-1601), art and crafts show, weekend fish fry; **Manchester Sidewalk Bazaar** (283-1601) (races, parade of sail); **Hellenic Festival** at the Hellenic Center, Route 1A, Ipswich (food, dancing, children's games); **Annual Crane's Beach Sand Castle Contest.**

September: **Annual 15-mile Road Race** around Cape Ann (281-2439); **Essex Clamfest** (283-1601), chowder festival, clam shucking contest, clambake.

October: **North Shore Antiques Show** (281-0572), major display by area dealers at Woodman's Function Hall in Essex; **Rockport Fine Artists Art Walk and Open House.**

December: **Christmas in Rockport:** ice sculpture, tree lighting, strolling carollers and minstrels, climaxing with Christmas pageant; also **Annual Santa Claus Parade** (283-1601) in Gloucester.

MEDICAL EMERGENCY Addison Gilbert Hospital (283-4000), 298 Washington Street, Gloucester.

Cable Emergency Service (356-4366), County Road, Ipswich. Provides 24-hour acute emergency care, staffed with skilled physicians, nurses, and professional support personnel; administered by Beverly Hospital.

Cape Ann

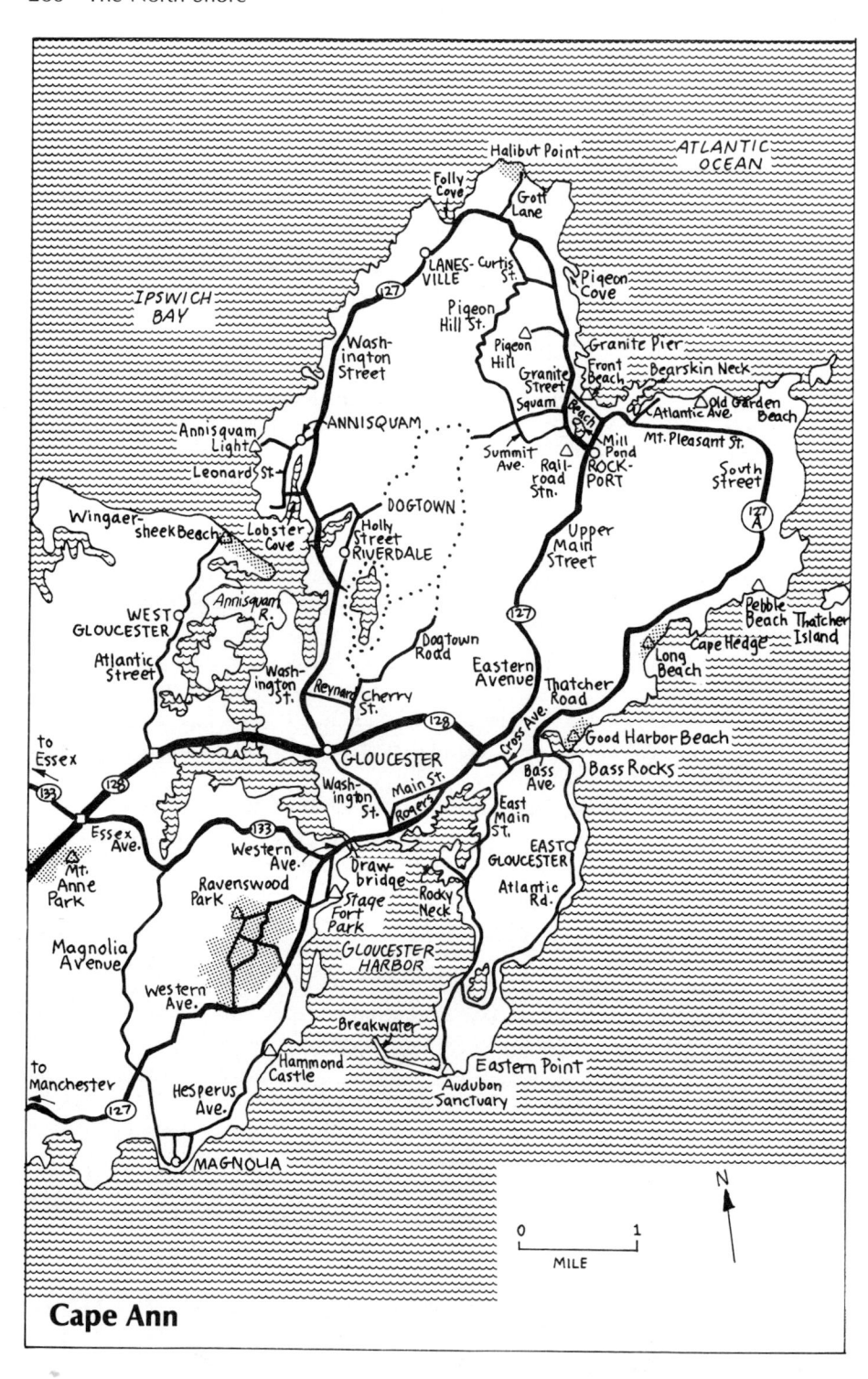

The Newburyport Area

The Bay State's smallest city has an up and down history and topography. An early shipbuilding center, Newburyport was one of New England's richest, most populous towns. Local fortunes were lost in the Revolution, but in the Federal era an even larger group of merchant princes appeared, building themselves the two-mile lineup of mansions still to be seen along High Street.

During this, the city's golden era, there was a deep split between the High Street Federalists and the Republican craftsmen and mariners who lived above their shops down by the river. Each party supported its own fire company, bank, masonic lodge, and militia company.

In 1930 when a five-volume study focused on this "Yankee City," the "upper uppers" were still living on High Street and social status sloped downward through five distinct strata to the "lower lowers" along the waterfront. Hometown novelist John P. Marquand reacted by satirizing the study and its subject in "Point of No Return," in which Newburyport appears as "Clyde," the city in which "Everyone instinctively knew where he belonged."

Both portraits are now drastically altered. In the 1960s urban renewal razed old distilleries and post-Civil War factories along 20 acres of the city's waterfront, then turned menacingly to the city's brick commercial rows, which date from 1811. Newburyporters of every ilk rallied in protest. The Newburyport Rehabilitation Authority began restoring rather than destroying. Market Square, the old waterfront centerpiece, has now been entirely restored and landscaped. The granite Custom House is a maritime museum. Hundreds of old homes have been restored by newcomers, and so many boutiques, restaurants, and galleries have opened that some people now refer to Newburyport as the "Yuppie" instead of "Yankee" city.

Newburyport is, without exaggeration, a jewel of an early nineteenth-century city, and its setting is quite beautiful: with a vast beach and National Wildlife Sanctuary on Plum Island; the salt marshes and old homesteads of Newbury; long, colorful Salisbury Beach; and the quiet riverfront parkland in West Newbury. Newburyport is also the departure point for whale watching and fishing boats.

AREA CODE 617

GUIDANCE Northern Essex County, Greater Newburyport Chamber of Commerce (462-6680), 29 State Street, Newburyport 01950. Open daily 9–5. **Summer Informaton Booth,** on High Street at Bartlett Mall, open mid-June through late September, daily 11–7.

GETTING THERE By bus: Greyhound bus offers frequent commuter service from its Boston Terminal (423-5810).

TO SEE AND DO In Newburyport: **Cushing House** (462-2681), 98 High Street. Open May to November, 10–4, except Sunday 2–5; closed Monday. Open in winter by appointment. This brick mansion, built in 1808, was the home of Caleb Cushing, our first ambassador to China. Twenty-one rooms are filled with elegant furnishings, silver, paintings, vintage clothing. Exhibits of old Newburyport industries are in the basement; $2 admission.

Custom House Maritime Museum (462-8681), 25 Water Street. Open weekdays year-round 10–4; closed weekends mid-December to mid-March. Built in 1835 of Rockport granite, designed by Robert Mills (architect of the Washington Monument and Treasury Building), this handsome building was sold in 1913 and used for hay storage and eventually as a junk shop; it is now a fine museum. Exhibits support Newburyport's claim to be "birthplace of the Coast Guard" and depict trade with exotic ports. In the Far East Hall we were fascinated by the detailed figures brought home by Captain Robert Pearson from Calcutta. The nautical exhibits fit nicely with the view of the Merrimack from the windows. There is also a Marquand Library, furnished and filled with the novelist's treasures. The admission ($1.50 adults $1 seniors, $.75 children) is not necessary for access to the gift shop.

Bartlett Mall, High Street. The high-splashing fountain here is known as Frog Pond; the mall as a whole was the gift of a merchant in 1800. The adjacent brick courthouse was designed by Charles Bulfinch; the old Hill Burying Ground across the way contains many of Newburyport's most memorable residents. The Old Jail (north end of the mall), built of Rockport granite, dates from 1823.

Unitarian Church (465-0602), 26 Pleasant Street. This 1801 structure is thought to have been designed by Samuel McIntyre and has an unusually graceful facade and spire with a Paul Revere bell. The interior is also graceful and airy. Services are held every Sunday.

Old South Presbyterian Church (465-9666), 29 Federal Street. Built in 1756 with a bell cast by Paul Revere, this dignified church has a whispering gallery; at one time it boasted a sea captain "at the head of every pew on the broad side."

In Amesbury: **The Whittier Home** (388-1337), 85 Friend Street. Open May–November, Tuesday–Saturday 12–5. John Greenleaf

Whittier (1807–1892) lived here for 46 years, and the house conveys a genuine sense of the poet and his poems.

Bartlett Museum (388-4528), 270 Main Street. Open June to October, Tuesday–Sunday 1–5. This town historical collection includes Indian artifacts.

Scenic Drive. Follow Main Street down under Route 495 to the river; turn left and drive to Route 1, there turning north to Salisbury or south to Newburyport. You will pass old mills, mill housing, and old homes with fine views of the river.

In Newbury: **Coffin House** (in Boston: 227-3956), 14–16 High Street, Route 1A. Open June through mid-October, Tuesday, Thursday, Saturday, and Sunday 12–5. This weathered house began circa 1654 and grew considerably over the next two centuries. Its old kitchens and early wallpaper, as well as furnishings, are interesting. Owned by the Society for the Protection of New England Antiquities. $2 admission.

Scenic Drives. Follow Route 1A-High Road by old homes and farmland that stretches east through the salt marshes to the sand dunes of Plum Island. Drive west on Route 1 by the campus of Governor Dummer Academy, the Parker River, and the old community gathered around an old brick church.

GREEN SPACE **Plum Island.** A string bean-shaped, 8½-mile-long barrier island accessible via Water Street, which turns into the Plum Island Turnpike. Open dawn to dusk, year-round. Two-thirds of the island is now the **Parker River National Wildlife Refuge** (465-5753), containing 4,650 acres of dunes, bog, tidal marsh, and beach. A seven-mile gravel road bisects the refuge, with parking areas strung along its length, adding up to just 150 in the summer season (tern-nesting season). On summer weekends these can fill by 10 AM, even in green-fly season (mid-July to mid-August). This is a famous place for surf fishing but not a good place to bring small children: it's a hike over the dunes, and the surf and undertow are unusually strong. In September and October people come to pick the wild plums and cranberries, in March and October to watch the migrating wildfowl: 300 species of birds have been sighted. In winter there are still a surprising number of birds; also deer and rabbits. A self-guided wildlife trail at **Hellcat Swamp** (Parking lot #4) is rewarding any time of year. Leashed dogs are allowed only September 20–April 20. Free.

North Beach, north end of Plum Island, a popular spot for fishing and wading out into the sandbars at the mouth of the Merrimack River; beware of currents near the jetty. $3 per car.

Plum Island State Reservation (462-4881), at the end of the seven-mile gravel access road on Plum Island (see above) is a 72-acre area with a sandy beach backed by rolling dunes and a small hill called

Bar Head. Parking is limited to 50 cars (attendants at the gate to the National Wildlife Refuge keep tabs on availability).

Old Town Hill Reservation. In Newbury turn left off Route 1A at Newman Street, far end of the Green, first left after crossing the Parker River. The Trustees of Reservations own these 230 acres. The steep path takes less than a half hour round-trip, and it is one of the most delightful walks in the state. You climb gradually, following old stone walls and wild rose bushes; benches are scattered along the way and the view is not only of Newbury and Plum Island but (on a very good day) as far north as Mt. Agamenticus in Maine and south to Cape Ann.

Maudslay State Park (369-3350), West Newbury. From Route 113 take Story Lane 1 $\frac{2}{3}$ miles to its junction with Geoffrey Hoyt's Lane; turn right and follow signs. A new state park, just purchased for $5 million in 1985, this 476-acre property includes nineteenth-century estate gardens, rolling agricultural land, and mountain laurel. It also includes two miles of frontage on the Merrimack River in one of its loveliest segments. The mansions (one had 72 rooms) are gone, but the formal gardens (designed by Charles Sprague Sargent, who also designed Harvard's Arnold Arboretum in Boston) remain, along with the glorious mountain laurel that inspired John Greenleaf Whittier to write a number of poems, among them "The Laurels" and "June on the Merrimack." Over eight miles of carriage roads and trails provide hiking, biking, cross-country skiing, and horseback riding.

AIR RIDES **Air Plum Island** (462-2114), Plum Island Turnpike, offers sightseeing rides; $12 per adult, $10 per child for 15 minutes in a four-passenger plane, $20 per person in a 1927, two-person biplane, $20 per person in a one-passenger ultra-light craft. Inquire about helicopter rides, flight instruction, charters, plane rentals.

AMUSEMENT RIDES An old-time carnival boardwalk atmosphere prevails with **Shaheen's Fun Park** (465-0801), claiming "more major facilities per square foot than anywhere else in the country."

BICYCLING **Calypso Excursions** (465-7173), 12 Federal Street, Newburyport, offers bicycle rentals, repairs, and tours; both locally and in Maine.

BOAT RENTALS **Yankee Marine Corporation** (462-8850) offers hourly, daily, weekly, and seasonal boat rentals; April to December.

CAMPING **Salisbury Beach State Reservation** (462-4481) offers more than 500 campsites for trailers. $5 per site, first-come, first-serve.

FISHING EXCURSIONS **Hilton's Fishing Dock** (465-9885/462-8381), 54 Merrimac Street, Newburyport. There is ample free parking on the wharf, also a shop from which you can set out for a full day of fishing, daily at 6:30 AM May through mid-October; Tuesday, Friday, weekends, and holidays March 30–April 30 and October 14–

December 1 (fall trips leave at 7 AM. Rods and reels for rent, free bait ($25 per adult, $3 for rod; $15 for children under 12, $4 discount for seniors). Half-day fishing trips (departing 7:30 AM and 1 PM daily, Memorial–Labor Day; Saturday, Sunday, and Wednesday in May; weekends in September and October) are available aboard the 60-foot *Victor E*, $12 per adult, $8 per child; night fishing is also offered on Wednesdays and weekends, June through September.

The *Barracuda* (465-3022), Merrimac Marina, Newburyport, a 28-foot sport fishing vessel, is also available for deep-sea fishing, whale watching, and cruising; takes up to six. $395 for a full day of tuna fishing; $185 for a half day of fishing for bass, blues, cod, or macs; $125 for an evening cruise. Equipment available but extra.

HARBOR TOUR   Capt. Bill Taplin (948-2375) runs **Yankee Clipper Harbor Tours** all summer, departing every hour, 11 AM–7 PM from the Boardwalk (wharf next to Hilton's) in Newburyport. $4 per adult, $2 per child. Special sunset tours and charters.

SAILING   **Capt.'s Dave and Pam Stickney** (465-0028), 46 High Road, Newbury 01950, take up to six passengers on their 55-foot classic topsail schooner *Heart's Desire* for full and half-day trips; also sunset sails. Embark on the Newburyport waterfront. Day cruises $400; sunset (5–9 PM) $200.

SWIMMING   See **Plum Island** under Green Space. Four-mile-long **Salisbury Beach State Reservation** (462-4481), off Route 1, Salisbury, is a 3.8-mile-long expanse of sand; frequently crowded in summer. Facilities include bathhouses, picnic facilities, boat launch, and interpretive programs (ranging from guided walks to live entertainment). $3 parking fee.

WHALE WATCHING   **New England Whale Watch, Inc.** (465-7165 or 465-9885), Box 825, Hampton, NH 03842, departs from Hilton's Fishing Dock, Newburyport. One of the oldest and best-known of the region's whale-watch excursions, founded by Scott Mercer, who does much of the narrating. The 85-foot *New Englander II* departs daily, late June through mid-September; weekends in May and June and late September through October. $20 per adult, $15 per child under 12.

Hilton's Fishing Dock (see Boat Excursions) runs its own whale watch; boat varies from year to year, departs twice daily July through mid-September; weekends in spring and fall; $20 per adult, $15 per child full day.

INNS AND BED & BREAKFASTS   In Newburyport 01950: **Morrill Place** (462-2808), 209 High Street. A three-story, Federal-style mansion built in 1806, Morrill Place offers 12 guest rooms with shared baths. The decor is a mix of formality and fun, and each room is very different. Some have sleigh beds, others four-posters and canopies; a few have working fireplaces, and a number have a third bed tucked discreetly in a corner. There is a formal parlor and dining room, also an inviting TV room, and a glass-sided winter porch. Continental breakfast and afternoon tea are included in $40–$70 per couple.

The Windsor House (462-3778), 38 Federal Street. The spacious kitchen in this eighteenth-century mansion was designed to be a ship's chandlery. Guests gather here in the morning for full breakfasts. The woodwork throughout the house is extraordinary, and the six guest rooms (three with private bath) are all nicely furnished. $58–$84 per room with breakfast. Innkeepers Judith Crumb and Jim Lawbaugh enjoy helping guests plan itineraries.

Garrison Inn (465-0910), 11 Brown Square. The atmosphere is that of a small, formal hotel (with an elevator and a room with facilities for the handicapped), rather than a New England country inn. The 24 guest rooms (private baths; color TV) are furnished with reproduction antiques; six suites have lofts with spiral or Colonial-style staircases. The two large dining rooms and pub overshadow any public space. $55–$110 per room.

Essex Street Inn (465-3148), 7 Essex Street. An apartment house rather than an inn feeling (no public space), but all 17 rooms are air-conditioned, with private baths, antiques. One-room suites have a fireplace and whirlpool; two-room suites have fireplaces, kitchen, and deck. $49–$135.

The Benjamin Choate House (462-3148), 25 Tyng Street. A classic Federal-style mansion, less central than others but handy to the waterfront. Two guest rooms have private bath, three share. Some pets permitted. Guests enjoy a full breakfast before a great old kitchen hearth. $40–$65 per room.

DINING OUT **Ten Center Street** (462-6652), 10 Center Street, Newburyport. Open for lunch and dinner daily. An eighteenth-century mansion with an informal pub atmosphere downstairs, more formal dining room upstairs with specialties like Veal Picatta ($9.95), Wiener Schnitzel ($12.95), and baked salmon ($15.95). You can also lunch on a hamburger ($3.95) or sup in the pub on a steak kebab or Chicken Chausseur ($6.95).

Scandia Restaurant (462-6271), 25 State Street, Newburyport. Open Monday–Friday for lunch and dinner; Saturday dinner only; Sunday brunch and dinner. White tablecloths and fresh flowers set the mood for New American cuisine with seafood specialties like Saffron Seafood Stew for lunch ($7.95) and Shrimp and Scallop Curry for dinner ($13.95).

Captain's Quarters Restaurant (462-3397), 54R Merrimac Street, Newburyport. Open from 5 AM–9 PM Sunday–Thursday; until 10 PM Friday–Saturday. THE place on the waterfront to my mind: deep booths, decks, right on the water, lunch specials like soup and sandwich ($2.50), mushroom quiche and salad ($3.95); seafood dinners from $4.75–$11.95.

The Grog (465-8008), 13 Middle Street, Newburyport. Open for lunch and dinner daily, usually crowded in the less formal pub space downstairs, slower-paced but the same menu upstairs in "Grog Too." You can lunch on enchiladas or grilled cheese, dine on roast duckling and lime pie ($2.95–$10.95). There was a time when The Grog was considered "Newburyport's living room," the place where many residents stopped to greet neighbors once a day. It's no longer that way but still a lively place, with nightclub entertainment downstairs after 8 PM.

Michael's Harborside (462-7785), Tournament Wharf (under the Salisbury bridge), Newburyport. Open for lunch and dinner, except Monday. An informal place right on the water with lobster from a tank, fried and broiled seafood, chowder; $4–$12.

Eagle House of Rowley (948-7177), just off Route 1A. Open year-round, daily 9 AM–9:30 PM; Sundays from noon. An attractively refinished old barn with two non-plastic dining rooms and a tavern. The chef prepares table-side specialties. Early bird menu, served 4 to 6:30, with entrees (including vegetable and salad) priced $7.50–$9.50, otherwise $9.95–$15.95; tavern menu: $2–$9.50. Specialties include Beef Wellington, Cesar Salad, and a daily fish dish.

Amesbury House (388-5249), 62 Haverhill Road (Route 110), Amesbury. Open for lunch and dinner weekdays, dinner on weekends. Fine dining and an extensive wine list; specialties include fresh seafood, beef, and poultry; $2.95–$9.95 for lunch, $9.95–$16.95 for dinner.

The Kendrick House (465-3767), Salisbury. Open for lunch weekdays, dinner daily, Sunday from noon. An eighteenth-century house with three antiques-furnished dining rooms. Lunch can be Plowman's Fare (soup, cheese, bread, and fruit, $3.25) or Broiled Sea Scallops ($4.95); dinner entrees include a Broiled Seafood Platter ($8.95) and N.Y. Strip Steak ($10.50).

EATING OUT **Fowle's Restaurant** (465-0141), 17 State Street, Newburyport. Open 6 AM–6 PM. Monday–Friday, from 7 AM on weekends, until 6 PM Saturday, 1 PM Sunday. I always end up lunching at the marble counter or in one of the small booths in this 1930s combo of a magazine and tobacco store with soda fountain. Like almost every store on State Street, it has changed in recent years but only to the degree that its art deco fountain (complete with an intricate wooden scene behind the counter) has been spiffed up and the menu has tipped to sprouts, veggies, and whole grain muffins. The soups are all hearty and freshly made, and the sodas come in ice-cream-parlor glasses. Prices range from $.45 to $4 and you pay at the Smoke Counter.

The Welsh Rabbit (462-4777), Liberty Street, Newburyport. Open 7 AM–4 PM Monday–Saturday. Bagels, croissants, cookies, and breads are all baked on the premises. Homemade soups and unusual deli-sandwiches (on bagels and croissants) are the specialty, $1–$6.

Riverview Fishmarket (462-7822), Route 1, Salisbury. Open Tuesday–Sunday 11–9,. Lobster from the lobster pool and steamed clams are the specialties, $1.95–$8.95.

The Agawam Diner (948-7780), Route 1, near the junction with Route 133. Open daily 5 AM–12:30 AM. Breakfast is served all day and there are blue plate specials, homemade cream and fruit pies, reasonably priced fried clams and shrimp. $1–$6.

ENTERTAINMENT **The Theatre of Newburyport** (462-3332 or 465-2983), PO Box 6027, Newburyport 01950. The theatre is at 75 Water Street but will be moving in '88 to the Firehouse on Market Square. This is a resident, professional company that stages a variety of year-round productions: classics, comedies, and one new play each year; also children's theatre. Curtain at 8 PM Thursday–Saturday, 7 PM Sunday. Tickets cost $8–$10.

The Playhouse (388-9444), 109 Main Street, Amesbury (town parking lot off Route 150). Near the junction of I-95 and Route 495 (exit 54). Dinner theatre performed by a resident troupe of 60 actors, classics like *Arsenic and Old Lace* and *Can-Can*. Dinner at 7 PM, show at 8:30 PM, also Sunday and Wednesday matinee ($12.50 for buffet and show); $6.50–$8.50 for show only, $18.50 on Friday and Saturday for buffet and show.

The Screening Room (462-3456), 82 State Street, Newburyport. A small, unusually comfortable cinema specializing in classic flicks.

SELECTIVE SHOPPING **The Newburyport Art Association** (465-8769), 65 Water Street, Newburyport. Open daily 1–5, except Mondays. The gallery shows and sells works by members.

Towle Silversmiths (465-8430), 1690 House, 268 Merrimac Street. Open Monday–Saturday 9–5:30. The business (now based in the adjacent, ivied factory) traces its origins to the 1690s. The 1690 House is filled not only with sterling and silverplate gifts but with a wide assortment of crystal.

Piel Craftsmen Company (462-7012), 307 High Street, Newburyport. Open weekdays 8:30–12, 1–4:30. Visitors are welcome to watch shop models of 1800s ships made by hand.

State Street and the **Inn Street Mall.** The lower State Street shops back onto a delightful pedestrian court and more shops, some on second floor. The buildings themselves, all built of sturdy brick after an 1811 fire destroyed this area, are delightful places to browse.

Gabriel of Newburyport (462-9640), 90 Pleasant Street. Open daily 10–6 weekdays, until 9 Thursday and Friday, 12–5 on Sunday.

A defunct movie house across from the waterfront has been transformed into a five-floor array of traditional work and sports clothing for men and women: all the big brand names at 20%–60% discounts; housewares on the fifth floor.

SEAFOOD STORES **Captain Red's** (462-3252), 54 Rear Merrimac Street, Newburyport (Hilton's Fishing Dock, same building as Hilton's Tackle). Open daily 9–6. Freshest fish, lobsters, and seafood, reasonably priced.

David's Fish Market (462-2504), Bridge Road (Route 1), Salisbury. Open daily 8–6. Fish, lobsters, native shell fish at good prices.

PRODUCE **Arrowhead Farm Stand,** High Road, Newburyport, open Easter to Christmas; retails vegetables, berries, plants, flowers, ornamental gourds, and Christmas greens from the farm, which has been in the Moulton-Chase family for over 300 years and whose story appears in an appealing history-cum-cookbook on sale at the stand.

Long Hill Orchard (363-5545), Main Street (Route 113), West Newbury. Open daily, year-round. Own vegetables in season, apples, cider, peaches, pears, blueberries, jams, honey.

SPECIAL EVENTS May: **Salmagundi Fair** (craft fair) Sunday and Monday of the Memorial Day weekend, includes food, dancing.

July–August: **Yankee Homecoming,** last week in July, climaxing first weekend in August, races, contests, sidewalk sales, concerts, buggy rides, fireworks.

September: **Annual Country Auction** at Upper Green, Newbury, high quality antiques, collectibles, and books attract bidders from throughout New England.

October: **Fall Harvest Festival,** Sunday and Monday of Columbus Day Weekend, craftsmen, performances, food, farm exhibits.

December: **Christmas celebrations** begin December 1 when Santa arrives by boat to lead the parade. Events are staged by merchants throughout the shopping season; also choral concerts and candlelight services the week before Christmas.

MEDICAL EMERGENCY **Anna Jacques Hospital** (462-6601), Highland Avenue, Newburyport.

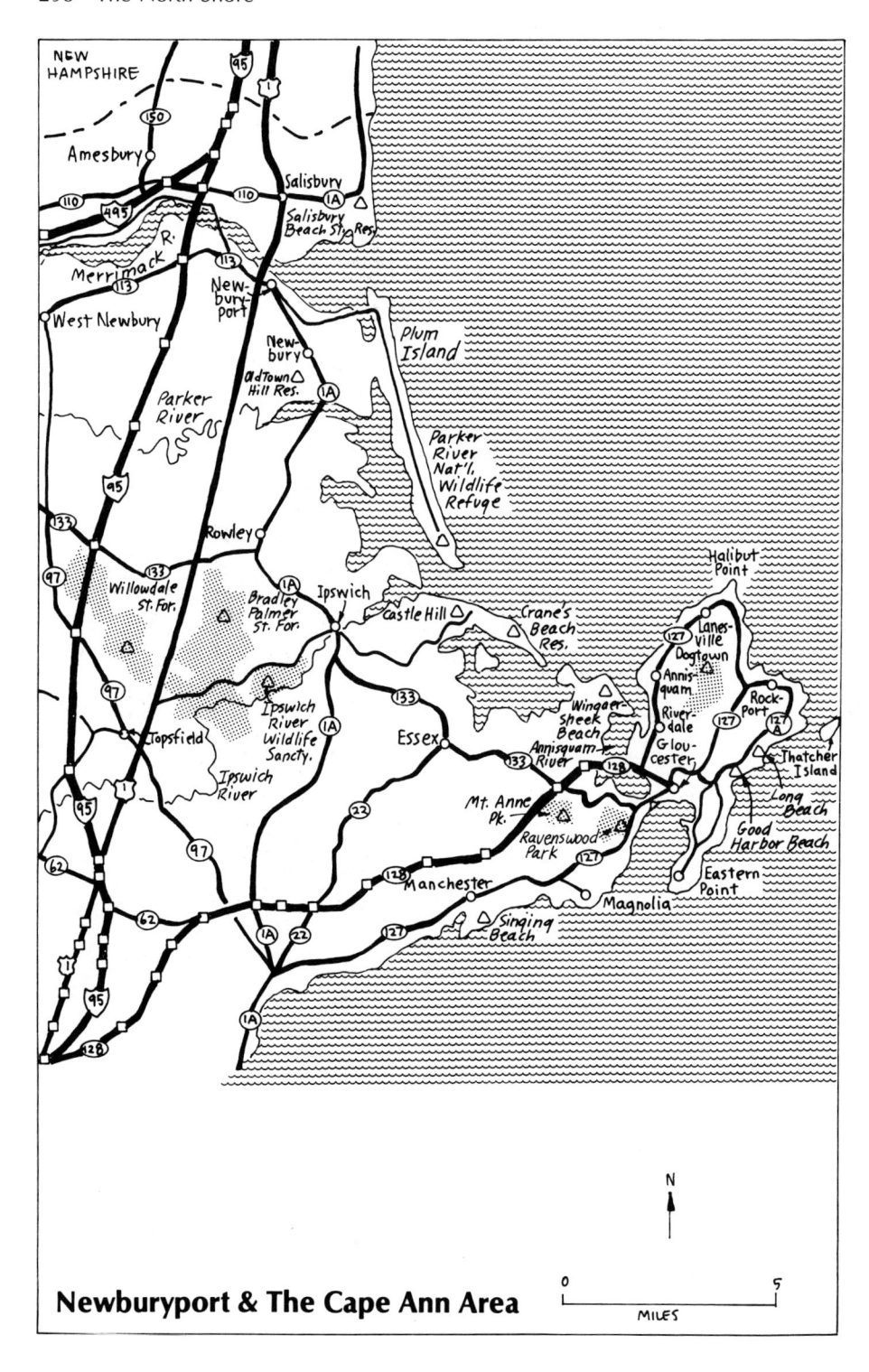

Newburyport & The Cape Ann Area

Plymouth

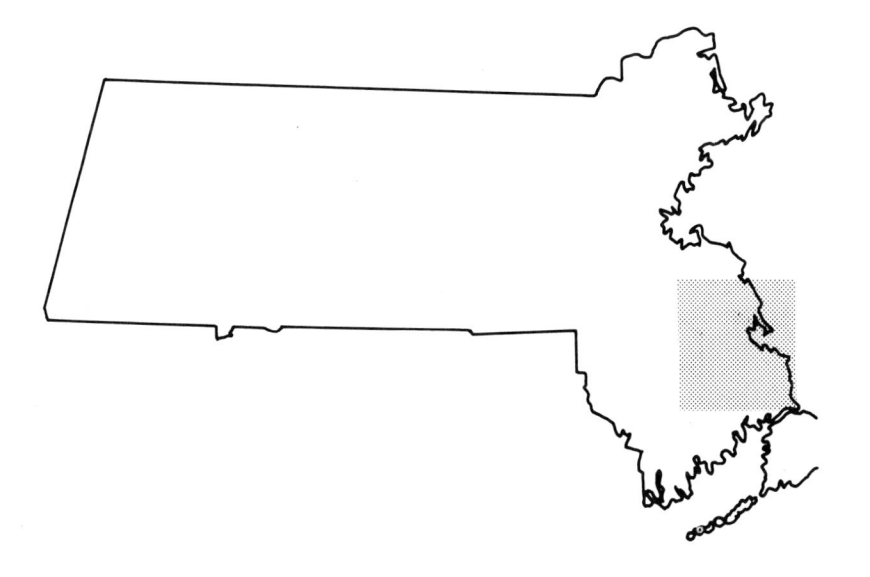

INTRODUCTION

Mayflower II is a brightly painted little tub of a ship, moored snugly behind flower beds and ticket booths near Plymouth's hot dog stands, traffic lights, and wax museum.

Despite the carnival trappings her message is jarring. Unnerved by her toy size, you can't imagine wanting to squeeze aboard her prototype, along with 127 others on a several months' ride across the autumn Atlantic.

It was mid-December by the time the *Mayflower* hove to beside the granite boulder now enshrined beneath a columned stone canopy labeled "Plymouth Rock." Passengers and crew hastened to build a "common house" and some "small cottages" along the lines of the tiny, airless replica now to be seen beside State Pier. Nearly half the company died that bitter winter and were buried secretly so that the Indians might not notice their dwindling number. But only the surviving crew opted for the comforts of home when the *Mayflower* sailed away in April.

America loves success stories, and this one is almost too well known to repeat. It is in fact our nation's first. Plymouth can and does boast that it is the oldest continuous settlement in the United States.

Leyden Street itself, the wide sloping thoroughfare along which the Pilgrims built their first permanent homes, remains a busy place graced with two churches and the town post office.

The idea of dramatizing the Pilgrims' daily life was conceived by Harry Hornblower. In 1945 Harry's father Ralph (a partner in the brokerage firm of Hornblower and Weeks) offered a founding gift, and his grandmother Hattie eventually donated her 100-acre estate, south of the original site, for a reconstructed village. The thatched homes and Fort-Meetinghouse within their diamond-shaped stockade are a modern pioneering effort in their own right. The plantation has rid itself of any authentic Pilgrim pieces, if they ever had them (samples are on view in Pilgrim Hall Museum).

Visitors to Plimoth Plantation (see To See and Do) are encouraged to sit on carefully re-created chairs and bedsteads and to thumb through Bibles. The staff are dressed in bright colors rather than in the blacks and browns in which Victorian artists picture them. Each has adopted a particular pilgrim to portray as authentically as possible. They freely admit that most of the buildings on view are far too tidy, built (as they were until recent years) with nails and modern tools. Subsequent additions are clumsily made with daub and alder wattling.

Not all visitors find their way to the plantation. They get bogged down instead on the quarter-mile Plymouth Waterfront—a hodgepodge of souvenir stands and fast-food places.

More than a million tourists pass through "America's Hometown" each year, but few realize its extent. Plymouth is actually the state's biggest town in the area. It is also an old summer resort: both its bay and lakeshores are lined with summer cottages, and in addition to more than 20 miles of saltwater beach there are public strands on Fearings and College ponds in the 16,000-acre Myles Standish State Forest. There are also a fleet of fishing and whale-watching boats, and a ferry to Provincetown.

The town of Duxbury, just a short drive up the coast from Plymouth, has its own Pilgrim sites and stately historic houses, more than its share of quiet woodlands and cranberry bogs to explore, and one of the state's outstanding beaches.

AREA CODE 617

GUIDANCE **Massachusetts Tourist Information Center** (746-1150/1152), Route 3, Plymouth. Open year-round, daily 9–5. A staffed, highway information center stocked with pamphlets; staff answer questions about the entire area.

Plymouth County Development Council (826-3136), PO Box 1620, Pembroke 02359, is the source of a handy *Plymouth County Hospitality Guide;* also leaflets on special events and dining.

Plymouth Area Chamber of Commerce (746-3377), 85 Samoset Street, Plymouth. The chamber itself is not geared to walk-in information inquiries but it maintains a seasonable (theoretically April through November) information booth (746-4779), open daily 10–5. Staff help with local reservations.

GETTING THERE By bus: Plymouth & Brockton Street Railway (773-9400 in Boston; 746-0378 in Plymouth) offers frequent service to Boston, Hyannis, and Plymouth County towns.

By car: Route 3 from Boston; take Route 44 (exit 6) for the Plymouth Waterfront and the specially marked Plimoth Plantation (exit 4) for the restored village. We suggest that you begin with Plimoth Plantation and drive back up Route 3A to the town, which, ideally, you should approach from Burial Hill (see Green Space), the better to compare the actual lay of the land with that of the Plantation.

By boat: Note under Boat Excursions that it is possible to come to Plymouth in summer by boat from Provincetown, which, in turn, is linked to Boston by a summer ferry.

GETTING AROUND **Plymouth Rock Trolley** (747-3419) circulates on a three-mile loop through town, Memorial to Labor Day, daily 9:30–5.

Plymouth is a walk-around town with historic houses conveniently clumped between the waterfront and Main Street.

TO SEE AND DO **Plimoth Plantation** (746-1222), off Route 3 on "Plimoth Plantation Highway" or three miles south of Plymouth on Route 3A. April through November, 9–5. We recommend starting here because the village provides the most authentic introduction to the Pilgrim story. Its elaborate new visitors center includes an audio-visual presentation and displays on the Pilgrims and their era. Within the stockade of the village we find ourselves in the year 1627 and in a colony that includes 50 families, 22 goats, 15 cows, and some 50 pigs. The debt to the London financiers has been substantially paid off in clapboards and beaver—the latter secured through trade with the Indians and a half-dozen outposts set up for the purpose. Now each family can farm for themselves rather than toil on communal plots. The settlement is about to burst from its fortified cocoon. Meander down beyond this enclosure and you find a Wampanoag Summer Campsite (open May–October), consisting of bark wigwams and resident Indians (see the introduction). The visitors center includes a gift shop and ample dining facilities (it's possible to dine on turkey and the fixings all year-round) for both individuals and groups. Admission: $6.25 per adult, $3.75 per child; a combination ticket with the *Mayflower* (see below) is $8.25 per adult, $5.25 per child. Free under age 5.

Mayflower II **at State Pier,** Plymouth waterfront. Owned and operated by Plimoth Plantation, open same hours except mid-June to Labor Day when it is open daily 9–6:30. $3 adults, $2 children aged 5–12 (see above for combination ticket with Plimoth Plantation).

Pilgrim Hall Museum (746-1620), 75 Court Street (Route 3A), Plymouth. Open daily 9:30–4:30, year-round. Billed as the country's oldest public museum, this is a fascinating collecton of things belonging to and relating to the Pilgrims: a chair owned by William Brewster, a cradle for the Fuller children, Peter Brown's tankard, and John Alden's halberd. $3.00 per adult, $1 children aged 6–15.

Plymouth Rock, Water Street, near the *Mayflower* replica. A stone-canopied and fenced rock; a recitation of its history is given by guides in summer months.

In Plymouth: **Antiquarian House** (746-9697), 126 Water Street, opposite Town Wharf. Open weekends in June and September to mid-October; daily late June to Labor Day; 10–5 Monday–Saturday, 12–5 Sunday. A gracious 1809 home with octagonal rooms, China Trade export porcelains, quilts, and children's toys. $2 adult, $.25 children.

Richard Sparrow House (747-1240), 42 Summer Street. Open late May to mid-October, Thursday–Tuesday 10–5. Built in 1640. The oldest surviving house in Plymouth overlooking Town Brook Park.

Our colonial heritage is very much alive at Plimoth Plantation

Since the 1930s the home of the Plymouth Potter Guild; you can watch the loading and firing of the hillside kiln. Donation.

Harlow Old Fort House (746-3017), 119 Sandwich Street. Open weekends in June and September to mid-October; daily late June–Labor Day weekend. Built in 1677 with beams believed to be from the Pilgrim fort, restored to its seventeenth-century look. Costumed guides demonstrate candle dipping, weaving, spinning, and yarn dyeing. $1.25 adults, $.25 children.

Mayflower Society Museum (746-2590). Open weekends in June and September to mid-October, daily late June to mid-September; Monday–Saturday 10–5, Sunday 12–5. An elegant home built in 1754, remodeled in 1898, features formal gardens, a "flying staircase," and nine furnished rooms. It is headquarters for the General Society of Mayflower Descendents. $1.75 per adult, $.25 per child.

Spooner House (746-0012), 27 North Street. Open late June to mid-September, Friday–Saturday 10–5, Sunday 12–5. A vintage 1749 home, owned by the same family until 1954, it reflects changing life-styles in Plymouth over two hundred years. The Spooners were prominent merchants and sea captains and the house is well furnished and alive with interesting local tales.

National Monument to Our Forefathers, Allerton Street, off Route 44. A late nineteenth-century rendition of Faith and her helpers.

Plymouth National Wax Museum (746-6468), 16 Carver Street. Open daily, March through November, 9–5. Twenty-seven tableaux, more than 180 figures, tell the Pilgrims' story from the time they left Scrooby up until the first Thanksgiving. $3 per adult, $1.50 per child.

Cranberry World Visitors Center (747-1000), Water Street, north of Town Wharf. Open April through November daily 9:30–5; also 5–9 Monday–Friday in July and August. A former clam-processing plant has become a showcase for Ocean Spray Cranberries, an 800-grower cooperative. Displays tell how the fruit came to be grown commercially in the 1820s, how a bog is made (not born), and how the cranberry has been picked over the years by Indians, Azoreans, and Yankees. Check with the center for a list of local bogs that welcome visitors to watch the harvesting in early October; it's a colorful process.

In Duxbury: Duxbury is more peaceful and aristocratic than America's Home Town. It was founded by Pilgrims Myles Standish, Elder William Brewster, and John Alden. You can visit the home built by John Alden's son, the site of the Myles Standish and Brewster homes, and climb the high old monument to Myles Standish on Captain's Hill. The town is also graced with a number of wealthy sea captains' homes. Duxbury Snug Harbor is a fashionable summer place, and nine-mile Duxbury Beach is one of the finest barrier beaches in New England (the public end is accessible only from Marshfield).

King Caesar House (934-6106). Open mid-June to Labor Day, daily, 1–4, closed Mondays. This is a classic Federal-era mansion built in 1807 by Ezra Weston II, better known as "King Caesar" because his wealth from shipbuilding and shipping was recognized by Lloyd's of London as the largest fortune in America. This house is finely constructed and detailed, and its front parlors, virtually unchanged, retain their original wallpaper, imported from France. There is a striking painting of Daniel Webster, who was a visitor here, and a fine exhibit about early nineteenth-century shipbuilding and Far Eastern trade. Across from the house stands the stone wharf where the family's ships were rigged; traces of the adjacent 100-acre shipyard can still be seen. $1 adults, $.50 students, $.25 children.

Captain Gershom Bradford House (934-2281), 931 Tremont Street. Open on summer Wednesdays 1–4, and by appointment. Another Federal-era sea captain's mansion, this one inhabited by four generations of Bradfords until 1968, when it was given to the Duxbury Rural and Historical Society.

Drew House (934-2378), junction of Washington Street, Powder Point Avenue, and St. George Street (at the flag pole). Open year-round, weekdays 8 AM–noon. This handsome 1826 house is headquarters for the Duxbury Rural and Historical Society. It includes period rooms and a small gift and bookstore.

John Alden House (834–6421), 105 Alden Street. Open late June to Labor Day, daily except Monday 10–5. This shingled house with a massive central chimney dates from 1653; the kitchen, borning room, and buttery are probably older, having been moved from their original position on a cellar hole to the rear. The house is maintained by the Alden Kindred of America and furnished to period.

Duxbury Art Complex (934-6634), Alden Street (off Route 3A), open Wednesday–Sunday 1–4. Built by the Weyerhaeuser family, partly to house their collection of pottery and Japanese artifacts. It is a striking building, wavy-roofed to suggest the sea and rolling hills of Duxbury, glass-sided to permit the seasons to be part of each exhibit. The permanent exhibits are Shaker furniture and Japanese pottery; other exhibits change monthly. There are also periodic lectures, concerts, and teahouse ceremonies.

In Marshfield: **Winslow House** (837-5753), corner of Careswell and Webster streets. Open July to Labor Day, daily except Tuesdays 10–5. We include this house because it is one of the most beautiful early homes in New England, and because it happens to be on the way to Duxbury Beach (the best in this area). Built in 1699 and remodeled in 1750, it retains its original staircase and hearths; furnishings include Pilgrim chests. A home until 1920, it then became a tearoom for a dozen years. There is a 1760 drawing room, Jacobean paneling in the bedroom, and a secret room for hiding Tories. Ask for directions to the nearby **Daniel Webster Law Office** (open in July and August, Wednesday–Saturday 1–4) in which Webster met with Lord Ashburton in 1842 and drew up the agreement establishing the boundary between Maine and Canada (thus ending the Aroostook War). The furnishings and mementoes are authentic. Webster's own house burned in 1848. He is buried in the nearby Winslow Cemetery (his memorial is a gift from the Trustees of Dartmouth College).

In Carver: Carver boasts more cranberry bogs than any Massachusetts town. Visit in early October and you will see billions of red berries bobbing on the surface of the bogs along Route 58 and Federal Furnace Road in South Carver.

Edaville Railroad (866-4526), Route 58, South Carver. Open daily June through Labor Day 10–5:30; weekends only in May noon–5; September through October weekdays 10–3 (using diesel trains), weekends 10–5:30 (using steam trains). Christmas Festival (of lights), mid-November through early January, weekdays 4–9 and weekends 2–9. Adults, $7.50, children, $5.00. The major attraction is a 5½-mile run in an authentic, steam-powered, narrow-gauge railroad, which originally carried lumber from Bridgton to Harrison, Maine, in 1882. The 30-minute ride meanders through an 1,800-acre operating cranberry plantation and includes a narration about the cranberry growing process. There is also a petting zoo, a variety of antique vehicles and rolling stock, a "Main Street" exhibit, a small working replica of a paddle-wheel riverboat with tours on Cranberry Lake, and a Bog Iron Nature Trail. There are also frequent special events. A snack bar features a chicken 'n' cranberry barbeque dinner.

In Middleborough: Cranberry processing is the big industry in this town that was home for midgets Tom and Lavinia Thumb. In the Historical Museum you learn that Mrs. Thumb was born Lavinia Bump in Middleborough, and that after her exotic travels with P.T. Barnum, she returned here with her second husband (also a midget) and opened a refreshment stand.

Middleborough Historical Museum (947-1969), Jackson Street (off Route 105). Open July and August, Wednesday–Friday 1–4. This is a complex of two twin mill houses, a small law office, and a carriage house. A reconstructed general store stocks penny candy and straw hats made in town, and there are costumes and tools. The midget collection is outstanding. You learn that Lavinia had four six-foot brothers (see above) and a midget sister. At the height of their career the Thumbs built a dwarf-size house across from the Bump home. Tom died as the result of fire and Lavinia married an Italian Papal Count. Their refreshment stand drew thousands.

A&D Toy-Train Village and Railway Museum (947-5303), 49 Plymouth Street. Open daily year-round 10–5. A collection of thousands of toy trains from 19 countries. They include 50 operating trains and miniature rolling stock from the 1850s to present. $2.50 per adult, $2 per senior, $1.25 per child aged 5–12.

In Kingston: Originally part of Plymouth, Kingston is a tranquil old seafaring town with its share of old "Captains' Houses" The weathered **Major John Bradford House** (585-6300), Landing Road, is open mid-June to Labor Day, Wednesday–Sunday 10–5. Built in 1674, this is a classic early saltbox with a massive central chimney. Its facade has a lopsided look because two windows are eighteenth-century sash-style, and three others are mullioned. You can swim here at **Gray's Beach** but it's $10 per car. **Van Bael's Wharf,** south on Route 3A, left at Howard Lane, is surrounded by a stone sea wall, offering a splendid view and a sense of this area in prosperous shipping days.

GREEN SPACE **Burial Hill,** Plymouth. Accessible from Obery Street or Route 44. The old graves top a hill above Plymouth. There are no guides, snack bars, or souvenir stands, and there is a splendid view and sense of dignity.

Brewster Gardens, along Town Brook from Water Street up to Jenny Grist Mill (just south of Plymouth Rock at the foot of Leyden Street). The Indians caught herring in Town Brook and taught the Pilgrims to place them in the soil to fertilize their corn. The Pilgrims used the reeds that grew along the banks for their thatching. You can still drink from the Pilgrim Spring near the Pilgrim Maiden Statue.

Myles Standish State Forest (866-2526), Cranberry Road, South Carver. Forest headquarters are open 8 AM–10 PM. This is a 15,000-acre recreation area, accessible from Exit 5 off Route 3. In addition to camping and swimming (see above) there are two pine-wooded picnic areas, fishing (at designated areas), and miles of roads for biking.

Manomet Bird Observatory (224-6521), PO Box 936, Manomet 02345. Begun in 1969 as a center for the study of bird migration, there are 26 acres of forest, wetlands, and fields maintained by a non-profit group, which offers guided tours, publicized visitors days, summer nature camps.

North Hill Marsh Wildlife Sanctuary, Mayflower Road, Duxbury. For details contact Massachusetts Audubon Society, South

Shore Sanctuaries (837-9400). This area includes a .6-mile loop and .9-mile-loop trail around a pond and cranberry bog. There are also designated canoe and fishing access areas.

Myles Standish Monument (866-2526), Crescent Street, Duxbury. From Route 3 take Tremont to Chestnut; left to the flagpole at Hall's Corner (a rotary at which you bear right onto Standish Street). A gate bars access by car from Labor Day to Memorial Day, but it is a short walk to the top of Captain's Hill. Picnic tables are scattered beneath the pines and it is 124 steps to climb to the top of the monument, topped by a larger than life Myles Standish. From here you can look off across Powder Point to Massachusetts Bay, across Kingston Bay and Plymouth to Cape Cod. The monument was completed in 1889.

In Duxbury: **Standish Cellar Hole.** From the Standish Monument continue along Crescent Street to Standish Street; take a left onto Standish, a right onto Marshall, and follow it to the end where the site of Myles Standish's home is marked. This is worth doing for the beauty of the spot and for the view across the bay to Plymouth. Captain Standish came here with his three small boys in 1628. A stone marks the house site, and a path leads over the hill to the site of the spring.

Brewster Lilacs. From the Standish Cellar Hole continue back up Marshall Street to the stone marker on the left, indicating the site of William Brewster's homestead. Walk in to look at the big lilac bush planted on the cellar hole. Brewster bought his plot in 1631 and the next year "gathered the parish," which became the town of "Duxburrow."

BOAT EXCURSIONS Boat trips: *Cape Cod Princess* (747-2400), Plymouth to Provincetown. Memorial Day weekend through Columbus Day, Sundays; June through Labor Day, daily; then Mondays, Wednesdays, Fridays through the end of September. Departs for Provincetown, 9 AM, returns 6:30. The cruise across Cape Cod Bay takes $2^{1}/_{2}$ hours, which leaves $4^{1}/_{2}$ hours in P'town before the return; adults $13.50, age 12–17 $10.50, ages 5–11, $7.50; bicycles, $2. Inquire about special evening Cape Cod Canal cruises.

Plymouth Harbor Tours (747-2400), June through September, narrated half-hour cruises depart regularly from the State Pier, $3.50 per adult, $1.50 per child.

Whale Watching and Deep Sea Fishing: Captain Tim Brady & Sons (746-4809), 254 Sandwich Street, Plymouth, offers April–November whale watching (departing 1:30 PM, also 6:30 PM in July–August) on the 45-foot *Mary Elizabeth;* also all-day open boat fishing (departing 7 AM–1 PM) $20 per adult, $17 per senior, $15 per child; whale-watching rates vary with time, $18 max per adult.

Capt. John Boats (746-2643), 117 Standish Avenue, Plymouth, offers whale-watching trips to the Stellwagen Banks aboard the 85-foot *Capt. John & Son II*, weekends in April, May, June, September, and October; two trips daily late June to September 1. $15 per adult, $13 seniors, $11 children. All day, half-day, and overnight fishing trips are also offered.

BOAT RENTALS **Rent-a-Boat** at Town Wharf offers paddleboards, outboards, deep-sea charters; **Tripp's Boat Livery** (224-2476), open daily 6–6, Manomet Point, offers rowboats, outboards, rods, and reels.

CAMPING **Scusset Beach State Reservation** (888-0859), Scusset Beach Road, from the junction of Route 3 and Route 6, offers 98 campsites. **Myles Standish State Forest** (866-2526) offers 570 campsites; $8 per night fee.

CANOEING Wampanoag Canoe Passage. A water trail used by the Indians has been revived by the Plymouth County Development Council; you can put in at Pembroke or Middleborough, paddle all the way to Dighton Rock on the Taunton River. A detailed brochure is available from the PCDC, PO Box 1620, Pembroke 02359.

GOLF **Plymouth Country Club** (746-0476), Plymouth. 18 holes.

FISHING See Boat Excursions; Scusset Beach under Swimming; Myles Standish State Forest under Green Space.

FLYING **Plymouth Airport** (746-2020) is base for a glider operation and flight school; air charters.

SWIMMING **Duxbury Beach** (387-3112) is a nine-mile barrier beach that has changed little since the Duxbury Beach Associates acquired it in 1931. There is a shingled bathhouse with baskets in which you can stow your clothes (also use the showers and changing room) for $.25. From Memorial to Labor Day lifeguards are on duty 9 AM–6 PM; parking is $2 weekdays, $4 weekends. Access is via Route 139 through Marshfield's Green Harbor section.

Plymouth Beach, Route 3A, three miles south of the village, is 3½ miles long, with rest rooms; parking for 200 cars, $3 weekdays, $5 weekends.

White Horse Beach, Plymouth (follow signs south of town to Manomet), is backed by cottages; offers only on-street parking (very limited) for which there is no fee.

Scusset Beach State Reservation (888-0859), Scusset Beach Road from Routes 3 and 6 rotary. A relatively uncrowded beach with snack bar, rest rooms, picnic tables, campsites, a fishing pier with bait shop, and seven miles of paved trails for biking. $3 parking.

Nelson Street Beach, Water Street, Plymouth. Just north of Cranberry World. Facilities include playground, lifeguard on duty, and parking: $3 weekdays, $5 weekends.

Stepher's Field, Route 3A, one mile south of Plymouth village; first left after the fire station. Facilities include playground, ball field. $5 weekends and holidays only.

Fresh water beaches: **Morton Park,** from Plymouth Center take Summer Street, heading west. Park entrance is 2½ miles on left. Facilities include rest rooms, lifeguards on duty. $3 weekdays, $5 weekends.

Myles Standish State Forest. Take Route 3 south from Plymouth to Long Pond exit. Go right on Long Pond Road; there are bathhouses and beaches at **College and Fearings ponds,** also picnic tables, fireplaces. $3 parking.

INNS AND BED & BREAKFASTS Around Plymouth Bay Bed & Breakfast (747-5075), PO Box 6211, Plymouth 02360, is a reservation service that arranges lodging in 35 private homes scattered from Scituate to Falmouth. Rooms range from $40–$50 single and $45–$75 double, breakfast included.

Be Our Guest, Bed and Breakfast, Ltd. (837-9867), PO Box 1333, Plymouth 02360, also offers lodging in 20 private homes in Plymouth and surrounding towns. Rates are $40–$50 double with a choice of full or continental breakfast.

Seaview Manor (746-7459), 259 Court Street, Plymouth 02360. A handsome, shingled home, four rooms with color TV, sea views, air-conditioning, breakfast served in the dining room; $40–$60 in season.

The Hall's Bed & Breakfast (746-2835), 3 Sagamore Street, Plymouth 02360. A pleasant home in the center of town (behind Friendly's), two rooms with shared baths, children welcome, $40 double includes breakfast.

Another Place (746-0126), 240 Sandwich Street, Plymouth 02360. Just off Route 3A between the village and Plimoth Plantation, a 1700s half cape furnished with antiques; set in a large garden, $50 double.

Morton's Park Place (747-2533), 1 Morton Park Road, Plymouth 02360. Four single rooms with shared baths, or two suites; $55 in summer with continental breakfast.

Winsor House Inn (934-2548), 390 Washington Street, Duxbury 02332. An 1803 tavern is now a popular restaurant with lodging upstairs. There are rooms with canopy beds, four posters, one with a fireplace; $80 double, includes a full breakfast.

Gurnet Inn (834-7121), Green Harbor, Marshfield 02050. A small, nineteenth-century summer hotel (revamped after the 1878 blizzard) offers eight apartments right on Duxbury Beach; pleasant atmosphere, maid service available May–September; $469 per week for a one bedroom, $534 for a two-bedroom unit, available by the day before and after July and August.

HOTELS AND MOTELS **Sheraton Plymouth** (747-4900), 180 Water Street, Plymouth 02360. A 177-room, four-story convention center. Facilities include a pub, attractive Apricots restaurant, health club, and indoor pool. The hotel is near the waterfront, behind its Village Landing Marketplace, a clustering of specialty shops. $80–$100 double, depending on room and season.

Cold Spring Motel (746-2222), 188 Court Street, Plymouth 02360. A half mile north of Plymouth Center; quiet, comfortable units, complimentary coffee and donuts in summer, $44–$56 double.

Blue Spruce Motel (224-3390), Route 3A, Manomet, Plymouth 02360. Six miles south of the village; 15 units include efficiencies, house, and cottage rentals. Facilities include a pool, shuffleboard, complimentary coffee. $42 double, $350–$450 per week for efficiencies.

Pilgrim Sands (747-0900), 150 Warren Avenue, Plymouth 02360. Right on Plymouth Beach, this two-story, 62-room motel has both an indoor and outdoor pool, rooms with refrigerators; $70–$87 in summer, less off-season.

DINING OUT **Mayflower Seafoods** (746-1704), Town Wharf, Plymouth. Open for lunch and dinner daily. A long-established seafood restaurant with nautical decor and early bird specials all day; dinner specialties include fish n' chips ($8.95) and a fried seafood platter ($10.50); entrees include soup and salad bar.

Scruples (747-3200), 170 Water Street, Plymouth. Part of the Village Landing (an extension of the Sheraton), open daily for lunch and dinner, brunch on Sunday. Slick, nicely decorated with a moderate luncheon menu: croissant sandwiches, soups, salads, gourmet burgers. Dinner is middle America: Hawaiian Chicken ($10.95), Teriyaki Beef Brochette ($12.95), and Fisherman's (deep fried) Platter, $13.95.

Station One (746-6001), 51 Main Street, Plymouth. Open daily for lunch, dinner, Sunday brunch. The town's old Fire Station One, with superb woodwork and brick walls, fern bar decor, sidewalk cafe. Crabmeat and avocado salad at lunch is $6.75; Shrimp Diane at dinner is $11.25.

Milepost Tavern Restaurant (934-6801), Route 3A, Duxbury. Open daily for lunch and dinner; dinner only served Sundays from 1 PM. The humdrum exterior belies an unusually attractive atmosphere within. Lunch can be homemade soup and salad or a sandwich. Dinner ranges from $8.50 (Broiled Scrod) to Steak Dijonnaise ($14.95); entrees average $12 and include a range of chicken, beef, veal, and seafood dishes.

Winsor House (934-2548), 390 Washington Street, Duxbury. Open Monday–Saturday for lunch, Monday, Tuesday, Friday, and Saturday for dinner. The dining room in this 1803 tavern has considerable charm and the low-beamed pub with hearth is genuinely cozy. The dinner menu is continental, $13–$18.

EATING OUT **Woods Fishmarket** (746-0261), Town Wharf. Open for lunch and dinner, year-round. At the end of the wharf, limited eating space, but there are benches on the wharf and great chowder ($1.25), $2.95 for three clamcakes; fishmarket next door sells live crabs and lobsters.

Mayflower Fish Market, Town Wharf, part of Mayflower Seafoods (see Dining Out) but the same food, less expensive. Open for lunch and dinner with ample seating space. The scallop roll is $4.95. Fresh fish also sold.

Lobster Hut (746-2270), Town Wharf. Open daily for lunch and dinner, February to December 20. Waterside with canopied eating area; lobster rolls cost $4.75, lobster salad plate is $8.25; luncheon specials include fried popcorn shrimp ($4.50, small portion).

Mama Mia's (747-4670), 122 Water Street, Plymouth. Open daily for lunch and dinner; Italian food, pizzas, subs.

ENTERTAINMENT **Priscilla Beach Theatre** (224-4888), Rocky Hill Road, Manomet. One of the country's oldest summer stock playhouses; live shows all summer.

Plymouth Philharmonic Orchestra (746-8008). For a program write Box 174, Plymouth 02360. Solo and chamber concerts at various locations year-round.

BOOKSTORES **West Winds Bookstore** (934-2128) Washington Street, next to Sweetser's Snug Harbor. The size belies the stock, crammed into every corner of this exceptional little store; good for children's titles, beach reading, regional books.

Annie's Book Stop (746-1405), 42 Main Street, Plymouth. Open daily. Half-price paperbacks.

The Yankee Book & Antique Shop, 10 North Street, Plymouth. Open daily. In an old house across from the library, specializing in hard to find books and Pilgrim history.

Note: Plimoth Plantation (see To See and Do) has an extensive gift and bookshop.

SELECTIVE SHOPPING **Commonwealth Winery** (746-4940), 22 Lothrop Street, Plymouth. Open daily, Monday–Saturday 10–5, Sunday 12–5; evening hours in July and August. Housed in an old industrial building near the Plymouth waterfront, a facility producing 16,000 cases of wine a year, 90 percent from Massachusetts grapes; also cranberry wines. Tasting bar, retail sales, bottles are priced $4.95–$9.95.

Plymouth Colony Winery (747-3334), Pinewood Road, Plymouth. Open April through December, Monday–Saturday 10–5, 12–5 on Sundays; January through March, weekends and holidays noon–5. The winery is a former cranberry screening house in the middle of a 10-acre cranberry bog. Tours, tastings, sales, picnic tables.

Sweetser's General Store, Washington Street, Snug Harbor, Duxbury. Open Monday–Saturday 8–8, Sunday until 6. A genuine village store with good picnic fixings, hot coffee, fresh pastries.

SHOPPING COMPLEXES **Jenney Grist Mill Village,** Spring Lane, Plymouth. Sited at the crossroads of the original Colony, the mill houses specialty shops selling gifts, crafts, gourmet ice cream. The Jenney Grist Mill Store features a working, water-powered mill.

Village Landing Marketplace (746-4600), Water Street. More than 20 specialty stores.

The Cordage Park Marketplace (746-7707), Court Street (Route 3A), North Plymouth. Open daily, year-round. Housed in a vast, nineteenth-century cordage mill, there are a variety of shops; the central area is served by a variety of food stands. **The Factory Shoe Outlet** (open Monday–Friday, 9:30–9, Saturday until 6, Sunday 12–5) stocks a wide variety of sports clothes for all ages as well as shoes.

SPECIAL EVENTS Late June: **Fishermen's Harvest Celebration,** Plymouth Waterfront; **Railfans Weekend,** Edaville Railroad; **Shallop Sail,** Plymouth Harbor; **Bathtub Derby and Grape Stomping Contest,** Plymouth Beach.

July: **Independence Day,** old-fashioned parade, Duxbury; **Arts and Crafts Fair,** Antiquarian House, Plymouth; **Wampanoag Wedding,** Plimoth Plantation.

August: **Pilgrims Progress Procession,** Fridays at 5 PM, costumed pilgrims process from Cole's Hill up Leyden Street to the site of the first church, on up to Burial Hill where psalms are sung and texts read. **Plymouth Rock Day,** first Saturday; **Marshfield Fair,** Marshfield Fairgrounds, mid-August; **Antique & Classic Auto Meet,** Competition, Edaville Railroad; **Mayflower Lobster Festival,** Plymouth Waterfront.

September: **Outdoor Art Show,** Brewster Gardens; **King Richard's Faire,** South Carver Faire-grounds, Route 58, weekends early September through mid-October, jousting, Medieval music and games.

Mid-October: **A Celebration with the Dutch,** Plimoth Plantation. A three-day harvest-time feast, includes games, sports.

November: **Thanksgiving Weekend Celebration** at Memorial Hall; reasonably priced turkey and fixings, served up continuously from 11 AM to 5 PM. There is usually entertainment before the meal and a square dance after.

MEDICAL EMERGENCY **Jordan Hospital** (746-2000), Sandwich Street (Exit 5 off Route 3, off Obery Street), Plymouth.

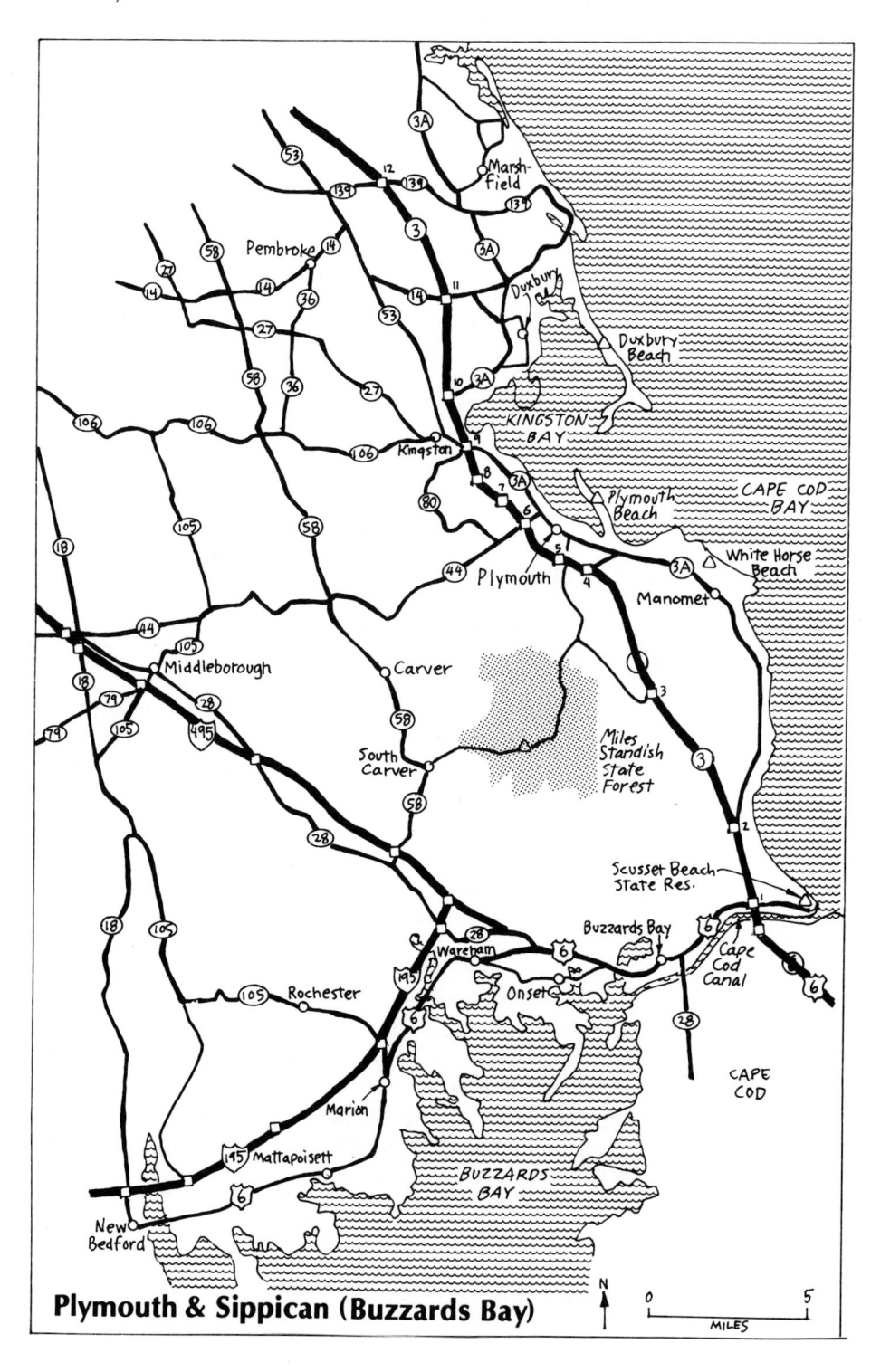

Plymouth & Sippican (Buzzards Bay)

Sippican

The lands of Sippican were settled in the 1630s. The 70- to 80-square-mile tract was named Rochester, after the Rochester in Kent, England, and incorporated in 1686. Before 1852 the town's harbor on Buzzards Bay provided a thriving coastal trade. Eventually the coastal towns of Marion and Mattapoisett became independent and other parts of the original territory became part of Fairhaven and Wareham.

Today relatively few people recognize the name "Sippican," but they readily agree that this Buzzards Bay area is a distinct land between the Plymouth and New Bedford tourist destinations, happily bypassed by most visitors.

Locally this delightfully ragged piece of coast is known as "the armpit of Cape Cod." Onset, begun as a camp meeting colony in 1876, remains a Victorian-style summer resort. Marion, an old shipbuilding port turned yachting resort, has a fine Arts Center and the Sippican Historical Society, and Mattapoisett, another old shipbuilding town, offers music and dancing in its Shipyard Park.

AREA CODE 617

GUIDANCE The **Plymouth Development Council** and the **New Bedford Chamber of Commerce** have jointly published a "Sippican" brochure, available from either (see Guidance under Plymouth and New Bedford).

The Onset Chamber of Commerce (295-1227), Main Street, Onset 02558, offers advice on finding local lodging.

GETTING THERE Route 6 is the high road of the area. It parallels I-195, which offers frequent access; a "strip" for much of the way, it in turn offers well-marked access to the various towns.

TO SEE AND DO **Mattapoisett Historical Society** (758-2844), 5 Church Street, Mattapoisett. Open July and August, Tuesday–Saturday. The old meetinghouse of the Mattapoisett Christian Church is now filled with exhibits on whaling and with local memorabilia, which spill over into the barn.

Sippican Historical Society Museum (748-0088), Front Street, Marion. Open mid-June through August, Wednesday 2:30–5, Saturday 11–5. Exhibits on Marion's whaling days, also on mystery boat *Mary Celeste*, found under full sail at sea in 1872 with all passengers missing.

Marion Art Center (748-1266), 60 Main Street. Open October through April, Tuesday through Saturday; May through September, Wednesday through Saturday 1–5, Sunday 10–2. There are changing exhibits as well as classes.

Fearing Tavern (295-0151), Elm Street, Wareham. Open July and August, Tuesday–Thursday 2–4. A 1690 historical house museum.

The Cape Cod & Hyannis Railroad (771-1145), 252 Main Street, Hyannis, operates between Braintree (accessible by Boston's MBTA system) and Hyannis on a regular summer schedule mid-May through foliage season, stopping at the Buzzards Bay (Route 6) depot in Bourne and the Depot, Main Street, Wareham. It's possible to ride to Sandwich or Boston and back. Price varies with length of trip.

BOAT EXCURSIONS **Cape Cod Canal Cruises** (295-3883), Onset Town Pier, Onset. May through October, varying schedule. The *Viking* offers regularly scheduled 2- and 3-hour cruises through the canal, $5.50–$7.50 per adult, $2.50–$3.50 per child aged 6–12; inquire about Sunday Jazz, Sunset, Lobster, and Dance cruises.

Fishing Expeditions: From Onset the *Trade Winds IV* (295-9402) sails out to fish April to mid-November (varying schedule), $15 per person, $25 parent and child special on Mondays, $2 for rod and bait.

From the Bourne Marina the *Sea King II* (291-0100) sails May through mid-September (varying schedule), $15 per adult, $12 per child, $1 for rod and bait, $25 Monday special for parent and child, $10 per extra child.

GREEN SPACE **Great Hill Farm** (748-1052), Delano Road in East Marion, is a 700-acre estate on Buzzards Bay. It includes woodland paths and 22 greenhouses, seven devoted to orchids. Flowering trees, exotic plants, and flowers are on sale.

Shipyard Park, Mattapoisett. This waterside park, middle of the village, occupies the site of the town's six defunct shipyards. The *Acushnet*, in which Herman Melville went whaling, was built here. Their flagpole is the mizzenmast from the town's last whaleship (*The Wanderer*, launched in 1878), and there is a golden whale weathervane on the bandstand, used weekly in summer for band concerts.

GOLF **Marion Golf Club** (748-0199), 9 holes.

Little Harbor Country Club (295-2617), Wareham, 18 holes.

Wareham Golf Course, Onset, 18 holes.

SWIMMING Aside from **Onset Beach,** accessible from the Onset Pier parking lot or on-street parking, this is disappointing beach country. Public strands are either small and uninviting or private. In Marion, **Island Park and Beach,** Front Street, is a tiny strand backed by a big stone pavillion, surrounded by boat brokers.

INNS, AND BED & BREAKFASTS **Mattapoisett Inn** (758-4922), Mattapoisett 02739, is an old summer hotel with a popular restaurant and three rooms upstairs; $50 double, $60 for a suite, year-round.

Ocean Crest/Anchor Inn (295-8763), 177 Onset Avenue, Onset 02558. This is a shingled old Onset cottage across from the beach, with four immaculate, nicely decorated rooms, sharing one bath; backyard grill, picnic area, outside shower, and changing room; also two apartments in annex cottage, $50–$60 per day.

Pineapple Hospitality (990-1696), 384 Rodney French Boulevard, New Bedford 02744, is a reservation service with listings in this area.

DINING OUT **L'Auberge de Marion** (748-2756), 450 Wareham Road, Marion. Open for lunch and dinner daily. French cuisine, daily specials, dinner entrees range $8.95–$17.95; specialties include Rack of Lamb, Bouillabaise, Veal Oscar, duck, and calves liver.

The Mattapoisett Inn (758-4922), 13 Water Street, Mattapoisett. Open April–November daily (closed Tuesdays) for lunch and dinner. A seaside old summer hotel with low-beamed dining rooms, atmosphere, early bird specials, Cajun cooking and Seafood Fettucini; Frogs Legs go for $13.50, Roast Duckling $12.95 at dinner.

Harbor Lights (295-6361), across from Onset Pier, Onset. Open Wednesday–Sunday 4–9, Sunday 1–9. A local dining landmark with an octagonal dining room in the heart of Onset Bay Grove. The menu includes Veal Picatta ($11.95), and Crab Stuffed Sole de la Mer ($12.95). Boiled lobster is $9.95.

EATING OUT **Oxford Creamery** (758-3847), Route 6, Mattapoisett. Open April–December daily, lunch menu until 8 PM. There is limited, inside seating, and a canopied patio. Cheerful, speedy young staff take orders and dish up the fried seafood and ice cream. Fish n' chips ($2.95), an overstuffed, chunky lobster roll ($4.50), and great ice cream.

Besse's Fish Market (295-0619), Onset, beside the bridge. A restaurant supplier with its own fried fish and clam eatery; locally loved, open daily for lunch and dinner.

Ansel S. Gurney House (748-1111), 403 County Road, Marion (Route 58). Open daily 11:30–5. Homemade soups and bread, salad bar, sandwiches, appetizers, and desserts.

ENTERTAINMENT **Gateway Players** (295-6738), Route 6, behind Town Hall, Wareham. Year-round repertory group performs in a restored freight station.

SELECTIVE SHOPPING **Tremont Nail Company** (295-0038), Elm Street, Wareham. Closed Mondays January through May, otherwise open Monday–Saturday, 10–5, Sunday noon–5. A tourist-geared, old-fashioned country general store, owned and operated by the world's oldest nail manufacturer (1819). **The Company Store** offers antique nails, colonial hardware, gourmet groceries, and nostalgia; nail-making film in summer.

Marion General Store (748-0340), Front Street, Marion. Open Monday–Saturday 8:30–6. A genuine, old-style store with a little bit of everything, including picnic fixings.

SPECIAL EVENTS September: **Festival of the Harvest Moon,** Onset (parades, exhibits, concerts).

MEDICAL EMERGENCY **St. Lukes Hospital** (997-1515), 101 Page Street, New Bedford.
Parkwood Hospital (995-4400), 4499 Acushnet Avenue, New Bedford.

Bristol County

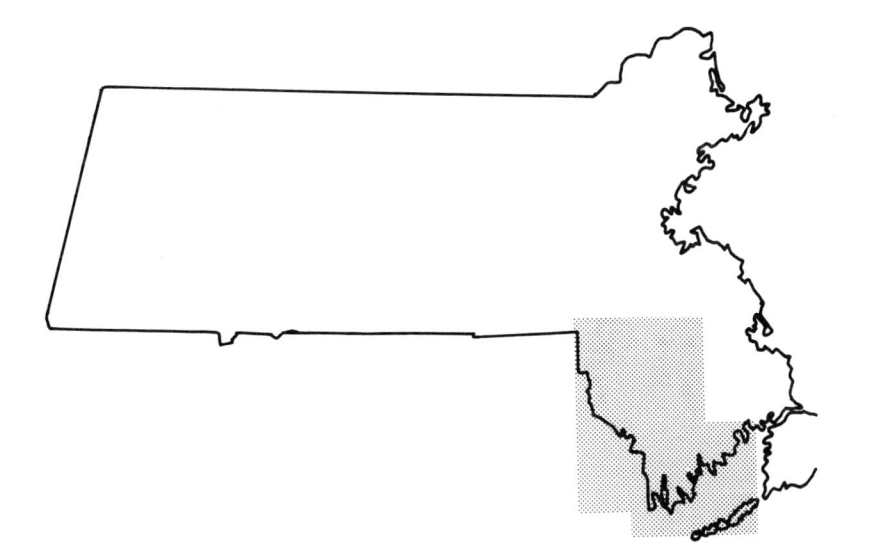

INTRODUCTON

The southeastern corner of Massachusetts is wedged between Rhode Island and highways which bypass its beaches, quiet coves, and seaside farms for Cape Cod. New Bedford actually offers easier access to Martha's Vineyard (both by ferry and plane) than the Cape, and its cobbled waterfront district offers fine museums and shops. But the fishing boats here are no tourist props. The world's former whaling capital remains America's leading fishing port.

The region's lure for many of its visitors is factory outlets. More than 100 genuine discount stores are now housed in New Bedford's brick mills and Fall River's granite mills. But even the bargain hunters are beginning to notice recent changes in these cities. Fall River's new Heritage State Park dramatizes the powerful story of how its mammoth mills have interwoven ethnic groups.

Between New Bedford and Fall River lies some of the most beautiful countryside in the state—green farmland webbed with narrow roads and spotted with peaceful, shingled villages: Westport Point, Russell Mills, and Padanaram. There is ample space to hike and a choice of beaches with and without surf. And offshore lies Cuttyhunk, one of the most convenient yet least-touristed of New England's islands.

AREA CODE 617

GUIDANCE **Bristol County Development Council** (997-1250), 70 North Second Street, New Bedford, operates regional information centers northbound on I-95 in Mansfield and eastbound on I-195 in Swansea; also staffs a seasonal information center at the Fall River Heritage State Park. For a guide to factory outlets, attractions, and events write: BCDC, Box BR-976, New Bedford 02740.

New Bedford

Known for its Whaling Museum and factory outlets, New Bedford now offers far more: a 14-block restored waterfront with more than its share of museums, restaurants, shops, and galleries; a class-act theater; a zoo; and pleasant lodging.

Just a decade ago, the waterfront was still visibly crumbling, and a highway had just severed the wharves of the early nineteenth-century warehouses and "manufactures" built to serve the world's largest whaling fleet. The Whaling Museum and the neighboring Seaman's Bethel, described by Herman Melville in *Moby Dick*, were the city's sole attractions.

Now, more than 90 buildings in this waterfront neighborhood—which happens to coincide with the city's original ten acres—have been restored. Streets have been cobbled and trees planted. The predictable gourmet restaurants, "fern bars," and gift shops have opened.

But New Bedford is still a working waterfront. In contrast to many recent harbor-side restorations, more than half of the businesses here are still sea-linked. New Bedford seamen may hunt small scallops now instead of mighty whales, but their 220 boats still add up to America's most lucrative fishing fleet.

Many of the city's more than 2,000 fishermen are descendents of Azorean and Cape Verdean seaman, who first saw the city from whaling ships. And Mayor John Bullard (who has dedicated his past ten years to restoring the waterfront) is a direct descendent of Joseph Rotch, who bought those original 10 acres as a base for outfitting whaling ships in 1765.

But New Bedford's faces are a varied lot. In the late nineteenth century (after the discovery of crude oil had obviated the need for whale oil), the city's 50 textile mills drew immigrants from all the world's corners.

"I'm an Irishwoman, married to a Greek, and we run a Jewish delicatessen" is the way our tour guide introduced herself. "That's the way it is in New Bedford. Everyone's very ethnic, but we're all mixed up together, very friendly."

The summer walking tours are free, led by volunteers who genuinely want you to like their town—which is especially appealing to children. In addition to the Whaling Museum there are Fire and Children's museums, beaches, and a great little zoo.

AREA CODE 617

GUIDANCE **New Bedford Visitors Center** (994-9905), North Second Street, New Bedford 02741. Open Monday–Saturday 9–5, Sunday 11–5. A walk-in center with an audiovisual introduction to the city; pamphlets.

The Bristol County Development Council (997-1250), 70 North Second Street, New Bedford 02741. Across the street from the visitors center, good for information on the entire county (see Bristol County introduction).

New Bedford Chamber of Commerce (999-5231), 838 Purchase Street, New Bedford, across from City Hall. Another source of pamphlets and general New Bedford information.

GETTING THERE By bus: **Bonanza** (800-556-3815) offers service to Boston, Providence, and New York.

By air: New Bedford Municipal Airport is served by **PBA** (800-282-3197) and by **Gull Airlines,** both connecting with Boston, New York, Cape Cod, and the islands. **Southeast Air** (992-1144) also serves the Cape and islands, and **Island Air Service** (994-1231), in Fairhaven, offers seaplane service to Cuttyhunk.

By car: From the west and New York City take I-95 to Route I-195 East at Providence, R.I. Exit 15 to Route 18, Downtown exit. From points north and Boston take Route 24 to Route 140 to Route I-195, Exit 15 to Route 18, Downtown exit. A shade slower but more pleasant from the north is Route 24 to I-495, Exit 5 to Route 18, via Lakeville and Acushnet.

PARKING The **Elm Street Garage** (on your left, just off the Downtown exit) costs less than a meter; max of $2 per day.

GETTING AROUND June through August trolleys circulate through the historic district; also go to **Buttonwood Zoo** and the beaches; $.25 a ride, free under age 5. The waterfront, shops, and County Street sights are all within comfortable walking distance of each other.

TO SEE AND DO In New Bedford: **Historic Waterfront.** Although the "Downtown Connector" (Route 18) disconnects the waterfront from the water, there are pedestrian crossways to the wharves where fishing boats are moored. In addition to museums, antiques shops, and restaurants, the neighborhood still has its share of chandleries and a Custom House that has been functioning since 1834. Free guided tours of the area depart from the Whaling Museum, late June to September, daily 10–3.

The New Bedford Whaling Museum (997-0046), 18 Johnny Cake Hill. Open Monday–Saturday 9–5, Sunday 1–5. Internationally known for its scrimshaw collection (more than 2,000 pieces), the museum displays vivid paintings of life aboard whaling vessels

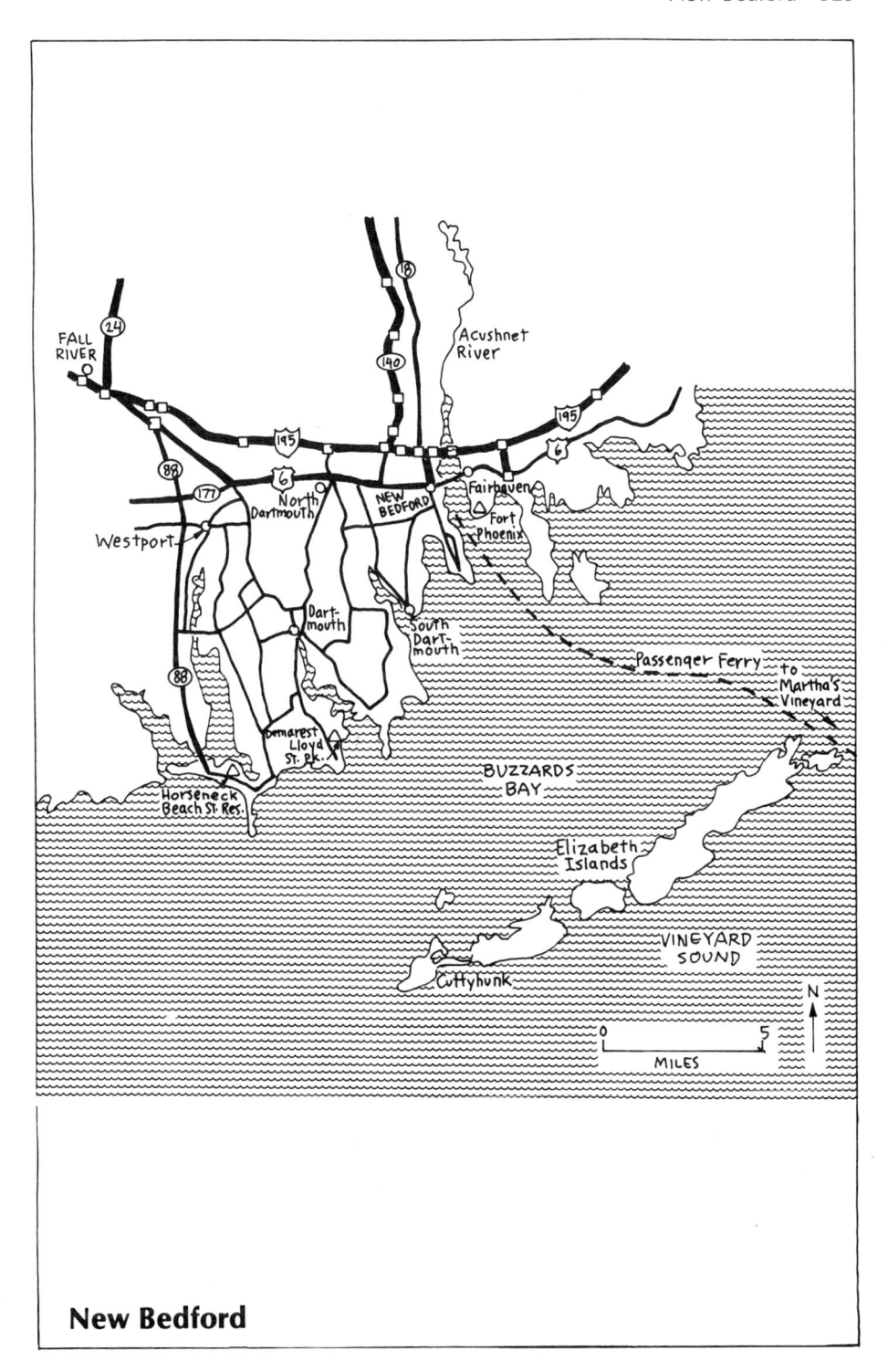

New Bedford

from Tahiti to the Arctic Circle. Whaling voyages are painted on a quarter-mile-long panorama (produced in 1848 to show in theaters), etched on whale teeth, and dramatized in movies (shown regularly in summer months). You can clamber aboard the world's largest ship model—a half-scale model of New Bedford bark *Lagoda*, fully equipped down to the skeleton of a humpback whale. Amid the figureheads and panoramas, hanging above a sampling of the museum's 1,080 logbooks, is the black-framed crewlist from whaleship *Acushnet*, dated December 30, 1840. It includes "Herman Melville, age 21. 5'9", dark skin, brown hair." $2.50 per adult, $2 seniors, $1.50 children aged 6–14.

Seamen's Bethel (992-3295), 15 Johnny Cake Hill. Open May–October, weekday afternoons and weekends. The pulpit, shaped like a "ship's bluff bows," such as Melville described, was actually installed after publication of *Moby Dick*. The remainder of the chapel conveys a sense of the men who prayed here (and continue to) before setting out to sea. The walls are covered with memorial tablets to men who have died in every watery corner of the earth. It is a Quaker-plain, moving place. The Mariner's Home next door, like the Bethel, is run by the Port Society, founded in 1830 "for the moral and religious improvement of seamen." The building itself dates from 1787 and there is a nominal charge to fishermen for a night's lodging.

New Bedford Glass Museum (994-0115), 50 North Second Street, open Tuesday–Saturday 10–5, Sundays 1–4. Also open Mondays, May through December. In the 1880s New Bedford became internationally known for its art glass. A collection of more than 2,000 pieces of Pairpoint and Mt. Washington glass are displayed here in a granite mansion built in 1820 by one of the city's leading merchants. $2 per adult, $1.50 seniors, $.50 for children aged 6–12. Across the street you can now observe glass being blown at New Bedford Glassworks (see Selective Shopping).

New Bedford Fire Museum (992-2162), corner of Bedford and South Sixth streets. Not far from the center of town, but a fire engine shuttles visitors up from the visitors center. Open July and August only, daily 9–5. Housed in a former stable next to nineteenth-century Fire Station #4, this is a collection of antique equipment: shiny pumpers, buckets, horns, and more. There is a corner for children to dress up in, and a pole for them to slide down (grown-ups are permitted to slide too). It is staffed by veteran fire fighters. $1 adults, free for children 12 and under.

Schooner Ernestina, ex-*Effie M. Morrissey* (992-4900), Coal Pocket Pier (next to Yesterday's Restaurant). Open June–August, Monday–Saturday 1–4 (when the ship is in port). Just across Route 18 at 30 Union Street, a museum exhibiting photos, artwork, and artifacts that trace the history of the ship, is open year-round, Monday–Friday 9–5 and by appointment. The schooner *Effie M. Morrissey* was built in Essex in 1894 and fished the Grand Banks into the '20s, establishing a reputation as a fast and lucky boat. Beginning in 1926 the *Morrissey* sailed to the Arctic on a number of scientific expeditions, serving as an Arctic supply and survey ship for the United States Navy during World War II. In 1948, after a brief period as a yacht (during which the ship caught fire, sank, and was raised again), the "Morrissey" became the *Ernestina*, carrying passengers and goods from the Cape Verde Islands (off Africa) to America. By 1975 she was the last sailing packet left in this trade. She was rebuilt by the Republic of Cape Verde and presented to the people of the United States. Since her arrival in New Bedford, the schooner has been further restored through funding from the state's Department of Environmental Management and a variety of other sources. Throughout the winter and spring she sails the Atlantic and Caribbean and in summer takes short educational cruises when she is not in port. A tour of the ship costs $1. The museum is free.

WHALE (996-6912), 13 Centre Street. The Waterfront Historic Area League, founded in 1962, is a non-profit preservationist organization that has saved dozens of buildings (both in the waterfront area and elsewhere in New Bedford) buying, restoring, and in some cases moving them and then selling them for appropriate uses. The offices, which welcome visitors and dispense information about special events and projects, are housed in the old Tallman Warehouse.

County Street. "Nowhere in America will you find more patrician-like houses," Herman Melville wrote, "brave houses and flower gardens . . . harpooned and dragged hither from the bottom of the sea." One of the oldest streets in the city, County Street runs along the crest of the hill from which the city slopes away to the Acushnet River. It was the obvious place for the wealthiest whaling merchants to build, and they were followed by textile mill owners. There are grand Federal mansions, spacious nineteenth-century homes, and turreted Victorians. Tours are offered Wednesdays at 11 AM during June, July, and August. Meet at the Rotch-Jones-Duff House (see below), $2 fee.

Rotch-Jones-Duff House and Garden Museum (997-1401), 396 County Street. In April–October, Sunday 1–4; in June–August, also open Wednesday–Friday. One of the finest County Street mansions, built in 1834 by Nantucket whaling merchant William Rotch, Jr. The 28 rooms are presently being filled with appropriate furnishings and the formal gardens (which fill an entire block) are filled with boxwood hedges and roses; there is a newly rebuilt gazebo and a beauty here that make it worth a visit. In July and August there are frequent concerts before which guests are invited to picnic. $2 admission.

Buttonwood Park Zoo (996-1852), Hawthorne Street and Brownell Avenue (Route 6). Open April 15–Labor Day, 10 AM–3:30 PM. Set in 97-acre Buttonwood Park (designed by Olmstead/Eliot, the firm that laid out New York City's Central Park), it includes seals, llamas, an elephant named Emily, deer, a mountain lion, and an assortment of other friendly animals. Also see Green Space.

In Fairhaven: Located just across the Acushnet River (take the Route 6 bridge) from New Bedford, Fairhaven is a proud old shipbuilding and whaling town. However its elaborate public buildings (most notably the Millicent Free Library on Center Street) are all gifts of a local boy who made his fortune in Pennsylvania petroleum rather than whale oil. Henry Huttleston Rogers left town a grocery clerk and returned a multimillionaire. In later years he saved Samuel Clemens from bankruptcy and in return "Mark Twain" laid the cornerstone for the town hall that Rogers donated and induced him to finance Helen Keller's way through Radcliffe College. Rogers also gave Fairhaven its grammar and high schools, its Masonic Hall, and its splendid Unitarian Church and library—each in a different revival style. The best view of New Bedford is from Poverty Point, the early 19th-century part of town where whaling ships were built. Fort Phoenix on the bay is the other site to see: pre-Revolutionary in origin, it claims the first naval engagement of the Revolution and remains a delightful place to sun. Two detailed pamphlets, *Walking in Fairhaven* and *Bicycling in Fairhaven,* are available from the Bristol County Development Council (997-1250), 70 North Second Street, New Bedford.

In Dartmouth: Just southwest of New Bedford lies some of the most beautiful seaside farmland in the state. From downtown head south across the Apponagansett River to Padanarum Village. This marks the spot of a seventeenth-century settlement. In the nineteenth century there were saltworks and shipyards; now it is a fashionable yachting resort with some fine little restaurants.

Children's Museum (993-3361), 276 Gulf Road, South Dartmouth. Open year-round, Tuesday–Saturday 10–5, Sunday 1–5. Housed in a huge old dairy barn (for many years Twin Silos, Gulf Hill Ice Cream), it is now filled with a kaleidoscopic range of hands-on exhibits (which include a walk-in kaleidoscope, beehive, spaceship, sailboat, and assorted animals). Outside are 50 acres of meadow, woodland, and salt marsh, with trails and exhibits. $1.50 per adult, $1 seniors and children aged 3–12. Phone for an update on frequent special exhibits and events.

Russells Mills. Continue on Gulf Road to Russells Mills Road; turn left and continue past the Apponagansett Friends Meeting House, a weathered building built in 1790. Stop here, even if it isn't open (there is a Sunday meeting in summer months). The graveyard is a quiet, moving place with the same names on the plain tombstones that appear on local mailboxes: Allen, Slocum, Gifford, Russell. Continue through the picturesque village where houses are scattered, each on their own rise of land around an old mill pond.

Russells Mills Doll and Toy Museum (636-5289), 1200 Russells Mills Road. Open May through October, Tuesday–Sunday. The 1824 church (which formerly housed the Children's Museum) is filled with Georgia Codin's collection of antique dolls, doll houses, and toys.

See Swimming for **Demarest Lloyd State Park** (just down Barneys Joy Road from Russells Mills), and note **Lloyd Ecological Center** under Green Space and **Lincoln Park** under Amusement Park.

CUTTYHUNK ISLAND Accessible by the *M/V Alert* (992-1432), which runs May–October four days a week ($12 per adult round-trip) from Pier 3 in New Bedford; also by Island Air Service (see Getting There), 14 miles offshore. Cuttyhunk is the westernmost of the 16 Elizabeth Islands, which together form the town of Gosnold. The islands trail off in a line from Woods Hole, dividing Buzzards Bay from Vineyard Sound. All but two of them have long been owned by the Boston Brahmin Forbes family, and they are very private. Cuttyhunk is little more than two miles long and an irregular three-quarters of a mile wide.

In Cuttyhunk's one room schoolhouse the pupils (who seldom number more than three) learn that their island is the site of the Bay State's first English settlement. Bartholomew Gosnold built a stockade here in 1602 and set about planting a garden and gathering sassafras (valued for medicinal uses). But Indians, lurking in the brush, made the would-be colonists jumpy. After a 22-day stay, they sailed away home. A stone tower, erected in 1902, now marks the fort's site on a mini-island in the middle of a salt pond (where oysters are presently being cultivated) at the western tip of the island. From town it is a pleasant hour or day's walk, depending on how frequently and how long you pause on the smooth boulders to watch the surf breaking or the sun glinting on beach grass. Your footsteps send countless rabbits scampering. (It's advisable to stick to the dirt road and avoid detours through the scrub because there are wood ticks, carriers of Lyme disease.)

Cuttyhunk is best known for game fishing. The world's record

73-pound striped bass was caught here. "Bass boats," with tackle, boat, and the guidance of their owners, can be rented by the day or the "tide."

You either love or hate this world to itself where people talk to each other, and where the air and water are clear. Most of Cuttyhunk's 90-odd houses are in the harbor-side town of Gosnold. There is a seasonal general store and just one place to stay: **Allen House** (996-9292), clean, simple, and homey. Open late May to early October, it offers seven rooms in the main house, six in an annex, and two cottages; $65 in summer, breakfast included.

There is a choice of two places to eat—**Allen House** (serving lunch and dinner) and the **Vineyard View Bakery and Restaurant.** Cuttyhunk's summer population falls below 400 and its winter people number less than 40. An ungainly, non-functioning windmill looms over the heath, beaches are stony, and the island is "dry." Bikes are useless on the sandy roads and there are only a few cars. Of course if Cuttyhunk were any more inviting, it would be mobbed. As is, it is as peaceful and remote as any island far Down East and rewards those who seek it out.

GREEN SPACE **Buttonwood Park** (993-5686). Aside from the zoo (see To See and Do), this 97-acre park includes tennis courts, picnicking space, and paddle boats.

Brooklawn Park (995-6644), Acushnet Avenue, New Bedford. There is a kiddie pool, tennis courts, and picnicking facilties.

Lloyd Center for Environmental Studies (990-0505), 430 Potomska Road, South Dartmouth. Extensive acreage, cross-country trails, and canoe excursions on the Slocum River.

Fort Phoenix, Fairhaven (from Route 6 take Green Street to the end). The story of the fort's role in the Revolution was apparently forgotten until the 1970s when Fairhaven fireman Donald Bernard began researching its history. Bernard's daughter had asked him how old the fort was, a question he discovered no one in town could answer. His research took him to England and back. His findings are now generally accepted in this state, but not in Machais, Maine, which also claims the first naval engagement of the Revolution. Fairhaven's first battle was May 14, 1775, and the fort was then built in its present shape; one cannon (still here) had been captured by John Paul Jones in the Bahamas. The fort was overrun in 1778 but fended off a British invasion party in 1814, and again saw service in the Civil War. The smooth rocks and small beach below the fort at the base of the Achushnet River breakwater are locally favored for sunbathing.

Fort Tabor, Rodney French Boulevard (the end), New Bedford. Follow Route 18 to Cove Road, bear left to the end of the street. This massive granite complex was designed by Captain Robert E.

Lee in 1846, long before his command for the Confederate Army.

AMUSEMENT PARK **Lincoln Park** (999-6984), Route 6, North Dartmouth. Open Memorial to Labor Day. Founded in the later nineteenth century by the Union Street Trolley Company of New Bedford, it retains its old picnic pavilion. There is bowling, roller skating, a variety of arcades, a big roller coaster, adult and "Kiddie Rides." No admission.

AIR RIDES **Balloon Adventures of New Bedford** (636-4846), 564 Rock O'- Dundee Road, South Dartmouth. One-hour champagne flights available year-round, $135 per person, $150 on weekends, May through October.

FERRY **Cape Island Express Lines, Inc.** (997-1688). Martha's Vineyard Island ferry *Schamonchi* departs daily (Memorial Day weekend through September), making between one and four runs (depending on the day and month) to Vineyard Haven. Shuttle service to the dock is available from the Elm Street Garage (daily parking rates are $2) to the dock at Billy Woods Wharf (take Route 18 south to Cove Road). Round-trip fare to the Vineyard is $12 adult, $7 one-way; $6 per child round-trip, $4 one-way.

FISHING **Captain Leroy** (992-8907) departs from the Fairhaven Bridge (Route 6) April–November, daily 7:30 AM, returning at 4 PM. His 50-foot and 65-foot party boats are equipped with fish and depth finders; rods and reels available for $2.

GOLF **Emerald Park Golf Club** (992-8387), North Dartmouth, 18 holes.
Whaling City Country Club (996-9393), New Bedford, 18 holes.
Heritage Hill (947-7743), Lakeville, 18 holes.
Hawthorn Country Club (996-1766), North Dartmouth.

HORSEBACK RIDING **Apache Ranch** (995-9866), 445 Old Fall River Road, North Dartmouth. Trail rides, $10 per hour.

SWIMMING **Demarest Lloyd State Park** (636-3298), Barney's Joy Road, South Dartmouth. This is one of my favorite state beaches, crowded on Sundays but otherwise relatively deserted, ideal for small children since there is no surf. There are roughly two miles of beach with a view of Cuttyhunk, picnic tables, grills, and fireplaces. A large sandpit jutting into the mouth of the Slocum River is a pleasant place to walk. In season there is a $3 parking fee.

Apponagansett Point Beach (parking fee for non-residents) is a small, pleasant beach on Gulf Hill Road, Dartmouth, near the Children's Museum.

See Fall River for details about **Horseneck Beach in Westport.**

New Bedford Beaches: Follow Route 18 south to Rodney French Boulevard. **Hazelwood Park** and **East Beach** both have changing rooms, snack bars; open late June until Labor Day, 9–6, free.

Fort Phoenix State Beach (992-4524), Fairhaven, take Green Street from Route 6. This can be windy but it is otherwise pleasant and

Fishing remains the number one industry in New Bedford

uncrowded on weekdays; an urban beach, bathhouse, lifeguards, $3 parking fee.

WATERSLIDE **Westport Waterslide** (636-6750), Westport, on Route 6 near Lincoln Park. Open mid-May to September; weekends until mid-June; then daily 10–8; six rides for $3.50.

BED & BREAKFASTS **Pineapple Hospitality** (990-1696), 384 Rodney French Boulevard, New Bedford 02744. "More than 200,000 visitors were coming to see New Bedford's waterfront and no one was staying here," says Joan Brownill about how she happened to found Pineapple Hospitality in 1980. Today the reservation service publishes a directory ($4.50) that describes (with pictures) 150 homes throughout New England, but its largest concentration remains in and around New Bedford. We have inspected these gracious homes in Fairhaven and Dartmouth and stayed at an 1857 Greek-revival home in downtown New Bedford. Each is very special and offers a taste of the good life in this southeastern corner of the state. $35–$45 double.

Edgewater Bed & Breakfast (994-1574), 2 Oxford Street, Fairhaven 02719. Parts of this unusual house, in Fairhaven's Poverty Point, were built as a store in the 1760s. It is now a rambling 1880s home, overlooking New Bedford Harbor. There are five rooms (each with private bath and water views), one with a private sitting room with fireplace, another with a canopy bed. The continental breakfast is served on the screened porch or in the dining room, and there is a comfortable, sunken living room for relaxing. $35-$50 double, $55 to $65 for suites.

Padanaram Guest House (993-9009), 4 Bridge Street, South Dartmouth 02748. Five guest rooms in a fine old house, one with private bath, four share; $30–$50 per night, breakfast included.

HOTEL AND MOTELS **Yesterday's Inn** (999-2700), 1 Merrill's Wharf, New Bedford 02744. The 18 rooms (private bath) are nothing special, but the location is right on the waterfront in the massive granite Bourne Counting House (built in 1848 for Jonathan Bourne, the whaling master who reputedly owned more whaling tonnage than any other man in the country). Yesterday's restaurant-lounge is on the glassed-in top floor, and the Cafe Estoril and Patio (ground floor) has a Portuguese and American menu. $37.50 double.

Skipper Motor Inn (997-1281), 110 Middle Street, Fairhaven 02719. Route 6 at the bridge. A two-story, 140-room motel. Each room has two double beds, color TV, and direct dial phones; facilities include an indoor heated pool and whirlpools, a restaurant, and banquet facilities. $54 double, $85 for suites, free under age 12.

Whaler Inn (997-1231), 500 Hathaway Road, intersection of Routes 140 (Exit 3) and I-195, New Bedford 02740. This is a 133-room, recently refurbished motel with a locally respected restaurant; outside pool. $55–$60 double.

DINING OUT **The Candleworks** (992-1635), 72 North Water Street, New Bedford. Open for lunch and dinner Monday–Saturday, 4–9 on Sunday. Regional fish like Poached Haddock in Mornay Sauce, Sauteed Scallops Matiche, and Coquille St. Jacques are the specialty. Filet Mignon and Steak au Poivre are also on the menu. Housed in a granite building built by Samuel Rodman in 1810 to produce spermaceti candles. Seasonal patio dining, a living room atmosphere inside; moderately expensive.

L'Auberge de Marion (728-2756), 450 Wareham Road, Marion (see Marion under Plymouth County), is the New Bedford area's current "in," and most expensive, dining spot.

Bridge Street Cafe (994-7200), 10-A Bridge, South Dartmouth. June to Labor Day, open daily for lunch and dinner, except Tuesday. A garage turned gourmet; the specialties are homemade pasta, seafood, and desserts. $8.95–$18.95.

Mike's (996-9810), 714 Washington Street, Fairhaven. Open 11:30–10:30 daily, Italian specialties, stuffed shrimp, lobster, prime ribs, $10 average for entrees, locally loved.

Huttleston House (999-1791), 111 Huttleston Avenue, Fairhaven. Open daily for lunch and dinner, specializing in veal, seafood, and beef dishes. Average $10.95 for entrees.

Twin Piers (996-3901), 1776 Homer's Wharf. Open daily for lunch and dinner, bar until 2 AM. Formerly Louie's, a longtime dining landmark, still unchanged; fresh seafood is the specialty, $2.95–$15.95, child's plates.

Tides at Padanaram (992-3608), 7 Water Street, South Dartmouth. Open Tuesday–Sunday 11:30–11; a long-established dining favorite for the area. Linen tablecloths, a view of the harbor in a cottage setting, with seafood specialties; $12 average for dinner entrees.

Freestone's (993-7477), 41 William Street, New Bedford. Open daily 11–11, Sunday brunch. This is both a casual and serious dining spot, depending on the time of day and what you order. Northampton couple Debbie Sequin and Kerry Mitchell dislodged a raunchy bar and restored this early nineteenth-century bank building, preserving the original mahogany paneling and working fireplace. A cup of prize-winning fish chowder is $1.75 and a full-course seafood dinner is $9.95 (same menu all day), now jam-packed for both meals; featuring hamburgers and fried fish at lunch, more ambitious fare at dinner.

EATING OUT **Davey's Locker** (992-7359), 1480 East Rodney French Boulevard. Open daily 11–10. Sited in the South End at Clark's Point, overlooking the water, this is generally agreed to be the best, reasonably priced place to eat fish in New Bedford. The clam chowder is outstanding and baked stuffed scrod with Creole sauce is $4.95.

The Phoenix Restaurant (996-1441), 140 Huttleston Avenue, Fairhaven. Open all night, from 11 PM to 2 PM (closed 3 PM to 11 PM). Breakfast is the specialty here; try scrambled eggs with linguica and home fries. Cheese rolls, Portuguese and Greek specialties; $3 or less for a meal.

The Main Event (992-0681), 252 Union Street, New Bedford. Open daily 11–11 and for Sunday brunch 11–2:30. This is an upbeat, downtown restaurant with hanging plants and nice artwork, but a reasonably priced menu: pocket sandwiches, linguica, and quiche for $3 and $4.

Maxie's New York Deli, Purchase Street, across from City Hall, New Bedford. Open 4 AM–2:30 PM. A bright, friendly eating and gossip spot, with fresh flowers on the counter, exposed brick walls, and hanging plants; the day's paper stacked for guests. Homemade soups, two eggs and toast, $1.05.

Portuguese Shanty (998-2645), 2980 Acushnet Avenue, New Bedford. Open daily for lunch and dinner, closed Mondays. Carne de Espeto, Cacoila, Bacalhau are the specialties, but you can also order chicken or chops. This is the best known of the city's Portuguese restaurants.

Joy's Landing Restaurant (992-8148), Water Street, South Dartmouth. Open daily 8 AM–9 PM, 24 hours on weekends. A shingled, waterside haven featuring fish and chips but also good for a linguica sandwich and kale soup or breakfast. $3 for lunch, $4 to $6 for dinner.

Shawmut Diner (993-3073), Shawmut Avenue, New Bedford, open 5:30 AM–7 PM daily, until 8 Thursday–Saturday. A chrome classic, but Roast Leg of Lamb is the specialty; $4.95 buys dinner.

ENTERTAINMENT Zeiterion Theatre (994-2900), 684 Purchase Street. All the Grecian friezes have been gilded in this 1923 Vaudeville theater. Its recent restoration has been a community effort, a symbol of the new New Bedford. The Zeiterion now has a professional summer and performing arts season, featuring musicals, jazz, dance, classical concerts, and children's performances.

Southeastern Massachusetts University (999-8000), Old Westport Road, North Dartmouth, stages cabaret theater (July through August) and a September Eisteddfod.

Local club and restaurant shows are listed in *Arts & Entertainment,* a quarterly magazine available from PO Box H-3045, New Bedford 02741. Single copies are $1, available by mail for an extra $.50.

SELECTIVE SHOPPING Antiques: **Brookside Antiques** (993-4944), 44 North Water Street, specializes in Pairpoint Glass, other things local.

Galleries: **Swain School of Design, Crapo Gallery** (997-7831), corner of Hawthorn and County Streets. Open Monday–Friday 10–4.

Bierstadt Art Society Gallery (993-4308), 1 Johnny Cake Hill, New Bedford. Open 12–4 daily except Monday. Area painters exhibit in changing shows.

Specialty Stores: **New Bedford Glass Works** (997-7928), 47 North Second Street, New Bedford. Open daily 10–6. In the rear of the Bourne Warehouse (a mini-mall housing croissant and chowder bars) is an open studio where you can watch Roy Wilson blow the intricate, colored pieces that he sells on the spot.

Moby Dick Specialties (994-5024), 27 William Street, New Bedford. Open Monday–Saturday 8–5. An old chandlery, crammed from floor to ceiling with an eclectic mix of kitsch, basic marine hardware and camping gear, brass ornaments, and salty souvenirs. The shop is supplied by a warehouse full of similar treasures, a wholesale source of nautical decor for restaurants.

FACTORY OUTLETS When petroleum replaced whale oil in the 1860s, New Bedford merchants put their money into cotton mills, which grew as whaling waned, reaching their peak prosperity in the 1920s. Then came a 49-year depression for the city. Now the picture is brightening again; major companies are occupying mill space and many of the old factories now house outlets. A **Textile Museum,** exhibiting machinery and cloth samples, is located in the Whitman Mills (see below).

Whitman Mills Outlet Center (997-2363), 1 Riverside Avenue, New Bedford. Open daily 10–6, except Sunday 12–5 and until 9 PM Thursday and Friday. Stores include **Old Mill** (ladies' sportswear); **DJ's** (women's shoe outlet—nothing over $15) and **Karen Anne Mfg.** (luggage, towels and athletic accessories).

VF Factory Outlet (998-3311), 375 Faunce Corner Road (the road is an exit off I-195), North Dartmouth. Open Monday–Saturday 9–9. This is a vast, hangar-like building filled with one of the best clothing outlets around. It was formerly known as "Kay Windsor," a line still carried in the large area that adjoins the Vanity Fair and Lee section (there are ample changing rooms and mirrors), with a great selection of jeans (including odd sizes) and sportswear for the whole family, all at savings that are genuinely half of retail. Down a long, tunnel-like corridor, **The Clothes Hound** carries better men's and women's sportswear (Ralph Lauren and Evan Picone); it's also a great source of boys' suits and jackets. **Misty Harbor,** down the line, sells its own label raincoats in an unusual range of styles. Shoes, luggage, children's clothing, and a cosmetics outlet complete the tempting scene.

Calvin Klein Outlet Store (999-1300), 100 North Front Street,

New Bedford. Open daily 10–5 and from noon Sunday; also until 8 Thursday and Friday. A wide selection of Calvin Klein sportswear for the whole family.

Gentlemen's Wearhouse (999-4033), 419 Sawyer Street, New Bedford. Open daily, weekdays 10–9, Saturday 10–6, Sunday noon–5. A great selection of styles and fabrics in men's suits, sportscoats, slacks, and shirts; also women's slacks, skirts, blazers.

Riverside Factory Store (999-1301), 661 Belleville Avenue. Open Monday–Saturday 9:30–5. Top quality men's slacks, sportscoats, tailored suits, also suits for women; expensive but 30 percent to 50 percent less than retail.

Bedspread Mill Outlet (992-6600), 69 State Street. Open Monday–Saturday 9:30–5:30, Thursday until 8. Blinds, balloon shades, drapes, sheets, comforters, blankets at 30 percent to 50 percent savings.

Dorothy Cox's Candies (996-2465), 115 Huttleston Avenue (Route 6), Fairhaven. Open daily 10–8, until 9 in summer. All recipes are made in small batches, cooked in heavy copper kettles. The specialties are buttercrunch and a variety of hand-dipped chocolates; in business since 1928; ships throughout the United States.

SPECIAL EVENTS   May: **Annual WHALE Auction** at the Zeiterion Theatre, artwork and antique furniture to benefit the Waterfront Historic Area League (early in the month).

June: **Annual House and Garden Tour** of a selected New Bedford neighborhood (first weekend of the month).

July: **Whaling City Festival** in Buttonwood Park, sunrise to sunset—giant flea market, car show, train rides.

August: **The Feast of the Blessed Sacrament,** music, dancing and FOOD—"the world's largest barbecue" (you rent a skewer and brown your own meat over a pit). There are fava beans, bacalhau in a variety of sauces, linguica, and other Madieran delicacies, plenty of Madieran wine, and a midway. The four-day happening is at Madiera Field in the North End (first weekend of the month). **Centre Street Summer Festival,** a major juried craft fair, street entertainment, ethnic foods (second weekend of the month). **Festival By The Sea,** at Piers 3 & 4, seafood, craft booths, live music, relays. On Sunday there is an ecumenical Blessing of the Fleet, followed by a parade of fishing vessels (third weekend of the month).

December: Celebrations at the Toych-Jones-Duff House (specially decorated for Christmas) and a downtown, outdoor choral sing.

MEDICAL EMERGENCY   **St. Luke's Hospital** (997-1515), 101 Page Street. **Parkwood Hospital** (995-4400), 4499 Acushnet Avenue. (Both in New Bedford.)

Fall River

From its source in the Watuppa Ponds, the Quequehan River (said to mean "falling water") drops 132 feet in less than a mile. You can see the river in very few places today but its effect has been dramatic.

Fall River remains one of the state's outstanding monuments to the textile industry. Its mammoth five- and six-story granite mills rise in tiers above Mount Hope Bay. Its first power loom was set in motion in 1817, and by the turn of the century the city boasted more than 100 mills and four million spindles. In 1900 Fall River produced enough yardage to wrap the equator 57 times.

In 1927 the industry sagged. Over the next few years millions of square feet of factory space were abandoned and fire wiped out the city's business core. Fall River went into receivership in the 1930s and was governed by a state-appointed finance board for a decade. The last mill shut down in 1965.

Today Fall River's mills are filled by "Needle Trades" (electronics and metals firms) and also by New England's largest concentration of factory outlets and off-price stores (more than 80). While the outlets draw bargain hunters, Battleship Cove (a lineup of naval vessels under the Braga Bridge) draws school and scout groups, some of whom discover the old mill building in Battleship Cove that has been refitted to tell the story of the Fall River Line, which from 1847 until 1937 was the city's proudest advertisement.

The new Heritage State Park in Battleship Cove is itself reason to visit Fall River. The mill-like, riverside building houses the multimedia show "The Fabric of Fall River," a moving dramatization of the way in which dozens of ethnic groups intermingled to form this unusual city.

More than half of Fall River's residents are still classified as "foreign stock." The spires of St. Anne's Church (a symbol for French Canadian residents) tower above the factory domes, and Columbia Street is lined with Portuguese shops, bakeries, and restaurants. The city is still divided into the dozen ethnic neighborhoods that began as self-contained mill villages.

AREA CODE   617
GUIDANCE   The **Fall River Heritage State Park** (675-5759), Battleship Cove. Open year-round, 9–4:30 daily except Mondays, until 9 P.M. Thurs-

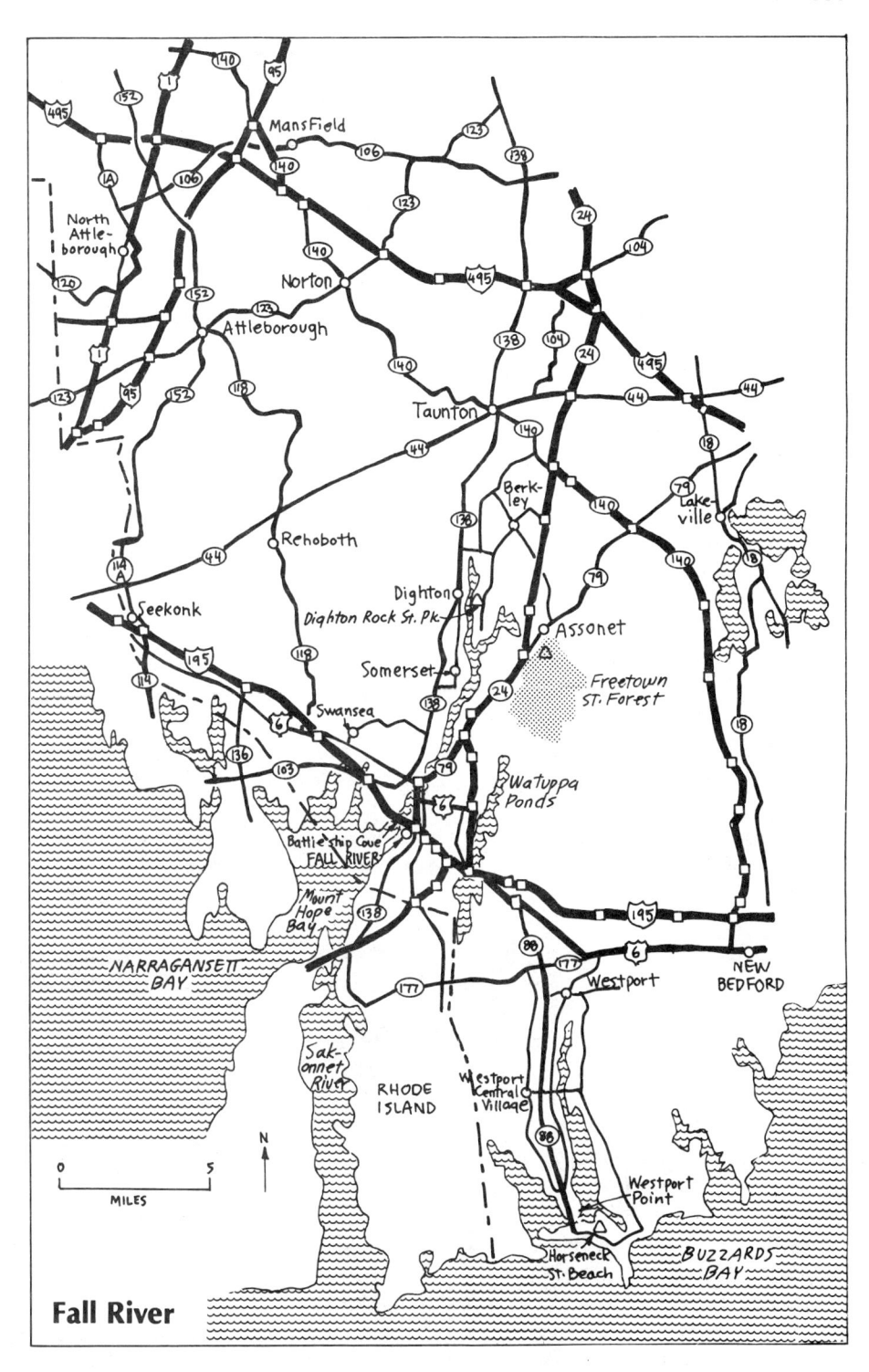

Fall River

days, 8 A.M.–8 P.M. daily Memorial Day to Labor Day. Staff answer questions about local sights, restaurants, and lodging.

Bristol County Development Council (see Bristol County introduction) maintains an information center (673-1311) in the Fall River Heritage State Park, Memorial Day–Labor Day, and will make reservations at member lodging places. Heritage State Park staff also perform these services when BCDC is not on hand.

Fall River Office of Tourism (679-0922), 72 Bank Street, Fall River 02720 (housed in the former Armory). Open weekdays 9–5; dispenses maps and brochures, sponsors walking tours in conjunction with the Heritage State Park.

GETTING THERE By bus: The SRTA Bus Terminal (679-2335), 221 Second Street, is served by **Bonanza,** connecting with Boston and New York, New Bedford, Padanaram, and Fairhaven.

By car: Route 24 or I-195 to Fall River and follow signs. From Route 24 take Route 79/138 and follow battleship blue indicator signs.

GETTING AROUND Thanks to one-way streets and the confusing way in which urban renewal has altered Fall River's downtown street pattern, the only hassle-free way around is on foot or by trolley. The trolley loops between Main Street and Battleship Cove at 20-minute intervals in summer months ($.25 fare). Off-season head for Battleship Cove first then drive to the Historical Society, on up to the mill complexes.

TO SEE AND DO **Fall River Heritage State Park** (675-5759), Battleship Cove. Open year-round, 8–8. Memorial Day–Labor Day, otherwise 9–4:30; closed Mondays, but open Thursdays until 9 PM. The handsome brick visitors center stands in an 8.½ acre landscaped park, the scene of frequent concerts and special events; the adjacent boat house offers a sailing program, also rental paddleboats. In the visitor center's 120-seat theater the 20-minute, multi-media, computerized "Fabric of Fall River" vividly traces the city's history, dwelling (more than do the other Heritage and National park shows) on the rigors of immigrants working 6 AM–6 PM shifts and on the accidents and death suffered by child workers. It also dramatizes the vitality of the city in 1911 when President Taft visited for the Cotton Centennial. Exhibits include a loom and a variety of historical photo blowups.

USS Massachusetts (678-1100), Battleship Cove. Open year-round 9–5, until 6 in July and August. The *Big Mamie* was saved from the scrap pile with $300,000 in nickels and dimes contributed by Bay State residents. Children now swivel the 40-millimeter gun mounts and clamber in and out of turrets. Women gawk at the 80-gallon stew pots. This one-time home for 2,400 men has a soda fountain, three dental chairs, a sick bay, repair shops, and four mess halls. Groups (mostly scout groups) can spend the night, September–June 1, for $23.50 per person.

World War II attack submarine **USS Lionfish** is moored next door. You can inspect the cramped living quarters for 120 men, the torpedo rooms, and the conning tower. Destroyer *J.P. Kennedy, Jr.*, also here, is the official state memorial to the 4,500 men and women who died in the Korean and Vietnam conflicts. There is also a tourist-trap gift store. $5 per adult, $2.75 per child under age 13 for admission to all the boats.

Marine Museum (674-3533), 70 Water Street, Battleship Cove. Open daily, year-round; Memorial Day–Labor Day, 9–7 weekdays, 10–7 weekends; otherwise 9–4:30 weekdays, 10–5 weekends. Housed in a former mill building of the American Print Works (once one of the world's largest textile mills), the museum is a fascinating collection of ship models. Exhibits include the Fall River Liner *Pilgrim*, "largest steamboat in the world" in 1884. Requiring a crew of 200 to serve her 1,000 passengers, she boasts 1,000 electric lights, rich carpeting, mirrors, potted palms, and a full band to drown the thunder of paddlewheels. Most passengers slept in open berths but a state room cost only $1 more. A four-course dinner, served on the boat's personalized china, included steak and lobster for $1.50; a glass of wine was $.15 extra. The mini-cruise was favored by business tycoons bound for Newport and New York City and by honeymooners and young swingers just for the live bands. On the northbound route $4 bought steerage and a new life. In all there are more than 100 ship models on display, including the 32-foot *Titanic* built by 20th Century Fox for a 1952 movie. Special slide presentations on the Fall River Line and the sinking of the *Titanic* are shown regularly and available for groups. $2 per adult, $1.50 per child.

Fall River Historical Society (679-1071), 451 Rock Street. Open March–December, Tuesday–Friday 9–4; April–November, Saturday and Sunday 2–4. Built in 1843 for mill owner Andrew Robeson, Jr., down near the mills, it was moved in 1870 to this height of land, acquiring a mansard roof and a French Second Empire interior. The rich woodwork, elaborately carved doors, period chandeliers, and the 14-foot ceilings in the front and back parlors are outstanding; the displays fill 16 rooms and include exhibits about the mills and life therein, the Fall River Line, and the Lizzie Borden murder. A fake bookcase hides the entrance to a secret space used for the underground railroad. Inquire about visiting the mid-eighteenth-century Thomas Durfee House, now a house museum at 94 Cherry Street.

St. Anne's Shrine (674-5651/678-5322), 818 Middle Street. Open daily. This was the first French-Canadian parish in the city. The basement chapel in which the shrine is located was completed in 1895, the remainder of the cathedral in 1906. The upper church is built of Vermont blue marble and dominates the skyline with twin onion domes. The shrine is the site of frequent novenas.

Walking Tours: A pamphlet guide to the Highlands Historic District streets, leafy streets lined with nineteenth-century mill owners' mansions, is available at the Heritage State Park and from the Chamber of Commerce.

In Westport: **Westport Central Village** and **Westport Point** are both picturesque, shingled villages. **The Westport Art Group,** housed in the school, stages a summer show and there are also fish markets (see Selective Shopping). **The Evergreen Artisans,** open Thursday–Sunday 10–4:30 (Memorial Day–Labor Day), is housed in St. John's Baptist Parish House.

GREEN SPACE Frederick Law Olmsted designed a park system for Fall River in the 1870s. It includes **Ruggles, North** and **South** (now John F. Kennedy) parks, as well as the **Durfee Green** in the Highlands, **Bradbury Green** in the South End and Northeastern Avenue. Both North and John F. Kennedy parks include picnic space, tot lots, and wading pools.

Bicentennial Waterfront Park, a short walk up along the Taunton River from the Heritage State Park, includes tennis courts and picnic grills.

Dighton Rock State Park (822-7537), Bay View Road, Berkley. There is a nineteenth-century-style pavillion under the trees and a vaguely Mediterranean building (open April–October, daily 9–8) sheltering the rock itself. Discovered in 1677, its significance puzzled Cotton Mather, and scholars still cannot agree on who drew the pictographs which can still be clearly seen. The most popular explanation in these heavily Portuguese parts is that it was done by Miguel Cortereal, a Portuguese explorer who disappeared in 1502 while sailing to Newfoundland in search of his brother Gaspar, who had failed to return from a voyage the year before. Miguel's signature, the Portuguese cross and the year 1511 are said to be clearly visible on the rock (it depends on how you look at it). One room in this mini-museum is devoted to the various interpretations of the rock's origin: Phoenician, Indian, and Norse, as well as Portuguese. There are picnic tables; the parking fee is $3 in summer if there is someone there to collect.

Freetown State Forest (644-5522), Slab Bridge Road, Assonet. More than 5,000 acres of woodland; wading pool, picnic tables with fireplaces. As you exit off Route 24 at Assonet (a picturesque old village with a mill pond) note signs for Profile Rock, a wooded state reservation where paths lead to a striking profile of an Indian jutting out from an 80-foot-high pile of granite.

AIR RIDES **Fall River Airways** (672-4953), 1 Airport Road, offers scenic rides, ultra-light rides.

AMUSEMENT PARK For details about **Lincoln Park** and **Westport Water Slide** see Fall River.

BOAT EXCURSION (675-5759) departs from the Heritage State Park boat house May–September daily at 1 and 3; cruises up the Taunton River to Dighton State Park and back; $4 per adult, $3 per child.

CAMPING **Horseneck State Beach** (see Swimming) offers 100 campsites, $8 per night fee.

GOLF **Fall River Country Club** (678-9374), 18 holes. **Dighton Golf Course** (669-6793), 9 holes. **Fire Fly Country Club** (336-6622), Seekonk, 18 holes. **Suspiro Country Club** (675-2539), Somerset, 9 holes.

In Rehoboth: **Hidden Hollow Country Club** (252-9392), **Middlebrook Country Club** (252-9395), **Inglewood Golf Club** (252-3817): all nine-holes; **Rehoboth Country Club** (252-6259), and **Sun Valley Country Club** (336-9825), both 18 holes.

HORSEBACK RIDING **Circle M Ranch** (947-6122), Route 105, Lakeville. Trail rides.

SWIMMING The big beach is **Horseneck State Beach** (636-8816), Westport Point, accessible from Route I-195 by Route 88. The highway stretches almost to the blacktopped parking lot and camping area and nearly to the futuristic concrete shower/rest room/snack-bar complex. There is even a blacktop strip between the dunes and beach. The vast

The 28-foot, one-ton model of the RMS "Titanic" draws enthusiastic visitors to the Marine Museum at Fall River

expanse of beach is spectacular, and the surf is just challenging enough. $3 admission. **South Street,** Somerset, visitors can swim for a fee. In Swansea non-residents can also pay to swim at the **Town Beach** on Ocean Grove Avenue.

DINING OUT **Lizzie's** (672-7688), 122 Third Street, Fall River. A vintage 1894 commercial building has become an attractive restaurant with a fern-bar atmosphere. Dinner is in the $10 range, but lunch is surprisingly reasonable; most sandwiches $2.75, chicken teriyaki $4.95.

White's of Westport (675-7185 or 993-2974), 66 State Road, Westport (Route 6). Overlooking Lake Watuppa, the large SS *Priscilla* dining room replicates the grand salon of the Fall River Line's most luxurious boat. Good for seafood dinners ($10 range) and for reasonably priced luncheons.

The Gangplank (679-8151), Battleship Cove (adjacent to the Heritage State Park), open daily for lunch and dinner, Sunday brunch, nightly entertainment. An attractive dining room overlooking the Taunton River; salad bar, prime rib, seafood; moderate.

Magoni's Ferry Landing (674-4335), 631 Riverside Avenue, Somerset (at the Brightman Street Bridge, Routes 6 and 138, across the river from Battleship Cove). Open 11–10 daily. The dining room is decorated with pictures of the old ferries that used to ply between Somerset and New Bedford. The menu is Italian but features prime rib, $10 entree range; sweet bread deep-fried with cinnamon is a specialty.

Captain P.J.'s (675-2000), Route 6, Somerset. Open Thursday and Saturday for dinner, Friday and Sunday for lunch and dinner. Seafood and prime rib are specialties, under $10 for dinner.

Ukranian Home (672-9677), 482 Globe Street, Fall River. Open Monday–Saturday 11–10. Galumbki, pierogi, kielbasa and cabbage soup, seafood; in business since 1958; casual, reasonably priced.

T.A. Restaurant (673-5890), 408 South Main Street, Fall River. Open for lunch and dinner daily, Portuguese specialties, under $10.

Moby Dick Wharf (636-4465), Westport Point, Westport. Open April–November (closed Tuesdays) for lunch and dinner. Right on the water near Horseneck Beach, with Cajun specialties weekends, early bird specials; seafood: Quohog Pie ($7.95), Coquille St. Jacques ($10.95).

Sagres Restaurant (675-7018), 181 Columbia Street, Fall River. Open for lunch and dinner; may be rowdy on Saturday nights. Portuguese specialties, under $10 for entrees.

Public Clam Bakes, Rancis Farm (252-3212), Rehoboth. Summer Sundays, rain or shine, but call to check. Prices vary with the market price of lobster but are generally under $10.

EATING OUT **China Royal** (679-2310) 542 Pleasant Street, Fall River. Open daily 11 AM–2 AM. A large, gaudy place with good chinese food, a strong local following, handy to mill outlets. $4–$12 for entrees.

Delightful Deli (679-6300), 10 Third Street, Fall River. Open for breakfast and lunch, an immaculate storefront deli with a cheerful dining area, triple decker specials like a corned beef and pastrami reuben for $3.70 (most sandwiches are less), soups, salads.

Beef, Bagel 'N' Brew (675-7676), 10 Purchase Street (at Bedford). Open Monday–Saturday 8:30–2:30. Hot and cold New York deli-style sandwiches, salad plates, soups of the day.

ENTERTAINMENT **Great Woods, Mansfield** (1-800-Beethoven or 239-2331), Mansfield 02048. Marked from Routes I-95, I-495, and 140. Opened in 1986, a summer theater with outdoor lawn eating; mid-June through August, big name performances and concerts by the Pittsburgh Symphony.

SELECTIVE OUTLET SHOPPING A "factory outlet" once meant a large mill building with a small room set aside for selling half-price "seconds." No longer. In Bristol County, outlet capital of New England, a number of large old mills have become self-contained malls, lined with a mix of genuine old-style outlets and "off-price specialty stores," most of them chains with similar stores in similar malls throughout the region. The better to serve bus loads of shoppers (chartered buses converge on this area from every point in the Northeast), more than 60 outlets now cluster within five blocks in the "Heart" or "Flint District." Here a former potato chip factory has been transformed into the **Quality Factory Outlet Center** (18 stores); adjoining granite bastions are now **The Tower Outlet Mill** (a half-dozen shops) and **Fall River Outlet Center** (21 shops). Name-brand clothing for the whole family plus luggage and housewares are priced 30–50 percent below retail prices.

The following Heart District outlets are open Monday–Saturday 9–5, some on Sunday 12–5.

In Quality Factory Outlet: **The Down Outlet** (676-1880). Down comforters, rugged outerwear for the whole family.

Handbag Factory Outlet (679-3999). Handbags, purse accessories, belts, hats, scarves, gloves.

Mackintosh of New England. Ladies' wool coats.

Revereware Factory Store (676-0066). Revereware pots, kitchen utensils, accessories.

Waraco Outlet (679-6363). Men's and women's clothing, name brands.

Fall River Factory Outlet, Wampanoag Mill: **The Bag Outlet** (674-0530). Large selection of average handbags, carry-alls.

Curtain Factory Outlet (678-6996). Curtains, drapes, bedspreads, shower curtains, window accessories.

Fall River Coats (672-2003). Thousands of coats and suits, samples, irregulars.

Garment Center Factory II. Name brands, featuring R&K (made here); women's dresses, petites, sportswear.

J.S.J. Adidas (679-3355). Sports apparel and shoes; irregulars, overruns.

Flint Mills: **Shirt World Fashion Factory** (675-3100). Ladies' blouses and shirts of all kinds.

Tower Outlet: **Carter Childrenswear** (672-6725). Carter's and other name brand children's clothes; heavy on smaller sizes.

D.J.'s Woman's Factory Shoe Outlet (673-2680). Brand name shoes below $15.

Eastern Tots to Teens (674-9155). Children's clothing, heavy on girls and smaller sizes.

Stafford Square: **Newport Harbor Coat Factory Warehouse,** 451 Quarry Street. Men and women's famous-maker, rainwear and outerwear.

Fall River Knitting Mills (687-7553), 69 Alden Street. Open Monday–Friday 9–9; Saturday 9–5. An old-style outlet piled high with 150,000 sweaters. The "world's largest sweater" graces the front wall and in the back there is a play corner: nine fish tanks, two parakeets, and a pile of toys. Through a window you can watch women stitching and sorting.

Karif Factory Outlet (678-5636), 135 Alden Street. Open Monday–Friday 8–3:30; Saturdays 8–12. In the factory itself, women's clothing.

Durfee Union Millplace. A 14-acre complex of granite Mills (some six stories) just two blocks from City Hall, sandwiched between Pleasant Street and Plymouth Avenue. Tenants include: **Fashion Shoe Outlet** (676-9190), open daily; **Happy Feet,** open daily with name brand sneakers including Nike, Reebok.

Copley Square Factory Outlet (679-5286), 240 Hartwell Street. Open Monday–Friday 9–4:30, Saturday 9–2; closed Saturdays in July. Women's blazers, skirts, and slacks in a wide variety of sizes at 50 percent off retail.

Milltowne Marketplace, 1567 North Main Street, Fall River. A dozen stores here are open daily, Monday–Saturday 10–6 (until 9 Thursday and Friday), Sunday 12–5. The basement is now one large **Men's and Women's Shop** (673-3289), selling a range of clothing, including top designer suits and dresses. There is also **Shoe Manufacturer's Outlet** (678-6110) and **Sheffield Shop,** selling locally made sterling and silver plate. **Budget Drapery** (822-3277), a branch of the Taunton mill store, has a wide selection of curtains and draperies.

Darwood (675-7462), 18 Pocasset Street, two blocks from Battleship Cove. Open daily 9–5, Thursday and Friday until 8, Sunday 12–5. A genuine factory outlet selling men's and women's suits.

Trina Factory Outlet (678-7605), Ace Street. Open Tuesday–Saturday 9–4; closed first two weeks in July and at 2 on Saturdays in summer. A block from Milltowne, also handy to Battleship Cove. Great women's travel kits: totes, sewing and laundry kits, cosmetic bags.

The Cotton Mill (674-9499), 109 Howe Street. Home furnishings: quilts, bedspreads, drapes, towels, area rugs, sheets at 20 percent–50 percent savings.

INNS AND BED & BREAKFASTS **Perryville Inn** (252-9239), 157 Perryville Road, Rehoboth 02769. An 1820s farmhouse, enlarged and Victorianized in 1897, now offering five guest rooms and three baths. All are furnished in antiques and share two large sitting rooms. $55–$75 double (private bath), $40–$50 (shared bath), continental breakfast included.

The Gilberts (252-6416), 30 Spring Street, Rehoboth 02769. This 150-year-old farm is set on its own 70 acres, surrounded by woods. There are three upstairs guest rooms, sharing a sitting room and bath. Guests are welcome to use the in-ground pool, and for children there are pony cart rides. Full breakfast includes fresh laid eggs. $40 double, $32 single B&B.

Colonel Blackinton Inn (222-6022), 203 North Main Street, Attleboro 02073. An 1850 house situated on the Bungay River with 16 guest rooms, two small dining rooms, a sitting room, den, sun porch, and garden. Breakfast is served to guests; lunch and dinner (by reservation only for a single sitting) are open to the public. $35–$50 for rooms with shared baths, $55–$60 with private bath.

Pineapple Hospitality (990-1696), 384 Rodney French Boulevard, New Bedford 02744, is a reservation service for homes in Lakeville, Assonet, Rehoboth, and Seekonk; $30–$50.

RESORT HOTEL **Johnson & Wales Inn** (336-8700), Route 114A and 44, Seekonk 02771. A former standard motel has been transformed by one of the nation's leading (Providence-based) culinary and hospitality schools. At present 62 rooms have been refurbished, most of them suites ($59 double) with their own whirlpools; more elaborate suites ($72) also include wet bars. The restaurant, Audrey's Tavern, attracts diners from the Providence area. There is an adjacent fitness center with an indoor pool, fitness club, tennis, racquetball, and also an adjacent 18-hole golf course; rooms from $46 double.

Note: Long before the current craze for factory outlets the towns of Taunton and Norton were known as places to shop for silver and Attleboro for jewelry.

Taunton Silversmiths (1-800-343-1190 or 824-6907), 90 Ingell Street (off Route 140), Taunton. Open Monday–Saturday 10–3. Sheridan silver and gold candles, crystal, closeouts, seconds, up to 75 percent below retail prices.

Najarda Pearls (695-9408), 13 East Street, North Attleboro. Open Monday–Saturday 10–5. Complete line of 14K jewelry; crystal at substantial savings.

For the Christmas shopping season a number of mills open outlets; request a current listing from the Bristol County Development Council (see Guidance).

SPECIALTY STORES Columbia Street is lined with Portuguese bakeries and shops selling Portuguese and Azorean imports.

SPECIAL EVENTS June: **Fall River Festival** at Bristol Community College, Fall River.

July: **Annual Book Fair,** Friends Meeting House, Central Village, Westport.

August: **Antique Car Meet,** Kennedy Park, Fall River (last weekend).

December: **Christmas Arts and Crafts Festival,** Durfee High School, Fall River.

MEDICAL EMERGENCY **Charlton Memorial Hospital** (676-0431), 7363 Highland Avenue.

For Emergency also call: 675-7411.

Index

Adams, 82, 93, 94, 96, 116
Agawam, 170
Agricultural fairs, 1
  Hilltowns, 55
Air rides, 1
  Central Uplands, 24
  Fall River area, 343
  Newburyport area, 292
  North Berkshire, 93
  Plymouth area, 309
  Quabbin Reservoir area, 36
  See also Ballooning
Alpine skiing:
  Central and South Berkshires, 117–118
  Central Uplands, 23
  Five College area, 157
  Hilltowns, 60
  Lawrence area, 234
  Mohawk Trail Country, 72–73
  Nashoba Valley, 210
  North Berkshire, 83
Alpine slides, 1
  Five College area, 154
  North Berkshire, 82
Amesbury, 290–291, 295, 296
Amherst, 147, 149–150, 152–153, 154, 155, 156, 157, 159, 160, 161, 162, 163, 164
Amusement areas, 1
  Central Uplands, 23
  Fall River area, 343
  Five College area, 343
  New Bedford area, 329, 331, 333
  Newburyport area, 292
  Salem and Marblehead area, 250
  Springfield area, 170
Andover, 232–233, 234, 235, 237
Animals, 1
  Blackstone River Valley, 201–202
  New Bedford area, 328
Annisquam, 265–266
Antiques, 1
  Cape Ann Region, 285, 287
  Central and South Berkshires, 107, 138–139
  Central Uplands, 27–28
  Five College area, 162
  Hilltowns, 64
  New Bedford area, 335–336
  Old Sturbridge Village Country, 189–190
  Quabbin Reservoir area, 39, 41

Salem and Marblehead area, 257
Upper Pioneer Valley, 50
Antiquities, 1
Appalachian Trail, 92, 93, 115
Apples, 1
  Mohawk Trail Country, 71
  Nashoba Valley, 208–210
  See also Orchards
Area codes, of Massachusetts, 2
Art galleries:
  Cape Ann Region, 266, 285–286
  Central and South Berkshires, 107
  Fall River area, 342
  Lowell area, 225
  Mohawk Trail Country, 76–77
  New Bedford area, 336
  Newburyport area, 296
Art museums, 1–2
  Central Uplands, 18
  Five College area, 147, 149, 150
  Lawrence area, 232
  North Berkshire, 81, 89
  Sippican area, 316
  Springfield area, 166–167
  Worcester area, 194
Ashburnham, 21, 23, 24, 25–26, 30
Ashby, 19, 22, 23, 26
Ashfield, 54, 57, 59, 62–63, 64, 65
Ashley Falls, 104, 114, 138
Assonet, 342
Athol, 33, 35, 36, 37, 38, 39, 41
Attleboro, 347
Auburn, 190
Auctions:
  Central and South Berkshires, 139
  Hilltowns, 64–65
  Old Sturbridge Village Country, 190

Baldwinville, 21–22, 29
Ballooning, 2
  Five College area, 155
  New Bedford area, 331
  Old Sturbridge Village Country, 182
Barre, 184, 185, 187, 188
Basketball, 2
  Springfield area, 167, 169
Battleship Cove, 338, 340–341, 344, 346–347

Beaches, 2
  See also Swimming
Bearskin Neck, 285, 286
Becket, 116, 119, 131–132
Bed & Breakfast, 2
Belchertown, 153, 156
Berkley, 342
Berkshire Common, 132
Berlin, 212
Bernardston, 45, 46, 47, 48, 49, 50
Beverly, 245–246, 250, 251–252, 256–257, 258
Bicycling, 2–3
  Cape Ann Region, 271
  Central and South Berkshires, 116
  Central Uplands, 23
  Five College area, 155
  Mohawk Trail Country, 72
  Nashoba Valley, 210
  Newburyport area, 292
  North Berkshire, 82
  Old Sturbridge Village Country, 182
  Upper Pioneer Valley, 45
Billerica, 222, 227, 228
Birding, 3
  See also Massachusetts Audubon Society; Nature preserves; Wildlife sanctuaries
Boat excursions, 3
Boat launches, 3
  Salem and Marblehead area, 250
Boat rentals, 3
  Cape Ann Region, 271
  Central and South Berkshires, 116
  Newburyport area, 292
  Plymouth area, 309
Boating:
  Central and South Berkshires, 116
  Five College area, 155
  Lawrence area, 233
  Old Sturbridge Village Country, 182
  Salem and Marblehead area, 251
  Springfield area, 170
Bolton, 209, 211
Boston, guides of, 3
Boylston, 196, 210, 211
Brimfield, 180, 182, 187, 189, 190
Brodie Mountain, 83–84

Brookfield, 182, 190
Buckland, 54–55, 57, 63, 65, 70

Camping, 3
Canals, 3
Canoeing, 3–4
  Blackstone River Valley, 202
  Cape Ann Region, 271
  Five College area, 155–156
  North Berkshire, 82
  Plymouth area, 309
  Quabbin Reservoir area, 36–37
  Upper Pioneer Valley, 46
Cape Ann Forge, 267
Cape Cod, guides to, 4
Carlisle, 210, 220, 222
Carver, 306
Chair lift rides, 4
Charlemont, 70, 72–73, 74, 75, 76, 77
Charlton, 182, 189
Chelmsford, 223, 227–228
Cheshire, 94
Chester, 57, 64
Chesterfield, 55, 57, 58
Chesterwood, 115
Chicopee, 169–170, 171, 172, 173
Chicopee Falls, 172
Children, activities for, 4
  Five College area, 152
  New Bedford area, 328
  See also Amusement areas
Christmas trees, 4
Clarksburg, 82, 93
Clinton, 210
Colleges:
  Five College area, 142, 147–150, 158–159, 160, 161, 162
  Lowell area, 224
  New Bedford area, 335
  North Berkshire, 81–82, 83, 84, 89
Colrain, 71, 72, 77
Conway, 55, 57, 63, 64, 65, 66
Covered bridges, 4
  Mohawk Trail Country, 70
Crafts, 4
  Cape Ann Region, 286
  Central and South Berkshires, 139
  Central Uplands, 28
  Five College area, 162
  Hilltowns, 65
  Mohawk Trail Country, 71, 76–77
  Quabbin Reservoir area, 32, 41
  Salem and Marblehead area, 258
  Upper Pioneer Valley, 50–51
  Worcester area, 197

Cranberries, 4
  Plymouth area, 304, 306
Cross-country skiing:
  Central and South Berkshires, 118–119
  Central Uplands, 23–24
  Five College area, 157
  Hilltowns, 60
  Lawrence area, 234
  Lowell area, 222
  Mohawk Trail Country, 73
  Nashoba Valley, 210–211
  North Berkshire, 83–84, 93
  Old Sturbridge Village Country, 182
  Quabbin Reservoir area, 38
  Upper Pioneer Valley, 46–47
Cummington, 54, 55, 57, 58, 60–61, 63, 64, 65–66
Cummington Village, 60
Cuttyhunk Island, 329–330

Dalton, 104, 114, 117, 132
Dance:
  Central and South Berkshires, 110
Danvers, 248–249, 250, 252, 253, 254
Dartmouth, 328, 331
Deerfield, 43–44, 46, 47, 48, 49, 50, 51
Dighton Rock, 309
Douglas, 202, 203, 205
Duxbury, 304–305, 307–308, 309, 310, 311–312, 313

East Blackstone, 202
East Brookfield, 182, 185, 188, 189
East Charlemont, 74
East Douglas, 204
East Gloucester, 262, 285
East Longmeadow, 170
East Marion, 317
Eastern Point, 268
Easthampton, 46, 154, 155–156
Egremont, 117, 122, 133, 137
Erving, 38, 39
Essex, 264, 269, 272, 279–280, 281, 283–284, 285, 287
Excursions:
  Cape Ann Region, 270–271
  Central and South Berkshires, 111
  Fall River area, 343
  Lowell area, 222
  Newburyport area, 292–293
  Plymouth area, 308–309
  Sippican area, 317
  See also Tours

Factory outlets, 4–5
  Blackstone River Valley, 205
  Central Uplands, 28–29
  Fall River area, 345–347
  Five College area, 163
  Lawrence area, 235–237
  Lowell area, 225
  New Bedford area, 336–337
  North Berkshire, 96
  Old Sturbridge Village Country, 188–189
  Worcester area, 197
  See also Shopping in Accomodations Index
Fairhaven, 328, 330, 331, 333, 334, 335
Fall foliage, 5
Fall River, 341–342, 343, 344, 345–347, 348
Farmers markets, 5
  Five College area, 163
Farms:
  Central Upland, 21
  Hilltowns, 58
  Quabbin Reservoir area, 33
  See also Orchards
Feeding Hills, 170
Fishing, 5
  Cape Ann Region, 271
  Central and South Berkshires, 116
  Five College area, 156
  Lawrence area, 234
  Mohawk Trail Country, 72
  Nashoba Valley, 210
  New Bedford area, 331
  Newburyport area, 292–293
  North Berkshire, 83, 93
  Plymouth area, 309
  Quabbin Reservoir area, 37
  Sippican area, 317
  Upper Pioneer Valley, 46
Fitchburg, 18–19, 21, 25, 26, 28, 29, 30
Flea markets. See Antiques
Florence, 153–154, 158, 160
Florida, 68, 72
Flying. See Air rides
Foxhollow, 117
Fruit. See Orchards; Pick your own; specific type of fruit

Gardner, 17, 18, 22–23, 25, 26, 27, 28–29, 30
Gill, 46, 47, 49
Gloucester, 261–262, 266–267, 270, 271, 272, 273, 277–278, 279, 380, 282–283, 284, 285, 286

Index 351

Golf, 5
  Blackstone River Valley, 202
  Cape Ann Region, 271–272
  Central and South Berkshires, 117
  Central Uplands, 23
  Fall River area, 343
  Five College area, 156–157
  Hilltowns, 59
  Lawrence area, 234
  Lowell area, 222
  New Bedford area, 331
  North Berkshire, 82
  Old Sturbridge Village Country, 182
  Quabbin Reservoir area, 38
  Salem and Marblehead area, 250
  Sippican area, 317
  Springfield area, 170
  Upper Pioneer Valley, 46
  See also Miniature golf
Goshen, 57, 58, 60, 63–64, 65
Grafton, 201, 203, 204, 205
Grafton Center, 201, 203–204, 205
Grafton Common, 205
Granby, 151
Great Barrington, 105, 109, 111, 114, 117, 118–119, 126–128, 134, 135, 136, 137, 138, 139
Green space:
  Blackstone River Valley, 202
  Cape Ann Region, 268–270
  Fall River area, 342
  Lawrence area, 233
  Lowell area, 220
  Mohawk Trail Country, 70
  Nashoba Valley, 210
  New Bedford area, 329, 330–331
  Newburyport area, 291–292
  Old Sturbridge Village Country, 180–181
  Plymouth area, 307–308
  Quabbin Reservoir area, 34
  Salem and Marblehead area, 249–250
  Sippican area, 317
  Springfield area, 169–170
  Upper Pioneer Valley, 45
  Worcester area, 195–196
  See also Heritage State Parks; Nature preserves; Public forests; Reservations; State forests and parks; Trustees of Reservations
Greenfield, 44, 46, 48, 49, 50, 51
Groton, 209, 210, 213

Hadley, 46, 150–151, 153, 155, 156, 159, 160, 163
Hamilton, 250, 257
Hampden, 169
Hancock, 83, 84, 85, 87, 101–102, 139, 140
Hang gliding, 5
  Nashoba Valley, 210
Hardwick, 190
Harvard, 206, 208–209, 213
Hay rides, 5
Haydenville, 57, 59, 64, 65
Heath, 71, 72, 77
Heritage State Parks, 5, 7
  Blackstone River Valley, 199, 201, 205
  Central Uplands, 17, 18, 22–23, 30
  Fall River area, 338, 340, 343
  Five College area, 146, 151–152
  Lawrence area, 231–232
  Lowell area, 219
  North Berkshire, 78, 92
  See also Green space; Nature preserves; Public forests; Reservations; State forests and parks; Trustees of Reservations
Hiking, 7
  Central and South Berkshires, 116
  Central Uplands, 23
  Five College area, 156
  Lowell area, 222
  North Berkshire, 82, 92, 93
  Old Sturbridge Village Country, 182
  Quabbin Reservoir area, 34, 38
Hinsdale, 117
Historical buildings:
  Blackstone River Valley, 201, 202
  Cape Ann Region, 266, 267
  Central and South Berkshires, 105, 107, 111–112
  Central Uplands, 19, 21
  Fall River area, 340–341, 342
  Hilltowns, 55, 57
  Lowell area, 220
  Middlesex Canal area, 227–228
  Mohawk Trail Country, 70, 71
  Nashoba Valley, 208
  New Bedford area, 326–327, 329, 330–331
  Newburyport area, 290
  Old Sturbridge Village Country, 179
  Plymouth area, 302, 305, 306
  Quabbin Reservoir area, 32
  Salem and Marblehead area, 244, 248
  Springfield area, 166, 167
Historical houses, 7
  Cape Ann Region, 262–264, 265, 267–268
  Central and South Berkshires, 102, 104–105, 107
  Five College area, 147, 150, 151
  Hilltowns, 54, 55
  Lawrence area, 232–233
  Lowell area, 219–220
  Middlesex Canal area, 228
  New Bedford area, 327–328
  Newburyport area, 290–291
  Old Sturbridge Village Country, 179–180
  Plymouth area, 302, 304, 305–306, 307
  Salem and Marblehead area, 244–245, 246, 248–249, 250
  Sippican area, 316
  Worcester area, 195
Historical societies:
  Cape Ann Region, 261–262
  Central Uplands, 19, 21
  Fall River area, 341
  Five College area, 151
  Hilltowns, 54–55, 57
  Lawrence area, 232
  Mohawk Trail Country, 70, 71
  Quabbin Reservoir area, 31–32, 33, 34
  Salem and Marblehead area, 245–246, 249
  Sippican area, 316
  Upper Pioneer Valley, 44
  Worcester area, 195
Holland, 180, 182, 184, 187–188
Holyoke, 142, 146, 151–152, 154, 157, 162, 163
Horseback riding, 7
  Blackstone River Valley, 203
  Cape Ann Region, 272
  Central and South Berkshires, 116–117
  Central Uplands, 23
  Fall River area, 343
  Five College area, 156
  Nashoba Valley, 210
  New Bedford area, 331
  North Berkshire, 82
  Old Sturbridge Village Country, 182
  Upper Pioneer Valley, 46
Hostels, 7
Housatonic, 134–135, 139
Hubbardston, 21, 26, 28
Hunting, 7
Huntington, 57, 62, 63, 64, 65
Hyannis, 316–317

352 Index

Ingleside, 163
Inns, 8
Interlaken, 108–109, 111
Ipswich, 264–265, 267–268, 269, 271, 272, 273, 282, 284, 285, 286, 287

Jiminy Peak, 82, 83, 84–85

Kingston, 307

Lakes, 8
Lakeville, 331, 343
Lancaster, 208, 209, 212, 213
Lanesboro, 85–86, 94, 137
Lanesville, 286
Lawrence, 230–232, 233, 234–237
Lee, 109–110, 111, 113, 116, 117, 119, 124, 129, 135, 136, 138, 139
Lenox, 105, 108, 109, 110–111, 113, 115, 116–117, 119–120, 121, 122–123, 124–126, 132, 133, 135, 136, 137, 138, 139, 140
Lenox Village, 138
Leominster, 22, 23, 28, 29
Leverett, 46
Leverett Center, 50–51
Littleton, 209, 210, 212
Longmeadow, 171
Lowell, 217–220, 222–225, 227
Ludlow, 170
Lunenburg, 21, 23, 27

Magnolia, 262–263, 272, 278
Manchester, 265, 269–270, 271, 272, 273, 278, 281–282, 284, 286, 287
Manomet, 307, 311, 312
Manomet Point, 309
Mansfield, 345
Maple sugaring, 8
  Hilltowns, 57–58
  Mohawk Trail Country, 71
  Quabbin Reservoir area, 34
  Upper Pioneer Valley, 45
Marblehead, 246, 248, 249, 250, 251, 252–253, 254, 255–256, 257, 258–259
Marblehead Neck, 249
Marion, 316, 317, 318, 334
Marshfield, 305–306, 310
Martha's Vineyard, guides to, 8
Massachusetts Audubon Society:
  Cape Ann Region, 268, 269
  Central and South Berkshires, 115
  Central Uplands, 22
  Mohawk Trail Country, 71

Plymouth area, 307–308
See also Nature preserves; Wildlife sanctuaries
Mattapoisett, 316, 317, 318
Mendon, 201–202, 204, 205
Metacomet-Monadnock Trail, 38, 156
Methuen, 235, 237
Middleborough, 306–307, 309
Middlefield, 57, 59, 65
Mid-State Trail, 23, 182
Mill River, 116, 134, 137
Millers Falls, 35, 36, 37, 41, 45, 46, 48, 50
Millville, 202
Miniature golf:
  Central and South Berkshires, 117
  Old Sturbridge Village Country, 182
Mohawk Trail, 68, 69, 70, 71, 72, 76
Monroe, 72
Monson, 184, 189
Montague, 45, 46
Montague Center, 45
Monterey, 112, 116, 117, 138
Monuments:
  Cape Ann Region, 266
  North Berkshire, 91
  Plymouth area, 304, 308
Mount Greylock, 91–92, 93, 96
Mount Wachusett, 22, 23–24, 26, 29, 30
Mount Washington, 112–113, 115
Mountains, 8
  Central and South Berkshires, 112–113
  Central Uplands, 22, 23–24
  Five College area, 156
  Mohawk Trail Country, 68, 70, 71
  North Berkshire, 83–84, 91–92
  Upper Pioneer Valley, 45
Museum villages, 8
  Central and South Berkshires, 101–102
  Lawrence area, 232
  Nashoba Valley, 206, 208, 213
  Old Sturbridge Village Country, 177, 179, 187, 188, 190
  Plymouth area, 302, 313
  Quabbin Reservoir area, 43–44
  Salem and Marblehead area, 245
  Springfield area, 169
Museums:
  Blackstone River Valley, 201
  Cape Ann Region, 262–263, 264, 267

Central Uplands, 18
Central and South Berkshires, 101, 102, 104, 107, 111
Fall River area, 341
Five College area, 147, 149, 150–151, 152
Hilltowns, 55, 57
Lowell area, 220
Mohawk Trail Country, 71
Nashoba Valley, 208
New Bedford area, 324, 326, 327–328, 329, 336
Newburyport area, 290, 291
Old Sturbridge Village Country, 179
Plymouth area, 302, 304, 306–307
Quabbin Reservoir area, 33
Salem and Marblehead area, 243–244, 245, 249
Springfield area, 167, 169
Worcester area, 194–195
See also Art museums
Music, 8
  Cape Ann Region, 284–285, 286
  Central and South Berkshires, 108–110
  Fall River area, 345
  Five College area, 161
  Hilltowns, 57, 64
  Lowell area, 224
  Mohawk Trail Country, 76
  Nashoba Valley, 213
  Plymouth area, 312
  Salem and Marblehead area, 257
  Springfield area, 172–173
  Upper Pioneer Valley, 50

Nantucket, guides to, 8
Nature preserves, 8–9
  Central and South Berkshires, 114–116
  See also Green space; Heritage State Parks; Massachusetts Audubon Society; Public forests; Reservations; State forests and parks; Trustees of Reservations; Wildlife sanctuaries
New Ashford, 83, 87, 89
New Bedford, 158, 211, 325, 326–328, 330–331, 333–334, 335, 336, 337
New Braintree, 188
New Marlboro, 113, 115, 122, 128–129
New Salem, 32, 33, 34, 39, 41
Newbury, 291, 292, 297

Index

Newburyport, 290, 292–295, 296–297
North Adams, 68, 71–72, 74, 76, 92–93, 94, 96
North Amherst, 155
North Andover, 232–233, 234, 235
North Attleboro, 348
North Dartmouth, 331, 335, 336
North Egremont, 116, 117, 134
North New Salem, 36
North Orange, 32, 39, 41
North Otis, 138
North Oxford, 179–180, 182, 188
North Plymouth, 313
North Reading, 233
Northampton, 149, 151, 154, 155, 156, 157–158, 159, 160–161, 162, 163, 164
Northbridge, 202, 205
Northfield, 44, 45, 46–47, 48, 49, 50

Old Deerfield, 48, 50
Old Sturbridge Village, 177, 179, 187, 188, 190
Onset, 317, 318
Orange, 33, 34, 35, 36, 37, 38, 39, 41
Orchards:
  Cape Ann Region, 285
  Old Sturbridge Village Country, 189
  See also Apples; Farms
Otis, 113, 116, 118
Oxford, 180, 182

Palmer, 187, 190
Pembroke, 309
Pepperell, 21, 28, 223
Peru, 114, 116
Petersham, 4, 32, 33, 34, 35, 36, 38
Petersham Common, 35, 39
Phillipston, 32, 33, 35–36, 38–39, 41
Pick your own, 9
  See also Apples, Cranberries, Orchards
Pigeon Cove, 269, 274–275, 286
Pittsfield, 101, 108, 110, 111, 113–114, 115, 116, 117–118, 131, 136, 137, 138, 139
Plainfield, 55, 57, 58, 63, 64, 65
Plainfield Village, 64
Planetariums:
  Central Uplands, 19
  North Berkshire, 81
Pleasant Valley, 203
Plum Island, 291–292, 293

Plymouth, 302, 304, 307, 308–309, 310, 311, 312–313
Polo:
  Salem and Marblehead area, 257
Princeton, 19, 22, 23, 24–25, 26
Princeton Common, 27
Provincetown, 308
Public forests:
  Quabbin Reservoir area, 34–36
  See also Green space; Heritage State Parks; Nature preserves; Reservations; State forests and parks; Trustees of Reservations

Quabbin Reservoir, 34, 37, 38, 153, 156

Racquetball:
  Central and South Berkshires, 117
Rehoboth, 343, 344, 347
Reservation services, Bed & Breakfasts, 2, 62, 85, 124, 127–128, 131, 158, 170–171, 196, 211, 223, 251–252, 310, 318, 333, 347
Reservations:
  Blackstone River Valley, 202
  Cape Ann Region, 269
  Central Uplands, 22
  Five College area, 152–154
  Hilltowns, 59
  Lawrence area, 233
  Newburyport area, 291–292, 293
  North Berkshire, 91, 93
  Plymouth area, 309
  Salem and Marblehead area, 250
  See also Green space; Heritage State Parks; Nature preserves; Public forests; State forests and parks; Trustees of Reservations
Richmond, 116, 129, 131
Riverdale, 268
Rock climbing:
  Blackstone River Valley, 203
Rockport, 263–264, 266, 267, 268–269, 270, 271, 272, 273–277, 278–279, 280–281, 283, 284, 285, 286, 287
Rocky Neck, 266, 271, 283, 285, 286
Rowe, 70, 75, 77
Rowley, 295
Royalston, 35, 36–37, 38, 41
Royalston Common, 31–32, 36

Sailboards, 9
  Cape Ann Region, 272
Sailing, 9
  Cape Ann Region, 272
  Newburyport area, 293
Salem, 243–245, 249, 250, 251, 252, 253, 254–255, 256, 257, 258, 259
Salem Bay, 250
Salisbury, 293, 295, 296, 297
Sandisfield, 113, 117, 124
Savoy, 74
Scuba diving, 9
  Salem and Marblehead area, 251
Seekonk, 343, 347
Self-improvement vacations:
  Hilltowns, 63
  Mohawk Trail Country, 75
Sheffield, 106, 109, 114, 115, 116, 128, 136, 138
Shelburne, 71, 74, 75, 76
Shelburne Center, 71, 74
Shelburne Falls, 70–71, 73, 74, 75–76, 77
Shrewsbury, 197
Shutesbury, 46
Skating:
  North Berkshire, 84
Ski touring, 9–10
Skiing, 9
  See also Alpine skiing; Cross-country skiing
Skyrides. *See* Air rides
Sleigh rides, 5
Somerset, 343, 344
South Asfield, 58, 59
South Auburn, 196
South Carver, 306, 307
South Dartmouth, 328, 330, 331, 333, 334, 335
South Deerfield, 45, 48, 50
South Egremont, 112–113, 118, 123–124, 132, 135, 136, 138
South Hadley, 147–149, 155, 156, 161, 163
South Lancaster, 209
South Lawrence, 235
South Lee, 112, 119, 120, 124, 131, 132–133
Southbridge, 179, 182, 187
Special events, 13
  Blackstone River Valley, 205
  Cape Ann Region, 286–287
  Central and South Berkshire, 139–140
  Central Uplands, 29–30
  Fall River area, 348
  Five College area, 163–164

Hilltowns, 65–66
Lowell area, 225, 237
Mohawk Trail Country, 71
Nashoba Valley, 213
New Bedford area, 337
Newburyport area, 297
North Berkshire, 96
Old Sturbridge Village Country, 190
Plymouth area, 313
Quabbin Reservoir area, 41
Salem and Marblehead area, 258–259
Sippican area, 318
Springfield area, 173
Upper Pioneer Valley, 41
Worcester area, 197–198
Spencer, 180, 182, 184, 186, 190
Sports. *See* specific type
Springfield, 142
Stallion Hill, 179
State forests and parks, 10–11
Blackstone River Valley, 202
Cape Ann Region, 269
Central and South Berkshires, 112–114
Central Uplands, 21–22
Fall River area, 342
Five College area, 152–154
Hilltowns, 58
Lawrence area, 233
Lowell area, 218, 219, 220, 222, 224
Mohawk Trail Country, 71–72
Nashoba Valley, 210
New Bedford area, 329, 331
Newburyport area, 292
North Berkshire, 92–93
Old Sturbridge Village Country, 180
Plymouth area, 307, 309, 310
Worcester area, 196
See also Green space; Heritage State Parks; Nature preserves; Public forests; Reservations; Trustees of Reservations
Sterling, 209, 211, 212, 213
Stockbridge, 102, 104–105, 107, 108–109, 110, 112, 115, 116, 121, 134, 136, 137–138, 139, 140
Stow, 210
Sturbridge, 177, 179, 180, 182–184, 185, 186, 187, 188–189, 190
Sudbury, 211, 212
Sugarhouses. *See* Maple Sugaring
Sunderland, 44–45, 46, 47, 49, 50
Sunderland Center, 45

Sutton, 202, 204
Swampscott, 251, 252, 256
Swansea, 344
Swimming:
Blackstone River Valley, 203
Cape Ann Region, 272–273
Central and South Berkshires, 117
Central Uplands, 23
Fall River area, 343–344
Five College area, 157
Hilltowns, 60
Lawrence area, 234
Lowell area, 222
Mohawk Trail Country, 72
New Bedford area, 329, 331, 333
Newburyport area, 293
North Berkshire, 82–83, 93
Old Sturbridge Village Country, 182
Plymouth area, 307, 309–310
Quabbin Reservoir area, 38
Salem and Marblehead area, 251
Sippican area, 317
Springfield area, 270
Upper Pioneer Valley, 46

Tanglewood, 108
Taunton, 347–348
Templeton, 19, 23, 26, 27, 29, 30
Tennis:
Cape Ann Region, 273
Central and South Berkshires, 117
North Berkshire, 83
Upper Pioneer Valley, 47
Tewksbury, 222
Theater, 11
Cape Ann Region, 284
Central and South Berkshires, 107, 110–111
Central Uplands, 27
Fall River area, 345
Five College area, 149, 161
Lowell area, 224, 225
Nashoba Valley, 208, 213
New Bedford area, 335
Newburyport area, 296
North Berkshire, 81–82, 89
Plymouth area, 312
Salem and Marblehead area, 256–257
Sippican area, 318
Springfield area, 172
Upper Pioneer Valley, 50
Topsfield, 269, 271
Tours:
Lowell area, 219

Newburyport area, 293
Salem and Marblehead area, 250
See also Excursions
Townsend, 19, 22, 24, 26, 28
Townsend Harbor, 21, 27
Train excursions, 11
Central and South Berkshires, 111
Trustees of Reservations, 11
Cape Ann Region, 268–269, 273
Central and South Berkshires, 104, 114–115
Central Uplands, 22–23
Hilltowns, 59
Lawrence area, 233
Newburyport area, 292
Old Sturbridge Village Country, 180
Salem and Marblehead area, 250
See also Green space; Heritage State Parks; Nature preserves; Public forests; Reservations; State forests and parks
Turners Falls, 46
Tyringham, 107, 115, 131

Upton, 202, 203
Uxbridge, 199, 201, 202, 203, 204, 205

Vineyards, 11

Wachusett Mountain, 22, 23–24, 26, 29, 30
Wales, 181, 190
Ware, 153
Wareham, 316–317
Warren, 189
Warwick, 32, 34, 35, 38, 41
Washington, 118
Waterfalls, 11
Central and South Berkshires, 115–116
Lowell area, 220
North Berkshire, 92
Quabbin Reservoir area, 36
Waterslide:
New Bedford area, 333
Wendell, 38, 39, 41
Wenham, 249, 256
West Boylston, 211–212
West Brookfield, 184, 185–186
West Chesterfield, 57, 58, 59
West Cummington, 58, 60
West Gloucester, 270, 280
West Hawley, 60, 71, 73

Index 355

West Newbury, 233, 292, 297
West Springfield, 162, 169, 171, 173
West Stockbridge, 111, 117, 122, 124, 133, 134, 135, 138, 139
West Townsend, 19, 21, 22, 28
West Warren, 188
Westborough, 212
Westfield, 162, 170, 173
Westford, 210, 222, 223
Westhampton, 158
Westminster, 23, 25, 26, 27, 29
Westport, 333, 342, 344, 348
Westport Point, 343–344
Whale watching, 11
  Cape Ann Region, 270–271
  Newburyport area, 293
  Plymouth area, 308–309

Salem and Marblehead area, 251
Whatley, 45, 46, 47–48
Whitinsville, 204
Wildlife sanctuaries:
  Cape Ann Region, 271
  Five College area, 154
  Mohawk Trail Country, 71
  Newburyport area, 291
  Old Sturbridge Village Country, 181
  Plymouth area, 307
  Salem and Marblehead area, 249
  Springfield area, 169
  See also Massachusetts Audubon Society; Nature preserves

Williamsburg, 55, 57, 59, 62, 64, 65, 124, 158
Williamstown, 80–83, 84, 85, 86–87, 89, 90, 96, 116
Wilmington, 227, 228
Winchendon, 21, 26, 27, 28, 29
Winchester, 227
Windsor, 59, 65
Woburn, 228
Worcester, 191–193
Worthington, 58, 59, 60, 61–62, 64–65
Worthington Corners, 57, 63

Yankee groups, 11

Lodging

Addison Choate Inn, 273
Allen House, 330
Alpine Haus, 184
The Amelia Payson Guest House, 253
American Youth Hostel, 48
Amity House, 126, 157
Anchorage Inn, 277
Andover Inn, 234
Another Place, 310
Apple Tree Inn, 122
Ashfield Inn, 62
Autumn Inn, 158
Avondo's Bed & Breakfast, 184

Bald Eagle Motel, 38
Barton Cove Nature and Camping Area, 38, 48
Bascom Lodge, 94
Beach Knoll Inn, 273
Beaver Pond Meadows, 84–85
Bed & Breakfast (Lowell), 223
The Beeches, 157–158
Bellefontaine, 120
The Benjamin Choate House, 294
Berkshire Green Acres, 63
Berkshire Hills, 86
Berkshire Hills Country Inn, 131
Berkshire Park Camping Area, 63
The Bernardston Inn, 47
Bernardston Motel, 48
Best Western American Motor Lodge, 185
Best Western Twin Light Manor, 277
Black Swan Inn, 132
Blantyre, 120

Blue Shutters, 277
Blue Spruce Motel, 311
Brook Farm, 125
Brookfield House Inn, 184
Bullfrog Bed & Breakfast, 63–63
Butternut Inn, 93–94

Caldwell's, 61
Campus Center Hotel, 158–159
Candlelight Inn, 124
Candlelight Resort Motor Inn, 48
Canterbury Farm Bed & Breakfast, 131–132
Cape Ann Campsite, 280
Cape Ann Marina Motor Inn, 279
Cape Ann Motor Inn, 279
Cap'n Jacks, 252
Captain Eddy House, 196
Captain's Bounty, 278–279
The Captain's House, 274
Carter-Washburn House, 212
Centennial House, 47
Centuryhurst Antiques, 128
Chanterwood, 119
The Charlemont Inn, 73–74
Charles Capron House, 203
Chicatabut Inn, 274
Chimney Mirror, 86
Clarksburg State Park, 94
The Coach House Inn, 252
Coffing-Bostwick House, 127
Cold Spring Motel, 311
Colonel Blackinton Inn, 347
Colonel Ebenezer Crafts Inn, 183
Colonial Inn, 62
Commonwealth House, 222–223
Commonwealth Inn, 184

Cornell House, 125
The Country Aire Campground, 74
Country Comfort, 74
The Country Inn at Jiminy Peak, 84
Country Inn at Princeton, 24
Cranwell Resort and Conference Center, 120
Cumworth Farm, 61

The Dalton House, 132
Deer Meadow Farm, 184
Deerfield Inn, 47

East Country Berry Farm, 126
Eastover, 119
Eden Pines Inn, 274
Edgewater Bed & Breakfast, 333
The Egremont Inn, 123
1896 Motel, 86
Elling's Bed & Breakfast, 126–127
Elwal Pines Motor Inn, 86
Erving State Forest, 38
Essex River House, 279–280

Federal House, 124
Fiske Dairy Farm, 73
Folkstone Bed & Breakfast, 211
Forest Way Farm, 74
Four Acres, 86
Fox Inn, 48
Foxhollow, 120
The Franklin Burrs, 61
French King Motor Lodge, 48
Friendly Crossways Youth Hostel, 212

The Gables Inn, 124
Garden Gables, 125
Garrison Inn, 294
Gateways Inn and Restaurant, 122–123
The Gilberts, 347
Gloucester, 279
Gnome Crossing, 171
Gold Leaf Inn, 62
The Golden Goose, 131
Good Harbor Beach Inn, 279
Gould, Helen and Donald, 62
The Grafton Inn, 203–204
Gray Manor, 277
Green Acres Motel, 185
Greenfield Howard Johnson Motel, 48
Greenmeadows, 127
Greer Bed & Breakfast, 131
Gurnet Inn, 310

The Hall's Bed & Breakfast, 310
The Hancock Inn, 85
Haus Andreas, 129
Hawthorne Inn, 254
Heritage House, 203
Heritage Park Inn, 25
Heywood House, 212
Hidden Hill Bed & Breakfast, 62
Highland Springs Guest House, 74
The Hill Gallery, 61
Hilltop Bed & Breakfast, 63
Hilltop Motel, 74
Hilton Inn, 158
Hilton Inn Berkshire, 132
Historic Valley Park Family Campground, 94
Holiday Inn, 170
Hollister House, 128
Horseneck State Beach, 343–344
Hotel Barre, 184
The Hotel Lafayette, 254
Hotel Northampton, 157
Howe's Camping, 25–26

Inn at Harrington Farm, 24–25
The Inn at Stockbridge, 121
Inn on Cove Hill, 274
Insight Meditation Society Center, 185
Ivanhoe Country House, 128

Le Jardin Inn, 85
Jericho Valley, 86
Johnson & Wales Inn, 347

King's Grant Inn, 254
Kingsleigh, 129
The Knoll, 158

Koala Inn, 234
Kripalu Center, 119–120
Lake Denison State Park, 21–22, 25
Lake Shore Bed & Breakfast, 185
Lake View House, 185
Lakeridge Campground, 38
Lamb City Campground, 38
Langhaar House, 128–129
Lawrence Marriott, 234
Linden Tree Inn, 274
Lindsey's Garret, 252
LittleJohn Manor, 127
Longfellow's Wayside Inn, 211
Lord Jeffery Inn, 157
Lowell Hilton, 222

Magargal, Raymond and Helen, 61
Marble Farm, 24
Marriott Hotel, 170, 196
Mattapoisett Inn, 317
Merrell Tavern Inn, 131
Middlerise Bed & Breakfast, 129
Millstones Guest House, 129
Misty Meadows, 184
Mohawk Park, 75
The Morgan House, 124
Morrill Place, 293–294
Morton's Park Place, 310
Motel 6, 48
Mount Greylock Reservation, 93
Munro's American House Guests, 131
Myles Standish State Forest, 309

Nathaniel Bowditch Guest House, 253
The Nautilus, 253–254
New Boston Inn, 124
North Adams Inn, 94
Northfield Country House, 47
Northside Inn, 86

Oak Lodge, 128
Oak n' Spruce, 120
Ocean Crest/Anchor Inn, 317
Old Corner Inn, 278
Old Farm Inn, 274–275
The Old Inn on The Green, 122
Old Sturbridge Village Motor Lodge, 183–184
Olde Rose Cottage, 211–212
Oliver Wight House, 183–184
The Orchards, 84
Otter River State Forest, 22, 25
Quincy Lodge, 126
Outlook Farm, 158
The Oxbow, 74

Padanaram Guest House, 333
Parson Hubbard House, 74
Paulson, Robert and Barbara, 62
Peaceful Acres, 26
Peaceful Pines, 26
Pearl Hill State Park, 22, 25
Peirson Place, 129
Perryville Inn, 347
Pilgrim Sands, 311
Pine Campgrounds, 26
Pine Knoll Farm, 85
Pineridge Campground, 38
Pleasant Manor Inn, 253
Pleasant Street Inn, 275
Pleasant View Motor Lodge & Pub, 204
Publick House, 182–183

Quabbin Gateway Motel, 38
Quaker Motor Lodge, 204

Ralph Waldo Emerson House, 275
Ramsey House, 129
Ranch Campground, 38
The Red Lion Inn, 121
Red Rose Motel, 74
River Bend Farm, 85
Rockport Lodge, 277
Rocky Shores, 275

The Salem Inn, 252
Salisbury Beach State Reservation, 292
Samuel Legro House, 253
Sandy Bay Motor Inn, 279
Savoy Mt. State Forest, 71
The Scott House, 63
Scusset Beach State Reservation, 309
Sea Lantern Inn, 279
Sea Ledges, 276
Seacrest Manor, 275
Seafarer Inn, 275
Seaview Manor, 310
Seaward Inn, 275–276
Seekonk Pines, 127
Seven Hills, 121
Seven South Street, 276
The 1797 House, 63
1777 Greylock House, 129
Shady Pines Campground, 74
Sheraton Plymouth, 311
Sheraton Rolling Green Inn and Conference Center, 234
Sheraton Sturbridge Inn, 185
Sheraton Tara, 170
Sheraton Tara Hotel & Resort, 254

Sheraton-Lincoln Inn, 196
Skipper Motor Inn, 333
Skyline Inn, 170
Spencer Country Inn, 184
Spray Cliff, 252
Springbrook Family Camp Area, 74
State Street Pilot House, 253
Staveleigh House, 128
Steep Acres Farm, 85
The Stephen Daniels House, 253
The Sterling Inn, 211
Sterling Orchards, 212
Stonehedge Bed & Breakfast, 212
Strawberry Hill, 126
Stump Sprouts, 73
Sturbridge Motor Inn, 185
Sunnyside Farm, 47–48

10 Mugford Street, 252–253
Thunderbird Motor Lodge, 25
Tidecrest, 253
Timberlost Farm, 24
Town House Inn, 222

Townry Farm, 85–86
Tuck Inn, 276
Tully Lake, 38
Turk's Head Motor Inn, 279
The Turner Inn, 253
The Turning Point, 127

Underledge, 126

The Victorian, 204
The Village Inn, 122

Walker House, 125
Warwick Inn, 38
Washburn House, 127
Weatherhead's Motel & Cabins, 48
The Weathervane Inn, 123–124
Westbridge Inn, 124
Westford Regency, 222
Westminster Village Inn, 25
The Whale Inn, 60
Whaler Inn, 333–334
Wheatleigh, 121

Whistler's Inn, 125–126
Whitcomb Summit Motel and Cottages, 74
White Birch Campgrounds, 48
White Horse Inn, 131
The White House, 278
Wildwood Inn, 158
Willard Brook State Forest, 22, 25
Williams Guest House, 277–278
Williams Inn, 84
The Williamsville Inn, 122
The Willows Motel, 86
Windfields Farm, 60–61
Windflower, 122
Windmill Motel, 48
The Windsor House, 294
Winsor House Inn, 310
Winterwood at Petersham, 38
Wood Farm, 24
Worthington Inn, 61–62

Yankee Clipper, 276–277
Yankee Pedlar Inn, 157
Yesterday's Inn, 333